# Buddha and the Spread of Buddhism in India and Abroad

These articles have been published in the Indian Historical Quarterly and the details of the articles is given below for reference:

| Issue | Year of Pub. | Page Nos. | Page Nos. in the present book |
|---|---|---|---|
| Vol. 8 (3-4) | 1932 | 600-605 | 1-6 |
| Vol. 17 (1-4) | 1941 | 149-159 | 7-18 |
| Vol. 32 (1-4) | 1956 | 27-30 | 19-22 |
| Vol. 3 (1-2) | 1927 | 60-67 | 23-30 |
| Vol. 3 (3-4) | 1927 | 508-509 | 31-34 |
| Vol. 3 (3-4) | 1927 | 803-807 | 35-40 |
| Vol. 4 (1-4) | 1928 | 530-533 | 41-44 |
| Vol. 5 (3-4) | 1929 | 715-720 | 45-50 |
| Vol. 6 (1-4) | 1930 | 334-344 | 51-60 |
| Vol. 7 (1-2) | 1931 | 150-160 | 61-70 |
| Vol. 8 (1-2) | 1932 | 247-252 | 71-76 |
| Vol. 10 (1-4) | 1934 | 551-559 | 77-84 |
| Vol. 28 (1-4) | 1952 | 41-50 | 85-94 |
| Vol. 27 (1-4) | 1951 | 239-249 | 95-104 |
| Vol. 4 (1-4) | 1928 | 791 | 105-106 |
| Vol. 9 (1-2) | 1933 | 76-87 | 107-116 |
| Vol. 4 (1-4) | 1928 | 110-123 | 117-130 |
| Vol. 13 (1-4) | 1937 | 132-136 | 131-136 |
| Vol. 4 (1-4) | 1928 | 667-677 | 137-148 |
| Vol. 7 (1-2) | 1931 | 193-195 | 149-152 |
| Vol. 8 (3-4) | 1932 | 591-594 | 153-156 |
| Vol. 7 (3-4) | 1931 | 657 | 157-158 |
| Vol. 8 (1-2) | 1932 | 377-379 | 159-162 |
| Vol. 32 (1-4) | 1956 | 168-169 | 163-164 |
| Vol. 7 (3-4) | 1931 | 683-702 | 165-182 |
| Vol. 37 (1-4) | 1961 | 177-182 | 183-188 |
| Vol. 26 (1-4) | 1950 | 152-158 | 189-196 |
| Vol. 32 (1-4) | 1956 | 341-351 | 197-206 |
| Vol. 37 (1-4) | 1961 | 93-104 | 207-216 |
| Vol. 3 (3-4) | 1927 | 747-756 | 217-226 |
| Vol. 26 (1-4) | 1950 | 333-336 | 227-230 |
| Vol. 27 (1-4) | 1951 | 144-150 | 231-238 |
| Vol. 31 (1-4) | 1955 | 68-75 | 239-246 |
| Vol. 32 (1-4) | 1956 | 163-167 | 247-252 |
| Vol. 5 (1-2) | 1929 | 14-30 | 253-270 |
| Vol. 32 (1-4) | 1956 | 179-210 | 271-300 |
| Vol. 32 (1-4) | 1956 | 211-222 | 301-312 |
| Vol. 32 (1-4) | 1956 | 297-303 | 313-320 |
| Vol. 2 (3-4) | 1926 | 673-689 | 321-334 |
| Vol. 3 (1-2) | 1927 | 429 | 335-336 |
| Vol. 32 (1-4) | 1956 | 314-318 | 337-342 |
| Vol. 25 (1-4) | 1949 | 229-262 | 343-374 |

# Buddha and the Spread of Buddhism in India and Abroad

## Collection of Articles from the Indian Historical Quarterly

### Vol. 2

Compiled by
Dr. Mahendra
P. Mittal

Introduction by
Prof. S. R. Bhatt

Originals
(an imprint of Low Price Publications)
Delhi-110052

Distributed by
**D.K. Publishers Distributors (P) Ltd.**
4834/24, Ansari Road, Darya Ganj,
New Delhi-110002
Phones: 3278584, 3278368, 3261465,
e-mail: dkpd@del3.vsnl.net.in
visit us at: www.dkpd.com


Articles first Published in the Journal from 1925-1963
First Published as a book
With an Introduction 2002
ISBN 81-7536-289-8

Published by
**Originals**
(an imprint of Low Price Publications)
A-6, Nimri Commercial Centre,
Near Ashok Vihar Phase-IV,
Delhi-110052
Phones: 7401672, 7452453
e-mail: lpp@nde.vsnl.net.in
visit us at: www.lppindia.com

Printed at
**D K Fine Art Press P Ltd.**
Delhi-110052



PRINTED IN INDIA

# Introduction

Prof. S.R. Bhatt

## A. Origin and Spread of Buddhism in India[1]

The origin and spread of Buddhism has been a landmark in the history of Greater India (*Mahā Bhārata* or *Bṛhattara Bhārata*) the boundaries of which covered a large part of Asia. As stated earlier, Śākyamuni, the Buddha, was the inheritor of an ancient, rich and varied cultural tradition of a very high order and he formulated and established a new culture out of it which was theoretically enlightening and practically redeeming from the labyrinth of suffering, imperfection, impermanence and other vicissitudes of life. He reconstructed an old path, as the Samyutta Nikāya puts it, a middle path which avoided all extremes. In his ideas, doctrines, and practices the proto-Vedic view of Reality and way of life blossomed forth in a fresh and invigourating form which attracted the elite and the masses alike. The rudiments of Buddha's teachings are well traceable to the Nāsadīya, Viṣṇu, Yama and several other Sūktas of the Ṛgveda. The earlier Upaniṣads and philosophical systems like Sāmkya-Yoga, Nyāya-Vaiśeṣika etc. had heavily influenced Buddha's thoughts. It is not unnatural that philosophical ideas and doctrines do not spring in a vacuum and grow out of old ideas. Oldenburg, a great authority on Vedic literature and Buddhism, has very pertinently and convincingly pointed this out in his works. Celebrated scholars like Mr. and Mrs. Rhys Davids have corroborated this fact. Apart from the Vedic sources, the contribution of Śramaṇa tradition and Ājjivikas etc. in the formulation of Buddha's philosophical view point has also been substantial. The Buddha had an open and assimilative mind and accommodated all those noble and sublime ideas available in the intellectual and meditational environment of his time which were agreeable to his experiences. There are many references to this effect in the Pāli canons which contain *Buddha-vacana* and in the biographical accounts of the Buddha. The basic teachings of the Buddha can be divided into two viz., philosophical and moral, or, theoretical and practical, and both have their ancestory in the Vedic thought. But the way the Buddha reformulated them is innovative and attractive and that is why he could impress upon and command respect and following both among the ruling elite and the masses.

## I

During his life time itself the Buddha was recognised as 'great saviour', an enlightened seer, who visualised and realized the summum bonum of life. He founded a new monastic order known as '*Samgha*' and gave a novel turn to the institution of *samnyāsa* directing it for universal well-being and happiness. A distinction can be drawn between monastic Buddhism and Buddhism of the non-monastic populace. Both the modes received great impetus during Buddha's life time. Even his royal parents and family members became his disciples. His popularity spread far and wide and his teachings provided solace and succor to the distressed people. He wandered from one place to another along with his disciples conversing with people in the language and idiom familiar to them. He mastered the art of discussion and debate and spread the radiance of his enlightened wisdom and conduct without taking any rest out of loving mercy and compassion for the suffering humanity. Of course, he encountered some opposition but he overcame it with his wit and wisdom, selfless service and benevolence. Though he did not write anything his teachings were preserved and subsequently codified by his disciples who very intelligently and diligently collated and compiled them with mutual consultation. His teachings were prolific and stretched over a long span of time but all these were retained in memory and recollected by his immediate disciples who always accompanied him during his travels from one place to another. This apart, his teachings were not theoretical and were exemplified in his conduct and in that of his disciples. Because of their practical nature it was easy to remember them. Almost the entire *Tripitaka* literature is a collection of sayings, utterances, narratives, rules of the order and other teachings known as '*Buddha vacana*'.

## II

Buddhism acquired popular recognition during the life time of the Buddha but soon after his Mahāparinirvāṇa it grew by leaps and bounds and continued to hold its sweep in India till 13th century A.D. when it ceased to be a distinct living tradition. During this period Buddhist councils were held to draw up canonical and other expository literature. A vast literature of varied nature was produced in India all of which is not fully available in modern times as it got extinct due to accidents of history. M. Winternitz in his 'History of Indian literature', vol. II, and Taranatha in his "History of Buddhism in India" have made an appreciable attempt to provide a brief thematic description of the extant part of it. An equally immeasurably vast literature came up in Buddhist countries outside India and it is the need of the time to attempt another compilation on a grand scale in a systematic, chronological and geographical order. It is a huge task to be taken up by a large team of scholars to be sponsored by international body like UNESCO.

The first great Council (*Samgiti*) took place, immediately after the Buddha's Mahāparinirvāṇa, at Rajagriha presided over by Mahākāśyapa in which along with him Upāli and Ānanda took major part. In this Council the three *Piṭakas*, or at least two of them, were compiled. This has been a landmark in the history of Buddhism as it provided a foundation to all subsequent developments in Buddhism as a philosophy, religion, culture and way of life. After one century the Second Council was held at Vaishali to further consolidate, purify and advance Buddhist faith. It drew up a new edition of *Piṭakas* and finalised composition of new treatises like *Nikāyas, Aṅgas* and *Dharmaskandhas*. It must also have attempted reconciliation among the differing or dissenting sections in the faith. The Third Council was organised under the auspices of Samrāt Aśoka who made phenomenal contribution to the preservation, propagation and spread of Buddhism in India and abroad. In this Council rigorous reformulation of Buddhist thought and practices was done by learned scholars well steeped in Buddhist lore. *Abhidharma* treatises, *Kathāvatthu* and other philosophical and sacred literature were composed. During Aśoka's time Buddhism became quite vibrant and predominant not only in Greater India but also in a large part of Asia. In a sense he was the first great royal patron, a staunch and ardent follower and a zealous propagator of Buddhism who sent missionaries, including his own children, to spread *saddharma* to near and far off places in Asia, Africa and Europe. Through rock-edicts, inscriptions, stone pillars etc. he enjoined people to lead pious life and follow the noble path of *dharma*. He provided great impetus to Buddhism and made it a truly universal religion. In the annals of Buddhism he will always be remembered with great love and reverence.

The Fourth Council was organised under the aegis of king Kaniṣka who ruled upto Afganistan and Iran. During his time *Vibhāṣā* literature was composed. He also attempted reconciliation among the eighteen Buddhist sects prevalent at that time. He made Sanskrit as the medium and prepared the ground for the rise of Mahāyāna Buddhism. In the history of Buddhism he comes next to Aśoka for the propagation of Buddhism and for enrichment of Buddhist thought and culture. Another king deserving mention is Harṣa who provided full protection to Buddhism. Among the ruling dynasties of early medieval India the Gupta, the Maurya, the Śunga, the Kaṇva and the Pāla were sympathetic to Buddhism and gave it patronage and encouragement. Though the base of Buddhism was Magadha and Kauśala, later on its centricity shifted to Kashmir and areas now under Pakistan and Afganistan. Buddhism flourished on the Indian soil till thirteenth century A.D. and thereafter ceased to exist as a distinct mode of thought as its basic tenets were absorbed in the Advaita Vedānta by Gauḍapāda and Śankara. Moreover, it had the same mythology and culture which was Paurāṇic and therefore was indistinguishable with other prevalent traditions. It also got extinct as a mode of living as it was primarily a monastic religion and with the invasion of foreign aggressors who were adherents of Islam, the monasteries and centres of learning were desecrated and destroyed. The lay followers who practised Buddhism were weak adherents and went back to the traditional fold.

However, there was revival of Buddhism and Buddhist studies in India in nineteenth century mainly due to European indologists. Several scholars in India and Europe studied Buddhist texts in Pāli and Sanskrit, translated them in English and other languages. Pandit Jawaharlal Nehru took keen interest in the re-establishment of Buddhist thought in India. Swami Vivekananda also appreciated the noble elements in Buddha's teachings.Smt. Indira Gandhi was a great admirer of Buddhism and thus Buddhist thought became popular in India over again. Dr. B. R. Ambedkar gave a new turn to Buddhism known as Neo-Buddhism. The coming of H.H. the Dalai Lama to India provided further stimulus to Buddhist studies. As a mode of thinking and a way of living Buddhism has a deep and unmitigated impact on Indian psyche and culture. That is why every Hindu cherishes great regard for Buddhism and reveres Lord Buddha as either incarnation of Viṣṇu or as identified with Śiva. It is a lopsided view that there was a decline of Buddhism in India. Buddhism constitutes the very core of Indian mind and has great potential in ennobling Indian culture provided it remains free from polluting political influence of the vested interests.

**B Spread and Influence of Buddhism abroad**

**(i)** We do not know the exact date of the introduction of Buddhism outside India and there are no definite historical records available to this effect. But there are positive evidences of Indian settlements in many parts of Asia practicing Vedic mode of living and this must have paved the way for the spread of Buddhism in those places. The prevalence of Vedic dharma before the rise of Buddhism provided the fertile ground in Asian countries for the acceptance and spread of Buddhism both through land and sea routes. The researches of B.K. Sarkar, Kenneth K.S. Chen, D.T. Suzuki, H. Nakamura etc. give sufficient clues in this matter which need to be examined closely with a positive mind.

From the point of view of cultural history of humankind it is indeed significant that originated in India Buddhism soon penetrated almost the whole of Asia, enamoured the hearts of the masses, influenced the intellects of the elite and won over the spirits of powerful rulers. Its intermingling with the local cultures and morass, its deep and pervasive impact on the minds of the native people have been so intense and immense that it not only moulded and reformulated the original thoughts, ideas and ideals, beliefs and practices of the countries of its *locale* but also brought about profound changes in their social, cultural and religions life. The people of these countries felt that Buddhism had something ennobling, enlightening and emancipating to offer. This apart Buddhism also acted as a catalytic force in transforming the social conditions, in forging national unity and in bringing about political solidarity in those countries. In this grand cultural interface there are a few points which deserve serious attention of world scholarship. The transmission to and acceptance, assimilation, modification and trans-creation of Buddhism outside India, its birth place and homeland, have been interesting and astonishing which need meaningful and gainful intercultural studies to find out a ground for world brotherhood. For the Indians it is really significant to know as to how and why Buddhism could get such a fascination and strong foothold outside India with notable and unmitigated impact on thought and culture of these countries. For the people of these countries it is instructive to be aware of the Indian roots of their Buddhistic view and way of life.

The Asian contribution in the preservation, propagation and furtherance of the Buddhist thought and culture cannot be underestimated. Once receptive of Buddhism these countries themselves became its exporters, so to say. The Indian seed yielded rich harvest on Asian soil. This apart it can be said with great satisfaction that some of the valuable Buddhist literature lost in India have been found preserved elsewhere either in original or in translation etc. It is the needed task for the Indian scholars to restore them back in Indian languages. It is well-known that China and Tibet have the proud privilege of preserving the largest and richest Buddhist cultural heritage. India and China along with other countries like Japan, Korea, Germany, United States, Thailand etc. can join hands and do a lot in sharing, preserving and enriching the same. Some of these have great literary, artistic, philosophical and religious value and can be regarded as classics in the world literature, culture and civilization.

The spread and influence of Vedic dharma and Buddhism in almost whole of Asia in the course of several centuries have been most fascinating. This evinces a common Asian mind set, shared modes of thinking and ways of living. Had there been no commonality of thought, belief-systems and value-patterns such a reception, absorption and intermingling would not have been possible. It is therefore not an exaggeration to say that there is something called Asian mind. Howsoever pluralistic and diversified it might be one can discern an underlying commonality which has made cross movement of ideas possible. Furthermore, the way, the ease and the swiftness with which this cultural appropriation and assimilation took place in the local cultures, atmospheres and environments, are suggestive of the metabolic dynamism of Asian psyche. It is, therefore, unfortunate that India and other Asian countries instead of directly interfacing each other and in a common way, view each other through a *tertim quid*. It is high time that we have now direct cultural understanding throwing off glasses of occidental indologists. In the hoary past we had direct linkages and cultural exchanges along with trade in material goods through land and sea routes. Trading in material goods has an ephemeral and transient value but exchange in thought and culture has a lasting impact. However, this should not be misunderstood as promotion of regionalism. Regional understanding is only a base for universal solidarity. Buddhism has been a universal religion and ecumenical character has been essential to it. It has displayed these features in its long history. It has tremendous potentiality to pave the way for world peace and co-existential beatitude among humans, sub-human species and nature on the basis of its cardinal principle of *pratitya samutpāda*, which is the principle of universal interdependence, interconnectedness and interrelationship. Perhaps at no other time in human history this message of the Buddha is more needed than at present to redeem the distracted humanity. In this venture the Western ways of thinking and Western knowledge of science and technology could be tempered and seasoned with Buddhist spirituality and meditational intuitions following the noble middle path.

**(ii) Spread and influence of Buddhism in China**

One of the most remarkable phenomena in the history of human relations is the introduction of Indian thoughts and institutions into China, opines Dr. Wing-Tsit-Chan[2]. India and China have the proud privilege to possess the most ancient civilizations of the world which are still alive, vibrant and thriving. These two cultural giants have thousands of years of mutual contacts and cultural exchanges with the Vedic dharma and its off shoot Buddhism as common bonds. Along with silk and other material commodities they traded with dharma, so to say, through land and sea routes. The people of China accepted the ideas and ideals, beliefs and practises propagated in Buddhism and assimilated them in their view and way of life. However, they continued to remain Confucian and Taoist while embracing Buddhism whole heartedly. In so doing they transcreated whatever they thought as non-essential in Buddhism without affecting the core of Buddhist thought. In fact they effected a remarkable synthesis of the three rich traditions without discarding or giving up any of their fundamentals. This resulted in a happy and wonderful cross-fertilization and a brilliant amalgamation of Indian Buddhism and traditional Chinese thought and culture. Confucianism, Taoism and Buddhism constitute three strands of the one composite Chinese culture and civilization. Buddhism thus took firm roots and prospered in China co-existing with Confucianism and Taoism, something which is unique is the world history. Buddhism made such a rapid and wonderful progress in China that according to B.K. Sarkar[3] it was said that as early as fourth century nine-tenths of the inhabitants of China were Buddhists.

The influence of Buddhism on Chinese life and thought has been manifold and tremendous. It was the characteristic of Buddhism and receptivity of the Chinese mind that very soon Buddhism got intermingled and integrated with the rich and ancient cultural traditions of China and became a part and parcel of the Chinese modes of thinking and ways of living. Keeping in view the pervasive and unmitigated influence of Buddhism on China one may wonder what kind of China it would have been had there not been introduction of Buddhism there. Further so much has been deep impact of Buddhism on Chinese life, character and culture that the history of China can not be properly understood if the role of Buddhism is ignored or misinterpreted. In the words of professor Ren Jiyu, former Director of Institute for the Study of World Religions "Buddhism has been introduced into China for nearly two thousand years and the Chinese people have come to regard it as part of their own tradition and not as a foreign culture. Its influence has far exceeded the scope of religion, and it permeates into Chinese philosophy, art, literature, language, dance, music, architecture, medicine and even family and social life. The two cultures mutually absorb each other, permeate into each other; each enriches itself and yet each retains its own distinguished features."[4]

It would really be interesting to know as to how and why Buddhism could get acceptance and strong foothold in China inspite of several hurdles and hardships. It is not unlikely and there are some positive evidences to support it that like in the rest of Asia in China also a fertile ground was already prepared by the prior influence of the Vedic thought. Dr. Wilhelm in his paper "On the sources of Chinese Taoism" in the journal of the North China Branch of the Royal Asiatic Society, Vol. IX, writes, "The suggestion lies near that Taoism and pre-Buddhistic Brahmanism may have something in common. It seems that many Brahmanic gods have found their way into Taoism even more easily than into Buddhism. Even the central notions of Taoism, *Tao* and *Te*, have an analogue in Brahman and Ātman. So we venture the suggestion that the affinity of Buddhism and Taoism may have for its reason certain Brahmanic influences on Taoism." A keen and careful observation of Buddhist monasteries and Buddhistic beliefs and practices may further lead one to think that what passes for Buddhism today in China is but varieties of the same faith that is known as Tantric and Pauraṇic Hinduism in so far as pluralism of god-lore, nature worship, mythology, iconography etc. and the personifying and concretizing tendency of Chinese Buddhism is concerned. One may wonder if the origin of the idea of Tao were not the result of the influence of the Vedic idea of Ṛta in so far as both these key concepts stand for cosmic order. It could also be that both these concepts are due to common thinking or mutual influence. It is remarkable to note that the same Pauraṇic Yakṣas and Yakṣiṇis, Dikpālas, Devatas, Nāgas, Kubera, Indra, Brahmā, Prajāpati, Gandharvas, Apsarās, Rākṣasas, piṣācas etc. are found in the Chinese Buddhist mythology and their iconographic depictios in the monasteries. So it may not be far from truth to say that the same 'Hindu' culture in general and Buddha cult in particular which prevailed in India, also came to stay permanently in China. During my official visit to People's Republic of China as a State Guest in 1986 I had the good fortune of witnessing the living and thriving Buddhism in a vivid and vibrant form.

The introduction of Buddhism in China might have been a matter of psychological necessity. It may also be that the religious consciousness of the Chinese have the same stuff as that of the Hindus. As stated earlier, there is no doubt that there is a common mindset, shared modes of thinking and ways of living. That is why one can discern an underlying commonality which has made cross movement of ideas possible. Buddhism introduced in China the doctrines of *Karma*, Karmic matter and force, *Samsāra*, ephemerality of the world and transcendental peace of *Nirvāṇa*, apart from certain fascinating pluralistic theistic beliefs which appealed to the literate and the illiterate alike. The emancipatory hope of eternal bliss was so enchanting that it fascinated almost all elderly people of China. The conception of one ultimate reality of Dharmakāya or Buddha-bhāva permeating everything, the notions of universal impermanence and suffering, non-substantiality of things, evanescence of worldly life, altruistic and noble code of conduct, universal compassion etc. deeply influenced the Chinese mind and heart. Buddhism not only evoked profound religious feelings and intense faith, it also inspired great imaginative works of art. As Kenneth K.S. Chen writes, "The decline of Buddhism in China during the last few centuries should not obscure the fact that when the religion was enjoying prestige and popularity it influenced the Chinese in very many ways and left lasting impressions on Chinese life. Neo-confucianism was stimulated in its development by a number of Buddhist ideas. Certain features of Taoism such as its canons and pantheon, were taken over from Buddhism. Words and phrases in the Chinese language owe their origin to terms introduced by Buddhism, while in astronomical, calendrical and medical studies the Chinese benefited from information introduced by Indian Buddhist monks. Finally, and most important of all, the religious life of the Chinese was affected profoundly by the doctrines and practices, pantheon and ceremonies brought in by the Indian religion."[5]

Though China's acceptance and assimilation of Buddhism coming from outside may be a wonder as China herself had a powerful civilization with a hoary past, it is a proof of metabolic dynamism of the Chinese culture. China appropriated Indian thought and adapted it to the Chinese environment. Even though after its introduction and spread in China Buddhism became more and more sinicised and adjusted itself to the Chinese cultural milieu its core and kernel remained Indian. Chinese Buddhism is Buddhism in its sinicised form. Its spirit has remained the same but its form has changed. Form is like an external shell which can be subject to modification as required by the circumstances. It can therefore be said to be the product of Indian seed on the Chinese soil. The Chinese contribution in the preservation, propagation and furtherance of Buddhist thought can not be underestimated. Once receptive of Buddhist thought China not only gave it a new look but also became its exporter. W.C. Mcgovern has truly remarked, "China once converted to the Buddhist faith turned missionary herself and most of the surrounding countries received their Buddhism through Chinese influences."[6] India and China are close neighbours who have interacted intimately for centuries togather with mutual borrowings and mutal enrichment in diverse fields. As a result of joint ventures they have made significant contributions to world culture and civilization and they still have tremendous potentialities to do so in a more meaningful and useful way. India and China should come together for this grand task. Due to accidents of history they are entangled in such a strange situation that in the cultural field they are looking at each other through some intermediaries rather than working in togetherness. Even though India is a homeland of Buddhism and China is the biggest repository of Buddhist literature, thought and culture, it is a travesty of fate that Indian scholars are not familiar with Chinese Buddhism and the Chinese scholars are not exposed to the Indian roots of Chinese Buddhism. A time has come for the beginning of a cultural renaissance and intellectual exchanges between the two great civilizations. "The Chinese scholars need to be introduced to the Hindu roots of their Buddhist heritage with a view to enable them to appreciate more of the spiritual roots and resources of their culture," as Prof. George McLean of the Catholic University of America opined when he at my invitation led a Chinese cultural delegation to India in the year 2000 for a series of colloquia with Indian scholars. As a *Kalyāṇa Mitra*, to use a Buddhist terminology, he made a noble attempt to renew cross-cultural interactions. He has given us the lead and it is for the scholarly people of the two countries to continue this task of mutual understanding and mutual enrichment through more and more exchanges and interactions.

**(iii) Spread and influence of Buddhism in Korea**

Korea has been an important Buddhist country practising Mahāyana form of Buddhism but having Hinayāna elements interspersed in it. It has reformulated Zen, Lāmāism of Tibet and Mongolia, Tantrayāna (Vajrayāna) etc. to suit Korean indigenous culture. Introduced first from India and thereafter influenced by Chinese form of Buddhism, there has been tremendous impact of Buddhism on the Korean national life and culture for about 2000 years. The mode and time of introduction of Buddhism in Korea is shrouded in mystery and there are no definite historical records available in this respect but according to one tradition it reached there by sea route around first century B.C. In ancient times Korea was divided among several small kingdoms. There was a kingdom by the name Gaya (or Garak) existing before Christian era which embraced Buddhism. Prof. Yong-kil Cho in his paper "Exchange of Buddhist Thought and Culture between India and Korea" presented in an International seminar organised by me in 2001 alludes to a work known as "Samgookyusa' (Records of Three kingdoms, Book 3, Chapter 4) written by Master Ilyeon of Goryo dynasty wherein it is recorded that an Indian princess from Ayodhya, then a Buddhist stronghold in India, was married to king Suro (42-199) of Korea. She was given the name "Queen Heohwangok'. She went to Korea by sea and took with her statue of the Buddha and materials to build a stone pagoda which was constructed in Hogyesa Temple in Kimhae, then the capital of Gaya kingdom. Later on this temple was renovated by the king Chilji in 452 A.D. The princess took Buddhist literature also along with her. This information is of vital significance so far as cultural contacts between India and Korea are concerned. The marriage of an Indian bride to a Korean bridegroom definitely implies a close and well-developed socio-cultural linkage between India and Korea. No Indian king will marry his daughter to an unknown and unfamiliar king at a far away place unless there existed close contacts, personal acquaintances and intimate social relations. Such an event must have been preceded by socio-cultural interface of quite a few centuries between the people of two countries. In ancient times such marriages among ruling classes in particular have not been uncommon but they were never among the strangers unless they were forced ones. The pertinent point is Buddhism reached Korea directly through sea route around first century B.C. or a little earlier. There are also some evidences of Indian settlements in Korea practising the Vedic faith. It is reported by Prof. Cho that in ancient Korea worship of Hwanin or Cheonie has something to do with the Vedic god Indra. Prof. Seo Yoon-gil reports about popularity of Indra belief in the paper entitled "Characteristics of Indra belief in Koryo Dynasty". Prof. Cho points out etymological affinity of Sanskrit word 'Agni' with Korean word 'Agungi' both representing the god of fire. The mode of fire worship was also similar in both the countries. He also hints at the influence of caste system of India on Korean society. He points out the inflow of Indian music and influence of Bharata's Nāṭya Śāstra venturing a suggestion of common origin of 'Nāṭya Śāstra' and Korean 'Young sanhoisang'. Prof. Rhi Ki-Yong an eminent scholar in his paper entitled "Buddhism and National culture in Korea" in an International conference organized by me along with others in 1986, writes that the word 'Seoul' has come from the Pāli word 'Sāvatthi (Skt. Śrāvasti) through its changed form 'So-Ra-Bo'. Unfortunately Indo-Korean scholars have not paid needed attention to these records which would definitely change our understanding of the dating and nature of Indo-Korean interface. There is a dire need to have a relook at ancient Indo-Korean history taking help of different literary, artistic and cultural resources which have remained untapped. If this is done, it will surely open up new vistas in Indo-Korean cultural relationship.

Though Buddhism and prior to that Vedic dharma existed in Korea before Christian era, it is generally believed that Buddhism was officially introduced in Korea in the year 372 A.D. Shilla Kingdom adopted it as official religion in 527 A.D. In the propagation of Buddhism in Korea China and later on Japan played an important role but initially there was direct exchange between India and Korea. For example, Master Gyeomic came to India by sea in 526 A.D., studied Sanskrit for five years and went back with an Indian monk. There were several other monks who visited India to learn Buddhism. In 6th century Buddha's statues and monasteries were constructed in Korea with steel and other material taken from India, particularly during the rein of Aśoka.

The influence of Buddhism on Korean life has been tremendous and unmitigated, in so far as it provided ideological foundation, cultural backup and socio-political solidarity and integration. In the words of Prof. Cho, "The influence of Buddhism on Korean thought and culture was so extensive that it can be said that we can not think of Korean thought without a reference to Buddhism which is in reality the very foundation of Korean thought and culture.

In addition to this, Buddhism in the early days in Korea provided a socio-political ideology for national integration, and inspired intellectual quests, academic activities, and creative arts of various genres. The aesthetic and spiritual values inspired by Buddhism predominated in the fine arts and the intellectual works in the kingdoms of those times."

The Korean contribution to propagation and reformulation of Buddhism has been quite significant. Once receptive of Buddhist thought Korea became its innovator and exporter. It will be very apt and appropriate to mention here as to how Buddhism got an entry into Japan from Korea. In 522 A.D. Buddhism was officially introduced to Japan from Korea at the behest of the King of Paekche, a former kingdom in South-West Korea, who sent a mission to the emperor of Japan which is as follows:

"The religion (Ho, Skt. dharma) is the most excellent of all teachings, though difficult to master and hard to comprehend, even the sages of China would not have found it easy to grasp. It brings endless and immeasurable blessings and fruits (to its believers) even the attainment of supreme enlightenment (bodhi). Just as the cintāmaṇi Jewel is said to fulfil every need according to desire, so the treasures of this glorious religion will never cease to respond in full to those who seek for it. Moreover, this religion has come to Korea from India and the people of the two countries are now ardent followers of its teachings and none are outside its pale" (Masaharu Anesaki, History of Japanese Religion P. 53).

This passage is significant in so far as it points out that Buddhism reached Korea from India and that it was held high in great reverence in Korea. Though the fundamental teachings of the Buddha remained the same, there are certain salient characteristics of Korean Buddhism which make it uniquely Korean. In fact this is so in all Asian countries which have adopted Buddhism, as the local culture and traditions transformed it. The reciprocal relationship between Buddhism and indigenous culture and faith has been of peaceful mutual adjustment of tolerance and assimilation. That is why Buddhism could make immense contribution to Korean national development and harmony. It has been regarded as 'Nation-protecting' religion in Korea. It received loyal patronage in all kingdoms and provided a socio-political framework to Korean rulers. The concepts of '*cakravarti*' and '*Buddha-kṣetra*' were handy to them for national unification and solidarity. It was recognised as state religion by many rulers. They firmly believed that their country was the land of the Buddha. The pursuit of harmony and unification were constant focal points of Korean Buddhism and therefore it was referred to as 'Tong bulkyo'.

The Buddhist influence in general and the Bodhisattva ideal in particular motivated Korean youths to patriotic and altruistic service. There were groups of young elites known as Hwarang (Flower Boys) who were builders of a new nation inspired by the Bodhisattva ideal. They helped in bringing about unification of the three kingdoms into one nation. Won-Kwang, a pioneer of Buddhist philosophy and an advocate of Saddharmapundarīka's Ekayāna, was their guide. Among several Buddhist thinkers of Korea Won-Hyo deserves a special mention. Won-Hyo was a great Buddhist Korean thinker who advocated holistic, integral and harmonised approach to reality and life. He was also inspired by Won-Kwang's writings and his advocacy of 'Secular Pañcaśīla'. Won-hyo was reveared as a nation-wide spiritual figure. He wrote 82 books, most of which were commentaries on Mahāyāna scriptures. He was proponent of peace and unity. He propounded the famous principle of 'hua-jaeng' i.e. peaceful integration through harmonisation of disputes. He regarded *pratītyasamutpāda* as the basic principle of cosmic process. He believed that *Dharmadhātu* is one and all dharmas are its manifestations within it. There is harmonious integration everywhere. For this view he relied upon the Avatamsaka Sūtra according to which "one is all, all is one; one is in all, all is in one." His exposition of the term '*Ātman*' one of the four *guṇas* of

*Mahāparinirvāṇa* (the other three are *nitya, sukha, vimala*), is really wonderful. *Ātman* is *Maheśvara* which is the nature of ultimate Reality as "Great self-existence". It is 'Hana' which means 'one unitary whole'. He emphasised meditation to experience oneness and altruistic service as its expression. The goal of life is establishment of such a society or *samgha* where there is harmonious integration without any conflict or disorder, where no body is deprived or alienated. This is *Mahāprajñā* and *Mahākaruṇā*. This is overcoming of the feeling of narrow selfish ego. This is *anātmavāda*. Won-Hyo cherished great faith in Bodhisattva Maitreya and Amitābha Buddha residing in Tuṣita. But these are all symbolic for him and not ontological. Expressing deep appreciation for Won-Hyo Prof. Rhi ki- Yong writes, "He was really a wonderful fruit that was grown on the Korean soil after the dissemination of the Indian grain. I personally hope as one of his unfitting disciples that once again this fruit grain could grow and flourish in order to illuminate this dark age of selfish materialism." The same sanguine hope is voiced by Prof. Cho who wishes that the religious tradition of India and Korea may be a major force in the future world playing an important part in furthering happiness of the human race with the spirit of non-violence.

**(iv) Spread and influence of Buddhism in Japan**

Japan is another important and presently very influential country which professes and practises Buddhism particularly of Mahāyāna variety. Buddhism has exerted an immeasurable influence on the thought and culture of Japan. Since its inception it has evolved into a form unique to Japan as it adopted itself to the local culture and ethos so as to best suit the needs and psyche of the people. It made adjustments with Shintoism and assimilated Shinto gods as various incarnations of the Buddha. Because of its catholicity, dynamism and openness it gained ground in the entire country and spread rapidly among both the elites and the masses. It gained the favour and patronage of the ruling class and soon after its introduction it became the state religion. It is believed that Buddhism known as 'Butsudo' was officially introduced to Japan from Korea in the year 552 A.D. but in the words of Dr. Amarnath Thakur, "Nonetheless this formal introduction of Buddhism did not represent the first contact of the Japanese people with the new faith. The traders and merchants or some of the immigrants from the Asiatic continent who had settled prior to the Paekche delegation also had brought the Buddhist teachings with them and very soon their religion made quite progress among the Japanese." In fact the same has been the situation in respect of Korea as well. There is a need to have a fresh look at the historical records and other available evidences. As per the present information, as stated earlier, a king of Korea sent a mission to emperor Kimmei of Japan with a message which we have described earlier in our treatment of Buddhism in Korea. He also sent some gifts in the form of statues of the Buddha and Bodhisattvas, Buddhist scriptures along with some priests, ceremonial articles etc. Afterwards prince Shotoku came to power and provided full royal patronage to Buddhism. He was himself a great Buddhist scholar who wrote commentaries on three Buddhist scriptures namely, Saddharmapundarīka Sūtra, Vimalakīrtinirdeśa and Śrīmalādevisimhanāda. He was an ardent follower and zealous propagator of Buddhism. With undefatiguable spirit he promoted Buddhism and during his rule there was phenomenal growth of Buddhist influence. Following the Lotus Sūtra he appreciated the Buddhistic conception of universal benevolence and distinguished it from the Confucian conception of propriety. He advocated the Buddhistic ideal of eradication of ego-centricity and cultivation of existential openness based on the principle of interconnectedness of all phenomena (*pratīyasamutpāda*). He emphasized the importance of realizing Buddhist truths within a concreate human nexus by establishing unity within the ultimate truth in daily life. It was world-affirming Buddhism, down to earth, and practical. His ideas are of great relevance to contemporary times in bringing about universal peace, prosperity and well-being. He is still remembered with great respect and reverence in Japan.

In the Nara period the Buddhist ideal of universal spiritual communion centred in Mahāvairocana Buddha got prominence following Avatamsaka Sūtra. Both the Saddharmapundarīka Sūtra and Avatamsaka Sūtra have heavily influenced Japanese, Chinese, Vietnamese and Korean Buddhism. During this time Saicho and Kukai came on the scene and gave a uniquely Japanese form to Buddhism. Saicho followed the Tien-tie or Tendai school based on the Saddharmapundarīka Sūtra. He advocated universality of salvation based on the *Ekayāna* theory. He insisted that the Buddhist practice is not divorced from everyday life. That is why he emphasized on the realization of ultimate unity of the whole universe in terms of 'Tathatā' in this very life. A contemporary of Saicho, Kukai founded Singon sect, a Tāntric school centred around Mahāvairocana Buddha, in which individual mystical vitalities were coordinated with cosmic vitalities contained in Mahāvairocana Buddha. This form of Buddhism is technically known as Vajrayāna according to which one can attain Buddhahood in one's life time through the regulative practices of body, speech and mind. With the help of two *mandalas*, *Vajra* and *Garbha*, Shingon Buddhism explains and correlates empirical (*samsāra, samvṛti*) and trans-empirical (nīrvāṇa, paramārtha). Kukai believed that *Dharmakāya* is personified as Mahāvairocana Buddha. *Dharmakāya* is the universal principle permeating the entire cosmos. All are manifestations of this principle and every one partakes in the same *Buddhabhāva*. Kukai was very much impressed by these noble ideas and on this basis he argued for the superiority of Buddhism over Confucianism and Taoism. Kukai was as famous as Shotoku and made considerable contribution to propagation and preservation of Buddhism in Japan. He also influenced Japanese art, culture and education. He was known for welfare activities. In Hein and Kamakura periods Genshin, Honen and Shinran popularised Sukhāvati Vyūha Sūtra and Amitāyur Dhyāna Sūtra. Meditation on and worship of Amitabha Buddha gained prominence. It is believed that he resides in the paradise Sukhavati or Tuṣita and he can cure all illness (which is symbolic). He is the Healing Buddha (*Bhaiṣaiya Guru*). During this time a new sect by the name Jodo (pure Land) came into existence. There was a difference of opinion between Honen and Shinran as to whether 'Nembutsu' (i.e. enlightenment) is innate or acquired. Honen maintained that it depends upon the mercy of Amida Buddha while Simran argued that the Buddha-nature is inherent in all of us and therefore only through self-effort this is attained. All of us have Amida Buddha indwelling in us. This is how Simran reconciled the Pure Land teaching with the traditional Buddhist doctrines. Like Nāgārjuna he insisted that there is no dualism between *samsāra* and *nirvāṇa*. Therefore he asserted tha it is possible to dwell in Amida Buddha's enlightenment while fully participating in *sāmsāric* activities. In 'Nembutsu' there is no difference between *samsāra* and *nirvāṇa*. He further maintained that one who practises 'Nembutsu' can do only good and no evil. D.T. Suzuki rated Sinran's sect, known as shin, as an outstanding Japanese contribution to the world culture. In the Kamakura period two new sects came into existence. One was Zen introduced by Eisai on the basis of Chan (Skt. Dhyāna). The Zen associated with him is known as Rinzai Zen which was popularised by Hakuin. The Rinzai Zen technique of 'Koan' is quite fascinating. In this students are given an apparently illogical question to think over. Then the teacher constantly presses them for an answer. This is followed by 'sesshin' which are intense sessions in which the teacher presses the students even harder. The purpose is not to seek any logical or rational answer and there may be none. The real aim is to get the ego of the students destroyed, or to make them realise that there is no logical answer to issues of life or to point out incorrectness of any particular answer. The same Koan can serve different purposes depending on the situation, the disposition of the student and the intention of the teacher.

The other variety of Zen known as Soto Zen was introduced by Dogen, another prominent thinker. He pondered over the vexed issue that if every one is endowed with the Buddha nature then why is there a need to train for and attain enlightenment. And the answer that he gave was, "This Dharma is amply present in every person but unless one practices, it is not manifested; unless there is realization, it is not attained". He opined, "To think practice and realization are not one is the heretical view. In the Buddha Dharma, practice and realization are identical. Because one's present practice is practice in realization, one's initial negotiation of the way in itself is the whole of original realization. Thus, even while one is directed to practice, he is told not to anticipate realization apart from practice, because practice points directly to original realization. As it is already realization in practice, realization is endless; as it is practice in realization practice is beginningless."

Thus there is no difference between practice and enlightenment. Enlightenment is not a goal to be attained at the end of practice for there is no end to practice. So if one is mindful in what one is doing then there is no distinction between practice and enlightenment. Take for example an accomplished artist. He does not cease to practice after becoming accomplished. Rather he displays greater and greater skill in producing newer master- pieces. In him enlightenment and practice go hand in hand.

Dogen further clarified that instead of saying that "All sentient beings have Buddha-nature" it should be said that "The whole of being is Buddha-nature". Similarly, he pointed out that redemption from *samsāra* is not to be confined to the sentient world only but it is to be extended to all existence. Thus he widened the basis of *nirvāṇa* from human to cosmic and made it trans-anthropocentric. He gave a very illuminating understanding of *nirvāṇa*. It is not mere transcendence of impermanence but realization of impermanence as impermanence. Mere transcendence of impermanence and reaching the state of permanence is not Buddhistic. Genuine *nirvāṇa* consists in realization of impermanence and working for enlightenment of suffering-affected *samsāra*-bound beings. This is the flow of *Mahākaruṇā* in which *samsāra* and *nirvāṇa* become one, as Nāgārjuna and Śāntideva have taught. This is what is meant by saying that. "Do not abide in *samsāra* or *nirvāṇa*." This 'no-abiding' is the true Buddhatva. It is not turning away from *samsāra* but realizing *nirvāṇa* in *samsāra*, a symbiosis of *Mahābodhi* and *Mahākaruṇā*.

Dogen advocated "deep mountain, quiet valley" approach to life. Rinzai monks, on the other hand, dwelled mainly in towns and cities. The essence of Zen teaching is, "Look into the mind and you will find Buddhahood." This practice of meditation and contemplation in day to day living has been emphasized by Dogen. The sum and substance of his teaching in his own words expressed in his master piece 'Shobo-genzo' is as follows:

"To study the Way is to study the self. To study the self is to forget the self. To forget the self is to be enlightened by all things. To be enlightened by all things is to remove the barriers between one's self and others".

In practice Dogen favours Zazen (sitting meditation) rather than Koan which is favoured by Hakuin. But emphasis on meditation and practice is common to them. It is believed that every being is possessed of *Bodhicitta* or the seed of Buddhahood. Every one is a sleeping Buddha and by meditation can realise enlightenment and gain a direct insight into the nature of reality.

Another notable thinker after Dogen is Nichiran. He was critical of Pure Land school and propagated faith in the Lotus Sutra. He wanted its promulgamation all over the world. He declared himself to be an incarnation of the Bodhisattva of Supreme Action. In the Tokugawa period we find a number of Buddhist leaders who revived, restated or reformed their own traditions and popularised Buddhism. Mention can be made of Suzuki Shosan who emphasised this worldliness and social action. He advocated faithful pursuance of one's own vocation. Realization of Buddhist truth in mundane activities entails appreciation of the practical activities of Buddhism within the human social nexus. But he wanted that care has to be taken that this should not degenerate into sheer utilitarianism of profit seeking activities. In modern times Nishida Kitaro, D.T. Suzuki, Takakusu, H. Nakamura, S. Mayeda etc. have made significant contributions toward proper understanding of Buddhism. All these thinkers have influenced and shaped the contemporary Japanese philosophy and the richness of their thoughts is yet to be adequately evaluated and fully appreciated. In recent years Japan has made substantial contribution in the spread of Buddhism in America and Canada. Several Buddhist temples have been constructed in many countries to popularise Buddhism and also for the benefit of Japanese living there. Thus after Korea and China Japan also became an exporter of Buddhism. Once receptive of Buddhist thought Japan became its zealous promoter and protector.

The contribution of Buddhism to Japanese national life, to its culture and civilization has been immense and valuable. It gave a new impetus to the development of arts, sciences, philosophy and literature.

It was not just a religion but an instrument of social service. Buddhist temples were seats of learning and social vocations. Society and temples were interrelated and they worked hand in hand for amilioration of the suffering of the people. The Buddhist monks provided community leadership. There was also perfect matching of Buddhism and state machinery. Shotoku's rule can be cited as an example. Under the influence of Buddhism the entire country was literary transformed. Buddhism helped in broadening the mental vista of Japanese people, elevated their spiritual level, refined their aesthetic sense and accelerated material progress. It is hoped that Buddhism will continue to thrive in Japan and with missionary zeal she may spread Buddhistic universal values of peace, cosmic unity and general well-being. Buddhism has taught Japan that there is a Deity who looks after the welfare of the whole universe and works for the redemption of all without discrimination irrespective of any particular tribe, clan or nation. Let Japan disseminate this learning all over the globe. The ideals of Buddha-land, Bodhisattva etc. stand for this. It is now for Japan to give the lead to the world in the field of spirituality apart from the fields of science and technology getting reinforcements from India. The present day Japan is facing the danger of extinction of its native culture nourished by Buddhism. The impact of Western consumerism and materialism has been devastating. India and Japan, and in fact the whole of Asia is engulfed in a crisis. A renewal of cross-cultural interactions will not only help and contribute to mutual understanding, mutual enrichment but it will also consolidate and vitalise common spiritual roots and resources. If we look back to our long past the wisdom of those times will help us to understand each other more intimately for our mutual benefit and enhancement.

**(v) Spread and influence of Buddhism in Tibet, Mongolia, Bhutan and Nepal**

The Buddhist influence on Tibet, Mongolia, Bhutan etc. has been strongest and most vivid so much so that Buddhism has not only become their national religion but has also entered deep into the hearts and minds of people and has shaped their entire culture and psyche. Though Buddhism went to Tibet and Mongolia from India, it was strengthened by Chinese influence and exchanges with other neighbouring countries. In Tibet it was accorded official recognition in 7th century A.D. but it reached there much earlier. After being introduced it replaced old traditional beliefs and practices and absorbed some of them in its Vajrayāna form. Indo-Tibetan scholars undertook the huge and stupendous task of Tibetan translations of Sanskrit works. Sanskrit-Tibetan dictionary known as Mahāvyūtpatti was composed to facilitate this work. Many prominent Indian scholars like Ācārya Śāntarakṣita, Ācārya Kamalaśila, Ācārya Atiśā Dīpankara etc. took active part in this enterprise and in the propagation and consolidation of Buddhism which later on assumed the form of Lamaism. There was monarchy in Tibet and the royal kings took keen interest in the spread of Buddhism in the masses. Later on priesthood became more powerful. In fourteenth century the great Tibetan scholar Tson-kha-pa founded Dge-Lugs-pa sect which till today dominates Tibetan Buddhism both spiritually and temporally through the institution of the Dalai Lama. The recognition of full and divine sovereignty of the Dalai Lama has been a turning point in the history of Tibet. The present Dalai Lama, now residing in India with a Government-in-Exile, has contributed a lot in spreading Buddhism in Europe, America, Canada, Australia and other parts of the world. By securing Noble peace prize he has become a world leader for peace.

Another sect by the name Bkah-rgyud-pa, having preponderance of *Dhyāna*, has also influenced the spread of Buddhism in Tibet. It got divided into several sub-sects among which Karma-pa and Hbrug-pa are important. The former is popular in Sikkim in India and the later in Bhutan. Mention may also be made of another old sect of Tibetan Buddhism by the name Sa-Skhya-pa which spread Buddhism in Mongolia, Siberia and other surrounding regions. The great scholar Bu-ston belonged to this sect. He was an erudite thinker and eminent commentator on Buddhist texts. He collected all the then existing Tibetan translations of Buddhist texts in several hundred volumes which are available now as Tibetan Buddhist Canon. Taranatha was another notable scholar-historian who contributed immensely by writing the history of Tibetan Buddhist literature.

Buddhism went to Mongolia both via Tibet and China but the Tibetan influence is stronger. Soon after its introduction the entire nation embraced Buddhism which became state religion. It accepted Lamaism and the Tantrayāna form of Buddhism. Buddhism is deeply rooted in Mongolia and has contributed to the spread of Buddhism in neighbouring regions of Manchuria, Siberia etc. Bhutan and Nepal are other Buddhist countries, bordering India. Nepal had the privilege of being the birth place of Śākyamuni. Though a Hindu kingdom it honours Buddhism which is not very much distinct from Hinduism. Nepal occupies a unique place in the history of Buddhism in so far as when there were Muslim invasions on India, Buddhist monks took shelter and refuge in Nepal. Nepal also served as a link between India and Tibet. Bhutan is exclusively a Buddhist country having much in common with Tibetan Buddhism.

### (vi) Spread and influence of Buddhism in Vietnam, Malay peninsula and Indonesia.

Though the countries south of India have predominance of Hinayāna or Theravāda Buddhism, Vietnam, Indonesia and Malay peninsula have major influence of Mahāyāna Buddhism. All these countries were adherents of Vedic Dharma before the introduction of Buddhism and Vedic remnants are still present there. In these countries the initial form of Buddhism was Sarvāstivāda which was transformed into Mahāyāna may be under Chinese influence. Indonesia has been a very important centre of Buddhist studies having close contacts with Buddhist centres in central India. Many Buddhist scholars came for studies to India and many went from India to Indonesia. Indian scholars like Dharmapāla, Atisa Dipankara visited Indonesia. Several monumental Buddhist structures like Borobudur still exist there. The Pāla kings from Bengal and the Chola kings from South excercised great influence. Mantrayāna, the Tāntric form of Buddhism, was also prevalent there. In Indonesia Hinduism and Buddhism still co-exist in some parts. There are conclusive evidences to show that before the advent of Buddhism the Vedic Dharma was holding its sway on the entire region including Laos and Cambodia. Śaivism was mostly popular there.

### (vii) Spread and influence of Buddhism in Ceylon, Burma, Thailand, Laos and Cambodia

Ceylon, also known as Sri Lanka or Simhala Dvipa, is another notable Buddhist country which is a stronghold of Hinayāna or Theravāda Buddhism. Though Buddhism must have reached there soon after the first Buddhist council in India, officially it was introduced by the son and daughter of King Aśoka. Before the introduction of Buddhism Hinduism was prevalent there and later on the two religions co-existed peacefully. The Buddhist influence has been so strong in Ceylon that practically the entire culture is Buddhistic. Buddhism has become interwoven into the very fabric of social, cultural and national life of the country. The Buddhist samgha has received royal patronage in the past and still it excercises great influence on national politics.

Ceylon has been a preserver and propagator of Pāli Buddhism. Not only she has preserved Pāli canon in its entirety, the Ceylonese scholars have written several commentaries on it. After India it is Ceylon which is regarded as homeland of Theravāda Buddhism. Like many other countries Ceylon also has been an exporter of Buddhism, and did not remain mere passive recipient. Her influence on Burma, Thailand, Cambodia, Vietnam, Laos, Malaya, Singapore and the countries south of India was so strong that with the exception of Vietnam all these countries mainly followed Theravāda Buddhism. Like Ceylon, Burma is another significant country practising Theravāda Buddhism. According to one local tradition Śākhya Muni himself went there to preach and two prominent merchants were his disciples. Apart from Theravāda, some adherents of Sarvāstivāda were also there. Vajrayāna also had some influence. The Burmese Buddhists developed a distinct form of *vipassana* meditation. There was a close contact between Burma and Ceylon in religious affairs.

Thailand like other South and South-East Asian countries initially adhered to Vedic Dharma but later on came under the Buddhist influence. The prevalence of Buddhism was so deep and strong that soon the entire country became popular and Pāli language flourished all over. Thailand is well-known for practising pure traditional Buddhism. It is both a national religion and a mass religion. The relation between the monarchy and the monks has been cordial. As a result of the spread of Buddhism the Vedic Dharma declined and almost disappeared. There was wholesale conversion to Buddhism and this happened with most of the countries of South and South-East Asia.

While concluding this part of the 'Introduction' it may be remarked that the prevalence of the Vedic Dharma in most of the present day Buddhist countries facilitated the introduction of Buddhism. Buddhism as a reformatory movement in the Vedic fold fascinated the elite and the masses alike. Its altruistic character and its path of redemption from suffering had a soothing effect on the minds of its adherents. Its impact in all these countries was so strong that it replaced the old traditional beliefs and practices. However, wherever Buddhism went, it became country-specific. It absorbed and assimilated local historical conditions suitably adopting itself to them. It did not come in conflict either with the Vedic dharma, which was mostly śaivism, or with the local and indigenous beliefs and practices. It retained and displayed the catholicity of Indian culture, its democratic mode of thinking and way of living. In 21st century Buddhism has tremendous potential and attracting power to have its sway all over the world with its noble ideas and ideals.

## References:

1. In preparing this write-up the author is indebted to the following works

(a) 2500 years of Buddhism (Ed.) P.V. Bapat

(b) Buddhism in China Kenneth K.S. Chen

(c) Chinese Religion through Hindu Eyes B.K. Sarkar

(d) Encyclopedia of Asian Philosophies Routledge Publishers

2. Foreword to Prof. K.S. Murthy's book, "Far Eastern Philosophies".

3. Chinese Religion through Hindu Eyes

4. Glimpses of Buddhist thought and culture (Ed.) S.R. Bhatt

5. Buddhism in China

6. Introduction to Mahayana Buddhism

References:

1. In preparing this write up the author is indebted to the following works

(a) 2500 years of Buddhism (Ed.) P.V. Bapat

(b) Buddhism in China Kenneth K.S. Chen

(c) Chinese Religion through Hindu Eyes B.K. Sarkar

(d) Encyclopaedia of Asian Philosophies Routledge Publishers

2. Foreword to Prof. K. Satchidananda Murty's book, "Far Eastern Philosophies"

3. Chinese Religion through Hindu Eyes

4. Glimpses of Buddhist thought and culture (Ed.) S.K. Bhat

5. Buddhism in China

6. Introduction to Mahayana Buddhism

# Contents

## *Chapter - 1*

# Some Problems of Pre-Buddhist History and Chronology

**H. C. Raychaudhuri**

It was the endeavour of the writer of the *Political History of Ancient India from the Accession of Parikṣit to the Extinction of the Gupta Dynasty*, part I (1919), to expose epic and Purāṇic tradition to the search-light of Vedic and early Buddhist evidence, and reconstruct a chronological frame-work for the pre-Bimbisārian period which, though opposed to certain traditional ideas, is in accordance with the testimony of the earliest literary treasures of the Brāhmaṇas and Śramaṇas. The author sought to prove that Janamejaya, son of Parikṣit, and his priests, Tura Kāvaṣeya and Indrota, flourished five or six generations before Janaka of the *Upaniṣads* and his contemporaries Uddālaka Āruṇi and Yājñavalkya. He pointed out that it was difficult to identify this Janaka with any of the kings of that name mentioned in the epic and Purāṇic lists. He noted no doubt the arguments that might be advanced in support of the view that he was the original of the legendary Sīra-dhvaja whom the *Purāṇas* represent as the father of Sītā. These, however, were not regarded as conclusive, and it was further pointed out that, in the absence of external corroboration, it was impossible to accept the entire Purāṇic list of Vaideha kings from Sīra-dhvaja downwards as reliable. The author went on to suggest that Śāṅkhāyana, who was two generations removed from Janaka of the *Upaniṣads*, was possibly a contemporary of Āśvalāyana and that Āśvalāyana was in all probability identical with Assalāyana of Sāvatthi mentioned in the early Pāli texts as a contemporary of Buddha and of Kakudha Kātyāyana, one of the leading sophists of the age.

These results have recently been challenged by Paṇḍit V. Vedāntatīrtha (henceforth abreviated as V.) in the *Annals of the Bhandarkar Oriental Research Institute,* April-July, 1932. He urges that "although Tura Kāvaṣeya stands at the 6th step in the series of teachers above Yājñavalkya and Janaka" Janamejaya himself should be placed "only a step above Janaka in conformity with several epic, Purāṇic and Vedic synchronisms." It is not necessary for us to discuss the Purāṇic synchronisms because V. himself speaks of the *Purāṇas* thus: "Collateral successions have sometimes been described in the *Purāṇas* as lineal; sometimes orders of succession (have been) reversed, (and) synchronisms misplaced." As to the epics it is well to remember that they refer to Paraśurāma as a contemporary of Rāma Dāśarathi as well as of Bhīṣma and Karṇa, and represent Hanumat and Vibhīṣana as having met Bhīmasena (*Mbh.*, iii. ch. 147-151) and Sahadeva (*Mbh.*, ii. 31) respectively. A critical study of these and similar statements in the *Mahābhārata* and the *Rāmāyaṇa* would convince any impartial student that it is extremely unsafe to depend for historical synchronisms on the uncorroborated evidence of such texts. We shall, therefore, confine ourselves to an examination of the Vedic evidence which, in the opinion of V., supports the view that "Janamejaya Pārīkṣita was…an older contemporary of Janaka Vaideha and Yājñavalkya Vājasaneya."

V. observes that the use of *laṅ* in the verb *bhu* in the interrogation "*Kva Pārīkṣita abhavan*" attributed to a contemporary of Yājñavalkya and Janaka, shows that the death of Janamejaya and his brothers happened during the lifetime of Yājñavalkya. But the question was not actually framed for the first time by a sage of Janaka's Court. He had heard about it and its solution from people in the Madra country. The passage, therefore, is what is termed by grammarians and others as a *mūrdhābhiṣikta udāharaṇa*, and it cannot be regarded as establishing the contempraneity of Janamejaya and Janaka. Moreover, persons with a real acquaintance with our ancient literature know that *laṅ* was often used in reference to events that happened in olden times.[1]

1. Cp.

चम्पस्य तु पुरी चम्पा।
या मालिन्य भवत् पुरा॥
हरिवंश, ३१, ४९.

तथांगस्यतु राजर्षे राजासीद्-दधिवाहनः।
सापराध सुदेष्णाया अनपानोऽभवन्नृपः॥
अथ चित्ररथस्यापि राजा दशरथोऽभवत्।
लोभपाद इति ख्यातो यस्य शान्ता सुताभवत्॥
वायुयुराण, ९९, १००-१०३.

Another argument brought forward to prove the synchronism of Janamejaya and Janaka of the *Upaniṣads* is that "a Vedic teacher named Dantabāla Dhaumra was...received by king Janamejaya Pārīkṣ-ita." 'Dantabāla Dhaumra' is represented as the corrupt form of the name 'Dantāla Dhaumya' which occurs in the *Jaiminīya Brāhmaṇa* as the designation of a contemporary of Somaśuṣma Sātyayajñi and, therefore, of Janaka. Now, the emendation of the name 'Dantabāla Dhaumra' into 'Dantāla Dhaumya' is as unjustifiable as the equation of Mādhavācārya, the author of the *Sarra-darśana-saṃgraha*, with Madhvācārya, the *Draita* exponent of the Vedānta. Moreover, as the reference to Dantabāla occurs in the mythical legend of Janamejaya and the two ganders, its value for chronological purposes may very well be discounted.

Writers who bring down Janamejaya, the contemporary of Indrota, to the time of Somaśuṣma, fifth in the decending line from that teacher, forget that in the time of Dṛti Aindrota, the son and pupil of Indrota, Janamejaya was obviously dead and the Kuru throne was occupied by Abhipratārin Kākṣaseni (*Vedic Index,* I, 373).

It will be seen that in his anxiety to support his theory V, has found it necessary to emend Vedic texts and blink over details that do not exactly fit in with his notions. But what is more regrettable is the attribution to the author of the *Political History* of views which he did not really entertain. Thus V, coolly suggests that the author has placed *all* the Videhas mentioned in the *Purāṇas from* Śīradhvaja to Kṛti, six generations after Janamejaya Pārīkṣita. As a matter of fact, the author, while not oblivious of the possibility of the Janaka of the *Upaniṣads* being the original of the Purāṇic Sīradhvaja, does not consider the identification as certain and regards the Purāṇic lists of later Vaidehas as of doubtful historical and chronological value. He says distinctly even in the first edition of his work (p. 38) that "with the exception of Ariṣṭa and Nemi or Nami none of the kings in the Purāṇic lists can be satisfactorily identified with the Videhan monarchs mentioned in the Vedic. Buddhist and Jaina literature. It is, therefore, difficult to say how far the Purāṇic lists are historical." The point has been made clearer in the later editions of the *Political History*, where it is stated that "as the identification of Sīradhvaja with the Vedic Janaka is by no means certain, it is not easy to determine which of the kings mentioned in the Purāṇic lists actually came after the contemporary of Āruṇi and Yājñavalkya."

The view, however, that has evoked the most bitter criticism is the identification of Āśvalāyana with Assalāyana, the contemporary of Buddha, with which is connected the problem of the identity of Kabandhī Kātyāyana. The identification of Āśvalāyana with Assalāyana was suggested on the following grounds:—

(1) Identity of names: Āśvalāyana=Assalāyana.

(2) Identity of the place of residence: Āśvalāyana was a man of Kosala (Kausalya). Assalāyana, too, was a man of Kosala, being an inhabitant of Sāvatthi in Kosala.

(3) Connection with the *Kalpa* literature: Āśvalāyana is a great master of the *Kalpa Sūtras* and his name is associated with the famous works on ritual known as the *Āśvalāyana Srauta Sūtra* and *Āśvalāyana Gṛhya Sūtra*. Assalāyana, too, is described as "*Tiṇṇaṃ vedānaṃ pāragū sanighaṇḍu ketubhānaṃ*" *Ketubha* is explained as "*kappa vikappo karīnaṃ upakārāya* satthaṃ," Kappa=Kalpa, 'the rules concerning rites, one of the Vedāṅgas.'

(4) Synchronism with the Philosopher Kātyāyaṇa who is called *Kabandhî* in the *Praśna Upaniṣad* and Pakudha or *Kakudha* in the Pāli texts. Pakudha (Kakudha) Kātyāyana was not a 'degenerate mediocrity' but "the head of an order, of a following, the teacher of a school, well known and of repute as a sophist, revered by the people, a man of experience, who has long been a recluse, old and well-stricken in years." (*Sāmaññaphala sutta, Dialogues of the Buddha*, I. 66).

Prof. Barua, who accepts the identity of Kabandhî Kātyāyana with Kakudha Kātyāyana, and traces a community of ideas in their philosophy, puts forward the suggestion that Kabandhî and Kakudha refer to the same physical deformity, viz. a hump on the shoulders (*Pre-Buddhistic Indian Philosophy*, 281). But he does not develop the point. In the *Atharva Veda*, however, Kabandha, when used in reference to a *Puruṣa* (X. 2. 3), means the part of the body that is "four-fold" (*catuṣṭayam*), with ends connected (*saṃhitāntam*), above the knees (*jānubhyāmūrdham*) and soft or pliant (*śithiram*). It is sharply distinguished from the *Kusindha* or trunk which supports the *aṃsau* (shoulders), and is *sudṛḍha* (firm). The *Kabandha* above the *knees*, which is *four-fold*, *śithira* and *saṃhitānta* (with ends connected), and is sharply distinguished from the *Kusindha* (trunk, not body) which supports the shoulders, must be identified, not with the belly or trunk, but with the *śroṇī* and the *urū* mentioned in the same verse (the two hips and the two thighs, four in all). And it is well known that *Kakudmatī*, lit. possessed of *Kakud*, refers, according to Amara, to the same part of the body (*kaṭo na śroṇī-phalakaṃ kaṭiḥ śroṇi kakud-matī*). It may also be noted here that in the Vedas (*Ṛg.*, V, 54, 8), *Kabandhin* is a special epithet of the Maruts who, by the way, are often styled *gomātāraḥ* 'having a cow for their mother' (*Vedic Mythology,* 78) and to whom the *Kakud* of the *ṛṣabha* ("bearing a *Kabandha*") is especially appropriated (*Atharva*, IX, 4, 38). Inpost-Vedic literature *kakud* frequently means a mountain peak (cf. *Raghu,* XIII, 47). The same idea may be conveyed by the word *Kabandhin,* 'cloud-capped' for according to Yāska (X, 4, 1) *Kabandha iti megha ucyate,* and *Parvatāśaya,* 'resting on mountains' means clouds and clouds alone according to the *Śabda-candrikā*. Megha-sakha, Meghmāla and Meghavat are well known mountain names (Cp. also the list of Meghanāmāni in the *Nighaṇṭu* (i. 10).

In this connection it is interesting to note that Kakudha Kātyāyana was a believer in 'seven things' that are 'steadfast as a *mountain peak*, as a pillar firmly fixed.'

Further, the word *kakudha* is frequently used in Pali literature to mean a *kakudha-bhaṇḍa*, which literally means a vessel, decoration or equipage (*bhājanādi parikkhāra*) with a projection or bulge (*kakud*) and is specially applied to the *uṇhīsa* and four other *insignia regis*. Now, the word *kabandha* has also the sense of a barrel, cask or large bellied vessel and, if the etymology of Kṣīrasvāmin (*kasya śiraso bandhotra kabandhaḥ*) is correct, it meant literally an *uṣṇīs*, rather than an *apamūrdha kalevara.*

Lastly, in the *Mahāvaṃsa*, XV, *kakudha* is the name of a little *vāpi* (reservoir of water). According to Yāska and Amara, *kabandha* has the sense of water. So that *Kabandhin* may also mean a reservoir of water.

The chief reason why V. finds it impossible to accept the identity of Āśvalāyana and Kabandhî Kātyāyana with elder contemporaries of Buddha, is the apprehension that as a consequence of such identifications Hiraṇya-nābha will have to be placed in the sixth century B.C., and Yājñavalkya and his contemporaries will be brought down 'to only a step above Gautama Buddha.' It should be remembered by V. that Āpastamba (*Dh. S.*, 1. 2. 5. 4-6) clearly refers to Śvetaketu as an *avara* and that Pāṇini, a writer who knew the *Yavana* alphabet and made his mark, according to the *Kāvya*

Mīmāṃsā (p. 55), in the city of Paṭalīputra founded after the death of Buddha, does not include Yājñavalkya's works among Purāṇa-prokta Brāhmaṇas. (IV. 3. 105 read with Kātyāyana's *Vārttika*). Cp. also the commentator's statement *Yājñavalkyādāyo* hi na cirakālā ityākhyāneṣu vārtā (Goldstücker, *Pāṇini*, p. 106). The *Saṃhitās* and *Brāhmaṇas* are not works of single authors or the products of a single age, and though the bulk of these works may be very old (*purāṇa-prokta*), particular portions may be late as is suggested by the evidence of Pāṇini and others.

*Chapter - 2*

# Studies in Early Buddhist Historiography

**U.N. Ghoshal**

Buddhism introduced into Indian literature two of its branches till then imperfectly, if at all, developed. These were the branches of sacred biography and church-history. It is true that the antecedent Vedic literature was not wanting in enumerations of teachers and successions of teachers of the Brahmanical sacrificial ritual. The Brāhmaṇas contain *vaṃśas* (genealogies) giving lists of teachers, sometimes fifty or sixty in lineal succession, who are credited with handing down one or other portion of the ritual from the gods. Apart from these general lists, individual teachers like Yājñavalkya and Śāṇḍilya are quoted as authorities for distinct portions of the later Vedic Saṃhitās and the Brāhmaṇas. But these authors were essentially interpreters of the sacred tradition which had gathered into a great mass in course of time. It was therefore no wonder that the *vaṃśas* remained mere lists of names without even the elements of a biography. On the other hand the rise of various religious movements at the epoch of the rise of Buddhism, brought into the forefront a number of persons who were marked out from their predecessors by their more or less distinctive teachings, who personified as it were in themselves the whole of their message. Nothing, therefore, could be more natural than that the lives of these Masters should from the first form the subject of reverent investigations by their disciples. What we have said about the biographies of these teachers would apply in a like manner to the history of their religious orders. It is only with two of these religious movements, Buddhism and Jainism and more specially with the first, that the student of early Indian histriography is concerned.

It would obviously be improper to judge by the modern critical standards the old Buddhist historical or quasi-historical texts such as we find embedded in the Pāli and Sanskrit canonical literatures. They transport us to an atmosphere where heroic poetry was very much in vogue, where beast-fables delighted the hearts of the learned and unlearned alike, where the doctrines of rebirth and *karma* were held to have undisputed sway over the lives and actions of men. The pious monks, probably the reciters (*bhāṇakas*) of the discourses, who composed the texts long after the event, looked upon their Master as the great Pathfinder, possessed of the three-fold knowledge and the ten powers, who had qualified himself for his high calling by his strenuous striving in previous successive rebirths.[1] And yet it is not unprofitable to study their works if only to discover the successive layers of the legend and the principles of their growth. In the present paper I shall confine myself to a small portion of my subject, viz., the biography of the Buddha, reserving the lives of Buddhist saints and the history of the Buddhist Church for a separate treatment.

In the whole range of Pāli canonical literature, there is no connected biography of Buddha. Interspersed with the canonical texts on Doctrine and Discipline, however, is a number of episodes describing the Master's ancestry and birth, His infancy and youth, His renunciation, austerities and enlightenment, His career as a wandering preacher and lastly His *nirvāṇa*. The same appears to have been the case with the oldest parts of the Sanskrit canon. Out of these separate legends were woven in later times and with numerous additions, complete biographies of the Buddha, such as we find in the Pāli commentaries and chronicles as well as in the Sanskrit *Mahāvastu* and *Lalitavistara*.

The form and contents of the early Buddhist historical or semi-historical texts were determined by the circumstances of their origin. Like all expanding religions Buddhism was split up in course of time into a number of schools or sects. The present Pāli canonical literature represents the scriptures of only one of these schools, the Theravādins. There is good reason to believe that a canonical literature essentially similar to this one existed already in the time of Aśoka.[2] The canonical literature of other schools has been preserved in the form

1. For the conception of Buddha's personality in the Pāli canon, see E.J. Thomas, *History of Buddhist Thought*, pp. 148-150.

2. Cf. Winternitz, *A History of Indian Literature*, vol. II, p. 18; E.J. Thomas, *Early Buddhist Scriptures*, Introduction, p. xxi.

of Sanskrit fragments recently brought to light in Central Asia, as well as in Tibetan and Chinese translations. It is however a curious fact that the sacred works of these sects at first were handed down by oral tradition alone and were not put to writing till centuries afterwards. Thus according to a tradition of the *Dīpavaṃsa* and *Mahāvaṃsa* which has been accepted as trustworthy, the Pāli Tripiṭaka along with its commentaries was fixed in writing for the first time under the Siṃhalese king Vaṭṭagāmaṇi in the first century B.C.[1] Now the oral mode of transmitting the canon has been traditional in India since the early Vedic times and it has been shown in the case of the Vedic literature how it was possible by a series of elaborate arrangements to preserve the purity of the sacred texts with conspicuous success. In so far as the Buddhist doctrinal teachings are concerned, the oral transmission was attended with the same happy results. A comparison of the scriptures of the Theravādins with those of the Mahāsaṅghikas and the Sarvāstivādins shows not only a common doctrinal basis but also a common arrangement of discourses and monastic rules.[2] In the case of the stories and legends of Buddha's life, however, there was from the first a strong doctrinal motive for transforming his personality into that of a Superman. In this process of transformation, the authentic facts of the Teacher's life tended to be obscured or forgotten, while numerous legends gathered around the various incidents of his career from his conception to his *Nirvāṇa*. How early these legends found their way into recognition will appear from the fact that the romantic tales of Buddha's miraculous conception and birth and the dogmatic beliefs about the six preceding Buddhas occur in the texts of the Pāli as well as the Sanskrit canon.

Beginning with the ancestry of the Buddha, we have a Pāli canonical discourse, the Ambaṭṭha sutta of the *Dīgha Nikāya* which gives a story of the folk-lore type about the origin of the Śākyas. There the origin is traced to the eponymous ancestors, four brothers and their sisters, who, expelled by their royal father at the behest of their step-mother, took refuge on the Himalayan slopes where they intermarried with each other to preserve the purity of their race.[3]

1. Cf. Winternitz, *op. cit.*, p. 8.
2. Cf. E.J. Thomas, *Early Buddhist Scriptures*, Introduction, p. xii.
3. For the Ambaṭṭha sutta, see Text in *D.N.*, P.T.S. edition, vol. I, pp. 92-93; tr., Rhys Davids *Dialogues of the Buddha*, vol. I, pp. 114-15. On the relation of this legend to the Rāma story in the *Rāmāyaṇa* and especially in the *Dasaratha Jātaka*, see, E.J. Thomas, *Life of the Buddha*, pp. 10-12 and the authorities quoted there.

From the polemical way in which this story of Śākya origins is put forward—as an answer to a proud Brāhmaṇa's description of them as menials—it would seem that there was at this time some dispute about the ancestry of the Śākya people. Whatever that may be, the above story marks a deliberate attempt to ennoble the origin of the Buddha, which is not justified by the incidental allusions to the comparative insignificance of the Śākya stock in other parts of the canon.[1] Of the genealogy of the Buddha, the Pāli canon gives very slender details. Only in such admittedly late suttas as the Mahāpadāna sutta of *Dīgha Nikāya* and the *Buddhavaṃsa* involving the dogmatic belief in a succession of Buddhas, do we come across the names of Gautama's father and mother along with his birth-place. There is no trace in the Pāli canonical literature of any attempt on the one hand to connect the Śākyas with Mahāsammata, the first king of the present cycle according to Buddhist beliefs, and on the other to carry forward the descent of Śākya kings to Buddha. Such connected accounts are found for the first time in the Pāli commentaries and chronicles, in the *Mahāvastu* and in the Vinaya of the Sarvāstivādins.[2] There can be little doubt that these later developments were inspired by the Puranic accounts of the descent of royal houses from the fabled Manu, the son of Vivasvān.

Of the conception and birth of the Buddha, we have a number of stories or legends alike in the Theravāda (Pāli) canon and in the canon of the Sarvāstivādins and other sects. In its simplest and most general form it occurs in the Soṇadaṇḍa sutta of the *Dīgha Nikāya* where it is said that the Samaṇa Gotama is "well-born on both sides, of pure descent through the mother and through the father back through seven generations with no slur put upon him and no reproach in respect of birth."[3] With this contrast the elaborate account in the Acchariya-abbhuta-dhamma-sutta of *Majjhima Nikāya*, which Ānanda recounts to the assembled monks "exactly as he has heard it from the lips of his Master." The Bodhisattva lived in his Tuṣita form during the whole term of his existence. Leaving this form, he entered his mother's womb to the accompaniment of a measureless vast effulgence. As soon as he enters his mother's womb, four deities guard the four

---

1. Cf. E.J. Thomas, *op. cit.*, p. 20.
2. Cf. tr. of Buddhaghoṣa's commentary on Ambaṭṭha Sutta in Thomas, *Life of the Buddha*, pp. 7-10; *Mahāvastu*, vol. I, pp. 338ff.; Rockhill, *Left of the Buddha*, ch. I, etc.
3. Text in *D.N.*, P.T.S. ed., I, p. 115; tr. in Rhys Davids, *Dialogues*. vol. I, p. 147.

cardinal points to keep watch over the precious child, while the mother is freed from all physical and mental ailments. The mother gives birth in an erect position and the child as it issues out from his mother's womb is received by the gods and bathed with two jets of water starting from mid-air. Then he takes seven strides to the north proclaiming his pre-eminence. This is attended as before by the outburst of supernatural effulgence.[1] The above extract, it will be seen, professes to trace Buddha's antecedent existence in the Tuṣita heaven ("Heaven of Delight"). To what extent this pious belief in the previous lives of the Buddha was developed thus early is shown by the existence of two separate works, the gāthā of the Jātaka and the *Cariyāpiṭaka*, as constituents of the canon. The characteristic incident of the Bodhisattva assuming the form of a white elephant, however, before entering his mother's womb, is not found till we reach the later works like the *Nidānakathā* and the *Lalitavistara*.

Another sutta of the Pāli canon, the Nālakasutta of the *Sutta Nipāta*, of which parallel versions occur in the *Lalitavistara* and the *Nidānakathā* introduces us to one of the most famous episodes of the Buddha's infancy. This is the visit of the sage Asita to see the Holy Child shortly after His birth. The metrical introduction (*Vatthugāthā*) of the Nālakasutta which contains this legend belongs to the class of metrical narratives or ballads out of which the later Buddha epic has grown.[2] Not only in its form but in its contents it anticipates the later works. For it describes, through the mouth of the sage, the Bodhisattva's possession of the external marks of the Superman and the famous prophecy of his attaining the summit of enlightenment.[3]

In the Mahāpadāna sutta of the *Dīgha Nikāya* the career of the Buddha is brought into relation with the Buddhist concept of the great time-cycles (*kalpas*) and their divisions which are marked by diminishing durations of the span of human lives. In course of these *kalpas*, we are told, there have arisen several Buddhas, viz., Vipassi, Sikhi, Vessabhu, Kakusandha, Konāgamana, Kassapa and Gotama. The

1. Text in *Majjhima Nikāya*, P.T.S. ed., vol. III, pp. 119-122; tr. in Chalmers, *Further Dialogues*, part II, pp. 223ff.; in Thomas, *Life of the Buddha*, pp. 30-31.
2. Cf. Winternitz, *op. cit.*, p. 96 and the authorities there quoted.
3. See *Sutta Nipāta*, 679-98; tr. in Thomas, *Early Buddhist Scriptures*, pp. 1-5. Cf. also *Nidānakathā*, V. Fausböll's ed. of the *Jātaka*, vol. I, pp. 54ff.; and tr. in Rhys Davids, *Buddhist Birth Stories*, pp. 157-160. Also Cf. *Lalitavistara*, Lefmann's ed., pp. 101ff. and tr. in Thomas, *Life of the Buddha*, pp. 39-41.

lives of these Buddhas follow a uniform pattern. For the text gives for each of them in identical phraseology his particular time-cycle, his *jāti* and *gotta*, his tree of enlightenment, his two chief disciples and his usual attendant, his parents and birth-place. What is more, the miraculous story of Gotama's conception and birth such as we have quoted from the *Majjhima Nikāya* text above-mentioned is found to be repeated *verbatim* in the case of the first Buddha.[1]

The lives or legends of the Buddhas are described at great length in another work of the Pāli canon to which we have referred above. This work is the *Buddhavaṃsa* which is incorporated in the *Khuddaka Nikāya*. It gives in as many chapters the legends of the twenty-four Buddhas supposed to have preceded Gotama in the past twelve *kalpas* and it winds up in the last chapter with a sort of autobiography describing in Gotama's own words his last earthly existence. The tendency towards schematization which was noticed above is still more prominent in the present text where the same principal incidents are repeated in a very monotonous fashion about the career of each of these Buddhas.

It will be noticed from the above that we have here, as in other cases, an initial stage of plain and matter-of-fact narrative. In the next stage the narrative has grown into a mythological account professing to trace the story to Buddha's antecedent existence in the Tuṣita heaven and claiming a supernatural conception and birth for the holy child. In the last stage the legend has been intertwined with Buddhist cosmological and cosmogonic concepts of *kalpas* with their outcrop of Buddhas and the whole has been standardised according to a uniform pattern.

The stories or legends of Buddha's renunciation, austerities and enlightenment are told in a number of passages in the Pāli canon. In the Ariya-pariyesana sutta ("Discourse of the Noble Quest") of the *Majjhima Nikāya*, the Bodhisattva tells us that he at first pursued what was subject like himself to rebirth, decay and the rest. Then when he reflected on their vanities, he was led to pursue "the consummate peace of Nirvāṇa which knows neither rebirth nor decay, neither disease nor death, neither sorrow nor impurity." He then started, despite the wishes of his parents who wept and lamented, to go forth from the householder's to the homeless life. He sought

1. Text in *Digha Nikāya*, P.T.S. ed., vol. II, pp. 2ff.; tr. in Rhys Davids, *Dialogues*, part II, pp. 5ff.

instruction successively from Ālāra Kālāma and Uddaka Rāmaputta, but finding no satisfaction he came to the township of Uruvela where he sought and won "the consummate peace of Nirvāṇa."[1]

Another equally connected account occurs in the Mahāsaccaka sutta of the *Majjhima Nikāya*, which speaks of the Renunciation in still more general terms and describes the austerities at great length. Here we are told that the Bodhisattva reflecting on the contrast between life at home and life in the open donned the yellow robes and went forth from the house-holder's to a homeless life. There flashed on him the three allegories which led him to practise the hardest austerities till at last, convinced of their futility, he renounced his fasting and was able to enter into the five successive trances and attain the supreme knowledge.[2]

In contrast with the above more or less general accounts we have other legends and traditions dealing with this specific episode of the Buddha's career. A passage in the *Aṅguttara Nikāya* attempts to give a dramatic turn to the incidents of the Renunciation. The Buddha, we are told, was a delicately nurtured youth having for himself three lotus pools and three palaces (one for the cold, one for the hot and one for the rainy season). There came to him the poignant reflection on old age, sickness and death and all the elation in life disappeared.[3] It seems unlikely that the above is based on a genuine historical tradition if only because of the essentially poetical character of the story of the three palaces which is likewise told of Vipassi Buddha in the Mahāpadāna sutta above quoted[4] and of the noble youth Yasa in the *Mahāvagga* of the Vinaya Piṭaka.[5] With the further development of the legend in which Gautama's abstract reflections are made to take the concrete shapes of an aged man, a sick man and a corpse, followed as a dramatic contrast by the sight of a contemplating hermit, we are not here concerned. It is, however, important to remember that even this development which is found

1. Text in *Majjhima N.*, P.T.S. ed., vol. I, pp. 160-175; tr. in Chalmers, *Further Dialogues*, Part I, pp. 113-118; in Thomas, *Early Buddhist Scriptures*, pp. 9-15, 23-29.

2. Text in *Majjhima N.*, P.T.S. ed., vol. I, pp. 240-249; tr. in Rhys Davids, *Dialogues*, pp. 173-178; Thomas, *Life of the Buddha*, pp. 62-68; Thomas, *Early Buddhist Scriptures*, pp. 19-22.

3. Text in *Aṅguttara N.*, P.T.S. ed., vol. I, p. 145; tr. in Thomas, *Life of the Buddha*, pp. 47, 51.

4. *Dīgha Nikāya*, vol. II, p. 21.

5. Vinaya Piṭaka, I, 7. 1.

in *Nidānakathā*,[1] the Sarvāstivādin Vinaya,[2] and other works, is anticipated in the story of Buddha Vipassi as described in the Mahāpadāna sutta above mentioned.[3]

The canonical texts above-quoted are silent about the temptation of Māra which plays such a conspicuous part in the later Buddhist works as well as in the Buddhist art from the Gandhāra school downwards. The Padhānasutta ("Discourse of Striving") of the *Sutta Nipāta*, however, of which parallel versions exist in the Sanskrit *Mahāvastu* and *Lalitavistara*, contain the first suggestion of this legend. In this sutta not only is Māra said to have vainly tempted Buddha while engaged in the performance of his austerities, but Lust, Aversion, Hunger and Thirst are personified as Māra's armies and Māra himself is said to have surrounded Buddha with his elephant arrayed in battle.[4] It is easy to understand how the dramatic rendering of Buddha's spiritual struggles during his strivings developed in the later legend into the story of an actual conflict between the Bodhisattva and the Power of Evil at the moment of the former's attaining the supreme enlightenment.

The story of the Buddha's last year, his *nirvāṇa* and his funeral is told in a number of texts in the Pāli as well as Sanskrit canonical literature. These consist, on the one hand, of the Sagātha sutta of the *Saṃyutta Nikāya* and the oft-quoted Mahāparinibbāṇa sutta of the *Dīgha Nikāya* and on the other hand, of the Nirvāṇa sūtras of the Sanskrit *Saṃyukta Āgama* as well as those of the Vinaya of the Sarvāstivādins and Mūla-Sarvāstivādins. Of these, the Sanskrit *Saṃyukta Āgama* and the Mūla-Sarvāstivādin Vinaya are preserved in translation in the Chinese Tripiṭaka while the Sarvāstivādin Vinaya is preserved in the Dulva section of the Tibetan Bkah-gyur. To the French scholar Jean Przyluski belongs the credit of the most thorough examination of the different Parinirvāṇa texts, making it possible to trace the gradual accretions of the legendry matter therein. Thus, in the first place, regarding the so-called 'stanzas of lamentation' uttered by various personages, human and divine, immediately after Buddha's death, Przyluski observes:

---

1. Tr. in Thomas, *Life of the Buddha*, pp. 52-53.
2. Rockhill, *Life of the Buddha*, pp. 22ff.
3. Text in *Digha Nikāya*, vol. II, pp. 21-29; tr. in Rhys Davids, *Dialogues*, pp. 18-22.
4. Text of Padhānasutta in *Sutta Nipāta*, 425-429; Cf. *Mahāvastu*, vol. II, p. 238 and *Lalitavistara*, p. 327.

"In the canon of the Sthaviras as much in that of the Mūlasarvāstivādins, we discern in the last analysis two parinirvāṇa sūtras: one very short, almost entirely recorded in verse (*Saṃyukta Āgama* and Pāli *Saṃyutta Nikāya*), the other, which reproduces the stanzas of the first, while inserting in it long developments inprose (Vinaya of the Mūlasarvāstivādins and the Mahāparinibbāṇasutta)."[1]

Proceeding further with his analysis of the stanzas abovementioned, Przyluski points out that while the versified portions of the *Avadānaśataka* and the Mūlasarvāstivādin Vinaya predicate of the Buddha a simple funeral, the prose portions of the Mūlasarvāstivādin Vinaya and the Pāli Mahā-parinibbāṇa Sutta attribute to him a pompous funeral like that of cakra-vartins. His view on this point may be explained in his own words as follows:

"Before being deified Śākyamuni was in the eyes of the faithful not essentially different from other men. He was a *bhikṣu par excellence*. The most ancient tradition accordingly recorded that he had the funeral of a religieux and was shrouded in the cīvaras. Meanwhile the popular con-science had conceived a type of kings superior to the greatest monarches of the earth.... This grant movement of ideas had a profound repercussion upon the legend of the Buddha. The legend of King Mahāsudassana is perhaps the most typical example of this kind. It was bodily inserted in the *Ta-pan-nio-p'an-king* and the other nirvāṇasūtras. But the redactors of *Dīgha* preferred to isolate it for making it an independent sutta. This legend had for its object to show that Śākyamuni in his past existences was a puissant *cakravartin* king. The ancient ceremonial of Buddha's funeral appeared from that time to be very vulgar. The sacred body, marvellously beautiful, could not have been shrouded in coarse clothes, common and slovenly. Ere long it was admitted that the funerals of Śākyamuni had been as pompous as those of *cakravartin* kings. It was even pretended that shortly before his death, he had clearly expressed his intentions on the subject."[2]

In the above account we can trace the development of the conception of Buddha's personality from an ordinary monk to a Superman, the equivalent of a universal Emperor. Another line of evolution may be traced in the account of the last journey of Buddha

---

1. *Le Parinirvāṇa et les funérailles du Buddha* in *Journal Asiatique* Mai-Juin 1918, pp.511-512, English tr. by the present writer.
2. J. Przyluski, *op. cit.*, pp. 514-515, English tr. by the present writer.

forming the prelude to the closing scenes of his life in the different redactions of the Nirvāṇa-sūtras. On this point again we can quote the views of the French scholar just mentioned.

"The udānas (verses of the Mūlasarvāstivādin Vinaya) enable us to go back to an epoch when the Magadha kingdom was the citadel of Buddhism. At this stage which we might call the era of Rājagṛha, the account of the last journey of the Buddha consisted essentially of a series of discourses which Bhagavat was supposed to have pronounced in course of the route.........Vaiśāli was then in contemplation only for mentioning the last look cast at it by the Master and perhaps also for the reception of Buddha by the courtesan Ambapāli. The diffusion of Buddhism in the Vṛji country marked the beginning of a second period. Vaiśāli acquired a puissant influence in its church. It attracted, while giving them an original turn, a certain number of traditions till then localised elsewhere. A new episode of the biography of the Buddha, the scenes of 'the rejection of life,' was likewise laid at Vaiśāli. The theologians introduced into the account the words of blame addressed to Ānanda and a new theory on the stages of the moral life.........All these traits which characterised the period of Vaiśāli are much more accentuated in the Mahāparinirvāṇasūtra than in the Parinirvānasūtra of the Mūlasarvāstivādins. Finally, the new faith spread into new regions and stretched to the foot of the Himalayas. The opulent city of Śrāvastī, ennobled in its turn, attracted to its territory a great number of legends and edifying scenes. Under the influence of this new current the account of the last journey of Buddha broke up, and some of its elements, transported towards the north, were finally gathered up by the compilers of the Sanskrit Ekottara-Āgama."[1]

Let us conclude this brief survey with some general remarks on the nature and services of early Buddhist Histriography. We have seen how the canon presents us as yet not with a connected narrative of the Buddha's biography, but with detached notices relating to the most striking episodes of his career. These notices obviously do not belong to the same chronological or intellectual stratum. Some texts (or portions of the same text) are simple and matter-of-fact accounts, while others are embellished with much legendary and dogmatic matter. We have thus on the one hand the picture of a very human Teacher, earnest in imparting his message to all and sundry,

1. Przyluski, *op. cit.*, Nov.-Dec. 1918, pp. 455-456.

remorseless in vanquishing his opponents with his logic and withal overflowing with human sympathy and kindness. On the other hand there is conjured up before our eyes a Superman having a long series of prototypes in the remote past, the chief incidents of whose career are marked by miracles and legends. In so far as the oldest narratives are concerned, we may grant that they are not the compositions of eye-witnesses, but we have no doubt that they have handed down the genuine tradition of the Founder's career. The strange view of R.O. Francke which looks upon Gautama Buddha as but a dogmatic conception has been condemned on just and proper grounds.[1] To the other arguments advanced against Francke's view, we may add one derived from the analogy of Caitanya's biography. It is a fact that the biographical notices of this great Bengali saint of the late 15th and early 16th centuries, unlike those of the Buddha, go back to the Teacher's own life-time. One of these contemporary writers, Murāri Gupta, tells us how Caitanya, after the great spiritual crisis of his career (his visit to Gayā and initiation by Īśvarapurī) was proclaimed as a portion of Viṣṇu. What is more, he was consecrated as a deity in the presence of a large number of his disciples and his own image was set up for worship in a number of different places almost immediately after he had assumed the vow of *sannyāsa.*[2] If such was the fate of Caitanya in his own life-time, it was no matter for surprise that the historical Buddha should have been invested with extra-human attributes in the course of oral transmission of his teachings. For the rest, the stories of the Buddha's life in the Pāli canon are not without interest for subsequent times. They lay down in broad outline the legend which was filled in by the authors of the *Aṭṭhakathās*, the source-books of the Pāli commentaries and chronicles and by the later compilers of Sanskrit quasi-canonical works. Thus was formed what may be called the standard biography of the Buddha which dominated Buddhist art and literature till it was thrown into the shade by the rise of Docetic ideas in the schools of Mahāyāna Buddhism.

1. See Winternitz, *op. cit.*, pp. 598-601 and the authorities there quoted.
2. See Biman Bihari Majumdar, *Caitanya-Cariter Upādān* (in Bengali). Published by the Calcutta University, 1939, pp. 590-605.

## *Chapter - 3*

# 25th Centenary of the Buddha

**Narendra Nath Law**

### A. The 25th Centenary of the Parinirvāṇa of the Buddha

This year was witnessed the 25th centenary of the Parinirvāṇa of Gautama Buddha—the apostle of peace and love. Torn as the world is today by strife and violence in many places, the teachings of the great Buddha have a special importance for mankind.

The *Pañca-Śīlas* inculcated by the Buddha have a great significance for the human society. They enjoin avoidance of (1) Killing, (2) Stealing, (3) Speaking falsehood, (4) Incontinence, and (5) Intoxication. The *Neo-Pañca-Śīlas* suggested by our Prime Minister for application to inter-national relations owe their affiliation to the teachings of the Buddha regarding *Maitrī* (amity), *Karuṇā* (mercy), and *Upekṣā* (equanimity). It is a matter for gratification that these precepts for the regulation of relations between nations have caught the imagination of many of them. The precepts are:—(1) Recognition of independence and sovereignty, (2) Non-aggression, (3) Non-interference in the internal affairs of other countries, (4) Mutual respect, and (5) Peaceful co-existence. The immense potentialities of the implementation of these *Śīlas* will have to pass through a course of trials through hard realities before they can actually transmit their beneficence. It is, however, hoped that in the long run, success will result, and the combined efforts of the nations will lead to lasting good will and peace in these days of threats from the lethal use of atomic energy.

### B. Unity and peace within India

India today is united geographically and knit together as never before in her history by the enormous improvement in the means of transport and communication through the application of modern scientific developments in those fields. But social unity and amity depend on several factors, some of which make for separatist tendencies. Our Government is trying its best to keep down or remove the sources of these adverse forces in various ways including suitable social legislation, which it has taken within its purview after the attainment of freedom. Greater speed is however, not possible in a matter like this, if evil consequences are to be avoided.[1]

### C. Problems re. M. and H. Relics.

Several decades have passed since the discoveries made by excavations at Mohenjo=Daro and Harappa. Recently, a Report of the Department of Archaeology (1955-56) shows that many finds of various descriptions, including seals with the Indus scripts and motifs, have been unearthed, as also various structures, evidencing that they are the Southern Extension of Harappa culture. The sites in which discoveries have been made are:—

(1) *Lothal* in Kathiawad (Ahmedabad District), and Rangpur,—30 miles to the south-west.

(2) *Lakhaaval*, in Halar District, but 9 miles north-east of Jamnagar. It is one of the 14 small Harappa settlements in the District.

(3) *Amra*, 3 miles away from site no 2.

(4) *A group of 5 mounds called Nagar,* extending for a distance of 3000 ft., about 2 miles south-east of Prabhas Patan (Somnath, South District).

A large mass of data relating to the relics has long accumulated and many scholars have already expressed their opinions, and propounded their theories, as to the social, economic, religious, and other aspects of the culture of the people who were their authors. A good deal of labour has also been put in to solve the riddle of the Scripts. An accidental discovery of the trilingual Rosetta Stone helped the decipherment of the Egyptian Hieroglyphics. It contains the text in hieroglyphics, a Demotic version of the same, and a Greek translation. Strenuous efforts were made by the eminent scholars, Young and Champollion, one after another, to study the language of the Copts, which retained elements of the ancient Egyptian tongue. This, together with the two versions, helped the scholars to get at the phonetic value of the components of the picture-writing, and the meaning behind the enigma. In the ordinary course, we cannot hope that Luck will be so propitious as to bring within our reach an

---

1. K.M. Panikkar, *Hindu Society at Cross Roads*, 1955, (related portions), and *The State and the Citizen*, 1956, pp. 51 ff., 82 ff.

inscription of that sort. Scholars should therefore carry on their labours, and grope on for the light that will shed its luminance on the meaning behind the enigmatic Scripts, and other problems connected with the Mohenjo-Daro and Harappa culture. An intensive search for any clan or tribe in the areas between Mohenjo-Daro and Mesopotamia to find out whether its language and writing can help in the solution of the problem regarding the Scripts should not be ruled out.

It is felt that we should have among ourselves Indian scholars with intensive knowledge of the history and antiquities of Chalden and neighbouring places, and also those of ancient Egypt with emphasis on inscriptions. For the purpose, to begin with, one or more of the Universities should award scholarships, tenable at a time, for, say, 2 or 3 years, to study the subjects. If possible, they may be associated with the work of excavations in Mesopotamia, or Egypt, for a period, by negotiations with the authorities concerned. To ensure continuance of these scholars in the research-line after their return to India, the scholarships should be awarded to selected teaches of history in the higher classes of colleges, having a zeal for the study of the aforesaid subjects.

**D. Handicap due to scarcity of essential books for research**

I want to point out that scholars are being very much handicapped for want of many books that are essential fore researches on Indology. They have been out of print, and the last World War has dislocated the trade in second-hand books on Indology here as well as in Europe. It is fortunate that some publishers have already given their active attention to this inconvenience, and have recently reprinted by photo-process the *Encyclopaedia of Religion and Ethics,* and Monier-Williams' *Sanskrit-English Dictionary*, which had become scarce, their pages having turned yellowish and brittle. Many other important works are in the same condition. They should be reprinted as soon as practicable.

In *conclusion*, I thank you all for the patient hearing you have given me. I invoke now the blessings of the Goddess of learning, of whom we are all votaries, with prayer that this History Congress may grow from strength to strength, and its members may serve the nation individually or in combination in the true spirit of service through their activities in the field of history, and that the proceedings and functions of this Congress at the present Session may be crowned with complete success.

# Chapter - 4

# Tāranāth's History of Buddhism in India

***(Translated from the German version of A. Schiefner with additional notes)***

**U.N. Ghoshal & N. Dutt**

[The *History of Buddhism in India* written by the learned Tibetan Lama Tāranātha (fl. latter quarter of the 16th and early part of the 17th century A.C.) deservedly occupies a high place in the history of the expansion of Indian Buddhism. Notwithstanding its admitted defects consisting mainly in a fanciful setting of history and geography and an extraordinary proneness to faith in miracles, it is a vast storehouse of Buddhist legends and traditions. It passes under review the whole epoch from the time of king Ajātaśatru to that of the Sena kings of Bengal, and numerous are the allusions it makes to the great figures and centres of the Buddhist faith. Its value has been recognised by the frequent references made to it by Western scholars ever since it was first made accessible in a European language.

It is now more than half a century since the Russian and the German versions of Tāranātha's work made their appearance almost simultaneously in print. The enormous advance made in every branch of Buddhist studies during the interval is too patent a fact to require mention. We have therefore thought it desirable to present to the readers of the Indian Historical Quarterly an English translation of the *History of Buddhism in India* from the German and to supplement it with our notes where necessary.

To the Russian Academy of Sciences we owe our sincere acknowledgments for its kindness in permitting us to make the present translation. Our thanks are also due to Prof. Theodore Stcherbatsky for his help in this connection.—Tr.]

### Schiefner's Foreword

In the first volume of his work upon Buddhism, Prof. Wassiljew has repeatedly noticed the *History of Buddhism in India* written by

Tāranātha, and he has given specially on pp. 47f. a short summary of this work. These notices made it desirable that the whole work should be published. Therefore in the year 1868 I edited the Tibetan text on the basis of four manuscripts which were at my disposal and as I remarked in the foreword to the text edited by me, I derived great benefit from the Russian translation placed at my disposal by Prof. Wassiljew which was to appear simultaneously with the present German version. Already on the 9th April, 1866 Prof. Wassiljew had presented this translation to the Academy, but different other works which he had to edit for the benefit of his audience in the local University and specially his Chinese Dictionary, retarded its printing so that it could be brought to an end only during the last eight months. Through this circumstance it was possible for me to add as an appendix to the present German translation—of which the printing was finished before the end of a year—most of the notes which Prof. Wassiljew contributed out of the rich store of his knowledge of the Tibetan and Chinese Buddhist literature in the course of printing of his own translation.

Tāranātha gives at the end of his work the 34th year of his life as the time when his work was finished; it is the "earth-monkey-year"[1] corresponding to the year 1608 according to the Christian reckoning; the year of his birth was therefore the "wood-pig-year" (1573). Both these dates are found mentioned in the chronological table of the work *Kalpasuvrkṣa*. Since the notice of his birth is limited shortly to "Jo-nang Tāranātha Keen-snjingh," the following remarks may be made for the elucidation of Prof. Wassiljew's Preface. To the different schools which were thrown into the back-ground with the appearance of the Yellow Caps (or Yellow Church[2]—Gelugpa) founded by Tsoṅ-kha-pa[3] belonged likewise to the school of Jo-nang; it derived its name from

---

1. The Tibetans have evolved their chronological system from those of India and China. They have adopted the Indian method of calculation by sixty-year cycle and twelve-year cycle, denoting the year of the twelve-year cycle by the Zodiacal beast of the year. From the Chinese system they have borrowed the five elements, wood, fire, earth, iron and water. For denoting a particular year they tag on to the elements of the Chinese system a Zodiacal beast of the Indian system. See Waddell's *Lhasa and its Mysteries*, App. I, pp. 449-450.—Tr.

[In the present version our own notes are always distinguished as above.]

2. The monks of this church wore *Yellow* coloured hats and girdles in order to distinguish themselves from the monks of the older conservative church, who used *Red* caps and girdles (while the Bons used *Black* caps).—Tr.

3. Tsoṅ-kha-pa (1368-1419) was a reformer of Tibetan Buddhism. He adopted as far as possible the monastic discipline of Hīnayāna Buddhism and thoroughly revised the Tibetan Buddhist liturgy. For details of his life see Eliot, *Hinduism and Buddhism*, iii, pp. 358-9; *J.A.S.B.*, 1882, PP. 53-7, 127; Huth, *Buddhismus in der Mongolei*, ii, pp. 175ff; *E.R.E.*, vii, p. 787.—Tr.

the place Jomonang where stood a monastery in which a certain Dolbupa, having separated himself from the Saskyas,[1] found his refuge. In his work called the *Ocean of the True Sense of the Mountain-teaching* he based the teaching of this school upon a particular form (essentially another form) of nothingness. Although Tsoṅ-kha-pa along with one of his immediate disciples and the disciples of that disciple had heard of the Kālacakra and the Pāramitā, the teaching of the special form of nothingness was rejected by the Yellow Caps. After the time of Tsoṅ-kh-pa, Kun-dra-grol-mstschog* and specially his re-incarnation Tāranātha propagated the Jonang teaching.[2] There was founded the monastery *r*Tag-*b*stan-phun-tshogs-gling, images were set up and wooden blocks were incised of Rin Spung, called Karm-*b*stan-*s*kjong-*d*vang-po, came forward as the protector of this teaching, its popularity greatly increased. But when his power came to an end, the fifth Dalai Lama, after the death of Tāranātha, annexed the Jo-nang monastery to the school of Yellow Caps, and the wooden blocks were sealed up so that at present of the Jonang school only two works of Tāranātha are known, viz. the *Sādhana* and the *History of Buddhism.**

To the above information, which Prof. Wassiljew has drawn from the history of Tibetan schools, he adds from the same work the following passage: "In Khalkha Prince (Khan) Usutai founded the monastery Erdeni Jowo, after he has met the third Dalai Lama. The son of his grandson Tushijetu Khan was the re-incarnation *r*Je-*b*tsun-dam-pa *b*lo-*b*sang-pai-*r*gyal-*m*tshan, the glory of Khalkha, who received great honour from the Manchu emperor (Kanghi); he founded the monastery Ri-vo-*d*ge-*r*gjas-*g*ling and he series of his incarnations continued still further."

1. The Sas-kyas were one of the most powerful sects of Tibet. Their monastery known also as the Sas-kya monaster was founded by a royal prince of that name at a distance of about 50 miles to the north of Mt. Everest. Kublai Khan after his conversion to Buddhism by the abbot of this monastery conferred upon him (usually known as Śaskya Paṇḍita) the temporal rulership of W. Tibet. The abbots of this monastery wielded great influence, both political and religious, over the whole of Tibet from 1270 to 1340. Eliot, *Hinduism and Buddhism*, iii, p. 354; *E.R.E.*, vii, s.v., *Lamaism*.—Tr.

* Born 1493, died 1566.

2. Jo-nang is a sub-sect of the Sas-kyas, another being Ngor-pa. *E.Ṛ.E.*, VII, P. 788.—Tr.

* The Sumbum of *g*Long-*r*dol-*b*lama (see Wassiljew, Historical & Philosophical Bulletin, vol. XI, *Mélanges Asiatique*, II, p. 354), which is really called Ngag-*d*vang-*b*lo-*b*sang comprises briefly both works. We observe also in the same place the full name Kun-*d*ga'-*s*ning-po (=Ānandagarbha), and where the series of re-incarnations since the time of Śākyamuni or Kun-*d*ga' *s*njing-po is the 16th. In the Tanjur we find the name Tāranātha as well as Kun-*d*ga'-snjing-po. In vol. lu of the Sūtra he is mentioned several times as translator, according to Jonang, as well as the epithet.

Now as far as the history of Buddhism written by Tāranātha is concerned, it appears from the plan of the work as well as from the casual remarks of the author that we have to deal with a mere compilation. Besides the Indian works which he himself mentions, he also makes use of indigenous works. When the separate volumes of the Tanjur with its numerous historical notices are properly investigated, it will be easy to trace back to their sources the numerous stereotyped passages which was found about individual occurrences in the work of Tāranātha as well as of other later writes. Probably one may succeed also in reconstructing a number of Indian and other names in their true forms or at least in finding out the origin of the present corrupted forms. In the Index I have printed in brackets the names and Indian words occurring in Tāranātha's Tibetan text in order to distinguish them from words authenticated from some other source or gained through retranslation. As the latter cannot always be relied on, I have marked the doubted cases with an asterisk. Sanskrit offers different probable forms for the Tibetan words, as for instance, I have retranslated Devendrabuddhi, while in Tanjur it is Surendra-bodhi;* in the place of Buddhadiś, a form which occurs in Wassiljew's *Buddhism* (p. 20), the form Buddhapakṣa which also occurs in the same work (p. 56) is perhaps the right one, it is probably an epithet derived from the *Mahjurśrīmūlatantra*, so also are the names Dharmika, Yogin, etc.

For 'Kāla' the synonym 'Kṛṣṇa' can well be put, the Chinese prefer for it the word 'Mecaka' which name I have restored as Kṛṣṇacārin† and which name is found in the later Tibetan works in the form Kālacarya; on the other hand Tāranātha's Kṛṣṇarāja appears to have arisen from a misunderstanding of the word Kaliṅga. It is difficult to decide whether the Jayabhadra or the Jinabhadra has the greater probability. Instead of Viśrutadeva, the later Tibetans use Vikhyātadeva (Thob jig, vol. III, p. 244). If after all I have written in the translation 'Bhaṅgala,' I have retained the form which occurs in all Tibetan works. To be frank there are many strange forms, e.g. 'Vikramalaśīla' instead of 'Vikramaśila,' 'Bharadhvaja', instead of 'Bharadvāja', and so on.

As we cannot always depend upon the different forms of single names, I have in the translation, wherever practicable, put them in a better form than what the manuscripts offer. The chronological account is also in an evil condition. Very gladly I would have complied with the wishes of those who had desired a synchronistic table as a supplement to the translation, if such a one could have been produced

* A similar fluctuation is found between the names Nāgabuddhi and Nāgabodhi, Indrabhūti and Indrabodhi.

† Also Kālacārin at p. 278.

with ease. A greater evil is that in the chronological account prophecies in the *Mañjuśrīmūlatantra* have been mostly admitted as the end and basis of chronology.

Notwithstanding these shortcomings Tāranātha's work, although it is not suited to be a sure guide for the history of Buddhistic regions in India, furnishes the occasion for further researches through it numerous, though often short, notes on some celebrities of Buddhism and their mass of legends. Perhaps one may succeed in collecting the works of Bhaṭagati, Indradatta and Kṣemendrabhadra mentioned by Tāranātha or at least in gathering accurate information about them. Even if this should not come to pass, occasion may be found for elucidating what is as yet little known and for finding out what is unknown about the rich Buddhist literature that is contained in the Kanjur as well as the Tanjur and the different works to which the notes to this translation refer. May young energy be found possessing the requisite means and perseverance to follow up this task.

St. Petersburg, 27 May (8 June), 1869. A. Schiefner

## INTRODUCTION

TREASURE OF WISHES OF THE NECESSARY NAMED DISTINCT EXPLANATIONS OF THE MANNER IN WHICH THE MINE OF HAPPINESS, THE GEM OF EXCELLENT TEACHING WAS PROPAGATED IN ĀRYADEŚA.[1]

Om, salvation to living creatures ! distinct explanations of the manner in which the mine of happiness, the gem of excellent teaching adorned with resplendent fortune, was propagated in Āryadeśa, and the treasure of wishes of the necessary things was known.[2] Adoration be to the Buddha along with his sons and disciples !* I bow down to the chief hermit, the head cloud† that came from the domain of beings to the domain of gods, that is adorned with the marks and signs of the rainbow and sends down the soft nectar-rain of deeds. Here also those versed in the year-books and antique lore, when arranging the stories of Āryadeśa, recognise in the drying up of their skill the basis of their poverty just like the poor man in the presence of goods exhibited for sale. As I have noticed along with some other scholars many serious

---

1. More accurately "The holy and precious religion, how it flourished in the Āryadeśa clearly explained, which is therefore called Ratnacintāmaṇi"—Tr.

2. Better, "The holy and precious religion decorated by the glory, how it flourished, Āryadeśa, clearly explained, which is called Ratnacitāmaṇi:—Tr.

* The most distinguished followers of Buddha and the most renowned Lamas are thus called.

† Literally in Tibetan "before the king of hermits, the first of clouds," so that Munindra and Meghendra may be compared with each other.

mistakes in the explanation of sources of the teaching, I have prepared in brief this arrangement of stories capable of removing mistakes for the benefit of others.

Here are the contents of the principal facts. In the line of king Kṣemadarśin there are four, namely, Subāhu, Sudhanu, Mahendra, and Camasa; in the line of Aśoka four: Vigatāśoka, Vīrasena, Nanda and Mahāpadma; from the line of Candra came forth Hari-,Akṣa-, Jaya-, Nema-, Phaṇi-, Bhaṃsa-, Śāla- with the subjoined (affix) Candra. Thereafter Candragupta, Bindusāra and his nephew Śrīcandra are named. To (the names) Dharma, Karma, Vṛkṣa, Vigama, Kāma, Siṃha, Bāla, Vimala, Gopī and Lalita also, Candra is annexed at the end. If Bindusāra is not counted in the list, there are 19 with the name Candra. Of these Akṣacandra, Jayacandra, Dharmacandra, Karmacandra, Vigamacandra, Kāmacandra and Vimalacandra are known as the seven Candras with the addition of Candragupta, Gopīcandra and Lalitacandra they are celebrated as the ten Candras. Descending from the Pāla line: Gopāla, Deva-, Rāsa-, Dharma-, Vana-, Mahī-, Mahā-, Śreṣṭha-, Bheya-, Neya-, Āmra-, Hasti-, Rāma-, Yakṣa-, all with the affix Pāla, are fourteen in the Pāla lineage. The kings Agnidatta, Kaniṣ -ka Lakṣāśva, Candanapāla, Śrīharṣa, Śīla, Udayana, Gauḍavardhana. Kanika and Turuṣka, the Śākamahā-sammata, Buddhapakṣa, Gambhīrapakṣa, Cala, Caladhruva, Viṣṇu, Siṃha, Bharṣa, Pañcama-Siṃha, Prasanna, Prāditya, Mahāsena, Mahāśākyabala, these stand single. Masurakṣita Caṇaka, Śāmupāla, Śāntipāla, stand singly in the Pāla line, Lava, Kāśa, Maṇita, Rāthika are the four Senas. In the South appeared in Kāñcī and the other different kingdoms Śūkla, Candrakṣ -obha, Śālivāhana, Maheśa, Kṣemaṅkara, Manoratha, Bhogasubāla, Candrasena, Kṣemaṅkarasiṃha. Vyāghra, Budha, Buddhaśuca, Sanmukha, Sāgara, Vikrama, Ujjayana, Śreṣṭha, Mahendra, Devarāja, Viśva, Śiśu, Pratāpa. In the South appeared the following Brāhmaṇas, Balamitra, Nāgaketu, Vardhamāla, Gaggari, Kumārananda, Matikumāra, Bhadrānanda, Dānabhadra, Laṅkādeva, Bahubhuja, Madhayamati; these are the old Mahācāryas. As the followers of the victorious teachers are generally known the following seven persons, Madhyānika counting as the eighth, Uttara, Yaśas, Poṣada, Kāśyapa, Śānavāsa. Mahāloma, Mahātyāga, Nandin, Dharmaśreṣṭha, Pārśvika, Aśvagupta, Nanda are the Arhats protecting the teaching. Uttara, Kāśyapa, Sammatīya, Mahīśāsaka, Dharmagupta, Suvarṣa, Vātsīputrīpa, Tāmraśāṭīya, Bahuśrutīya, Dharmottara, Avantaka, Jetavanīya, Sthavira, Dharmatrāta, Vasubandhu Ghoṣaka, Śrīlābha, Buddhadeva, Kumaralābha, Vāmana, Kuṇāla, Śaṅkara, Saṅgha-vardhana, Sambhūti, are the disciples of the great Bhadantas.* Jaya, Sujaya, Kalyāṇa, Siddha, Adarpa, Rāghava, Yaśika, Pāṇini, Kuśala, Bhadra, Vararuci, Śūdra, Kulika, Mudgaragomin, Śaṅkara, Dharmika, Mahāvīrya, Suviṣṇu, Supramadhu, the second Vararuci, Kāśijāta, Caṇaka and Vasunetra. Śaṅku, Bṛhaspati, Makṣika, Vasunāga, Bhadrapālita, Pūrṇa, Pūrṇabhadra, these are the great Brāhmaṇas honoured for the teaching.

The Āryas of Mahāyana teaching are not mentioned in this list since they are generally well known but they will be mentioned in the course of this history. The six jewels of Jambudvīpa have a great celebrity. Sūra, Rāhula, Gaṇaprabha, Dharmapāla are called the four great ones, Śāntideva and Candragomin are praised by the learned as the two miracle-performing Ācāryas. The designation of the two most excellent ones is unknown in India. The designation of the six Jewels and of the two most excellent ones is known through the Tibetan. jñānapāda, Dīpaṅkarabhadra, Laṅkājayabhadra, Śrīdhara, Bhavabhadra, Bhavyakīrti, Līlāvajra, Durjayacandra, Samayavajra, Tathāgatarakṣita, Bodhibhadra, Kamalarakṣita,—these twelve are the Tantrācāryas of Vikramaśīla. Thereafter came the six Door-paṇḍits and different Ācāryas of the secret teaching.

Keeping the above well in mind one will easily understand the history set forth below through its entanglements.

While the genealogy of the kings before the entrance of our teacher, the fully enlightened Buddha, into the world can be obtained credibly according to circumstances from the Vinaya, the Abhiniṣkramaṇasūtra and partly from the Lalitavistara and other works, the series of kings, ṛṣis, etc. who lived at the time of Stayayuga, Tretāyuga and the Kaliyuga are here not put into writing form the works of Tīrthikas, since these, although many in number, are partly mixed up with untruth and may not be simply believed, and as no connection with the history of the excellent law exists and no requisites for the thoroughly pure design are evident. But if one asks for the works of their teacher, these are the Bhārata with more than 100000 ślokas, Rāmāyaṇa consisting of 100,000 ślokas, the 18 Purāṇas in more than 190,000 ślokas, the poetry Raghuvaṃśa in 86,000 ślokas, etc. Here are only explained the histories of the things which refer to the teaching of the Teacher.

---

* According to Wassiljew the renowned persons of Buddhist hierarcy during the time of Mahāyāna were called Bhadantas; they stand among the Arhats but must be directors and founders of schools, propagators of the teaching and authors of words; cf. however Burnouf, Introduction A l'histoire du buddhisme Indien, p. 567.

## *Chapter - 5*

# Tāranāth's History of Buddhism in India

## *(Translated from the German version of A. Schiefner)*

**U.N. Ghoshal & N. Dutt**

### II

### The Time of King Ajātaśatru

At the time when the words of the fully enlightened teacher were put together for the first time, the gods praised it in the world of men, happiness and welfare prevailed everywhere, and gods and men lived in peace. King Kṣemadarśin, who was also called Ajātaśatru augmented his merit by virtue of his character, and brought under his subjection without fighting the five cities with the exertion of the Vṛjis. When the Tathāgata and the model pair alone with 168,000 arhats passed away peacefully and when also Mahākāśyapa disappeared from existence, all men became sorrowful. The bhikṣus, who had seen the face of the Teacher, simple people who grieved that they had not through lack of diligence attained distinction while Buddha was still living, applied themselves energetically to the study of the law; so also did those who carried on the sacred teaching. The young bhikṣus who had not seen the face of the Teacher thought that on that account they would not have sufficient strength to instruct personally, unless they devoted themselves to the teaching, roamed about and directed their whole energy to virtue. Therefore the number of those who attained the four fruits considerably increased every day. As now from time to time the venerable Ānanda handed down instructions in the teaching to the four groups (of disciples), those who comprehended the *Tripiṭaka* and delivered the teaching together with all who entered on the priestly office lived in purity; the Teacher gave the teacher's office to Mahākāśyapa, who however made it over to the venerable Ānanda of the greatest purity. Kings and other householders, kings whose virtue it is difficult to measure, were filled with sadness at the reflection that the Teacher no longer lived within their field of vision and considered that they has seen earlier the excellent Teacher of the world but now saw his disciples and the group of their disciples. Hence they came to know the excellence of the Buddha, the Dharma and the Saṅgha, showed them veneration and respect, and devoted themselves to virtue; there was no division or anything of the kind, and in this way the world lived in virtue for 40 years.

After the lapse of 15 years since the venerable Ānanda exercised the Teachership, the youth Kanakavarṇa attained Arhatship; his history has been described in the *Kanakavarṇāvadāna*. At that time the king Ajātaśatru thought the venerable Ānanda to be a Śrāvaka equal to the Buddha since he had fixed one Kanakavarṇa in the Arhathship easily and without hindrance, and the king provided the venerable Ānanda along with 5000 bhikṣus with every requisite through five years. At this time there came to Magadha from the town of Kimmilamala in the south Bharadvāja of the line of Jambhala who was greatly skilled in magical arts, and he began to contend with the bhikṣus in transformation. He produced by magic in the presence of the king and other persons four mountains of gold, silver, crystal and Lazuli stone, four jewelled pleasure-groves on each mountain, in each pleasure-grove four lotus-ponds which he filled with diverse kinds of birds; but the venerable Ānanda magically produced many wild and uncontrollable elephants who ate up the lotuses and trampled the ponds; then he sent forth a strong wind which threw down the trees; a shower of rain with thunderbolts destroyed the hedges and mountains without leaving any trace. Thereafter the venerable Ānanda showed 500 bodily forms of which some gave light out of themselves, others rain; some performed the four movements in the air, others let the fire flame from above and the water stream from below, and after they had shown these and other transformations, he drew them up again within himself. He delivered the teaching repeatedly in the course of seven days to Bharadvāja related to Jambhala and to other groups of men who became believers (in the religion). He then initiated Bharadvāja at the head of 500 brāhmaṇas and other 80,000 men into the truth. Thereafter at another time when the venerable Ānanda was dwelling at Jetavana, the householder Śaṇavāsika gave to the clergy a great five-yearly feast and at last through the instruction of the venerable priest he became gradually the supporter of the *Tripiṭaka* and from the first two steps of Arhathood he attained complete emancipation. When in this way Ānanda sooner or later had raised ten thousand bhikṣus to the Arahat status, he be took himself to the middle of the Ganges flowing between two countries in order that the Licchavis of Vaiśāli and king Ajātaśatru might each obtain a portion of his bodily relics and there he created an island in the middle of the river when 500 ṛṣis entered into the priesthood. When the 500 bhikṣus collected there and he by his magic-power consecrated them in a single hour and placed them in Arhathood, they were called the five hundred, midday or the midwaterly priests. The most prominent of them is called the Great midday (Mahāmadhyāntika) or Great-midwaterly. When he had passed out of existence his corpse consumed itself by self-produced fire and dropped down just as a jewel-ball in two parts, which the waves carried to the two banks. The portion that was carried to the north was taken by the inhabitants of Vaiśāli, and that to the south was taken by Ajātśatru; and in each of the countries was erected a caitya (grave-monument). Ānanda carried on the teachership for 40 years; a year after him, king Ajātśatru also died. In a trice he was reborn in Hell, from there he passed away (lit. separated himself) and was reborn among the gods, and thereafter he heard the teaching from Śaṇvāsika and attained the grade of a Srota-āpanna.

The first section, the time of king Ajātaśatru.

# *Chapter - 6*

# Tāranāth's History of Buddhism in India

## (*Translated from the German version of A. Schiefner*)

U.N. Ghoshal & N. Dutt

## III

### Events of The Time of King Subāhu[1]

Thereafter Subāhu, the son of Ajātaśatru, exercised the rulership for ten years and held the teaching of Buddha in respect. When the venerable Śānavāsika[2] had held the teachership for a short period, the

---

1. Tāranātha mentions as the chronological frame-work of this part of his work four successive reigns. These are the reigns of (1) Subāhu, son of Ajātaśatru (10 years); (2) his son Sudhanu (23 years); (3) his son Mahendra (9 years); (4) his son Camasa (22 year). The more authentic accounts of the Sinhalese Mahāvaṃsa and the Brāhmaṇical Purāṇas know nothing of these kings. According to the former the immediate successors of Ajātaśatru were (1) Udayabhadda (16 years), (2 and 3) Anuruddha and Muṇḍa (8 years), (4) Nāgadāsaka (24 years). In the Purāṇas their names are Darśaka (24 years), Udāyin (33 years), Nandivardhana (40 years) and Mahānandin (43 years). See Geiger's English tr. of *Mahāvaṃsa*, Introduction, p. xli, and V. Smith's *Early History of India*, 4th ed., p. 51. Evidently Tāranātha's sources had lost sight of the authentic historical tradition so that there was no other alternative than to insert fictitious names to fill up the gap between Ajātaśatru and Aśoka. Tr.

2. Śāṇavāsika (with variant forms of this name) is well-known in the Northern Buddhist tradition as the third Buddhist partriarch receiving the guardianship of the teacher from Ānanda and in turn transmitting it to Upagupta (cf. besides Tāranātha above cited, Rockhill, *Life of the Buddha*, p. 161; Rājendralāla Mitra, *Sanskrit Buddhist Literature of Nepal*, p. 10 etc.). Tāranātha's account of his early life as given above (I.H.Q., vol III, p. 500) occurs in a fuller form in the Tibetan Vinaya (Dulva). See Rockhill, *Life of the Buddha*, pp. 161-167. The term Śāṇavāsika literally means "wearer of the linen" and a legend is told by Hiuen Tsang to account for this strange designation (Watters' Yuang Chwang, vol. I, p. 120). A Sambhūta Śāṇavāsin is known both to the Northern and the Southern tradition as playing a conspicuous part in connexion with the Council at Vaiśālī (sec Cullavagga, xii, 1, 8ff. of the Pāli Vinaya Piṭaka; Dīpavaṃsa, v, 16ff.; Mahāvaṃsa, iv, 18ff.; Rockhill, *Life of the Buddha*, p. 176 etc.). He is the reputed author of a few verses occurring in Theragāthā (see Ibid., no cxcii). Tr.

venerable Madhyāntika,[1] who lived at Vārāṇasī,[2] imparted the teaching in an excellent manner to the four groups[3] and he preached the law to the brāhmaṇas and house-holders. At another time many brāhmaṇas and house-holders of Vārāṇasī took offence at the large number of mendicant bhikṣus and reviled them saying, "Was there no other region for alms and was there no city as prosperous as Vārāṇasī" We are obliged to support you, but you do not give us the least in return." As they said so, the venerable Madhyāntika encompassed by a group of 10,000 arhants betook himself, soaring through the air, to the mountain Uśīra that lay in the north. There the householder Aja assembled all the monks of the four regions and maintained them for one year, and thus 44,000 arhants were there together. Through this cause the teaching was spread specially in the north. In this way Madhyāntika delivered the teaching on the Uśīra mountain for three years. At that time Śāṇavāsika lived in Śrāvastī and through his preaching of the law to the four groups nearly 1000 persons became arhants. Formerly there were at the time of Ajātaśatru two men of the brāhmaṇa caste of the name of Pana and Napa[4] who had no knowledge of the law, were wicked and cruel, observed no distinction between pure and impure food and killed different living beings. As these two had committed theft in a house and the king had their hands cut off, they grew very angry, and after giving a midday-meal to many arhants they wished that as a result of this good deed they might become Yakṣas for destroying the king and the inhabitants of Magadha. After some time both were struck by an epidemic, cut off and were reborn as yakṣas. About 7 or 8 years after, when king Subāhu was ruling, both of them acquired the position of Yakṣas in Magadha and sent forth into the land a great infectious disease. When many men and cattle perished there and none could stop the epidemic, and when the astrologers ascertained the real state

---

1. Tāranātha's account of the miraculous conversion of Madhyānika and his 500 followers by Ānanda at the time of his death (I.H.Q., vol. III, p. 509) agrees substantially with that of the Tibetan Vinaya (Rockhill, *Life of the Buddha*, pp. 166-167). Both agree in making Madhyāntika a contemporary of Śāṇavāsika and therefore of Ajātaśatru and his immediate successors. On the other hand the Ceylonese tradition as embodied, e.g., in the Mahāvaṃsa, xii, 3ff. and the historical introduction to the Samantapāsādikā (P.T.S. ed., vol. p. 63) makes him (Pāli Majjhantika=Sans. Madhyāntika) a contemporary of the Thera Tissa, the son of Moggali, and hence of Asoka. Thus the N. tradition antedates Madhyāntika by three centuries. For the Uśīra mountain situated near Mathurā (see Watters, *Yuen Chwang*, vol i, p. 308). Tr.

2. More properly, Bārāṇasī. Tr.

3. Bhikṣus Bhikṣuṇīs, Upāsakas and Upāsikās. The corresponding Sanskrit terms are *catasṛṇām pārṣadānām*. Tr.

4. We may compare the account communicated in the Biography of Śākyamuni, p. 68 (298) which occurs also in the Karmaśataka (IX, 9).

of things, the inhabitants of Magadha invited the venerable Sāṇavāsika from Śrāvastī and begged him to subdue the two Yakṣas. He on his part came to the mount Gurva where the two Yakṣas lived, and stepped into the Yakṣa-cave. The Yakṣas however had gone at that time to the habitation of another Yakṣa and were called hither by another Yakṣa. When they returned, they got angry and let fall the rocks of the cave; but there came into existence another cave and in the same was seated the venerable Śāṇavāsika. When this happened three times, they let off a flaming fire; but the Arhant let off a still more powerful flaming fire in the ten directions, where-upon the Yakṣas were terrified; as all regions were on fire, they found no place of refuge, and when they gave themselves up to the protection of Śāṇavāsika, the fire was extinguished. Thereafter, as the teaching was preached to them, they became very believing and were initiated into the Seeking of Refuge (Śaraṇāgamana) and the doctrines. Immediately afterwards the epidemic ceased. This piece of magic was witnessed by a thousand brāhmaṇas and householders.

The second section, the events during the time of king Subāhu.

## III
## Events of The Time of King Sudhanu

When the king died, his son Sudhanu came to rule simultaneously with the conversion of Kāśmīra by Madhyāntika. This Madhyāntika reached Kāśmīra through his supernatural power settled down on the banks of a lake inhabited by the Nāgas. Then the Nāga king Auduṣṭa with his retinue got into anger and sent down a heavy shower, but it could not move the fringe of the holy robe; when the rain of different projectiles coming from different directions was changed into a flower rain, the Nāga appeared and asked what the Venerable desired. When the latter demanded a piece of land and the Nāga asked "How big a piece?", the Venerable said "A piece of land that I can cover by sitting cross-legged"; and that was granted to him. When by a supernatural crossing of legs he covered the nine regions of Kaṣmīra, the Nāga said" How large is the following of the venerable?" "Five hundred." "If there be one wanting, I shall take back the land?" "This land was chosen before by the Teacher as a place suitable for deep contemplation.[1] Since where there are givers, there are also mendicants, brāhmaṇas and householders must also be settled." After these words,

1. The corresponding Sanskrit term is *Vipaśyanā* which Wassiljew (quoted by Schiefner in the additional notes at the end of his German p. 285) explains as a meditation in which the spirit is sunk in metaphysical thought. The equivalent term in Pāli is *Vipassanā*. See Kern, *Manual of Indian Buddhism*, p. 60.

he betook himself to Kāśmīra with the 500 Madhyāntikas from Uśīra and also with many hundred thousand brāhmaṇas and householders believing and devoted to the law from Vārāṇasī. Thereafter many men came gradually to Kāśmīra from different lands and at the time when Madhyāntika lived, this land was adorned with nine great cities, many villages of mountain-dwellers, with a royal residence and twelve Vihāras containing very numerous monks. He, then, through his supernatural power led the groups of men from Kāśmīra to Gandhamādana and subdued the Nāgas by means of a fire-magic. When he had persuaded them to give saffron covering the shadow of the clerical robe, the Arhant magically made the robe large. When he had covered the saffron with this shadow and when all men had taken it up, he came back in the twinkling of an eye to Kāśmīra, filled the land with colonies of saffron, and gave the command that this would increase their wealth by preference. He then converted all the inhabitants of Kāśmīra to the teaching and vanished from existence. He preached the law for 20 years in Kāśmīra.[1] When Madhyāntika came to Kāśmīra, the venerable Śāṇavāsika taught the law to the four groups of men dwelling in the six towns. After a reign of 23 years king Sudhanu one day passed out of this existence. After him the officials and retinue of this king, one thousand in number stepped into the priestly office through Śāṇavāsika. With these and very many others he passed the summer at the cemetery of Śītavana; after they had meditated on the cemetery-ground at the conclusion of the Varṣa, all obtained the *aśubha-samādhi*[2] and attained afterwards the completion of the highest form of knowledge (lit. consciousness or conviction), and became Arhants. Thereafter Upagupta, son of a spice-dealer, was ordained as a priest and perceived the truth; after seven days he attained the complete emancipation from two of the Arhant-stages.[3] When Śāṇavāsika had given over the teachership to Upagupta he passed out of existence in the land of Campā. Instructed by this Śāṇavāsika sooner or later in the doctrines,

---

1. The above description of the miraculous conversion of Kāśmīra by Madhyāntika and his introduction of saffron into that country occurs also in the Tibetan Vinaya (See Rockhill, *Life of the Buddha*, pp. 167-170; Feer, Fragments extrailts du Kandjour, pp. 83-86). There the Nāga is called Hu-lun-ta. The Ceylonese account is somewhat different (see Mahāvaṃs, XII, 9-28, Samantapāsādikā, P.T.S ed. pp. 64-66). It makes out the Nāga king's name to be Aravāla.

2. The practice of *aśubha* contemplation was known to Buddhism from early times. It consisted in meditation on the basis of some impure object. For an explanation of this term see S.Z. Aung' and Mrs. Rhys Davids, *Compendium of Philosophy*, p. 121, *n.* 6. Tr..

3. The stages of Arhantship in their ascending order are as follows: Srota-āpanna, Sakṛdāgāmin, Anāgāmin, and Arhat. Tr.

100,000 became Arhants. In this matter the people of Kāśmīra maintain the Madhyāntika must be counted in the succession-list of teachership, since while Madhyāntika held the teachership for 15 years in Madhyadeśa, the venerable Śāṇavāsika had only a few disciples. When Madhyāntika went to Kāśmīra, Śāṇavāsika held the teachership, so that there were eight 'handlings-down' of the teaching. Others maintain that the teacher had prophesied the conversion of Kāśmīra by Madhyāntika, that Ānada would teach him the word, that Ānanda would hand over the teachership of Śāṇavāsika, and that there would be only seven "handlings-down" of the teachership; this opinion the Tibetans also follow.[1]

The third section, the events during the time of king Sudhanu.

1. The sevenfold "handling-down" of the teaching mentioned above as in accordance with the Tibetan tradition is apparently based upon the following succession of Buddhist patriarchs after Śākya Buddha:—
(*a*) Kāśyapa, (*b*) Ānanda, (*c*) Śāṇavāsika, (*d*) Upagupta, (*e*) Dhītika, (*f*) Sudarśana. These early patriarchs are distinguished in the Tibetan Vinaya as 'elephants' i.e. mighty ones (see Rockhill, *Life of the Buddha*, p. 170 and *n*. Tr.

# *Chapter -7*

# Tāranāth's History of Buddhism in India

**(*Translated from the German version of A. Schiefner*)**

**U.N. Ghoshal & N. Dutt**

## IV

### Events of The Time of The Venerable Upagupta

Thereafter Upagupta crossed the Ganges and came northwards into the Videha country which was a region to the west of Tirahuti (sic). He established himself in a Vihāra erected by the householder Vasusāra,[1] where the Saṅgha of the four regions was entertained; and he spent the summer there. While he delivered the teaching at that place, the number of those who attained the grade of an Arahant in three months amounted to a thousand. Having gone thence to the prince of the Gandha mountain,[2] he taught the law, and initiated innumerable men into the Truth. When he reached the city of Mathura that lay on the north-western frontier of Madhyadeśa, the Malla elders and head-merchants Naṭa and Bhaṭa held consultations [among themselves] at the crowded place before the gate of Mathura. After praising the Venerable Upagupta they expressed the wish that he might establish himself in the Vihāra on Mt. Śiras[3] that had been erected by them in the time of the Venerable Śāṇavāsika. When upon a certain time they saw Upagupta from a distance, they exclaimed, "O wonder, he who is coming here from a distance with subdued mind and full of glory is indeed the Venerable Upagupta." After they had taken counsel, they went out a little to meet him, and after bowing down before him they enquired whether he was the venerable Upagupta. When he said

---

1. I cannot indicate whether the Sanskrit name found in the text has its correct form; the Tibetan translation of this name that is found on p. 88 of the Bu-ston agrees with that of Hiraṇyagarbha.

2. Perhaps Gandhamādana is meant.

3. The Tibetan text Śira, i.e., head, is the Uśīra mountain already mentioned on p. 10 [of Schiefner's text].

that he was so called in the world, they made over to him the Naṭabhaṭika Vihāra that lay on the Mountain Śiras, and provided him with every requisite. When Upagupta delivered the teaching at that place, many bhikṣus and laymen perceived the Truth. When at another time at a gathering of 100,000 men he delivered the teaching, Māra Pāpīya[1] sent a shower of fruits into the city. Many people accordingly went away into the city, but the rest heard the law. When on the second day a shower of clothes fell, many men likewise went away into the city, and when on the third, fourth and fifth days there fell successively the showers of silver, gold and the seven precious stones, the number of those who heard the law was very much decreased. On the seventh day Māra Pāpīya himself took the form of a divine dancer and as his sons and daughters also assumed the forms of male and female dancers; thirty-six dancers, male and female, appeared in the city and distracted the minds of all men through their various modes of dancing and magical performances, their lovely songs and their instrumental music, so that there remained nobody to hear the law. At that time the venerable Upagupta also came into the city, and said, "O brave men, as your dance is so beautiful, I will decorate you with garlands". With these words he bound a garland over the head and neck of each. Immediately afterwards through the magical exercise of the venerable Upagupta, the Sinful One with his whole company became decrepit and repulsive with torn clothing, and on the head (of each) there appeared a rotten corpse and on the neck a decomposed dog's carcase, which spread their stench through the ten world-regions and caused nausea through their very sight. Then all the men who had not yet renounced their passions turned away full of vexation, dread and nausea, while holding fast their noses. Then Upagupta asked the Evil One as to why the latter had injured his company. The Evil One answered, "O Venerable One, grant (us) pardon, and free us from the bonds."—Upagupta said. "If you do not come close to my group, I shall do it." He answered, "I will not injure you, even if my body were to be annihilated." Immediately afterwards the body of the Demon obtained peace. He said, "When I injured Gautama at the Bodhimaṇḍa, he dwelt in the samādhi of mildness, but his younger auditors were exceedingly fierce; then as I wished to play a few of my pranks, the Venerable [Upagupta] has bound me." Then Upagupta entered into a religious conversation with the Evil One, and said, "As I have doubtless seen the spiritual body[2] of the Teacher but not His material body

1. The evil demon, the tempter; with regard to Upagupta may be compared the 7th chapter of the Dsanglun. [The Dsanglun, or more accurately, the Hdsangblun is a Tibetan work of which the title means 'the wise man and the fool'.—Tr.

2. These correspond respectively to the terms *dharmakāya* and *rūpakāya*. —Tr.

while thou hast seen it, show me the form of His body." When the Demon thereupon assumed the form of the Teacher, great devotion was awakened in Upagupta; embarrassed with bodily trembling and with tears, he wished to lay the joined palms of his hands on his head; saying, "I bow down to the Buddha". The Evil one, [however], could not bear it, and falling into a swoon, he sank in a heap. Then the Demon vanished and in this way all the men, being filled with repentance, became still more believing; while the [i.e., Upagupta], having begun from the roots of the fruit, expounded the law through the whole night of the sixth day to all the men that had assembled from the four quarters and were impelled from the roots of their former virtues; on the seventh day 1,800,000 men perceived the Truth. Then he lived in the Naṭabhaṭika Vihāra to the end of his life-time. Into a cave that was 18 yards long, 12 yards broad, and 6 yards high, each Bhikṣu that had stepped into the religious life, cast, under his orders, on attaining the grade of an arhant, a slip o wood 4" long. Thereupon the cave was afterwards so filled up by men with slips of wood that there remained no intervening space. When at a certain time the venerable Upagupta vanished from existence, and his corpse was committed to the flames along with these slips, the remaining relics were carried off by the gods. He had been prophesied by the Teacher himself as a Buddha without [the characteristic] signs, i.e., as one who, while lacking only the signs and marks of the Buddha, brought to all living being benefit equal to that of the Buddha; and after the Tathāgata had vanished from existence, there arose no one who was of greater benefit to the world.[1] The time during which Upagupta held

1. The traditional account of Upagupta given above agrees in the main with other accounts derived from Chinese and Tibetan sources. The Tibetan Dulva, e.g., mentions the same famous prophecy of Gautama Buddha about Upagupta's being born as a Buddha without his characteristic signs [i.e., without the thirty-two signs of the great man] [See Rockhill, *Life of the Buddha*, p. 164]. In the various versions of the Aśokāvadāna we have almost identical accounts of Buddha's prophecy about Upāgupta, of Māra's attempt to interrupt Upagupta's teaching at Mathura by means of miraculous showers of precious things, of his subsequently showing Upagupta the physical of Gautama, and of the cave in which were cast the wooden slips by Bhikṣus attaining the Arhatship under Upagupta's direction (See Przyluski's tr. of the A-yu-wang-tchonan, in his *La Légende de l' Empereur Aśoka*, pp. 353-362). Hiuen Tsang, while visiting the Mathura country, was shown a hill-monastery situated close to the capital which was attributed to Upagupta, and near it a cave wherein were gathered the relics of those who attained Arahatship under Upagupta's direction (Watters, Yuan Chwang, vol-I, p. 306. It should, however, be observed that while Tāranātha calls the hill on which stood the Naṭabhaṭikavihāra Śiras (i.e., Uśīra), other accounts give it the name of Urumaṇḍa which was translated into Chinese as the Great Cream. The puzzle is sought to be solved by Watters who observes (op. cit., p. 308), "The Uśīra hill was at the side of the Urumaṇḍa hill, and the latter may have included the two hills and the wood or forest adjoining."

the office of the Teacher, synchronised for the most part with the time when Mahendra, son of king Sudhana exercised sovereignty for 9 years and his son Camasa exercised it for 22 years in Aparāntaka. At that time there lived in the west of India the Arhant Uttara whom the king Mahendra honoured very believingly. The inhabitants of Bagala built a Vihāra in a Kukkuṭapāla[1] forest and presented it to him; it is called by the name of Kukkuṭārāma.

1. So literally according to the Tibetan text; it must have been called Kukkuṭapāda; the building of this vihāra is otherwise ascribed to king Aśoka.

# Chapter - 8

# Tāranāth's History of Buddhism in India

## *(Translated from the German version of A. Schiefner)*

## U.N. Ghoshal & N. Dutt

The most renowned of his disciples was the Arahant Yaśas. When king Mahendra died and king Camasa was installed in the kingship, there lived, not far from the land of Magadha, a Brāhmaṇi Jassā[1] by name who was nearly 120 years old. She had three sons, Jaya, Sujaya and Kalyāṇa. The first worshipped the great god Maheśvara, the second Kapilamuni and the third, the perfect Buddha. When they became versed in their own sacred books, they wrangled daily in one and the same house. Then their mother said, "Why do you wrangle (among yourselves), since I give you unstintedly food, clothing and all other requisites?" They said to their mother, "We have no quarrel about dwelling and things of that sort; we quarrel in regard to the teacher and his dharma." Then the mother said, "If you, through the power of your own insight, do not know what teacher and doctrine is good or bad, ask some other wise people." They obeyed their mother, and going into different regions, asked people, but were unable to find anything conclusive. When finally they came to the Arhat Uttara, each of them explained his story to him. Both Jaya and Sujaya narrated the praise of Mahādeva, of his destruction of the three cities[2] etc. Although they deprecated[3] Kapilamuni, they praised the greatness of his might. They, did not, in fact, deprecate Śramaṇa Gautama, but they declared him to be powerless, as he performed no penance and

---

1. The text has the peculiar form dsḥ-śa with which I can only compare the names occurring in the *Rājataraṅginī*, viz., Jāsaṭa (viii. 543); Jassarāja (vii. 536). [The correct references are Rājata, viii. 542 and vii. 535 respectively—Tr.] But perhaps there is some other corruption or something from Jayasenā?

2. I.e. Śiva. Cf. Böhtlingk-Roth, Sanskrit-Wörterbuch, under Tripura. [The text refers to Śiva's destruction of the three cities (groṅ khyer) of gold, silver and iron built for demons by Maya in the sky, air and earth.—Tr.]

3. Lit imprecated, Tib, *mod. pa*—Tr.

was therefore unable to conquer the Asuras. After they had spoken these and other words, the Arhat answered, "What does penance signify to those whose inner nature is excited through passion? As here the wicked and cruel Dākiṇīs and Rākṣasas act without restraint so must be those blamed whose morality has fallen into degeneracy; those who kill, bind, injure and do other evil deeds, etc., will beyond doubt fall a prey to death; their instigations to kill are very foolish, being similar to the (conduct of) fools who threaten the sinking sun with a cane and exalt themselves boastingly. Listen, moreover, O Brāhmaṇas, to the teaching of the Buddha, who sought the welfare of the world and is without evil; whoever follows him patiently is also called righteous. He continually performed beneficial works, and therefore after attaining full insight, he worked for salvation without doing any harm and induced his followers also to work for good. There cannot be any spiteful talks in respect of Brāhmaṇas as well as Śramaṇas as well as the words heard by others. This is the way of complete virtue. That Ugra likes to dwell in the cemeteries, devours human flesh, marrow and bone, is cruel, and takes pleasure in killing living beings—this is taught by the law of Mahādeva himself. When the basic-text is thus sullied by wrong views and whoever is believingly attached to it indulges continuously in sinful pleasures, what sensible man will have his joy in it? When bravery itself is a virtue, must not the lion, the tiger, etc. be treated with veneration? Pacified state of mind[1] alone is a virtue. This is the primary proposition." When he had repeated to them the five hundred lines of the 'Introduction to the Teaching', describing the difference between virtue and vice, both Brāhmaṇas perceived the truth and became exceedingly believing with regard to the Three Treasures.[2] The Brāhmaṇa's son, Kalyāṇa, however, increased his faith (in the Buddha) still more than it was before. All the three brothers, having formed the same views, went back to their house and spoke to their mother, "As we know the virtue, every one of us wishes to build a temple in which the Teacher's image is to find place. Thou, mother, tell us the place for it." Thereafter, in accordance with the advice of the mother, the Brāhmaṇa Jaya erected a temple at Vārāṇasī[3] with the image (inside it) at the place where was preached the law. Of the vihāras in which the Teacher himself had lived, and which, by virtue of the supernatural nature in their essence, were visible through magic, there were at this time no more traces left because of palpable mutilation and other mishaps incidental to living beings. For this

1. Tib. *shi-war-sems-pa*. Schiefner translates by 'Sanftmuth'—Tr.
2. i.e. Buddha, Dharma and Saṅgha—Tr.
3. i.e. the Deer Park at Sarnath—Tr.

reason the Brāhmaṇa Sujaya erected an image and a temple in the Bamboo grove at Rājagṛha. But the youngest brother Kalyāṇa erected the most holy temple with the Mahābodhi at the Vajrāsana Gandhola.[1] The workmen were the divine artists who came down in human forms. The workmen who erected the Mahābodhi were divine artists and Kalyāṇa was inside, and they had agreed that no other person should be allowed to come in till the seventh day. When the sixth day came, the mother of the three brothers arrived there and knocked at the door. The people told her, "As now no more than six days have expired, to-morrow the door will be opened." The mother replied, "As I must die this evening and as I alone on this earth have seen the Buddha, others later will not know whether the image of the Tathāgata has or has not the exact likeness, therefore open the door at once." When the door was opened, the divine artists vanished.[2] After looking at the image closely she said that it was wholly like the Teacher except at three points: it was without the streaming forth of light, it was not teaching the law, and it was only in the sitting posture and not in any other of the three postures of the body.[3] It was declared that the image was similar to the real Buddha. As the seven days had not expired, some portions were not completed, some noticed that the toe of his right foot was missing, others said that the curling of the hair on his head was not right, these were executed later on. The Paṇḍitas also said that the hair of the body, and the robe, which did not touch the body, were not completed. Paṇḍita Kṣemendrabhādra[4] also said the same. On the same evening the brāhmaṇī Jassā vanished out of the present existence without any suffering. When shortly thereafter the brāhmaṇa Kalyāṇa went away to some place, he found one of the self-luminous emeralds. He thought that if he had found it before the erection of the Mahābodhi, he might have made out of it a stone for the eyes, but it was not then found. While he was thus thinking, there

---

1. Corrupted from Sans. Gandhālaya. The perfumed room occupied by Buddha is called Gandhakuṭi in Pāli. It generally refers to the room made by Anāthapiṇḍika in Jetavana—Tr.

2. A similar legend is told by Hiuen Tsang (Watters' *Yuan Chwang*, vol. ii, p. 116) of the construction of the image of Gautama Buddha in the temple to the east of the Bodhi tree at Bodh Gayā. Mahābodhi here, as in the accounts of Hiuen, I-tsing and other Chinese travellers, is the name of a *Vihāra*, and not of a temple (See Watters' *Yuan Chwang*, vol. ii, pp. 118-119)—Tr.

3. Buddha's images are usually built in all four or any one of the four postures, viz., Preaching, Reclining, Walking and Meditating. Some of the recently built temples at Colombo have images of Buddha in all these four postures.—Tr.

4. Tibetan sa. dhaṅ. bjaṅ. po; can he be identical with the Kṣemendra mentioned in Burnoul's *Introduction* etc., p. 555? See also, Rājataraṅgiṇī, I, 13 where he is mentioned as an author of a table of princes (*nṛpāvali*).

appeared immediately a self-formed hole in the place of the eyes (of the image of the Buddha). When the people were on the point of spliting up the precious stone into two parts, there appeared of itself a second one like the first, so they were set in the places of both eyes. In the same manner he found a luminous Indranīla and fixed it in the ring of hair between the eye brows. Through his magical power illuminating light shone forth in the interior of the Mahābodhi temple continuously through the night up to the time of king Rāthika. The three Brāhmaṇa brothers thereafter maintained 500 bhikṣus in their three Vihāras and provided the whole brotherhood with all necessaries. The fourth section, the events of the time of the venerable Upagupta.

## V

## Events At the Time of the Venerable Dhītika.

The venerable Upagupta handed over the teachership to the venerable Dhītika. This is his history. In the land of Ujjayinī there lived a sagacious and wealthy brāhmaṇa. He had a son called Dhītika, highly intelligent, wise and upright, and versed in the four Vedas and the eighteen sciences. When his father, full of joy, furnished him with a house and sought a wife for him, he prayed for permission to enter into the priestly office, as he had no desire for a household life. His father said that if he positively wished to become a priest, he should not do it before his death and in the mean-time, train up a group of 500 brāhmaṇas. He complied with his father's wishes and by living a life of purity in the house, he instructed 500 brāhmaṇas in the various sciences without any prejudice. When his father died at a certain time he distributed the whole wealth of the house among the Śramaṇas and Brāhmaṇas, and he himself with a following of 500 betook himself to a wandering life, passed through sixteen great cities, asking the most famous brāhmaṇas and tīrthikas about the way of the perfect purity of life,[1] but he could not obtain a satisfactory answer. Finally he asked the venerable Upagupta in Mathura. There he became very believing, entered into the priestly order and was ordained as a bhikṣu. As Upagupta delivered the seven kinds of instructions, the 500 brāhmaṇas obtained Arhathood in 7 days. The venerable Dhītika gave himself up to the contemplation of the eight *vimokṣas*.[2] He led many distinguished brāhmaṇas of the widely different regions into the most excellent belief in the Buddha's teaching. When the venerable Upagupta delivered to him the teachership he gave admonitions to the fourfold assemblies of

1. Tib. tshaṅs, par. spyod generally refers to the purity of life in reference to perfect abstinence from female company—S.C. Das's Tib. Dic.

2. See Mahāvyutpatti, lxx, for enumeration and explanation—Tr.

the six cities, and greatly propagated the teaching of Buddha, leading all living beings to happiness. At that time there lived in the land of Tukhāra, the king Minara.[1] All the inhabitants of that land honoured the God of Heaven, but they knew no difference between virtue and vice. At the time of their festivals they used to offer to heaven the great smokes arising out of the burning of rice, clothing-stuff, precious stones and scented wood. With a company of 500 Arhats, Dhītika flying through the air went to the place of sacrifice and settled themselves down in the dining hall. The people thinking, that he was the God of Heaven, fell at his feet and offered him riches; but when he delivered the teaching, the king at the head of 1000 men perceived the truth and innumerable men were initiated in the formulas for seeking refuge and the main principles of the teaching. Having lived there for 3 summer months, he increased the number of bhikṣus immeasurably and the result was that a thousand bhikṣus attained Arhathood. Later on when the route between this land and Kāśmīra could be travelled safely, many Sthaviras came from the land of Kāśmīra and the teaching spread yet more. At the time of this king and his son Imasya[2] 50 great Vīharas were filled up with an innumerable crowd of priests. In the east also in Kāmarūpa the brāhmaṇa Siddha who was equal to great king in respect of his riches, brought offerings to the Sun with a company of many thousands. Once when he made offerings to the Sun, the venerable Dhītika showed a magical feat, as he came out of the midst of the Sun's disc and with much light streaming forth he placed himself before the brāhmaṇa, who took the former to be the Sun-god, brought him offerings and showed veneration to him. After the teaching was delivered to him and great faith was roused in him, the venerable Dhītika appeared in his own form. When he again preached the law, the brāhmaṇa perceived the truth, and living full of great faith, he built the Mahācaitya Vihāra, gave a great feast to the brethren of the four regions and spread the teaching of Buddha considerably in Kāmarūpa. At that time the brāhmaṇa Adarpa[3] was exercising the rulership in the west in Malwa without wearing the crown. He killed daily a thousand goats and offered a sacrifice of flesh and blood to the fire. He had a thousand sacrificial altars. He made the brāhmaṇas belonging to his circle to bring goats for sacrifice according to their means and the non-brāhmaṇas to gather materials for the sacrifice. Once when he wished to make an offering of cattle, he invited to the sacrifice the Ṛṣi Bhṛgurākṣasa of the Bhṛgu lineage,

1. It is natural here to think of Menandros. See Lassen, *Ind. Alter.* II, p. 323ff.
2. Might we here think of Hermaios? See Lassen, *op. cit.*, p. 334.
3. Tib. dregas med, "the pride-less," also dregas bral in Mañjrśrī-mūlatantra, leaf. 343.

gathered two thousand white cows, invited also other brāhmaṇas and procured many other sacrificial requisities. When the sacrifice was about to be performed the venerable Dhītika came to that place. The fire could in no way be kindled to a flame and the cattle could in no way be killed, and the brāhmaṇas, when they wished to repeat the Vedas and the formulas of prayer, could not bring forth any sound. Then Bhṛgurākṣasa said that the performance of the sacrifice was prevented by the craft of the Śramaṇa who was present there. All of them threw stones, clods and dust at him, but when they saw that these things were turned into flowers and sandal powder, they became very believing, showed him veneration and begged forgiveness asking what they should do. The Venerable One said "Hear, O Brāhmaṇas, and let it off, why these sinful offerings? Distribute gifts and practise meritorious deeds, while you yourselves being gods of brāhmaṇa lineage are obliged to perform the duties of a mother, how can the gods have anything to do with the killing of fathers and mothers? If the brāhmaṇas cannot touch the unclean flesh of the cow, can the gods be satisfied with the same? Oh Ṛṣis, away with this sinful law. If you have longing for flesh-food why should you need this fire offering and shedding (of blood). The magical formulas which teach salvation through illusion are only a deception of the world." After he had clearly delivered this and similar teachings, they felt repentance for their sinful deeds, they became ashamed of their conduct, they cast down their faces and being overpowered they asked for a means by which they could restrain their sins. For these purposes they were all initiated according to the teaching of the Venerable in the refuge formulas and the five tenets. On the site of the pleasure grove of the householder Ghoṣavanta there was built a great Vihāra, and they strove for the seven kinds of blessings accruing from the right application of wealth. In this manner did Dhītika spread the teaching very much in the land. Not long before this time King Aśoka was born. Dhītika gradually brought 500 brāhmaṇas to the faith in the three jewels and after he had guided the Buddha's teaching for a long time and worked for the salvation of living beings he gave up the teacher's office to the venerable Kāla, he vanished from the present into the region of Ujjayinī, which was a part of Malwa. The fifth section, the events of the time of the venerable Dhītika.

## *Chapter - 9*

# Tāranāth's History of Buddhism in India

### (*Translated from the German version of A. Schiefner*)

**U.N. Ghoshal & N. Dutt**

### VI

### The Biography of King Aśoka

This is about the time of the young days of King Aśoka. His biography is as follows:—King Nemita with 500 ministers ruled, wielding great power over the lands lying in the north of the country of Campārṇa,[1] belonging to the series of extreme border-lands. He had at the beginning six sons, Lakṣmaṇa, Rathika, Śaṅkhika, Dhanika, Padmaka, and Anūpa.[2] Later on a merchant's wife by having intercourse with the king became pregnant. As this child was born of the wife of the merchant on the day of expiry of the period of mourning, which was due to the death of the king's mother, the king named him Aśoka, because he was born on the day when the period of mourning ended. As he grew up, he became very proficient in the sixty sciences, eight crafts,[3] art of writing, calculation etc. And once in the midst of men, the ministers asked a brahmin, who was an astrologer,[4] as to which of the king's sons would get the rulership; in reply he said: "It is he who eats the best food, puts on the best garment and sits in the best place." Thereupon both the prime ministers asked him in secret and he replied that the best food was the rice porridge, the best dress was the rough felt and the best seat was the earth. While the other sons of the king lived in abundance of wealth and riches, Aśoka had only ordinary food and dress, hence they understood that he would become the king.

---

1. Perhaps derived from Campā-karṇa. [The derivation suggested by Schiefner does not help as much. The Tib. name is *tsa. mpa. a. rna* which may be equated to Sans. Campārṇa (mod. Campāran), a place near the Nepalese Terai—Tr.]
2. In Tib. dge. va. can, śiṅ, rta. can, duṅ, can nor. can, padma. can, sor. can.
3. Tib. *b*rtag. pa—Tr.
4. Ger. seher, Tib. ltas, mkhan.—Tr.

In the meantime many hillmen of Nepal and Khaśa[1] became rebellious. Aśoka was sent with an army to subdue them, he conquered the hillmen without any difficulty, arranged for taxes, hostage and tribute and made them over to the king. The king said: "As I am pleased with your wisdom, power and bravery, I shall give you whatever you desire." He replied: "As here in this place other brothers will encroach upon my rights, may the town of Pāṭaliputra as the dwelling place and all requisites wished for be given to me". When the father had granted this, he made in the town 500 pleasure gardens, surrounded himself with 1000 female musicians and spent day and night in the gratification of desire. As then in the land of Magadha King Camasa died and none of his twelve sons, although chosen, assumed the throne, the minister and Brāhmaṇa Gambhīraśīla carried on the rulership for one year. At that time king Nemita got into enmity with him and there was a great fight on the bank of the Ganges in which the six elder sons of the king took part, but the king died at the time. Apprehending (lit. in the supposition) that if the news of death of the king became known, the people of Magadha would gain in power, both the ministers kept it secret and they themselves carried on the government but when the inhabitants of the city came to know it after seven days, they began to disobey the orders of both the ministers. Remembering what the Brāhmaṇas had prophesied, they sent for Aśoka and made him the ruler. When the six sons of the king had conquered the people of Magadha and taken the six towns, they heard on that day that Aśoka had been installed in the rulership. They refrained from going to the countries north of the Ganges and ruled with their 500 ministers in these six towns, Rājagṛha, etc. to which Aṅga was the sixth.[2] Of the sons of the king the first revered the secret teaching of the Lokāyatikas, the second Mahādeva, the third Viṣṇu, the fourth the secret-teaching of the Vedānta, the fifth the Nirgrantha Piṅgala,[3] and the sixth the Brāhmaṇa Kauśika Brahmacarya; each of them gave to the teaching honoured by him a place of abode. Aśoka believed in the words of those who held in veneration the Dākiṇīs and Rākṣasas of the Bhṛgu family and held Umā besides the Cemetery-mother as divinities. As he gave himself up for one year to the enjoyment of pleasures (kāma), he was called Kāmāśoka. As he got into enmity with his older brothers,

1. Tib. kha. śya. Cf. Burnouf, *Introduction*, p. 362, n. 2, besides the form Khāsya in *Lalitavistara*, p. 123 (transl. Foucaux).

2. The six cities are Śrāvastī, Śāketana, Vārāṇasī, Vaiśālī, Campā, Rājagṛha. Of these cities Campā lay in the Anga country. See Lassen I, p. 143, and Csoma in Asiatic Researches, XX, p. 61.

3. The Tibetan Text has gser, can which I consider to be a corruption of gser, skya, = Piṅgala. The last appears in Burnouf, op. cit., p. 360.

he carried on a fight with them for several years and at last killed the six brothers with their 500 ministers, conquered also many towns and ruled over the whole land between the Himālayas and the Vindhyās. He was so very ill-tempered and cruel that before he had inflicted punishment he could neither have his sleep nor take his food. From the morning (lit. commencement of the day) he inflicted punishment such as killing, binding, beating and the rest, and then if his mind obtained peace, he sat for food. Kṣemendrabhadra said that although there were very many stories of the king's warlike deeds, he did not relate them thinking them to be unnecessary, so I too, although various Indian stories have reached my ear, have not written them down here. Guided at the time by Brāhmaṇas with perverted views, Aśoka devoted himself to the offering of living beings. He erected an offering-house particularly at the instruction of Ṛṣi Gokarṇa of the Bhṛgu family, who said that if he could bring an offering by killing 10,000 men, he would be able to extend his dominion, and at the same time he would attain emancipation. While searching for a man who was able to kill 10,000 men, he for some time could not find one. At last he met at Tīrahuti, a man of Caṇḍāla caste whom he ordered to bring into that house all who deserved death, and kill them until the number 10,000 was full. This, as the king himself declared, would be an offering-vow made in favour of Umā.

In this ways when he had killed one or two thousand men, he went out of the city of the dead and met a bhikkhu who with the hope of bringing a change in his life, told him various stories of the sufferings of hell which one has to undergo in consequence of killing, without however awakening in him the root of virtue. That hangman thought that he had so long killed men by hanging, now however, after hearing the stories of the bhikkhu, he could likewise kill in a different way, viz., by burning, cutting, lynching and so forth and in these manifold ways he killed 5000 men in the offering-house. For this reason his former name was changed and he came to be known as Caṇḍāśoka[1] or the cruel Aśoka. At that time a disciple of the Arhant Yaśas, who was a learned Śrāmaṇera, and lived in contemplation of the Yoga-ways, came by mistake (lit. not knowing the way) into the interior of the offering house. As the hangman wanted to slay him with the sword, he asked for reasons. When the hangman had related to him the previous circumstances the Śramaṇera begged that he might be killed after 7 days; in the meanwhile he would not go anywhere and dwell in the offering house. The hangman agreed to it; and the Śrāmaṇera saw the

1. See Burnouf, *op. cit.*, p. 365.

offering place wholly filled up with flesh, blood, bones and intestines, and as a result of this he realised the 16 kinds of truth[1] as well as the impermanence of everything etc., and before the lapse of 7 days he attained the rank of an Arhant and performed supernatural feats. On the day of expiry of the sevenday's respite the hangman thought that as he had not seen any man of such description before this he would arrange also for a sort of death not happened before. He put the Śrāmaṇera in a big cauldron filled with sesame oil, made a fire and sought to burn him, but although the fire burnt day and night, it could not injure his body in the least. The hangman reported the matter to the king who became astonished and went into the offering house to see this. The hangman seized his sword and went up to kill him. On the king's asking the reason of it, he said that the vow, pronounced by the king himself, was that before 10,000 men were killed, all that might come into the house must be put to death. The king replied: "Much more must thou, because thou camest here before me, be killed first." When they were thus quarrelling with one another, the Śrāmanera sent down a rain and produced lightning. He passed through the air and showed other magical feats whereby both the king and the hangman became very faithful, touched his feet and awakened in themselves the seed of knowledge. On his delivering a discourse the king became repentant for his misdeeds and destroyed immediately the offering-house. In order to atone for his sins, he invited the Śrāmaṇera to stay. He, however, said that he was not in a position to offer the remedy for the sins and further said that in the East in Kukkuṭ-ārāma lived the teacher and arahant Yaśodhvaja who was in a position to absolve the king of his sins. Hearing this king sent to the Arhant a message with the request that the Venerable. One may come to Pāṭaliputra and absolve him of his sins and in the event of his not coming he himself would go to him. As the Arahant knew that if the king himself came, he would hurt many persons so he himself went to Pāṭaliputra, taught the king the law all day long; in the night after coming to the vihāra he gave instructions to the four classes of his disciples. Since the meeting of the king with Arahant Yaśa, the king became very believing, spent his time, day and night, in virtuous works, and daily supplied food to 30,000 clergymen. At the time when Arahant Yaśa was staying in Magadha and the neighbouring regions, it happened that the king had sent 500 merchants to fetch jewels from the Jewel-island. They got their ship well-equiped, filled the same with various kinds of valuables and returned home. When on this side of the coast

1. 16 kinds of truth evidently refer to the 16 kṣaṇas into which the four truths are divided. See La Vallée Poussin's transl. of the *Kośa*, ch. v. Intro.—Tr.

they sat for rest, the Nāgas sent a sea-wave and carried away all their goods into the sea. They gradually improved by throwing their lives on the charity of foreigners. As it was said that the merchants would reach Pāṭaliputra after 7 days, and as no one had heard what happened to them, Brāhamaṇas, Parivrājakas and a mass of innumerable men gathered together to see the colour of the jewels and their wonderful qualities. When the king together with the great crowd of men came to the pleasure garden on the 7th day, the merchants appeared with only the upper portion of their bodies covered and looked exhausted and as this was quite contrary to the expectation, the crowd of men dispersed with derision. On the king's questioning the merchants, they narrated the events. "O, Your Majesty, if thou dost not subdue the Nāgas, nobody in future will have the desire to fetch jewels; it is therefore proper, O King, that thou shouldst inflict punishment." Being urged in this manner, the king thought of the matter and questioned in various ways about the means. As the Brāhmaṇas and Pari vrājakas had no information, a gifted Arahant with six Abhijñās (Ger. Klarsichten) gave himself up to meditation and came to know that the house-god would teach the means, but in order to show that the king himself had thought over the matter so that people might not have the conviction that he (the king) had sided with the bhikṣus, and that the Tīrthikas might not spread calumny, he (the Arahant) said to the king that there was a means, which the house-god would point out in the same evening. Just at sunrise the house-god hovering in the air said, "O king, show to Buddha great veneration, he will subdue the Nāgas." There upon said the gods dwelling on the earth, "Honour the saṅgha of Arhants, they will perform the subjugation." On the following day when the whole crowd of people had assembled, he announced the prophecy of the gods and asked what was to be done. The ministers replied: "Ask the Arhant himself who gave you the advise yesterday." When he had stepped in and had been asked, he said that he would devise and effective means. On a copper-plate he wrote, beginning thus: "O Nāgas, hear the command of King Aśoka" and continuing it thus, "Give back to the merchants the jewels kept by you." This plate was thrown into the Ganges and some golden images of the King and of the Nāgas each within a cover made of eight metals (*aṣṭadhātuḥ*, Tib. *snod*—Tr.) were placed on the top of a high rock at a very prominent crossing of the city. On the following day one noticed that the Nāgas had got enraged and thrown the copper-plate by a strong whirlwind at the gate of the palace, the image of the king however, was bent towards the Nāga-images. On the king's asking the Arahant, the latter admonished him saying, that "As yet the (religious) merits of the Nāgas are greater than those of the king, the latter, in order to increase his own merits, must honour the Buddha and the Saṅgha. And when the king showed sevenfold greater veneration than before to the Buddha image and the Caitya, the Arhant betook himself in the twinkling of an eye to the regions of gods and Nāgas and gave the information to all the Arhants. After the king had erected a big house for the entertainment (of bhikṣ -us) and the Arhant had struck the gong, all Arhants assembled there from Sumeru and its neighbouring places. The king maintained the 60,000 Arhants with all requisites for three months long. At that time the image of the king grew higher and higher every day and in 45 days it attained a height equal to that of the image of the Nāga. There upon the image of the Nāga shrunk daily likewise for 45 days and bent itself down at the foot of the king's image. All men, however, were very much astonished at this and saw how great must be the merit of venerating the three *ratnas*. When one had thrown the former copper-plate into the Ganges, a messenger of the Nāga came in human form with the message that the jewels had been conveyed to the bank of the ocean and the merchants might be sent in order to fetch them. When the king was about to follow them, the former Arhant said: "O king, this is not a great wonder. If thou commandest them (the Nāgas) to bring the jewel on their shoulders in seven days and if this is carried out, it will be a great wonder." As the king acted according to the instruction of the Arhant, the Nāgas in the form of merchants brought the jewel on the expiry of 7 days amidst the gathering of kings and a crowd of countless persons and bowed down before the feet of the king. This was a spectacle for the crowd of people. The king also arranged for a great feast. When the king had completed the magic formula of Yakṣa-Yāna[1] there appeared horses as big as elephants, men as high as palm trees, and even a powerful fourfold (*caturaṅga*—Tr.) army of Yakṣas. With these he brought under his control without harm the lands, etc. lying south of the Vindhayas. He ruled all the provinces of Jambudvīpa in the north of Himālayās, the snowy mountains lying on the other side of the Li country, and extending up to the ocean on the east, south and west and besides 15 small *dvīpas*. Thereupon Arhant Yaśas told him the prophecy made by the Teacher, the fully enlightened Buddha, and encouraged him to decorate the surface of the earth with caityas containing the relics of the Tathāgata. As Buddha-relics became necessary, the king and the arhant Yaśa with a great crowd of men went to Rājagṛha in order to unearth the relics hidden there by Ajataśatru under the ground of the great caitya. But

1. In *Mañjuśrimūlatantra*, leaf 321 appears simply de. nas. gnod. sbyin. śiṅ, rta. grub. (thereupon he perfected himself in Yakṣa-way).

when they had gone three men's depth into the earth, they could not find the spot on account of an iron wheel which was revolving violatently producing fire. Then an old man of the region showed an expedient, (namely) that if one could lead to the spot a stream of water from a mountain situated 3 yojanas west of the same place, the wheel would cease to turn and the fire would disappear. When the earth was again dug, the king saw there on a copper-plate the inscription recording that in future a needy king would bring up the Magadhan portion of relics of the Tathāgata kept there. So the king on account of his pride thought that he was not the same person who would unearth the relics, but it must be some other person. He was on the point of turning back, when on the request of the Arhant Yaśas, the earth was again dug to the depth of seven men's height. Seven coffins, one within another, the first one of which was made of iron, were opened. The middle of the Teacher's skeleton, which had been originally the Magadhan portion increased to a measure of six loads. As the king saw in the four corners of the coffin precious stones which were placed in special offering vessels and which cast light one yojana wide and the worth of each of which could not be measured by the entire riches of the entire kingdom of Aśoka, the pride of the king was broken. He took form there a great quantity of relics, put the coffins at the place as before, concealed them and placed also the iron wheel again at its place. Then the mysterious water was led again to its former course, the fire burnt as before and the wheel whirled, whereupon its top was covered. He then issued orders to the men of every region, while he despatched messengers and executors with the help of the highly powerful Yakṣas. He erected Caityas in the eight principal places, an enclosure in Vajrāsana and he built Caityas with the Muni's [i.e., Buddha's—Tr.] relics in all northerly countries lying on this side of the Li country and in all countries of Jambudvīpa. On the same day the 84000[1] caityas were completed. Thereupon he sent orders to all lands that 1000 lights, incense and flower-garlands be offered daily to the caityas. Offering 10,000 gold, silver and vaidūrya pitchers filled with scented water and the five kinds of nectar to the Bodhi tree, he paid his respects to it from a distance with 10,000 incense-pots and lights. For three months he daily supplied with all requisites 60,000[2] Arhants whom he had invited, and who hovered in the air over Pāṭaliputra. He maintained the venerable teachers and ordinary

1. This figure is based on the tradition that Buddha preached 84,000 dhammakkhandhas in 45 years, *Saddhamma Saṅgaha* (J.P.T.S., 1890), p. 65; *Mahāvaṃsa*, p. 36.—Tr.

2. Cf. *Mahāvaṃsa*, p. 36.—Tr.

bhikkhus all over the earth. At last he gave to every bhikkhu a robe worth 100,000. On the evening of the same day the king and his retinue, wishing to see the caityas, were carried on the shoulders of the powerful Yakṣas and in seven days they visited the caityas of the *(tri)ratnas* of all lands of Jambudvīpa one after another and showed tenfold more honour to them. To the caityas of Buddha and the Śrāvakas he gave gold decorations while he decorated the Bodhi tree specially with all jewels. On the eighth day the king as a result of his meritorious service expressed repeatedly the desire to become a Buddha, the best of men.[1] When he invited the people to have pleasures and rejoicings, many of them thought that these enterprises of the king attended with so much trouble were but of small gain and, as the king in the meanwhile had not yet obtained the highest and complete insight, it was questioned as to whether the king's prayer would be fulfilled. The king then said "Should this prayer of mine be fulfilled, may the great Earth quake and may a rain of flowers come down from heaven." Immediately after these words were uttered, the Earth quaked, a rain of flowers came down. At this the men became faithful and the wish was confirmed. On the day when the arrangements for Bhikṣu-maintenance for three months in honour of the consecration of the caityas came to an end, the king gave to many ordinary bhikṣus who had all come there a great feast in the pleasure-garden and showed special attention to the oldest bhikṣu sitting at one extremity of the bench. This bhikṣu was very dull, simple, and unable to quote a single śloka; among the young bhikṣus there were, however, many who knew the tripiṭakas. After the meal-time was over, those sitting at the bottom of the bench asked the old bhikṣu whether he knew the reason why the king was showing him honour. The old bhikṣu replied in the negative. They said, "We know it; as the king wished to hear the law, he would come immediately, and you must teach him the law." At this the old bhikṣu was troubled within his innermost heart. He thought that since his consecration he had not learnt a single śloka in 60 years. If the king on account of that reason only had given him the excellent food, he would have given it to other bhikṣus and looked for an expositor of the law. Now he has eaten the food and does not know what he should begin, and thus he was caught with remorse. The god dwelling in that garden thought that the king should not become unfaithful before that bhikṣu, and appeared in another form before that bhikṣu, and said to him that if the king came to him to hear the law, he should tell him, "O great King, if the Earth with its mountains will vanish, how much more should the power of the king? This is to be thought of seriously".

1. This is a general epithet of Buddha, *Narottama*, see Mahāvyut. p. 2

In due course the king came and put on him a gold-coloured double garment and sat down to hear the law. When the bhikṣu had spoken as above, the king, as he was very faithful, thought that it must be very true. A shudder came over him and he pondered over its sense. Thereupon the god of the pleasure-garden said to the old bhikṣu that he should not eat the least particle of food offered to him by the faithful. As the bhikṣu prayed for instruction and had concentrated himself to meditation, he obtained in three months the grade of an Arhant and spent the summer in the region of thirty-three gods in the Pārijāta garden. When he came again to Pāṭalīputra in the middle of the monks and the crowds of people, he filled all the regions with perfume, as the garment bestowed by the king was imbued with the Pārijāta perfume. When the other bhikṣus had enquired of the cause and he had narrated the events that happened; all were astonished. Then by and by the king also heard it and as he thereby saw the power of the law—that even a very dull-minded bhikṣu can obtain the grade of an Arhant—as also what a garment given by him had achieved and what usefulness would accrue out of other gifts, he arranged again a great feast of five years' duration for 300,000 bhikṣus. In the first part of the forenoon the Arhants, in the second the Venerable Teachers and in the third the ordinary bhikṣus were supplied by him with excellent food and dress. Thereupon the king vowed to give at the end of that time 1000 millions of gold to each of the clergy of Aparāntaka, Kashmir and Tukhara, and gave it in full measure to the clergy of Kashmir and Tukhara as well as other requisites in equal measure. To the clergy of Aparāntaka, however, when the king had yet to grant 40 millions of gold and requisites, he was attacked by a serious illness. The king's descendant (grandson) Vāsavadatta (nor. lhas. byin=Vasu-deva-datta—Tr.), however, who was the keeper of the gold treasures, disobeyed the king's order and did not give the rest of the gold to the clergy. As at the time many arhants and bhikṣus came to the king, he in order to quench his thirst (of giving) gave them with a believing heart a half handful of myrobalans.[1] The Arhants then cried out in one voice, "O king, the merit of this gift is much greater than the former gift of 960 millions of gold at the time when thou hadst the rulership." A maid-servant overpowered by the heat of the day fell into slumber and let drop from her hand a fan having a handle of precious jewels and it touched the body of the king. At this he got into rage at the thought that formerly great kings washed his feet but now a low maid servant showed him disrespect in such a manner, and died. In

1. Āmalakī, cf. Hiouen Tsang, II, 428 and Burnouf, op. cit., 428, where the name of the nephew is given differently.

consequence of this anger he was reborn in Paṭalīputra in a big lake as a Nāga. When the Arhat Yaśa reflected as to where a king so devoted to the religion could be reborn, and saw that he was reborn in that lake as a Nāga. The Arhant came to the bank of the lake, and as the Nāga as a result of his former passions for pleasure had come to the surface of the lake and had seated himself near the Arhant and was about to devour the birds and other excellent creatures, the Arhant asked him to control himself. As he now denied himself food, he died and was reborn among the gods of Tuṣita heaven. This king spread the Buddha teaching on all sides through the establishment of monasteries in all lands ruled by him and many seats of learning. As he obtained faith in the Buddha teaching his former name was thence forward changed and he was called the Dharmāśoka, the Righteous Asoka. As he could not give to the bhikṣus of Aparāntaka more than 960 millions of gold, a clever minister mentioned to the king that there was a means in as much as he could give to the clergy his whole kingdom and then it would be 100 koṭis. As the king saw its justness, he gave over the rulership to the clergy. In order to increase the merit to the king, the clergy carried on the rulership for two days. Then the clergy was given unaccountable gold and property, and the rulership was taken back, and Aśoka's grandson Vigatāśoka[1] was selected for the rulership. In Kṣemendrabhadra's historical work his life history is narrated in full and in the seven Avadānas belonging to the Śrāvaka-piṭaka, viz., (1) in Aśoka Avadāna, (2) in Avadāna of Asoka's conversion (Tib. btul=Vinīta—Tr.), (3) in Avadāna of Naga subjugation (Nāga vinaya—Tr.) by Aśoka, (4) in Caitya or Stūpa-Avadana, (5) in Avadāna of Utsava (dus-ston—Tr.), (6) in Avadāna of gold gift (Suvarṇopahāra —Tr.) and (7) in Kunāla-Avadāna. Of these the second and the seventh have been translated into Tibetan. Of the other I have seen Indian texts. The Avadāna of a gold-gift and the other stories are found also in the work Desire-creeper (Kalpa-latā evidently referring to Kṣemendra's Avadāna-kalpalatā). The sixth section: the life history of King Aśoka.

---

1. This is perhaps another name of Sampadi. In the Indian Avadānas the brother of Aśoka is called Vītāśoka (see Burnouf,*op. cit.*, pp. 415 ff.)

# Chapter - 10

# Tāranāth's History of Buddhism in India

## (*Translated from the German version of A. Schiefner*)

**U.N. Ghoshal & N. Dutt**

## VII

### Events Contemporaneous With King Aśoka

Before handing over the charge of teaching to the Venerable Kāla,[1] the Venerable Dhitīka while dwelling in Kauśāmbī in the land of Malava and suffering from sickness, imparted various instructions to the four classes of persons.[2] The bhikṣus of Vaiśālī thought that perfect instruction could not be obtained from an ailing Sthavira, so they did not betake themselves to him, and held that the ten improper measures,[3] practised by them, were according to the Law, the Vinaya and the Doctrines of the Teacher. The Arahant Yaśa and 700 other

---

1. Tib. Nag-po. in Buston is found Kahnava, which can be traced back to Kṛṣṇa.
2. I.e. monks, nuns, lay disciples and female devotees; cf. Pāli, catasso parisā—Tr.
3. In the Tibetan text of *Vinayakṣudraka* the ten improper acts are mentioned thus:

(1) the exclamation of surprise '*Aho*';
(2) to incite the bhikṣus to frivolities;
(3) to dig with one's own hand and to let others dig;
(4) to mix and eat the salt consecrated for life whenever needed;
(5) to go away one Yojana or a half, assemble there and eat, alleging it to be a journey;
(6) to eat with two fingers the food which is (so small as) not to be left over;
(7) to sip in intoxicating drink in the manner of a leech and seek excuse on the ground of sickness;
(8) to mix one *droṇa* of sweet milk and one *droṇa* of sour milk and drink it out of time;
(9) to make a new cushion without patching or mending an old and strong pillow of the size of Sugata-span (?);
(10) to place on the head of a Śramaṇa at the cross roads one round begging bowl, filled with fragrant essence and sweet smelling incense, decorated with flowers, and to invite people to give gold, silver and jewels, telling them that great reward awaits such givers. Cf. Lassen, II, 84, Koppen, *Religion des Buddha*, p. no. 7.

arahants denounced them and arranged for the second collection of words (i.e. the Second Council) in the Vihāra of Kusumpurī,[1] of which king Nandin, who came of the family of the Licchavis, was the patron (*dānapati*). At the time of determination of the boundaries of the six cities,[2] 700 arahants, all of whom belonged to the region of Vaiśālī, had obtained the two sanctificatory stages of emancipation and were vastly learned.[3] The collection therefore is surely a partial one. As the essentials of this history may be very fully known from the *Vinayakṣudraka*[4] it has not been here described. That this collection took place at the time has been told by Bhaṭaghaṭī and Kṣemendrabhadra. In the Vinaya which is still existing in Tibetan, it is stated that 110 years after the demise of the Teacher the second collection, according to the tradition, took place and that the collection was made suited to one school. In the Vinaya of another school it is seen that the second collection was arranged 210 or 220 years after the demise of the Teacher. In order to ascertain here the right mean, one must take into consideration the fact that in some of the extant Indian historical works the Venerable Dhitīka and the others have been made contemporaries of Aśoka, and that after Sudarśana had passed out of existence and Aśoka died, the second collection was to have taken place. It (this discrepancy) is due to the faulty interpretation of the words of *Kṣudrāgama*: "When he gave over the teaching to Sudarśana, the elephants (i.e. the great beings) had entirely vanished out of existence, at that time 160 years had passed since the Nirvāṇa, etc. In Sanskrit *yadācit* through the power of word-combination can as well mean "at which time" as also "and at the time."[5] This passage one must have translated as "at which time." The Guru Paṇḍita said that if it is put as 200 years, etc. then a half-year has been calculated as a full-year and it should therefore be taken as 100 years. According to the adjusted[6]

---

Cf. Rockhill's *Life of Buddha*, pp. 173 ff.; for the Pāli version of these ten breaches of the rules of discipline see Dutt's *Early History of the Spread of Buddhism and Buddhist Schools*, pp. 226-7; La Valleé Poussin, *Le Muséon*, N.S., vi (1905); Ind. Ant. 37 (1908); *Mahāvaṃsa* (transl.) pp. 19-20.—Tr.

1. In the text Kusma-puri. The name of the Vihāra is different in the *Mahāvaṃsa*, see Lassen II, 86. The name is Vālikārāma—Tr.

2. It seems that this passage is not quite incorrupt. There were six citites besides Vaiśālī, from which places the Arhants assembled to take up the task of expulsion of bhikṣus.

3. Schiefner has taken it be the proper name of Bahuśrutīya School. The Tib. is man-du-thos-pa, meaning 'vastly learned'. While the Tib. name for the School is man-thos.—Tr.

4. Kanjur, vol. II, leaves 323-330.

5. So Tāranātha thinks to be the cause; one notices there from how differently he uses from the Sanskrit in Sanskrit. *Yadācit* is primarily a Tibetan fabrication.

6. Tib. gtam. gyi. sbyor. wa: German: Geschictsharmonie.—Tr.

report of Paṇḍita Indradatta, it is said that Upagupta appeared 50 years after the Nirvāṇa of the victorious (One), but 110 years after the Nirvāṇa the hierarchical succession came to an end.[1] Then while speaking of the appearance of Aśoka, etc. he says obviously that as this is in contradiction with the prophecy and the sources of the adjusted tradition of Āryadeśa, although everything appears to have been properly mentioned, yet it is not credible.

In the east in the land of Aṅga lived a wise and very well-to-do householder, and in his house grew through the power of his deeds a tree from which fell jewel-fruits. As he was without any child, he used to bring offerings continually to the great god Viṣṇu in the form of Kṛṣṇa, in consequence where of the self-same Kṛṣṇa was born as his son. When he had grown up he became desirous of going out to sea. He then with 500 merchants, taking all equipments of a ship, went to the jewel-land and filled the ship with goods. In this way as he had gone to the sea six times and returned quickly with loaded ship without any difficulty, all regions were filled up with fame of the merchant as being endowed with great merits. At the time when his parents were dead and he had become a faithful devotee of the Venerable Dhitīka many merchant came to him from the far north and requested him to go again to the sea. Although at first he declined saying that he would not go as he did hear of anybody having loaded a ship for the seventh time, but on their persistent request he at last sailed and reached the jewel island, loaded the ship with treasures and returned home. On an island of the ocean the merchants saw a green grove existing and so they went there to recuperate themselves. But they were caught there by Krauñca Kumārī, the foremost Rākṣasī of the Rākṣasī family dwelling in the sea. They then took refuge in the Venerable Dhītika, who came to the island through supernatural power. The Rākṣasīs, not being able to endure his glory, ran way, and the merchants returned happily to Jambudvīpa. At this place the merchants supplied the clergy of the four regions for three years with all requisites, and at last entered into the priesthood. They were ordained by the Venerable Dhītika and all of them soon attained the grade of Arhatship. Then on the passing away of Dhītika, the venerable Kṛṣṇa, who belonged to the family of merchants joining the priesthood, took charge of the teaching; he delivered instructions to the four groups, and the acquisition of the four fruits suffered in interruption.

At this time appeared Bhikṣu Vatsa[2] of Kasmira, of Brāhmaṇa caste, very wicked, but learned. He took pleasure at the Ātmaka theory,

1. Tib. gtad. rabs. rdsogs. zin.—Tr.

2. Tib. gnas. pa. cf. Wassiljew, Der Buddhismus, p. 62 of the German translation.

travelled over all regions, and turned the simple people into his bad teaching and thus raised a little dissension in the saṅgha. Therefore Dhītika collected the clergy of the four regions in Vihāra Puṣkariṇī, a part of the Maru land, the yakṣa Kapila providing them with the necessary sustenance, corrected the errors, and re-iterated the Anātmaka theory in the assembly of the monks. As three months passed, all the bhikṣus who were converted by the Sthavira Vatsa to the Ātmaka theory, were completely purified, beheld the truth and at last, Sthavira Vatsa himself was converted to the unshakeable teaching.

Far off in the island of Siṃhala was the king Āsana-Siṃhakośa (Tib. khri. ldan-seṅ-geḥi. mtsod—Tr.). Once when he was in an assembly, a merchant of Jambudvīpa made over to him a wooden image of the teacher. As he asked what it was, the merchant recounted to him (the events) beginning from the Teacher up to the Venerable Kṛṣṇa of the dignitaries. Then the king wished to see the Venerable Kṛṣṇa as also to hear the excellent teaching and so sent a messenger. When this (messenger) came near the Venerable, the latter set out with a following of five hundred through the air by means of his supernatural power, whereupon the messenger held himself fast to the corner of the holy robe and let himself down on the border of Siṃhaladvīpa. As he sent the messenger before, the king came to meet him with others. He entered the chief city, where he diffused differently coloured rays of lights, shone forth and showed other wonders. On this island he preached the Law for three months, filled it with vihāras and clergymen, and made many partakers of the four fruits. Although the Teacher formerly had trodden over this island with his feet, the teaching after his death gradually disappeared, the Venerable Kṛṣṇa, however, greatly spread it afresh. After handing over the teaching to the Venerable Sidarśana, who came of the royal family, he vanished to the country of Kuśavana in the north. Now follows (the story of) Sudarśana.

In the west in the land of Bharukaccha, there was a kṣatriya Darśana, sprung of the Pāṇḍu line. He had extraordinary riches; his son was called Sudarśana. As he grew up, he became possessed of prosperity like that of the gods: he had 50 pleasure gardens, 50 picked women, each of whom had 5 maid-servants and each of them again had five female playmates. He spent daily 5000 gold paṇas on flowers alone, not to speak of his other riches. Once when he had gone to the pleasure-garden, surrounded by that group, he saw the Arhant Śukāyana going on the way with numerous followers, became exceedingly faithful and bowed before him, and took his seat by his side. When the Arhant had taught him the Law, he obtained on that very seat the grade of an

Arhant. When he asked for reception into the clerical order, the Arhant explained to him that was not possible for one living as a householder, that the circumstances were not suitable and that he should inform his father beforehand. As he requested his father for permission to enter into the priesthood, his father flew into rage and wanted to put him in iron-fetters, but just at that moment he raised himself in the air, displayed the stream of light and showed other wonders. Thus he converted his father, who said: "O son, as you have attained such a high grade of virtue, enter into the priesthood and thereby give me pleasure." After he had entered the priesthood, he delivered the teaching to his father, who then realised the truth. Then he chose Kṛṣ-ṇa as his Ācārya, and he lived in his company for a long time. Then Kṛṣṇa died and Mahā-sudarśana began to discipline the four groups by means of his teaching.

At that time there lived, in the west in the country of Sindhu, a yakṣiṇī Hiṅgalākṣī of great strength and supernatural power. She was spreading epidemics in different regions. She obstructed the way of those who wanted to go away somewhere else. She appeared in a dreadful form, whereupon the people offered her daily a wagon-load of food drawn by six bullocks, one excellent horse, one man and one woman.[1] When Sudarśana came to know of this and also of the fact that the time to subdue her had come, he came to his place of residence after he had collected his alms in the city of Sindhu, and ate his food. She took him to be a Śramaṇa who had lost his way. When at last he poured out the water, with which he had washed his bowl in her house, she flew into rage and sent a shower of stone and weapon, which however on account of his being absorbed in compassionate meditation (maitrībhāvanā—Tr.), he turned into a shower of flowers. Then through the power of the wish of the Venerable, all sides were set on fire and the yakṣiṇī herself was greatly terrified and sought for refuge to the Venerable. He taught her the Law, initiated her into the precepts, and from that time up to the present day no offering of flesh and blood was made to her. Further, Sudarśana knew that later on there would be no subduer, so he converted to the teaching 500 unbelieving Nāgas and Yakṣas. Thereafter the Venerable visited all the towns in the south, provided them with vihāras and monks. On many small islands he established the Buddha's teaching, and afterwards in Mahācīna and other lands he spread the teaching gradually and led innumerable living beings into bliss, and at last he vanished from existence into the "niravaśeṣa-nirvāṇadhātu."[2]

---

1. A similar yal.ṣa-offering is mentioned in the biography to Śākyamuni, p. 298 (68).
2. As restored from Tibetan. Schiefner renders it by "in dem restlosen Stoffe der Verdienstanhäufung".—Tr.

It is to be observed that the time of youth of king Aśoka corresponded to the last portion of the life of the Venerable Dhītika; the time of his sinful way of living with the time of the Venerable Kṛṣ-ṇa; the time when he became Dharmarāja was the time when the Venerable Sudarśana protected the teaching; when Mahāsudarśana vanished out of existence, King Aśoka also died. From the Venerable Ānanda up to Sudarśana there are wellknown *avadānas*; their contents Kṣemendrabhadra had collected and described. This series (of teachers) protected the teaching perfectly and their teaching agreed with that of the teacher, the Buddha himself. Thereafter appeared, it is true, many Arhants but they did not perform things which fully agreed with Buddha's teachings. The seventh section, the events contemporaneous with king Aśoka.

## VIII

## The Events At The Time of King Vigatāśoka

Of the eleven sons of king Aśoka, the most excellent was Kuṇāla,[1] whom a ṛiṣi had given this name on account of the similarity which his eyes had with those of the bird (named) Kuṇāla dwelling in the Himālayas. At the time when he had become master of all sciences, Tiṣyarakṣitā, the wife of king Aśoka, fell in love with him and wanted to seduce him artfully. But as he was pure and would not agree to it (her proposals), Tiṣyarakṣitā flew into rage. Later on when King Aśoka was suffering from diarrhœa and vomitting excrements, Tiṣyarakṣitā heard that just the same (illness) had happened to a common man of a mountain-village. She ordered his death, and when the stomach was cut open and examined, it was found out that a many-limbed ugly worm by going up and down caused the diarrhœa and vomitting. This worm did not perish by any medicine except when treated with a white garlic. Thereupon Tiṣyarakṣitā gave the king a white garlic as the remedy. Although the Kṣatriyas cannot eat white garlic, he was however allowed to take[2] for healing the sickness, and he soon recovered. At this the king vowed to grant her an excellent (boon). She said that she would ask for it not then but at some other time. Once upon a time in the north west in the Aśmaparānta country lying far off, king Gokarṇa revolted and the king's son Kuṇāla was sent there with an army for his subjugation. When he had subjugated the king, Tiṣyarakṣitā said to Aśoka: "O king, the time to grant me the boon has come now, give me the rulership for seven days." When he had granted her the same, she wrote an order to extract the eyes of

---

1. See Burnouf, Introduction, p. 403 f. Hiouen Tsang, Memoirs, vol. I, p. 154 f.
2. Burnouf, *loc. cit.*, p. 150.

Kuṇāla, sealed it with the stolen seal of the king and sent a messenger to Aśmaparānta.[1] Although the king of that place read the letter, he did not dare extract the eyes of Kuṇāla. When however Kuṇāla himself read the letter and became aware of the command of the king as also of the fact that one was ready to extract the eyes, he ordered accordingly the man to take out one eye and place it in his hand. What happened was made known to him before by an Arhant (that it would so come to pass). He had been many times initiated into the teaching which had the doctrine of impermanence as its beginning and which also brought firmness to his mind, As a result there of, he became a Śrotāpanna as soon as he saw the eye. After dismissing his servant, he took a lyre and wandered through different countries, and at last came to the Elephant controller at Pāṭalīputra. There the elephant gifted with insight recognised him and showed him respects. The men could not recognise him; on the daybreak the elephant guards asked him to play on the lyre. And as he had played the melody Gamaka on the lyre the king came to know from the top of his palace that the voice was similar to the voice of his son; on the morning he had enquiries made and learnt the actual state of things. When he had found out the cause, the king flew into rage, ordered Tisyarakṣitā to be locked up an burnt in the Lākṣā house. But Kuṇāla dissuaded him from it and he declared the true-wish: 'If I who love Tiṣyarakṣitā and my son in equal manner, and have no hatred in my mind, then let the eyes be as before'; and Kuṇāla obtained his eyes better than before. He than entered into the priestly office and obtained the Arhant grade.[2] Therefore the rulership could not devolve on him but his son Vigatāśoka was selected for the rulership. At this time appeared in the kingdom Oḍiviśa, the brāhmaṇa Rāghava having great wealth; he acknowledged the three treasures (ratnas) as his teaching. He was informed beforehand by a god in a dream that on the following day a bhikṣu would come to his house fo beg for alms, and that as his supernatural power was great, he would be able to collect the Venerables of all regions and so he should ask him (to do that). When another morning the Arhant Poṣadha came to his house he implored him. He maintained for 3 years the congregation of 80,000 Venerables. The gods being greatly delighted at the teaching let fall down in his house a rain of flowers. He satiated 100,000 bhikṣhus daily up to the end of his life. The eighth section: the events at the time of king Vigatāśoka.

1. In the other recensions of this story, it is known as Takṣaśilā which is restored from Tibetan rdo. hdsog (stone-accumulation).

2. This story of Kuṇāla with slight variations is found also in the *Divyāvadāna* (27), *Aśokāvadāna* and *Avadānakalpalatā* (59).—Tr.

# IX

## Events of The Time of Second Kāśyapa

After him the Arhant Kāśyapa, who was born in the North, in the land of Gāndhāra, worked for the salvation of living beings through three kinds of religious works. At that time there lived, the son of Vigatāśoka, Vīrasena,[1] who through the favour of Vaiśravaṇa's wife, the goddess Lakṣmī, possessed inexhaustible riches without doing even the least harm to living beings. He supported bhikṣus of the four quarters for three years, and offered a hundred kinds of sacrificial requisites to all caityas existing on the face of the earth. At that time in Mathurā, the Brāhmaṇa Yaśa[2] who was very much devoted to the teaching, erected the Vihāra Śarāvatī,[3] and maintained 100,000 monks; in that Vihāra the Arhat Ślanavāsa (Śāṇavāsika or Śāṇavāsa)[4] taught the Dhamma to a large number of bhikṣus of all regions gathered there. At that time there lived, in a region of the kingdom of Maruṭa,[5] the son of a merchant, Mahādeva, who had committed the three unpardonable (ānantarya) sins,[6] viz., patricide, matricide and murder of an Arhant. Tormented by his conscience he went to Kasmira.[7] After concealing his ways of life he became a bhikṣu. With his sharp intellect he became very learned in the three Piṭakas, felt strong repentance, and practised samādhi in solitude. Thereafter, by the power of Māra, all took him to be an Arhant, and this greatly increased his gain and fame; he them came to Śarāvatī with a group of bhikṣus; the bhikṣus recited the Prātimokṣasūtra by turn, and when the turn came to Mahādeva, he said at the end of his recitation that "gods are deluded through ignorance, the path proceeds out of the sound-stream, the sceptics are possessed by others' (wrong views)[8]—this is the teaching of Buddha." When he had taught this, the Venerable ones and old

---

1. Tib. dbaḥ. woḥi. sde with it variant dbaṅ-poḥi. sde (Indrasena); is it not a corruption of Vṛṣasena ? See Lassen II, 27, the Mañjuśrī-mūlatantra (leaf 323) attributes to him a reign of 70 years, and to his predecessor 76 years.
2. Text: Yaśika (grags-ldan),
3. The river Śarāvatī is mentioned in the Divyavadāna (p. 21) as one of the boundaries of the Madhyama Janapada of the Buddhists; see S.N. Mazumdar's edition of Cunningham's Geography, p. xliii, Vinaya, Mv., I, p. 197.—Tr.
4. Yul. slan. pa. Cf. Mahāvaṃsa, p. 22: Sambhuūta Sānavāsi.—Tr.
5. The kingdom was probably named after the ruler and he is Maruṇḍ? See Bohtlingk and Roth, *Sanskrit Dictionary* s.v.
6. In the Abhindharma-mahā-vibhāṣā-śāstra and other works Mahadeva's life is related. Watters has summarised it in his *Yuan Chwang*, vol. I, pp. 267-9.—Tr.
7. In the Chinese sources Pāṭaliputra is mentioned instead of Kasmīra. See Watters, *op. cit.*, p. 268.—Tr.
8. Lha. rnams. ma. rig. pa. yis. bslus. Lam. ni. sgra. yi. rgyun. las. byun. The tsom. can. rnams. gzan. gyis. hjug. —Tr.

bhikṣus said that these were not the words of the sūtras; but the majority of the young bhikṣus sided with Mahādeva, and thus there appeared a division. After Mahādeva had explained falsely the sense of many other words of the text and had passed away, the bhikṣu Bhadra, whom men took to be a reincarnation of Māra Pāpīya, also succeeded in introducing many contradictions and doubts regarding the sense of the scriptures, and he announced five facts, viz., (1) the answer, (2) ignorance (3) doubt, (4) temptation (5) the restoration of individuality and he gave these out to be the teaching of Buddha.[1] Different ways of explaining the word appeared in consequence of the many special opinions, and on account of doubts and misunderstandings the division became manifold, and also on account of the fact, that the teachers of the different sūtras in the language of different regions changed a little the succession of letters and connection of words, and introduced many different long and short word-beginnings.

Although the Arhants and many learned people tried to reconcile this division, the ordinary bhikṣus were overpowered by the Demon and the division did not cease. When Mahādeva and Bhadra died, the bhikṣus came to know their character. After Kaśyapa II had vanished from the present, the Venerable Mahāloma took charge of the land of Mathurā and the Venerable Nandin, the affairs concerning the teaching. The ninth section, the events of the time of Kāśyapa II.

1. See Dutt's *Early History etc.*, p. 229, for the interpretation of Mahādeva's five tenets.

## Chapter - 11

# Tāranāth's History of Buddhism in India

**(*Translated from the German version of A. Schiefner*)**

**U.N. Ghoshal & N. Dutt**

### X

### Events of The Time of The Venerable Mahāloma And Others

Soon after the time when the Venerable Mahāloma and Nandin were in charge of the teaching, king Vīrasena died and his son Nanda inherited the rulership which he carried on for 29 years. As the king had invoked the Piśāca Pīlu, his hand was filled with precious stones whenever he clutched at the sky.[1] There lived at that time in the land of Svarṇa-prastha (Gold-Droṇa),[2] the Brāhmaṇa Kuśala who gathered together all the bhikṣus of the four regions and entertained them for seven years. Thereafter, the king himself entertained the bhikṣus with food through many years in Kāśī-Vārāṇasī. At that time the learned bhikṣu Nāga began to speak highly of the five propositions (*pañcavastu*)[3] again and again and the division among the clergy became wider, giving rise to four schools. The Venerable Dharmaśreṣṭha then attained Arhathood and he left the company of quarrelling clergymen with a group of very peaceful bhikṣus and betook himself to the region of the North.

---

1. The *Mañjuśrīmūlatantra*, leaf 323 mentions this invocation. Cf. *Mañjuśrīmūlakalpa*, p. 611:—

तस्याप्यनन्तरो राजा नन्दनामा भविष्यति ।

... ... ... ... ... ...

तेनापि साधितो मन्त्र पिशाचः पीलुनामतः

तस्य मन्त्रप्रभावं तु महाभोगे भविष्यति ।—Tr.

2. gSer. bre, perhaps Hemavaddroṇī, shortened to Hemadroṇī, see Böhtlingk-Roth, sv. Droṇa.

3. Evidently it refers to the well known five points of Mahādeva which brought about the division in the Buddhist Church. For the five points, see *JRAS.*, 1910, p. 416. Dutt, *Early History* etc., p. 229.

One of king Nanda's companions was the Brāhmaṇa Pāṇini, who was born in the west at Bhīrukavana. Once he asked a palmist whether he would learn all the teachings of the world and he was answered in the negative; so he made a line on the palm of his hand with a sharp knife; he approached all the teachers living at that time on the earth, and learnt everything from them. But as he was not still satisfied,[1] he invoked, through concentration (of mind),[2] his protecting deity. As the latter showed his face and uttered *a*, *i*, *u*, he acquired all the words (*sgraḥi gnas* =*śabdapada*—Tr.) to be found in the three worlds. The heterodox people (lit. outsiders= *phyi-pa-rṅams*—Tr.) maintain that the deity was Īśvara, but have no special ground therefore, while the orthodox (lit. insiders—Tr.) hold that it was Avalokiteśvara, and have for their ground the following prophecy in the *Mañjuśrīmūlatantra* (leaf 323): Brāhmaṇa's son Pāṇini will surely obtain *Śrāvakabodhi* (Tib. *ñes-par-ñan-thos-byaṅ-chub-tu*—Tr.) according to my prophecy, and invoke the majesty of the lord of the worlds through his magical charms.[3] This Pāṇini compiled the grammatical sūtra known as the *Paṇini-Vyākaraṇa* which contained two thousand ślokas, one thousand ślokas being devoted to etymology and the other thousand to explanation. This is, as it were, the root of all grammars. Before him there was no written śāstra on etymology. As there did not exist any system which brought the facts under observation, the individual linguists who set about forming combinations of one and all separate words,[4] were reckoned as specially learned. Although it is said in Tibet that *Indravyākaraṇa* is older, it will be seen as stated below, that it probably existed earlier in the divine regions but not in Āryadeśa. Although paṇḍitas maintain that in Tibetan translation the *Candravyākaraṇa* agrees with Pāṇini and the *Kalāpavyākaraṇa* with *Indravyākaraṇa*, it may be stated generally that the *Pāṇinivyākaraṇa* in particular on account of its extraordinary minuteness of explanations

---

1. Tib. legs. par. bslabs. śin. śes. kyaṅ. da. duṅ. ma. tshim. ste.—Tr.
2. Tib. rtse. geig. tu.—Tr.
3. Cf. *Mañjuśrīmūlakalpa*, p. 613:

तस्य (नन्दस्य) अप्यन्यतमः सखा पानिर्नाम मानवः ॥
नियतं श्रावकत्वेन व्याकृतो मे भविष्यति ।
सोऽपि सिद्धमन्त्रस्तु लोकीशस्य महात्मनः ॥
साधयेत प्रज्ञाकामस्तु क्रोधं हालहलं द्विजः ।

The word लोकीश in the above verse is, I think, the point of contention referred to by Tāranātha.—Tr.

4. Tib. re-re-gñis-gñis=one and all, one with another, indiscriminately. Schiefner writes: wenn jene von zwei bis zwei Verbindungen anfangend einzelnes zusammenbrachten.—Tr.

and its full and systematic observations, is something very exceptional.[1] The tenth section, the events of the time of the Venerable Mahāloma and others.

## XI

## Events of The Time of King Mahāpadma

In the north, in the borderland Vanāyu (nags. khi. sa) there lived a king Agnidatta who for more than thirty years supported three thousand monks with the Arhant Dharmaśreṣtha at their head. The venerable Mahātyāga (gtoṅ-ba-chen-po=*mahādātā*) guarded the teaching in Madhyadeśa, and Mahāpadma, son of the king Nanda, maintained the whole saṅgha in Kasumapura. Bhikṣu Sthiramati, a follower of Sthavira Nāga proclaimed again the *Pañcavastu* increased the discord and the schools began gradually to split up into eighteen. The friends of king Mahāpada, the Brāhmaṇa Bhadra and the Brāhmaṇa Vararuci both showed veneration to the clergy. The Brāhmaṇa Bhadra betook himself through the skill of his magical charm to different regions, and wherever he came he took away all the riches of the non-human beings (i.e. yakṣas, etc) and served 1800 brāhmaṇas, 2000 bhikṣus, and other wandering monks and beggars, 10,000 in all, daily with all requisites. Vararuci, however, had a pair of boots of tree-leaves which he had obtained through the power of his magical charm; when he put them on, he could procure excellent things from the dwelling-places of gods and nāgas and with these he satisfied many beggars. Once when he lost his friendship (mi. mdsaḥ. bar. gyur Tr.) with the king, and the latter thinking that he might apply evil charms against himself, sent a messenger to kill him, he put on his boots and escaped to the city of Ujjaini. At length he was outwitting by the king, because when a woman stole his boots and he could no more fly, he was killed by the hangman. To atone for the guilt of murdering a Brāhmin, the king erected 24 vihāras and established by their side fully equipped religious halls (chos kyi. gshi—Tr.). Some say that the third collection of Buddha's teaching took place at that time, but evidently there is little possibility for it. This Vararuci wrote many explanatory work (*vibhāṣā*) and distributed them among the preachers of the Dharma. Books containing the words of Buddha existed already at the time when the Teacher lived, but this was the beginning of the explanatory śāstra put in book-form. The meaning of *vibhāṣā* is detailed explanation; in accordance with the text as delivered by the Teacher himself and the instruction imparted by him, the sense of the words

---

1. The only grammatical work existing in Tibetan translation in Tanjur, see Schiefner's essay "on the logical and grammatical works in Tanjur." *Bullet. histor.-philol.*, vol. IV, 18, 19.

has been given in it. The *vibhāṣā-śāstras* are not special śāstras, these are easier to understand than the sūtras, but they were composed later in the interest of beings living in the future. Some think that at the time of Upagupta they were composed by the Arhants in universal agreement; other maintain that this had been done by Yaśa, Sarvakāma and several others. It is evident that on account of the mixture of both these earlier opinions, the Tibetans have taken them to have been composed by Sarvakāma, Kubjita[1] and five hundred other Arhants living in Naṭa-Bhaṭika vihāra on the Vindhyā mountain in the north. Whatever that may be, it was through these Arhants that the words have been put together, and having been transmitted from ear to ear by the sthaviras, they were afterwards put in witting. According to the opinion of the Vaibhāṣikas, the seven Abhidharma sūtras should be held as Buddha's words, and the Vibhāṣā be regarded as the beginning of the explanatory sūtras. According to the view of the Sautrāntikas, the seven Abhidharma sūtras, which the Vaibhāṣikas look upon as being handed down from earlier times, were composed by the imperfect śrāvakas[2] and were wrongly given out as Buddha's words collected by Śāriputra and others and counted as the beginning of the explanatory śāstras. Some ācāryas assert that the seven sūtras might have been the words of Buddha himself, but the compositions of imperfect śrāvakas were interpolated into it, as was the case with the sūtras of different schools. According to this view one must look upon those parts which are not in agreement with the three pramāṇas and diverge from them as later interpolations. One may say that, as in Mahāyāna the Abhindharma forms a separate piṭaka so also it must be among the Śrāvakas; and although it is true that the contents of the Piṭakas are connected with one another, as there are separate books for the two other Piṭakas, there is no reason why it should not be the case with the Abhidharma. Although this last assumption is very proper, we have in the meantime followed the other tradition in as much as Ācārya Vasubandhu seems to have agreed with the opinion of the Sautrāntikas. The view that it is not the word of Buddha because so many mistakes are found, but that it was a composition of Śāriputra and others, is very stupid. If one of the ideal pair had already died before the Teacher, so, in the life-time of the Teacher there could not be any explanatory śāstra of his words. And if the teacher himself were still living, it would be too much to say that wrong exposition of the sense of his

1. Sgur. po: it occurs in Kandjur, vol. XI, 1. 325, and corresponds to Kujjitasobhito (=Pali: Khujja-sobhita) of the *Mahāvaṃsa*, p. 19.

2. Tib. ñan. thos. so. so. skye. bo=śravakas who are pṛthagjanas, i.e., not yet sṛotāpa mas. The German translation "einfachen Śrāvakas" is not accurate.

words had already appeared. Let us accept that as the commentaries were on the basis of the approved teaching of Buddha, the difference between Buddha's words and the commentaries was merely in name though the words had appeared when the Teacher himself was living, and the commentaries after he had passed away from existence. If, however, the ideal pair and others had wrongly explained the Śāstras, and all the contemporary men (who could be taken) as witnesses, had died, and if it is not reasonably possible to ascertain the persons who were contemporaries (and so be regarded as) witnesses, and if the Arhants did not know the truth (*de ñid*), then it follows that in the school of the Śrāvakas nobody could realise the Truth.[1] If the great Arhants, who arose through the transformation of the Teacher, were, willingly in the wrong, it was due to the demons. Shortly after the time of king Mahāpadma, there lived in the land of Oḍivisa, King Candragupta to whose house the venerable Mañjuśrī came in the shape of a bhikṣu and delivered the different Mahāyāna teachings and even left behind a book. The Sautrāntikas maintain that it was the *Prajñāpāramitā* of eight thousand ślokas but the Tantra School maintains that it was the *Tattvasaṃgraha.*[2] Whatever may be the case, I think, without wishing to contradict anything, that the first view is proper. This is the beginning of the appearance of Mahāyāna among men after the passing away of the Teacher. The eleventh section, the events at the time of king Mahāpadma.

---

1. As there is much ambiguity in both the Tibetan text and the German translation, a free translation has been give here—Tr.
2. In Tanjur vol. *ḥe* occur the *Sūtras* called the *Tattvasaṅgrahakārikā* by Sāntigupta and *Tattvasaṅgrahapañjikā* by Kamalaśrī.

Recently both the text (Karika) and its commentary (Pañjikā) have been published in the Gœkwad Oriental Series. The opinion of the Tantra School is evidently wrong—Tr.

words had already appeared. Let us accept that as the commentaries were on the basis of the approved teaching of Buddha, the difference between Buddha's words and the commentaries was merely in name, though the words had appeared when the Teacher himself was living and the commentaries after he had passed away from existence. If, however, the local pa[illegible] and others had wrongly explained the Śāstras, and all the contemporary men (who could be taken) as witnesses, had died, and if it is not reasonably possible to ascertain the persons who were contemporaries (and so be regarded as) witnesses, and if the Arhats did not know the truth (de-nyid), then it follows that in the school of the Śrāvakas nobody could realise the Truth. If the great Arhats, who arose through the transformation of the Teacher, were wittingly in the wrong, it was due to the demons. Shortly after the time of king Mahāpadma, there lived in the land of Odiviśa king Candragupta, in whose house the Venerable Mañjuśrī came in the shape of a bhikṣu and delivered the different Mahāyāna teachings and even left behind a book. The Sautrāntikas maintain that it was the Prajñā-pāramitā of eight thousand ślokas but the Tantra School maintains that it was the Tattvasaṁgraha.[1] Whatever may be the case, I think, without wishing to contradict anything, that the first view is proper. This is the beginning of the appearance of Mahāyāna among men after the passing away of the Teacher. The eleventh section, the events at the time of king Mahāpadma.

1. As there is much ambiguity in both the Tibetan text and the German translation, a free translation has been given here. [illegible]

2. In Tibetan [illegible] called the Tattvasaṁgraha-kārikā by Śāntarakṣita and Tattvasaṁgraha-pañjikā by Kamalaśīla.

Recently both the text (Kārikā) and its commentary (Pañjikā) have been published in the Gaekwad Oriental Series. The opinion of the Tantra School is evidently wrong. [illegible]

# Chapter - 12

# Tāranāth's History of Buddhism in India

## (*Translated from the German version of A. Schiefner*)

U.N. Ghoshal & N. Dutt

### XII

### Events of The Time of The Third Collection

After this time there lived in Kashmir a king Siṃha (*Seṅ. ge*) who took ordination (*rab. tu. byuṅ=pravrajyā*) and assumed the name Sudarśana (*legs. mthoṅ*). He obtained arhathood and taught the had heard law in Kashmir. When Kanishka, the king of Jalandhara, this (teaching), he became very believing, came to Kashmir, which lay to the north, heard the teaching from the venerable Siṃha-Sudarśana, showed great veneration to all the *caityas* of the north and entertained many times the Bhikṣusaṃghas of the four regions. At that time the bhikṣu Sañjayin (=*yaṅ. dag rgyal*) having learnt much from an arhat, became influential, and obtained from the householders and brāhmaṇas, ample provisions, and carried on religious discussions with 200,000 monks. At this time there took place (in the Saṅgha) the division into eighteen different schools but they lived together without much quarrel. In Kashmir there lived a Brāhamaṇa (called) Śūdra, possessing an inconceivable store of requisities (*yo. byad=pariṣkāra*-Tr.) (for mirians with his company of 5,000 bhikṣus, and thus spread the three school of Vaibhāṣika with his followers, and to the foremost of the Sautrāntikas (the monk called) Sthavira, highly respected by the Kashmirians with his company of 5,000 bhikṣus, and thus spread the three piṭakas widely. The Āgamas of the Sautrāntikas at this time were *Dṛṣṭāntamālāgama* (*luṅ. dpeḥi. ḥphreṅ. ba*), *Piṭakadharmamuṣṭi* (*sde. snod. ḥtijin. pa ḥi dpe. ḥkhyud*), etc. At this time there came from the east Ārya Pārśva who was an arhant and an accomplished scholar. He gave out the prophecy-(*vyākaraṇa-*)*sūtra,* the *Kāñcanamālāvadāna*, which was preserved by some learned Sthaviras, and contained the dream of king

Kṛkin,[1] as well as several other very rare sūtras. When king Kanishka heard this, he gathered all bhikṣus in the Kuṇḍalavanavīhāra (*sna. rgyan. nags kyi. gtsug. lag. khaṅ*) of Kashmir, and prepared (as is said by the Kashmirians) the third collection of the words. Others however say that the collection took place in the Kuvana monastery in Jalandhara, and most scholars agree with this last view. According to the narratives of the Tibetans, 50 Arhats, 500 Bodhisattvas, 500 ordinary Paṇḍitas gathered together and prepared the collection; although this does not contradict the Mahāyānic view, the foremost Buddha-scholars, however, were at that time called 'Mahābhadanta' since the designation of Paṇḍita did not exist; for this reason the designation of 500 Paṇḍitas is not correct; more correct appears to be the tradition that Vasumitra and 400 bhadantas were present there as is stated on a page of "the abstract of a detailed history of the succession of the teacher," an Indian work, translated by ḥGos. gshon. nu. dpal. But also this Vasumitra should not be taken to be the same as the great teacher of the Vaibhāṣ -ikas. Further, as these persons had taken pains with regard to the teaching of the Śrāvakas, it is well to suppose, in agreement with the history of the Śrāvakas, that although it is said that 500 Arhants and 500 Tripiṭakadhara Mahābhadantas prepared the collection, 500 Arhants were added here in order to increase the importance of the teaching; in any case, however, the number of Arhants was less and that those who had attained the fruits, namely, the Srotāpannas, etc., made up the number of 500. Before the appearance of Mahādeva and Bhadra, the number of those who used to attain the fruits was great, but after these two had brought, confusion into the teaching and a disruption had set in the number of those who attained fruits greatly decreased because the bhikṣus did not devote themselves to *yoga* but gave their thoughts to the strife. Therefore, the number of Arhants at the time of the third collection was small. Towards the end of the life-time of king Vīrasena and during the whole period of the reign of kings Nanda and Mahāpadma, and at the beginning of the life-time of king Kanishka, i.e., during the life-time of these four kings, the schism in the Saṃgha took place; the bitter quarrel lasted for 63 years but (calculating) with the earlier or later, this or that, the schism lasted nearly 100 years. When this strife was made up at the time of the third collection, all the eighteen schools were recognized as so many forms of teaching;[2] the *Vinaya* was put into writing, the *Sūtras* and the *Abhidharma,* which were in earlier times not put into writing, were so

1. For the dream, see Buston, transl. I, p. 98.
2. Buston, transl., I, p. 98.

recorded, but that which had been recorded were purified. At this time there appeared among men all Mahāyāna texts, which some bhikṣ-us who had attained *anutpattikadharmakṣānti* carried forward for a little while but as this did not spread very much the strife among the Śrāvakas ceased. The twelfth section: the events of the time of the third collection.

## XIII

## Events At The Beginning of The Great Propagation of Mahāyāna

After the Third Collection had taken place and king Kanishka had died, there lived, in the north in the land of Aśmaparānta, to the west of Kashmir, and near Tukhāra, a householder Jaṭi possessed of immeasurable wealth. He showed veneration to all *caityas* of the north. Inviting the Vaibhāṣika-bhadanta Vasumitra, belonging to Maru, a country lying in the west, and Tukhāra-bhadanta Ghoṣaka, (*dbyaṅs. sgrog.*), he maintained 300,000 monks for twelve years, and at last he had the wish to obtain the highest insight. As an indication of the fulfillment of his wish, the flowers given (by him) as offering remained unfaded for one year, and the lamp lasted as long; the sandal powder as well as the flowers flung away remained held up in the air, the earth quaked, musical sounds were heard, and so forth. In his Puṣkalāvatī palaces, the son of king Kanishka maintained one hundred arhants and 10,000 bhikṣus continuously for five years; in the east in Kusumpura lived the brāhmaṇa Viduḥ, who made ready innumerable books of the Tripiṭaka and offered them as gifts to the bhikṣus. In each of the Tripiṭakas there were 100,000 ślokas, such 1,000 copies were prepared by him, and to each of these copies was attached (*spel. ba*=conjoined—Tr.) an offering of requisites in inconceivable quantities. In the town of Pāṭaliputra lived the Arhant Ārya Aśvagupta who had cast away astrology [*dus. mi sbyor*] and meditated upon the eight vimokṣas (*de.ni. rnam. par. thar. pa. brgyad. la bsam. gtan. paḥo*). As he learned the teaching, Nandimitra and other Arhats by proper exertion (*ci.rigs= yathāyogaṃ*—Tr.) realised the truth in various ways. In the west lived the king Lakṣāśva who exerted considerably for the teaching of Buddha. In the south-west, in Saurāṣṭra there was a brāhmaṇa Kulika (*rigs. ldan*); when he heard that the Sthavira Arhat Nanda had comprehended the Mahāyāna teaching, he invited him in order to hear from him the Mahāyāna discourses. At this time appeared all at once in divergent regions numberless *Kalyāṇamitras of Mahāyāna* teaching; all these had heard the teaching from Āryāvalokiteśvara, Guhyapati, Mañjuśrī, Maitreya, etc., and acquired the *Dharmasantāna-*

*Samādhi* (*chos. khi. rgyan. gyi. tiṅ-ñe. ḥrtjin*); there appeared Mahābhadanta Avitaraka, Vigatarāgadhvaja, Divyākaragupta, Rāhulamitra, Jñānatala, the great upāsaka Saṅgatala and other teacher of the Law, 500 in number. At this time there were the *Ārya Ratnakūṭ-adharmaparyāyaśatasāhasrikā* in 1,000 sections, *Āryāvataṃsaka in* 100,000 discourses and 100 chapters; *Ārya Laṅkāvatāra* in 25,000 ślokas, *Ghanavyūha* in 12,000 ślokas, *Dharmasaṅgīti* in 12,000 ślokas, and a number of other works being portions of the Sūtras procured from the gods, nāgas, gandharvas, rākṣasas and various other regions, but mostly from the land of nāgas.

The brāhmaṇa invited a number of these teachers; when the king Lakṣāśva heard this news, he became more faithful and wished to invite the 500 teachers of law. He asked the ministers how many teachers of law (*dharmadeśakā=chos. smra. ba*) there were, and was answered "five hundred" and how many hearers of the law, the answer was "five hundred."

The king thereupon thought that there were many teachers of law but few students (*slob. ma*). He therefore erected upon the top of Mt. Abhu, five hundred Vihāras to each of which he invited a preacher of the law (*dharmavācaka*) whom he provided with all requisites. From the pariṣad of the king himself, as many as five hundred persons with strong disposition took ordination (*pravrajyā*) and increased the number of students of Mahāyāna. Thereafter the king wished to have books written and enquired how many books formed the Mahāyāna piṭaka (*de. snod*). When he was told that generally, they cannot be measured but there were now 10 million ślokas, the king said that although so many, he wished to have them written down. He had them written down and gave them to the bhikṣus. Later on these works were taken to Śrī Nālandā. Thereafter these, 1500 bhikṣus who followed the Mahāyāna teachings composed numberless sūtras. They were of irresistible understanding, (*apratihatabuddhi=blo. gros. thogs. pa. med. pa*) and had developed faith (*kṣānti*) and were able to exhibit before the people their miraculous power and make a little display of higher knowledge (*abhijñā-vikrīḍā*). Thereafter the fame of Mahāyāna spread in all directions and as this did not please the Śrāvakas, they declared that the Mahāyāna teaching was not the word of Buddha because the followers of Mahāyāna applied their minds to meditation (*yogāvacara*), they took ordination (*pravrajyā*) according to the 18 different schools, and lived mostly with them. Though there were only a few Mahāyāna teachers among the thousands of Śrāvakas, yet the Śrāvakas could not suppress them. At that time there were in

Magadha two brothers, the brāhmaṇas, Mudgaragomin Siddhapati and Śaṅkarapati who rendered offerings to the family deity Maheśvara but were nevertheless versed in the hetorodox as well as orthodox systems. Mudgaragomin alone had doubts (*vicikitsā*) and held Maheśvara in honour; Śaṅkarapati on the other hand was very believingly devoted to Buddha. They procured for themselves on the advice of their mother the swift-footed (*kṣripra-pādā*) and betook themselves to the king of mountains,—Kailāśa. There in the abode of Maheśvara they perceived the white bull which he rode and the goddess Umā plucking flowers, etc. At last, they saw the god Maheśvara himself sitting on a lion and giving discourses. At that moment there came flying from the Mānasa Lake 500 Arhants. Mahādeva showed them veneration, washed their feet, entertained them and then heard their teachings. Although they now came to know that there were none superior in knowledge to Buddha, and Mahādeva also told them in reply to their question that the salvation could be obtained only through the Buddha-mārga and not through any other way. Full of joy they returned home, gave up their Brāhmaṇa dress, adopted the precepts of an upāsaka and thoroughly learnt the principles of all yānas. In order to distinguish between the merits and demerits of the believers in Buddha and Tīrthikas, Mudgaragomin composed the *Viśeṣastava* (*khyad. bar. du. ḥphags. paḥi. bstod. pa*) on the merits and Śaṅkarapati composed *Devātiśastotra*[1] (*lha. las. phul. du. byin. bar. bstod. pa*) and when these had spread to all market places and royal palaces, the people began mostly to recite them (i.e. the *stava* and the *stotra*). Mudgaragomin and his brother made provision for living requisites for 500 bhikṣus of the Śrāvaka (yāna) in Vajrāsana and for 500 Mahāyānists in Nālandā. It was Nālandā which was formerly the birth place of the venerable Śāriputra and it was also the place where he finally vanished from existence with 80,000 Arhants. In the meanwhile the Brāhmaṇa village became deserted and there remained only the caitya of the venerable Śāriputra to which king Aśoka made large offerings and built a great Buddha temple. When later on the first 500 Mahāyāna bhikṣus counselled together and came to know that they had delivered the Mahāyāna teaching at the place of Śāriputra they took it to be a sign that the teachings of the Mahāyānists would spread widely; but when they further learnt that the same was also the place of Maudgalyāyana, they took it to be a sign that the teaching would be very powerful; but the teaching did not prosper very well. Both the brāhmaṇa brothers and the teachers erected 8 Vihāras and placed there

1. Cf. Buston, trans., II, p. 181.

the works of the whole Mahāyāna teaching. Thus, (we see) that the first founder of Nālanda Vīhāra was Aśoka, the developer of the place of learning was the 500 Ācāryas, Mudgaragomin and his brother, the next enlarger was Rāhulabhadra and the greatest expander was Nāgārjuna. The thirteenth section: events at the beginning of the great propagation of Mahāyāna.

## XIV

## Events of The Time of The Brāhmaṇa Rāhula

King Candanapāla was the ruler of Aparāntaka. This king is said to have lived 150 years and reigned for 120 years. He brought to the temples and the Saṅgha great offerings and it appears, according to the accounts, that no one rendered more services than him to the religion of Buddha. At that time the brāhmaṇa Indradhruva, friend of the king, after invoking the king of gods, received from him the science of words (Grammar). As it was written down as he delivered it, it was known by the name *Indravyākaraṇa.* It contains 25,000 ślokas and the work is known as the grammar taught by the god. At the time when the king was appointed to the rulership, the great Ācārya and brāhmaṇa Rāhulabhadra came to Nālandā. He took ordination from paṇḍita Kṛṣ ṇa and learnt the Piṭakas of the Śrāvakas. Some, however, say that he was ordained by the Bhadanta Rāhulaprabha and that Kṛṣṇa was his paṇḍita (teacher). But this Kṛṣṇa is not the same as the one whose name occurs in the succession of teachers. Although, he heard the teachings from Ācārya Avitaraka (*rnam. par. mi. rtog*) and some others, he learnt the Sūtras and Tantras of Mahāyāna mainly from Guhyapati and other higher gods, and spread the Mādhyamika teachings. Simultaneously with this Ācārya, lived the eight Mahābhadantas of the Mādhyamika teachings, viz., Bhadanta Rāhulagarbha, Ghanasa and others. The venerable Sarvanivaraṇa-viṣkambhin appeared in person to Bhadanta Prakāśadharmamaṇi after the latter had acquired *anutpattikadharmakṣānti* (Geduld in der Lehre des Nichtgeborenwerdens). He procured from the under-world the ancient *Mahāsamaya* (see Burnouf, *op. cit.*, p. 222) in 100,000 sections and 1000 chapters. Further many disciples of the first 500 Ācārya acquired many Sūtras and Tantras, hitherto unknown, and since this time all the three forms of Tantras were established, *viz., kriyā-, caryā-,* and *yoga-tantras,* and diverse works on the *Anuttarayoga, viz., Guhyasamāja, Buddhasama-yoga, Māhājāla,* etc. At this time appeared in the city of Sāketana the bhikṣu Mahāvīra, in the country of Vārāṇaśī the Vaibhāṣika Mahābhadanta Buddhadeva, and in the land of Kashmir the great Sūtra-Ācārya Bhadanta Śrīlābha. By them the Śrāvakayāna was propagated. It should be noted that the four Bhandantas Dharmatrāta, Ghoṣaka, Vasumitra and Buddhadeva were regarded as the great Ācāryas of the Vaibhāṣikas, and every one of them is said to have had 100,000 disciples. The following were valued as the leading works of the Vaibhāṣ-ikas, *viz., spel. ,a. gsu,. gyi. phreṅ, gdams. ṅag. brgya.* be which were enlarged by the Ācāras. One must not confuse this Dharmatrāta with Dharmatrāta, the complier of *Udānavarga,*[1] and this Vasumitra with two others of the same name, of whom one is the author of *Samayabhedoaracanacakra*[2] (*gshun. lugs. kyi. bye. brag. bkod. paḥi. hkhor. lo*). According to the tradition of the Guhyasamāja school one should place at this time the king Viśukalpa in the country of Oḍiviśa as the contemporary of Candanapāla. At this time in Kuru land was brāhmaṇa Dharmika, who in this land and the surrounding regions established 108 Buddha temples and gave them away for residence to the preachers of Mahāyāna-*dharma.* In the town of Hastināpura, the brāhmaṇa Yogin, (*brtson. ldan*), who was considerably rich, built 108 temples and made them seats for 108 Dharma-preachers of the Vinaya School (*hdul. ba. rtzin. pa=Vinayadhara-Tr.*). At the time appeared in the east, in the country of Bhaṅgala, king Haricandra, the first of the line of Candra. In the *Mantramārga*, he obtained *siddhi*, built palaces with the five kinds of jewel stones and decorated the surrounding walls with representations of the three kinds of existence (*tri-bhava-Tr.*); in wealth he vied with the gods, he erected the temple of Vidyādhara, around which there were 1000 steps. It was the time of Srī Saraha or the Mahābrahaman Rāhula Brahmacārī and the time of appearance of the 500 Yogacaryā teachers. Lastly during his life-time, most of the Mahāyāna-sūtras with the exception of the *Śatasāhasrikāprajñāpāramitā* came into existence. The 14th section, the events of the time of the brāhmaṇa Rāhula.

---

1. The work is found in Tanjur, vol. *du* of the Sūtras, with a commentary of Prajñāvarman.
2. Or *Nikāya-bheda-upodarśama-saṃgraha.* See Buston, transl. I, 122.

## Chapter - 13

# Tāranāth's History of Buddhism in India

**(*Translated from the German version of A. Schiefner*)**

**U.N. Ghoshal & N. Dutt**

### XV

### The Events of The Time When Ārya Nāgārjuna Was in Charge of The Teaching

Thereafter Paṇḍita[1] Nāgārjuna maintained[2] the teaching and spread extensively the Mādhyamika-system. He rendered great service to the Śrāvakas, specially after having turned out a number of Bhikṣus and Śrāmaṇeras, who had transgressed many disciplinary rules and who had great influence in the Saṅgha and who are said to have been about 8,000 in number. Thereupon all sects acknowledge him as their master. At this time, appeared Bhadanta Nanda, Bhadanta Paramasena,[3] Bhadanta Samyaksatya.[4] These three had grasped the Yogācāra thought and had written Śāstras; and as they obviously preached the *ālaya*,[5] these three Bhadantas are called the old Yogācāryas and Asaṅga with his brother are counted as later ones; and it is clear that they were not his successors. Paṇḍita Nāgārjuna granted maintenance to 500 dharma-preachers of Mahāyāna, teaching in Śrī-Nālandā for many years with the wealth which he had obtained by the gold transforming essence. He succeeded in invoking Caṇḍikā. When this goddess was about to take him with her to heaven and to lead him into the dwellings of the gods, he told her that for the time being it would not be necessary to go there; but that he had acquired the *siddhi* in order that the goddess (Caṇḍikā) might give support to the priests of the Mahāyāna as long

---

1 སློབ་དཔོན། 2 བསྐྱངས། 3 དམ་པའི་སྡེ།

4 ཡང་དག་བདེན། 5 ཀུན་གཞི།

as the doctrine would exist. According to these words she settled down to the west near Nālandā in the form of Vaiśyabhadrā.[1] The Paṇḍita drove a great Khadira-wedge,[2] weighing one man-load, into a very high, thick wall of the Mañjuśrī-temple built with stone and solicited her to maintain the clergy until this wedge was transformed into ashes. After she had supplied the clergy with everything for twelve years, it happened, that at last an worthless Śrāmaṇera who did the service made repeated proposals of love to her, but she answered nothing. She told him once, that she would come to him if that Khadira-wedge could be transformed into ashes. When that Khadira-wedge had been burnt and transformed into ashes by that evil Śrāmaṇera, the goddess disappeared at once. Thereupon the Ācārya erected 108 centres of Mahāyāna teaching in the 108 temples, put up an image of Mahākāla in each of them, and entrusted the god with the protection of the doctrine. Further at the time when an elephant in Vajrāsena did great harm to the Bodhi tree, he erected two stone-pillars behind the Bodhi-tree, and so no more damage occurred. The stone-pillars were put up, each with a Mahākāla riding on a lion and holding a club, which proved very useful for some years; when damage occurred again, the tree was enclosed with a stone-railing, behind which 108 Caityas were set up with images of gods. The blessed fruit-giving Caitya[3] was surrounded by a wall and within the wall 108 temples were erected. At the time when water had done great damage to the eastern side of the Vajrāsana, seven stone-blocks were put up in the shape of a dam, on which a large image of Muni[4] with face backwards was engraved, and the damage of the water was warded off in this way. They were called the seven Dam-Munis. As the word *Chulon*[5] is a designation of the dam, only ignorant persons say that the images are so called because these were made in the shape resembling the image seen in water. If one says that these images were made at the time when King Uttayana[6] was converted, this would not be in conformity with the Vinaya-text, and it makes obvious the value of the two traditions.

About this time, king Muñja with a following of 1000 men obtained the Vidyādhara *Kāyasiddhi* in the country of Oḍiviśa,[7] and

---

1. རྗེ་རིགས་མ་བཟང་མོ།  2. སེང་ལྡེང།
3. དཔལ་ལྡན་འབྲས་སྤུངས་ཀྱི་མཆོད་རྟེན,།
4. ཐུབ་པའི་སྐུ་བརྙན་ཆེན་པོ།
5. ཆུ་ལོན།  6. ཨུ་ད་ཡ་ན།  7. ཨུ་ཊི་བི་ཤ།

in the west in a part of Mālava called Ṭoḍhahari, King Bhojadeva with 1000 followers gained the Siddhi. They could make themselves invisible and so forth by uttering mantras but could not gain all *siddhis*. The Āryas acquired many Dhāraṇīs and the *Śatasāhasrikāprajñāpāramitā* the composition of which the Śrāvakas attributed to Nāgārjuna. After this time no new Mahāyāna-Sūtras were added. In order to put an end to the quarrel of the Śrāvakas, who believed in the existence of the matter, he composed the five *Nyāya-saṃgrahas* and other works. The Tibetan histories record that 1,20,000 ślokas were mentioned in a Śāstra called *Nyāyalaṃkāra* which was written by Bhikṣu Kṣemaṅkara[1] (or Śaṃkara) in order to refute the Mahāyāna; in three Indian historical books, however, the corresponding statement is that there were 12,000 ślokas. In the east many temples were erected in Paṭaveśa or Pukam[2] and in Oḍiviśa, Bhaṅgala and Rāḍhā. At this time, Brahmin Suviṣṇu erected 108 temples in Magadha, in Śrī-Nālandā, and 108 seats for the teaching of the Abhidharma (Mātṛkā), so that the Abhidharma of Mahāyana and Hīnayāna would not perish.

Towards the end of his life the venerable Nāgārjuna betook himself to the regions of the south and after having converted King Udayana he protected the doctrine for many years. In the south, in the country of Dravaḍi[?], there were two Brahmins, Madhu and Supramadhu, who were possessed of inconceivable wealth. They vied with Ācārya Nāgārjuna in the sciences of the Brahmins, in the four Vedas and in 18 science, etc. The Brahmins, however, had not gained a hundredth part of the knowledge which the Ācārya possessed. The two Brahmins said: "O you son of a Brahmin, who has learned down to the bottom of all Śāstras referring to the three Vedas, why have you become a Śākya-Śramaṇa?" When Nāgārjuna explained to them that the Vedas were not to be praised, but that the teaching (of Buddha) should be praised, they became very faithful and rendered reverence to Mahāyāna. When the Ācārya had initiated them in the Mantras, the former, (Madhu) invoked Sarasvatī, the latter (Supra-madhu) Vasudhārā, and both of them maintained 250 Mahāyāna preachers; the first had the *Prajñāpāramitā* which contained 1,00,000 ślokas copied in 1, 2 or 3 days etc., and gave many copies to the Bhikṣus; the second supplied the clergy with all requisites. As this Ācārya upheld the excellent doctrine in every possible ways by preaching, contemplating, erecting of temples, supporting the clergy, working for the benefit of the non-human beings, refuting the attacks of the Tīrthyas, etc., he should be

---

1 བདེ་བྱེད། 2 པ་ཊ་བེ་ཤ་དཾ་པུ་ཀཾ།

regarded as the incomparable benefactor of Mahāyāna-doctrine. As I have given the biography of the great Brahmin[1] and of Ārya Nāgārjuna in the account of the seven-sectioned Tantras it may be regarded as well-known.

King Udayana lived for 150 years; this Ācārya, however, lived, as some people presume, 71 years less than 600, according to others, however, 29 years less than 600; if we follow the first opinion, he is supposed to have lived in Madhyadeśa for 200 years, in the south for 200 years, in Śrīparvata for 129 years, obviously a rough calculation, about which my teacher and Paṇḍita was of the opinion, that half a year had been counted as one whole year. The other opinion resembles the previous one in every respect; it only supposes that he lived in Śrīparvata for 171 years. As he had conjured the life-giving balsam, his skin took the colour of jewels.[2] By contemplation in Śrīparvata he obtained the first Bodhisattva-stage and his body was adorned with the thirty-two marks.

A friend of the Ācārya was the Ācārya and Brāhṃin Vararuci, who lived as a *purohita* of King Udayana. At this time a younger wife of the king knew a little grammar while the king did not learn it. At the time when they played in water in the pleasure-grounds and the king splashed her with water, she said to him: "*modakāsiṃca*"[3] i.e. don't splash me with water." The king, however, understood this accordance with the language of the south, made a cake of peas and boiled it in sesame-oil and gave her such a cake. The queen thought, it would be better to die than to live with such an ox-like king and got ready to kill herself, but she was stopped by the king, who set about to learn the language and diligently learnt it with the Brahmin Vararuci, but as he did not make much progress, he took lessons also from Ācārya Saptavarmā.[4]

The history of Ācārya Vararuci is as follows: The Brahmin, who was eagerly devoted to Buddha, doctrine and to *Ṣaṭ-karma*[5] and who became acquainted with the venerable Nāgārjuna at the time when he (Nāgārjuna) was Paṇḍita in Nālandā, came from the country of Rāḍhā[6] which was situated to the east of Magadha. When he had recited the

---

1. Rāhulabhadra or Saraha.
2. ནོར་བུའི་མདོག་ལྟ་བུར་གྱུར། ।
3. Cf. *Kathāsaritsāgara*, I. 6: "*modakaiḥ paritāḍaya*" The same story is told here in connection with King Sātavāhana and his queen. For "*modakaiḥ*" see Līlāvai: Intro. The king was Sātavāhana whose guru was Nāgārjuna.
4. Cf. Ācārya Śarvavarmā in the *Kāthāsaritsāgara*.
5. ལས་དྲུག་ལ། ।
6. ར་རའི་ཡུལ = Rāḍha, and not "*chāgala*" as suggested by Schiefner.

sacred *Avalokiteśvaramantra* for twelve years and had at last offered him (Avalokiteśvara) appeared and asked what he wanted "I wish to bring about the welfare of all living-beings through the great Siddhis and that you make Mahākāla my servant." When this was granted to him, he could accomplish every charm as he desired and through the eight Siddhis, *Bindu*, etc.[1] he rendered thousandfold service to the living beings; the eight *Siddhiprāptas* recognized him as their teacher and he was thoroughly acquainted with all sciences without having studied them. When he had then betaken himself to the south, he lived in the country of the very wealthy king Śāntivāhana and, and when living there rendered service to the living beings through Mantras and Tantras. He rendered still greater services to the living beings, when he came to Vārāṇaśī, where ruled at this time King Bhīmaśukla.

Kālidāsa's life is fitted in at that time. As he had then come to the south and King Udayana wanted to learn the language, but could not find a teacher who knew Pāṇini's book completely, and when he had heard that the Nāgarājaśeṣa knew the Pāṇini completely, the Brahmin Vararuci called him through the power of Mantras and made him give a detailed explanation of the whole meaning of Pāṇini in 1,00,000 ślokas, which the Ācārya wrote down; both, however, were separated by a curtain. When 25,000 ślokas were done, the Ācārya wanted to see what sort of body it had, he lifted the curtain and saw a big, stretched out snake, which ran away, out of shame. Thereupon, the Ācārya himself continued writing the explanation, but there were not more than 12,000 ślokas. These two works together are known by the name of the grammar taught by the Nāgas. In it there is much teaching of language and other sciences. It is said that at last Mahākāla took him on his shoulders and carried him to the summit of the Sumeru to Parijātaka. As King Udayana did not trust the explanation which had been made by the Ācārya Vararuci, he ordered the Brahmin Saptavarman to invoke the Ṣaṇmukhakumāra. When he was conjured up, he asked the Brāhmin what he wanted. "Give me the *Indravyākaraṇa*." When the god had only pronounced the words "*Siddhovarṇasamāmnāya*,"[2] he comprehended the meaning of all sounds. Formerly it was told in the traditions current in Tibet, that Ṣaṇmukhakumāra had dictated the first four chapters of *Kalāpa* and the *Kalāpa* was to be comprehended as joining together of the parts, as the differently coloured parts were joined together in the tail-feathers of the peacock. It is, however, not that *Kalāpa* was written by

---

1. རིལ་བུ་ལ་སོགས་པ་གྲུབ་པ་བརྒྱད་པོ།
2. Cf. *Kalāpa*, I.

Saptavarman himself and the meaning of collecting the parts is that all necessary parts were collected. Also the name of this Ācārya is written wrongly as a "Īśvaravarman," as also the form "Sarvavarman" has crept in by mistake; Saptavarman means "Seven-Armour".[1]

Kālidāsa's life-story is as follows: At the time when the Brahmin Vararuci had as honourable a position as Bhīmaśukla, the king the Vārāṇaśī, the king wanted to give his daughter Vāsantī in marriage to the Brahmin Vararuci. Vāsantī, however, out of pride, because she thought herself to be of higher learning, did not want to be subservient to him. So Vararuci intended to deceive her by a trick and said to the king: "Invite my learned teacher who is a hundred times wiser than me, and give him Vāsantī." He saw a cow-boy of beautiful figure from Magadha, who sitting at the end of the branch of a tree, struck with the axe the base of the branch; when he saw how stupid he was, he called him; after having bathed and anointed him carefully for some days, he dressed him in the costume of a Brahmin Paṇḍita, taught him

---

1. Cf. *Kathāsaritsāgara,* I, 2, in which Vararuci (*alias* Kātyāyana) gives his autobiography. It runs thus: Vararuci was born in a Brāhmaṇa family of Kauśāmbi. His father died when he was very young and so he was brought up by his mother with great difficulty. It was prophesied at the time of his birth that he would be a *śruti-dhara* (i.e. he could remember whatever he heard once). He was accepted as a student on account of his quick memory by the distinguished teacher Varṣa of Pat aliputra. He had two fellow-students. Indradatta and Vyāḍi. All of them stayed with the teacher for a long time and studied various śāstras.

Vararuci fell in love with Upakośa, the lovely daughter of Upavarṣa, brother of Acārya Varṣa. He was duly married to her, and the ceremony was perfomed at Paṭ aliputra in the presence of his mother who came from Kauśāmbi. After marriage the couple lived together happily.

About this time, Pāṇini, who had a very dull intellect, became a student of Ācārya Varṣa. But Pāṇini, through the blessing of the great god Śaṃkara, developed a fine intellect and became a great grammarian. On one occasion Vararuci joined issues with him but was defeated miserably and was enjoined by the great god Śaṃkara to accept and disseminate the grammar composed by Pāṇini. His grammar called *Aindravyākaraṇa* was therefore destroyed beyond recovery.

King Yogananda (better known as Nanda), made Vararuci one of his ministers. On one occasion, the king suspected illicit love between Vararuci and his queen and so he commanded his chief minister Śakaṭāra to put him to death, but the wise minister Śakaṭāra saved his life by an expedient and kept him concealed in his house. In course of time, when the king realised his mistake and repented for the death of a wise man like Vararuci, the chief minister Śākaṭāra disclosed to him that he had not killed Vararuci. The king thereupon sought the pardon of Vararuci and wanted to reinstate him as one of his ministers, but Vararuci declined the offer and became a recluse and went to the Vindhya forest for worshipping Vindhyāvāsinī goddess. At last he decided to lay down his mortal frame at Badarīkā. For *Aindravyākaraṇa* and dates of Vararuci and Pāṇini, see Belvalkar, *Systems of Sanskrit Grammar* (1915) pp. 10 ff.

only the sentence "*Oṃ svasti*" and ordered him, when he would stand in front the king and his court to throw flowers at the king and to say "*Oṃ svasti,*" but if somebody else asked him, any question, he was not to give any answer. When he did this and threw flowers at the king he said "*uśaṭara.*" Then the Ācārya explained the sense of the four letters and passed them off as a benediction:

*Umayā sahito Rudra, Śaṃkarasahito Viṣṇuḥ /*

*ṭaṃkāraŚūlapāṇiśca, rakṣantu Śivaḥ sarvadā //*

Thereupon Vāsantī began to ask him about the meaning of the words etc., but he did not give any answer. Vararuci, however said: "Why shall he, my learned teacher, answer the question of a woman?" After Brahmin Vararuci had confused his (the cow boy's) head in this way, he escaped to the south. When the husband was lead to all temples, he did not utter a word; a last, after he had seen the figures of different beings, he was very pleased to see the picture of an ox painted on the outside-wall of a temple and took the ways of a cow-boy. Then Vāsantī cried: "Alas, he is a cow-keeper." And she knew that she had been tricked. She thought: "If he is clever, I shall teach him the language," but when she examined him, she found that he was a dullard. Becoming very angry Vāsantī sent her husband daily to pick flowers. In some part of Magadha there was an image of the goddess Kālī made by a divine artist. Every day he brought plenty of flowers to it, bowed, and prayed full of devotion. Once when Vāsantī was offering sacrifices to the goddess and when he had gone by day-break to pick flowers, one of Vāsanti's maid-servants had hidden for fun behind the frame of the image, chewing areca nuts.[1] When the cow-boy was praying as before, this maid-servant put a piece of chewed nut into his hand; he, however, swallowed it, thinking that the goddess herself had given it to him. On the spot he received unhindered intelligence[2] and became a great expert in dialectics, grammar, and poetry. Once he held in his right hand a day-lotus (*padma*), in his left hand a night-lotus (*utpala*) and when Vāsantī asked him, which he wanted, whether the beautiful day-lotus with the thick stalk or the little night-lotus with the delicate stalk, he answered: "In my right hand the day-lotus, in my left likewise the night-lotus, whether with delicate or thick stalk, take which you like oh lotus-eyed one." When the wife now perceived that he had become learned, she began to honour him highly and as he had shown great reverence to the goddess Kālī, he was called Kālidāsa. At the same time he became the crown-jewel of all poets, wrote the eight

---

1. གོ་ལ།    2. བློ་གྲོས་ཐོགས་པ་མེད་པས།

Dūtakāvyas. Meghaduta etc.[1] Kumārasambhava and many other Kāvyas. He as well as Saptavarman both belonged to the heterodox sects.

At this time there lived in the country of Li, the Arhant Saṃghavardhana and further among many Vaibhāṣika-teachers in Ṯukhāra, Vāmana, in Kāśmīra Kuṇāla, in the middle of Aparāntaka Kṣ-emaṃkara, in the east Ācārya Saṃghavardhana; among the Sautrāntika Ācāryas in the west, Bhadanta Kumāralābha. Each of these had a number of disciples.

At this time King Haricandra together with his retinue had obtained a rainbow-body[2] and there was no offspring. It was the time, when his nephew Akṣacandra and his son Jayacandra were in power. Though both of them honoured the excellent law, there is no account of their substantial services to the doctrine.

In the south King Haribhadra with a retinue of 1000 men obtained the *Bindu-siddhi*. From the time of appearance of Mahāyāna up to this day out of 1000 men about 100 became Vidyādharas.

At this time the Turaṣka faith appeared for the first time. While some people say, that it was started at the time when the Bhadanta Śrilābha died, others maintain, that it was the time of a disciple of Kuṇāla. There was a very learned, but unbelieving Sautrāntika, called Kumārasena, who, when he had been expelled from the clergy on account of violation of the vows, became very enraged and decided to found a doctrine which could compete with the Buddha-doctrine. He betook himself into the country of Śulika situated at the other side of Tukhāra,[3] took the name Māmathār,[4] changed his costume and started the law of *hiṃsā* known as Turaṣka (Tīvarar or Anārya) doctrine, and kept it in the abode of the spirit *Bi. ṣli. mli.* of the family of Dānavas.[5] Blessed by the Māra he accomplished by frequent magic incantations victories over others. At this time a virgin from the Brahmin-caste in the country of Khorasan collected daily many flowers and after having accumulated them, she offered them partly as sacrifice to the gods, partly she sold them to others. Once a spirit[6] came out of the middle of a heap of flowers and penetrated into her body, whereby she became

1. སྤྲིན་གྱི་ཕོ་ཉ་ལ་སོགས་པ་ཕོ་ཉ་བརྒྱད་དང་།

2. འཇའ་ལུས་གྱུར་བས= the body of a saint vanishing in the manner of the colours of a rain-bow. See S.C. Das's Dictionary sv.

3. དགེ་ཡུལ་གྱི་རྒྱབ་ཤུ་ལིག །

4. མ་མ་ཐ་ར །

5. འཆེ་བ་ཆོས་སུ་སྨྲ་བའི་ཀླ་ཀློ་བའི་ཆོས་བརྩམས་ཏེ། ལྷ་མིན་གྱི་རིགས་ཀྱི་གདོན་ཆེན་པོ་བི་ཤླི་སྨླིའི་གནས་སུ་སྦས་ཤིང་གཏད་དོ།

6. བྱི་ལ་ཞིག a cat or the name of a spirit, see S.C. Das's *Dictionary*, s.v.

pregnant. After one year a very strong boy was born, who, when grown up, beat all the boys of the same age and killed all the animals, therefore, the chief of the place drove him out into the forest. But there also he put the men, whom he met, in bondage, made some his slaves, killed several wild animals and living beings of the forest and gave the meat, bones and skin to the men in bondage. When the king heard about it, made enquiries and questioned him, he said: "I am neither a Brahmin, nor a Kṣatriya, nor a Vaiśya nor a Śūdra, and as none have taught the custom of my caste and this has exasperated me. If there would be somebody, who would deliver to me the law followed by my caste, I would comply with his instructions." Questioned by the king who would deliver to him the law followed by his caste, he said, he himself would look for him. Instructed by Māra in a dream he found the work formerly hidden. When he had read the same, he faithfully adhered to it and pondered who would teach the same. On Māra's instruction he came in contact with Māmathār and received guidance from him. He also performed magic incantations and became along with a following of 1000 men Turuṣka saints who were called Paikhampa.[1] When he had betaken himself to the country near Makha, he taught his false doctrine to Brahmins and Kṣatriyas, and this is the origin of the royal-families of the Saita[2] and Turuṣka.[3] This teacher was known under the name of Ardho and this was the first beginning of the Turuṣka doctrine. The 15th chapter, the events of the time when Arya Nāgārjuna was in charge of the doctrine.

---

1. པཻ་ཁམ་པ།

2. སཻ་ཏཱ།

3. ཏུ་རུ་ཥྐ།

# Chapter - 14

# Tāranāth's History of Buddhism in India

*(Translated from the German version of A. Schiefner)*

U.N. Ghoshal & N. Dutt

## XXXVII

### The Events At The Time of The Four Sena Kings and Others

Lavasena's son was Kaśasena, his son Maṇitasena, his son Rathika-sena. Though the number of years which each of them ruled is not known, all the four kings taken together did no rule for more than about eighty years. During this time Buddha's doctrine was looked after by Śubhākaragupta, Raviśrījñāna, Nayakapśrī, Daśabalaśrī, and a little time after these, by Dharmākaraśānti, Śrīviśrutadeva, Niṣ kalaṃkadeva, Dharmodgataśānti, Abhayākara and his followers, who were all learned Siddhas and masters of Buddha-śāstras. At the time of King Rathikasena there appeared the so-called twenty four Mahantas,[1] the great Paṇḍita of Kāśmir Śākyaśrībhadra, Buddhaśrī or Nepal,[2] the great Ācārya Ratnarakṣita, the great Paṇḍita Jñānākaragupta, the great Paṇḍita Buddhaśrīmitra, the great Paṇḍita Saṃgamajñāna, Raviśrībhadra, Chandrākaragupta and others, who were devoted to the Sambara[3] and were Vajradharas and had crossed the sea of Śāstras.

The life of the great Paṇḍita Śākyaśrī is well known. The Nepalese Buddhaśrī was for some time the *sthavira* of the Mahāsaṅghikas in Vikramaśilā, but in Nepal he taught the Pāramitā and the secret Mantras. He followed the Tantric form of conduct.

The great Ācārya Ratnatakṣita is said to have been equal to Śākyaśrī in knowledge of the Pāramitā-yāna and the Śāstrśri is said to have been more learned in logic, but he was more learned in the secret

---

1 མ་ཧ་ནྟ། 2 བལ་པོ། 3 སྡོམ་བརྩོན།

Mantras, in conferring blessings and in exercise of magical powers they are said to have been equal; he belonged to the school of the Mahāsaṅghikas and was Mantra-Ācārya in Vikramaśilā; he visualised Cakrasambara, Kālacakra, Yamāri etc. Once he heard in Potala through the sound in music which the Nāgas and Asūras offered to Ārya Avalokita the explanation of the 16 kinds of Śūnyatās.[1] At the time of benedictions, he was able to create enthusiasm for knowledge in Logic. The Dākiṇis received the blessing sprinkles directly from him. When he turned his magic glance[2] at a mad elephant, its body became stiff. He prophesied the conquest of Magadha two years in advance and form this time onwards a great number of his disciples who believed in him went to Kāśmīra and Nepal. At the time of the fall of Magadha he went to the north and on his way to Tirāhuti[3] he brought a vicious buffalo, which had appeared in the forest, under his power by his magic glance, so that it licked his feet and accompanied him for about one *yojana*. For the benefit of the people of Nepal, he went to Tibet for a short time and there he wrote a commentary on Saṃvarodaya.[4]

Jñānākaragupta visualised Maitreya's face. Buddhaśrīmitra heard while asleep the doctrine from Vajravārāhī. He could subdue an elephant with a slap of his hand and by magic glance he could perform other miracles. All these were very proficient in all Śāstras, and they visualised the faces of great deities and obtained the merits for perfection and ultimate peace. I am unable to tell their life-stories as I have neither seen nor heard truthful biographies of every one of them.

Vajraśrī, Daśabala's disciple, reached at that time his 100th year, and then he lived again for about 100 years, worked for the welfare of beings and had not the appearance of infirmity or old age; in the south he brought many thousands who were worthy of it to maturity in the Mantra-yāna and helped them in obtaining emancipation.

During the time of four Senas the Tīrthikas increased more and more in Magadha and many followers of the Turuṣka-system of the Tajiks appeared.[5] In Odantapurī and in Vikramaśilā the king erected for some time a kind of fortress, and some soldiers were appointed for its protection. A Mahāyāna-school was founded in Vajrāsana and there appeared also some *Yogins* (meditators) and Mahāyāṇa-followers who

1. Cf. *Pañcaviṁśati P.P.*, I, p. 196-7.—Tr.

2. གྲུབ་པའི་ལྟས = सिद्धदृष्टि। 3. ཏི་རཱ་ཧུ་ཏི།

4. སྡོམ་འབྱུང་གི་འགྲེལ།

5. སྟག་གཟིག་ཏུ་རུཥྐའི་གྲུབ་མཐའ་འཛིན་པ་ཡང་མང་དུ་བྱུང་།

preached the religion. During the summer about 10,000 Saindhava-Śrāvakas gathered. Other centres of teaching mostly met with destruction. It is said that in Vikramaśilā and Odantapurī, there were as many inmates as at Abhayākara's time.

After King Rathika's death when Lavasena had taken up the government, some years passed in peace. Then there appeared in the country of Antarvedi[1] between the Gaṅgā and the Yamunā the Turuṣka-king Candra[2] and with the help of some Bhikṣus who were the king's messengers he formed a coalition with other small Turuṣka-kings living in Bhaṅgala and other parts of the country and conquered the whole country of Magadha. He killed many priests in Odantapurī, and destroyed it as well as Vikramaśilā. In the place of the Odantavihāra a fortress of the Tajiks was erected.

Paṇḍita Śākyaśrī went to the east to Jagaddala situated in Oḍiviśa. After he had stayed there for three years he came to Tibet. Ratnarakṣita senior went to Nepal, the great scholar Jñānākaragupta and the other great Paṇḍitas with about one hundred junior Paṇḍitas went to the south-west of India. The great scholar Buddhaśrīmitra and Daśabala's disciple Vajraśrī and many other junior Paṇḍitas escaped far to the south. The scholar Saṃgamaśrījñāna, Raviśrībhadra, Candrākaragupta and the other sixteen Mahantas and two hundred junior Paṇḍitas went further east to Rakhaṅ Muñaṅ, Kamboja and other countries. In Magadha the doctrine was as good as extinguished. Though there were many people learned in and devoted to *siddhis* at this time, there was no means to apply them to the welfare of beings. At this time the Yogins following Gorakṣa were mostly very stupid and in order to obtain honours from the Tīrthika-kings they became Īśvara-followers, and said that they would not resist even the Turuṣkas. Only Nateśvara's little school remained in the Buddha-doctrine.

Lavasena, his son Buddhasena, his son Haritasena, his son Pratītasena, etc. all of them were kings of very limited powers, as they had to accept orders from the Turuṣkas. In view of their limited power, they rendered a little service to the doctrine. At Buddhasena's time there lived the great Paṇḍita Rāhulaśrībhadra in Nālandā and had about seventy people who listened to the law. Bhumiśrībhadra lived after him, and after him Upāyaśrībhadra. At the same time with these Karuṇāśrībhadra and Munindraśrībhadra supported the doctrine of the saint with fervour. After Pratītasena's death his family ended and though it is said that some small kings were devoted to the doctrine, I have not seen any historical authorities about it.

---

1 ཨ་ནྟ་ར་བྷེ་དི།

2

After about a hundred years had passed after Pratītasena's death the energetic Cangalarāja[1] lived in the country of Bhaṅgala. He ruled over all Hindus and Turuṣkas up to Ḍili.[2] Though at the beginning he was devoted to Brahmanism, his mind was changed by his wife who believed in Buddha. He offered great sacrifices in Vajrāsena, re-established all destroyed temples, excellently restored four of the nine storeyed Mahā Gandhola,[3] which had been destroyed by the Turuṣkas. When Paṇḍita Śāriputra stayed there, he erected a religious institution. In Nālandā, too, he rendered great reverence to the temples, but he did not erect big institutions. This king lived for a long time. Since his death about 160 years have passed. I have not heard that there were kings in Magadha after him who rendered honour to religion; therefore I have also not heard if Sādhakas and Piṭaka-holders lived there. Later on there appeared in Oḍiviśa the King Mukundadeva who ruled also over a great part of Madhyadeśa; he did not establish any institution for teaching in Magadha, but he erected Buddhist temples in Oḍiviśa, and a few small institutions for teaching and he spread the doctrine a little. Since the death of this king thirty-eight years have passed, as it is well-known.

The 37th chapter the events at the time of the four Sena-kings and others.

## XXXVIII

## The Order of Succession of Vikramaśilā's Teacher

Now there are some minor matters to be told. From the time of the former King Śrīmant Dharmapāla until the time of Canaka during five generations, one great Mantra-Vajrācārya was in charge of the doctrine in Vikramaśilā. At the time of King Dharmapāla himself, Ācārya Buddhajñāpāda guided the doctrine at first, then Dīpaṃkarabhadra. His biography is related elsewhere. At the time of King Masurakṣita came the Laṅkā-Jayabhadra;[4] this Ācārya was born in the country of Laṅkā or Siṃhala and he was proficient in all Śrāvakapiṭakas and resided in this country as a Bhikṣu-Paṇḍita. He came to Magadha and became well-versed in Mahāyāna, he became especially very well-versed in the secret Mantras, in Vikramśilā he perfected himself in Cakrasambara-siddhi. Once he came to the south, to Koṅkana; there was a Caitya, called Mahābimba, which, it is said,

---

1 ཙཾ་ག་ལ་རཱ་ཛ། 2 ཌི་ལི་ཚུན་ཆོད་ཀྱི་ཧི་ནྡུ་དང་ཏུ་རུཥྐ།

3 ག་ནྡྷ་ལ་ཆེན་པོ། 4 ལ་ངྐ་རྒྱལ་བ་བཟང་པོ།

could not be touched, and of which there was a reflection hovering in space. He stayed there and recited many Mantra-yāna texts to some disciples. He wrote the commentary on Cakrasambaratantra etc. He obtained such magic power that when a vicious buffalo of the forest attacked him, he subdued it by his forefinger and the buffalo perished, and so on. In Vikramaśilā he became a Mantrācārya. After him came the Brahman Ācārya Śrīdhara. His biography is given elsewhere. When it was heard that he had performed great miracles in the south he was invited to Vikramaśilā. That this Ācārya was Jñānapāda's disciples [*tantra-dhara*[1]] becomes evident from the Rakta-and Kṛṣṇa-yamāri[2] works written by him. The Tibetans think him to the Ācārya Kṛṣṇacārin's disciple, and though this does not agree with the time of his birth, nevertheless he must have been his disciple as he visualised him. At the time Brahmin Śrīdhara was constantly engaged in sādhana. One morning the went outside in order to collect flowers and other objects for worship. When he had recognized in him Kṛṣṇacārin, he bowed at his feet and begged help to accomplish the *sādhana*. After reciting the Sarasvatī-Mantras, he gave him instructions and disappeared. Immediately afterwards he saw Sarasvatī in the northwest of the magic circle and not long afterwards he obtained the Siddhi.

After him there came Bhavabhadra. He, too, was generally proficient in all sciences, and especially well-versed in Vijñāna-siddhi[3] and he knew about 50 Tantra-sections. He was blessed in his sleep by Cakrasambara, visualised Tara, practised Bindu-siddhi[4] and in the end perfected himself in the same. Pursuing to the utmost the Siddhis and obtaining many *rasāyana*[5] (life-elixir) siddhis, he rendered great service to himself and to others.

Bhavyakīrti[6] came after him. He, too, had crossed the ocean of mantras and texts and he was known as the possessor of unobstructed knowledge [अप्रतिहत-अभिज्ञा].

Līlāvajra lived after him. He obtained the Yamāri-siddhi. One can also assume that the *Bhayakaravetālāṣṭakasādhana* in Tibetan translation has been written by him. When it was told at this time that a Turuṣka-army was there, he drew a Yamārimaṇḍala[7] and uttered a

---

1. བརྒྱུད་འཛིན། 2. གཤིན་རྗེ་གཤེད་དམར་པོ = a tutelary god—the Red Bhairava (see S.C. Das, *Dict.*)—Trs.

3. རྣམ་རིག་གི་གྲུབ་མཐའ་ལ། 4. ཐིལ་བུའི་དངོས་གྲུབ།

5. བཅུད་ལེན། 6. སྐལ་ལྡན་གྲགས།

7. གཤིན་རྗེ་གཤེད་ཀྱི་འཁོར།

spell for conquering the army. When the warriors had come to Magadha, all of them became mute for a long time, their bodies stiffened, etc. so that they turned back.

After him came Durjacandra. His story is related elsewhere.

After him came Kṛṣṇasamayavajra who has been mentioned above. Then came Tathāgatarakṣita; he obtained power over *Yamāri* and *Sambara;*[1] his best attainment was that, when he directed his attention to the main seat of his inner veins, he could understand the language of different countries, of animals, etc., and he could comprehend the Śāstras which he had not studied before.

After him came Bodhibhadra, who was well learned in all secret Mantras of dharmas of his own sect as well as of others. He was an Upāsaka. He visualised Mañjuśrī. He carried on *nāmakīrtan* and it is said that *nāmakīrtan* induced Samādhi. There were at that time many bearing the name Bodhibhadra; it is obvious that the Bodhibhadra of whom we are speaking was not so well known in Tibet formerly.

After him there came Kamalarakṣita. This Ācārya was a Bhikṣu. He learnt all *Sūtras* and *Mantras,* specially the *Pañāpāramitā, Guhyasamāya* and *Yamāri-Tantras*. In southern Magadha, on a mountain called Andagiri,[2] he accomplished Yamāri sādhana. In the meantime, several obstructing magic phenomena appeared; these disappeared, however, after he had contemplated upon Śūnyatā. Then he visualised Yamāri and when he asked what he wanted, he said: "Make me your koṣa (vault)." Whereupon Yamāri became one [विलीन] with his heart. From this time onwards all things happened as soon as he only thought to them, and he was able to accomplish difficult things, Every evening he visualised Yamārikāryavajradhara and heard from him the law. When he once wanted to arrange a Gaṇacakra on the cemetery of Vikramaśilā, he took with him a number of Mantra-disciples; some Yogins, however, came with the materials for the *sādhana*. They met on the way a minister of the Turuṣka-king from the Karṇa-country in the west, who with 500 Turuṣkas went out to plunder Magadha. They robbed the materials for the *sādhana*, but when they started to offend the Ācārya and his followers, the Ācārya became angry, came nearer and threw down a jug filled with water over which Mantras had been spoken. A great violent wind arose on the spot; out of the wind some black men issued forth armed with swords, who began to strike the Turuṣkas. The minister

1. ཤ་རི་གཤིན་རྗེ་གཤེད་དང་བདེ་མཆོག་ལ་མངའ་བརྙེས་པ་ཡིན

2. ཡད་གི་རི །

himself died spitting blood and also the others were overtaken by infectious diseases, so that none of them went back and great fright came over Turuṣkas and Tīrthikas. Further he is said to have carried out many other *abhicārakarma;* had he not carried out this *abhicārakarma*, he would have been transformed into a rainbow-body,[1] but an account of *abhicārakarma* even a great Yogin becomes infamous. This Ācārya was a very deserving teacher of the Jo-vo-rje of the Khyuṅpo yogins and others. He spent the last part of his life in constant *sādhana* in a forest not far from Nālandā and is said to have been occupied mostly with the contemplation of the way to perfection.

In this way, out of these twelve Ācāryas, i.e. excluding the first two, ten are said to have taken the (principal) seat, one after another, for twelve years each. After Kamalararkṣita, came the six learned guardians of the gate.[2] After them came many single Mantra-Ācāryas. The order of succession to the seat of the main-protector of the doctrine from Dīpaṃkarajñāna seems to be incomplete. After the six learned guardians of the gate, Nālandā had no Paṇḍitas for some years, except occasionally, one staying there. Then came Dīpaṃkaraśrījñāna; then Mahavajrāsana was the Paṇḍita for some time; then a certain Kamalakulīśa, was the Paṇḍita, then one called Narendraśrījñāna; then Dānarakṣita, then Abhayākara for a long time, then Śubhākaragupta, then Sunayakapaśrī then Dharmākaraśānti, then the great Paṇḍita of Kāśmīra, Śākyaśri, and then Vikramaśilā went to ruin.

The 38th chapter—the order of succession of the abbots of Vikramaśilā.

## XXXIX

## Propagation of The Teaching in The Eastern Koki-land

East India consists of three parts: Bhaṅgala and Oḍiviśa belonged to Aparāntaka[3] and are called Pūrvāparāntaka or the eastern countries. The northern lands Kāmarūpa, Tipura and Hasama being surrounded by mountains are called Girivarta. Proceeding thence to the east on the side of the northern mountain there are Naṅgata deśa, the Pukhaṃ countries, bordering on the ocean, Balku, etc., the Rakhaṅ country, Haṃsavatī, Markolādi, of Mu-ñaṅa country; further off Campā, Kambojādi. All these are generally known as Koki.

In these Koki-lands there existed since the time of king Aśoka, sections of the Saṃgha. In course of time, they increased until they

1. འཇའ་ལུས། = the body of a saint vanishing in the rainbow or in the manner of the colours of a rainbow (see S.C.Das, *Tibetan Dict.*)—Tr.

2. སྒོར་བྲུ་ཞིན་དྲུ །

3. ཉེ་འོག་ལ་གདོགས་པས །

became very many. At the time of Vasubandu's appearance there were only Śrāvakas. After some disciples of Vasubandu had spread the Mahāyāna teaching, it existed almost uninterruptedly. Many of the disciples resided in Madhyadeśa, when it was under king Dharmapāla. They increased in number at the time of the four Senas. About half of the Saṃgha residing in Magadha came from the Kokilands. Henceforth, Mahāyāna was propagated very much. The Mahāyāna and Hīnayāna were not so much separated as in the Tibetan regions. Since the time of Abhayākara the Mantrayāna was spread more and more. When Magadha was conquered by the Turuṣkas, the large section of scholars of Madhyadeśa went to that region and the teaching was further propagated there. At this time lived the king Śobhajāta[1] who erected many temples and founded about two hundred seats of learning. King Siṃhajāti, who came after him, brought the excellent teaching into repute even more than before, and the teaching was very much spread in all these lands, and when from time to time the Saṃgha gathered together in great numbers, there were about twenty to thirty thousand Bhikṣus and many Upāsakas. The Paṇḍitas Vanaratna and others, who later on went to Tibet, also came from this region. Later on lived the king Bālasundara. In all these lands, the teachings of Vinaya, Abhidharma and Mahāyāna were very much propagated. With the exception of the Kālacakra and the three Mālā-section[2] and some others the secret mantras became very rare. He sent about two hundred Paṇḍitas of this region to Khagendra country in the south to Mahāsiddha Śāntigupta[3] and others in order to learn the secret mantra texts and thus he established it again. His son Candravāhana is now in Khaṅ.[4] Atītavāhana ruled Cāgma,[5] Bālavāhana ruled Muñan,[6] Sundarahaci[7] ruled Nangaṭa[8] and the teaching is now very much spread in comparison with the earlier times.

## XL

## The Form of Propagation of The Teaching in Small Islands and Yhe Re-Propagation of The Teaching in The Southern Countries.

Further in Siṃhaladvīpa, Yavadvīpa, Tāmradvīpa, Suvarṇadvīpa, Dhanaśrīdvīpa, Payigudvīpa—in these small *dvīpas* the

1 ཤོབ་ཛ་ཏ།

2 འཕྲེང་བ་སྐོར་གསུམ་ལ་སོགས་པ།

3 གྲུབ་ཆེན་ཞི་བ་སྦས་པ་ལ། 4 ཁ་ང་།

5 ཙག་མ། 6 མུ་ཉང་།

7 སུ་ནྡྷ་ར་ཧ་ཙི། ནྃག་ཊ།

teaching was spread from the earlier times and it is very much propagated down to this day. In the Siṃhaladīpa there are partly the followers of Mahāyāna but mostly they are Śrāvakas. Even now at the time of Śrīpāduka celebration i.e. the festival of the footprint, about 12000 Bhikṣus, mostly Śrāvakas gather together. In Dhanaśrī and Payigu there were also some followers of Mahāyāna, on the other islands there are the followers of Śrāvaka. On the Dramila[1] island the teaching in earlier times did not exist continually and there it was first established by the Ācārya Padmākara; Dīpaṅkarabhadra also went there. Beginning from there appeared in the course of a hundred years very many Vajradharas out of Magadha, Urgyan,[2] Kāśmīra etc., and they very much spread the Mantrayāna. There were also many *tantras* which had disappeared in India because of their being hidden earlier at the time of king Dharmapāla and such as were brought form outside and had never been in India. Now the teaching of the four sections of the secret *mantra-tantras* spread as before; there were also Vinaya, Abhidharma and Pāramitā works in part. In the southern lands of India in Vidyānagara, Koṅkaṇa, Malyara, Kalinga, etc., since the time when Magadha was conquered by the Turukṣas, although very great seats of learning were not erected and the number of religieux was not very considerable, the exposition (of texts) and the *sādhana* went on without interruption, and the Paṇḍita called Narāditya[3] lived in a part of Trilinga, called Kalikar.[4] After the teaching had been thus introduced in the south-western kingdom by king Karṇa, and when Magadha was conquered by the Turukṣas, it was propagated through Jñānākara-gupta, etc. in Maru, Mewar, Citavara, Pihuva, Ābu, Saurāṣṭra, Gujrata etc. where many seats of learning were established and there are even now many bhikṣus. In later times especially through the blessings of Mahāsiddharāja Śāntigupta, the teaching was spread afresh in Khagendra and within the Vindhya mountain region. At the time of king Rāmachandra the Saṅgha was very much respected. His son Bālabhadra built many temples, Śrīratnagiri, Jitā, Ojana, Urvaśi, etc. He erected also many seats of learning for all subjects of study. It is said that in this land 2000 new Bhikṣus were found who continuously spread and elevated the explanation of the *Sūtras, Mantras, Sādhana* and *Nirvāṇa*.*

---

1 འགྲོ་ལྡིང་གི་གླིང་ །　　2 ཨུ་རྒྱན །

3 མི་འདི་ཉི་མ་ཨོ་དེ་ཡན །　　4 ཀ་ལི་དཀར །

* Translations of these chapters are being published (after collation with the original Tibetan) on account of their great importance for the history of the later period of Buddhism.—Trs.

# *Chapter - 15*
# Newly discovered Asoka Edicts

A momentous discovery of another recension in Brāhmī script of fourteen rock edicts of Asoka has just been announced by the Department of Archæology in India. The inscription have been found engraved on five large rocks in the Kurnool District of the Madras Presidency. Eleven of the fourteen rock edicts have already been identified. It is expected that a fuller report together with the photographs of the inscriptions will be available shortly.

# Chapter - 16

# Remarks on the fourth Rock Edict of Aśoka

Jarl Charpentier

When trying to establish, according to my humble opinion, the order of publication and the interrelations of the thirteen (fourteen) Rock Edicts of Aśoka[1] I pointed out that the Edicts III and IV are most probably only pieces of one original rescript. This seems to me to be proved by the identical words recurring in III, A-B, and in IV, K (cp. Girnār: *Devānampiyo Piyadasi rājā evaṃ āha dhādasavāsābhisitena mayā idaṃ āñapitaṃ* (III) with *dbādasa-vāsābhisistena Devānaṃpiyena Piyadasinā rāñā idaṃ lekhāpitaṃ* (IV). Further in III, D, Aśoka inculcates certain meritorious actions such as *ahiṃsā* and a decent behaviour towards relatives, ascetics and Brahmins, the very absence of which he deplores in IV, A. Because of these reasons I hold it as fairly sure that Rock Edicts III and IV should be read as one.

Now what I intend here is nowise to give any new and startling interpretation of Edict IV simply for the reason that I am not able to do so. I shall, however, try to establish, according to my lights, the meaning of certain expressions within the first three paragraphs of the Edict which still look somewhat dubious. Thus let us begin with quoting these paragraphs from the new edition of the inscriptions by the late lamented Professor Hultzsch; for practical reasons the Girnār version is referred to here.

A *atikātaṃ aṃtaraṃ bahūni vāsa-satāni vaḍhito eva*[2] *prāṇāraṃbho vihiṃsā bhūtānaṃ ñātīsu asaṃpratipatī brāmhaṇasramaṇānaṃ*[3] *asaṃpratipatī.*

---

1. Cp. *BSOS.*, VI, 313 ff.
2. K. *vā*; Dh. J. *va*; sh. M. *vo*.
3. K. *Samaṅa-baṃbhanānaṃ;* Sh. M. *Śvamaṇa-bramaṇana(ṃ);* Dh. *Samaṇa-bābhanesu.*

*B. ta aja devānaṃpriyasa Priyadasino rāño dhaṃmacaraṇena bherīghoso aho dhaṃmaghosa vimānadasaṇā*[1] *ca hastidasaṇā*[2] *ca aggikhaṃdhāni*[3] *dasayitpā janaṃ.*

*C. yārise bahūhi vāsasatchi na bhūtapuve tārise aja vaḍdhite Devānaṃpriyasa Priyadasino rāṇo dhaṃmānusasṭiyā anāraṃbho prāṇānaṃ avihāsā bhūtānaṃ ñātīnaṃ saṃpaṭipatī brāmhaṇa-samaṇānaṃ*[4] *saṃpaṭpatī mātari pitari*[5] *sustrusā thaira-susrusā.*[6]

What is first of all apt to attract our attention is the expression *otikātaṃ aṃtaraṃ bahūni habūni vāsasatāni vaḍhito eva prāṇārambho* etc., i.e. "in times gone by, for many centuries, there has ever been increasing the killing of animals" etc. To this corresponds the *bahūhi vāsasatehi* of C. The phrase *atikrāmtam antaram* is not a very rare one; it occurs in the Rock Edicts IV, V, VI, and VIII as well as twice in the Pillar Edict VII at Delhi-Toprā. But why 'for many centuries'? According to my humble opinion this does not simply mean a lump sum intended to express a high but unlimited number of years. Instead of that it means, as I venture to suggest, that for many centuries the Buddhist doctrine (*dhamma*)[7] had been in abeyance; after many hundreds of years, however, through the pious exertions of Aśoka it had again risen to its former height. As, according to the Rumindei inscription, Aśoka thought himself to be well aware of the Buddha's birth-place it might not be too venturesome a suggestion that he also believed the founder of Buddhism to have lived several centuries ago. Thus it comes to this: for several hundreds of years, since the time of the decease of Gautama the Buddha, his doctrine had been in a state of increasing decay until it was again lifted up to its former height by the reforms of Aśoka.[8]

---

1. Like Senart and Buehler I am unable to read here anything but *dasaṇā* (Hultzsch has *darsaṇā*).
2. K. *hathini,* Dh. *hathīni;* Sh. *astina;* M. *astine.*
3. Sh. *joti-kaṃdhani* (all other versions—except G.—*kaṃdhāni*).
4. Dh. *Samana-bābhanesu.*
5. K. *mātā-pitisu;* Sh. M. *mata-pituṣu;* Dh. *māti-pitu-susūsā.*
6. Sh. *vuḍhanaṃ suśruṣa; M. vudhrana suśruṣa; Dh. vuḍha-susūsā.*
7. Cp. Geiger, *Abhandl. Bayer. Akad. d. Wissenschaften, philol.—hist. Kl.*, XXXI: I, 33f.
8. In this connection we may also remember that in another passage Aśoka reminds us of the pious kings of yore (Delhi-Toprā VII, B): *Ye atikaṃtaṃ aṃtalaṃ lājāne husu hevaṃ icchisu kathaṃ jane dhaṃmavaḍhiyā vaḍheyā no cu jane anutupāyā dhaṃmavaḍhiyā vaḍhiṭhā.* Thus the exertions of these rulers came to naught, perhaps because their behaviour was rather that of the children of the world, cp. Rock Edict VIII, *A* (Girnār): *atikātaṃ aṃtaraṃ rājāno* (K. Sh. M. *Devanaṃp(r)iyā) vihāraṇātāṃ ñayāsu/eta magavyā añāni ca etārisāni abhīramakāni ahuṃsu//* Aśoka, however solely went on tours for preaching *dhaṃma* and thus achieved every sort of success.

Many different interpretations have been put forth of the words *bherīghoso aho dhaṃmaghoso* in B.[1] All sorts of more or less ingenious interpretations have been proposed and rejected; the difficulties to be surmounted, however, do not in reality seem very great. First of all we must, of course, interpret *aho* as=*abhūt* as was correctly suggested by Kern,[2] a suggestion that has been endorsed by most scholars. In spite of the great reverence that we still feel for the work of the immortal Burnouf there can be no doubt at all that his interpretation of *aho* as being an exclamation[3] is essentially a mistake. Thus *bherīghoṣo'bhūd dharmaghoṣaḥ* can mean nothing but: "the sound of drums became the announcement of *dharma* (i.e. the doctrine of Buddha)". And here we are reminded of the words of Professor Bhandarkar that "the sound of a drum invariably precedes either a battle, a *public announcement*, or the exhibition of a scene[4] to the people". The sound of drums thus preceded the proclamation of the Aśokan edicts; and as these contained the maxims of the simple and practical Buddhism taught to laymen such proclamations may well be called a *dharmaghoṣa*. As the first commandment of this Buddhism for laymen is *ahiṃsā,* the non-killing of living beings, we may well compare the *bherī* sounded by Aśoka's officials with the *māghātabheri* spoken of in a passage of the *Jātaka*. The king of Kosala, so we are told in the introduction to the *Aṭṭhasaddajātaka* (418; vol. III, p. 428) ff.), in the middle of the night heard a fearful sound; consulting the Master he came to know that he ought not to fear: ..... *"na hi, mahārāja, evarūpaṃ bhayānakam, avinibbhogasaddaṃ tvam ev' eko suṇi, pubbe pi rājāno evarūpaṃ saddaṃ sutrā brāhmaṇānaṃ kathaṃ gahetvā sabbacatukkayaññaṃ yajitukāmā paṇḍitānaṃ kathaṃ sutvā yaññaharaṇatthāya gahitasuṭe vissajjetvā nagare māghātabheriñ carāpesuṃ."*

In the *atītavatthu* the king of Benares also hears some dismal sounds: Brahmins persuade him to prepare an immense sacrifice but a wise and pious man (the Bodhisattva) explains to him the real cause of

1. Authorities dealing with this passage are Lessen *Ind. Alterthumsk.*, II,[2] 238 n. 3; Wilson, *JRAS.*, XII, 174 ff.; Burnouf, *Lotus*, p. 731; Kern, *Jaartelling*, p. 45 ff. (=JA., V, 261); Senart, J.A., X, 84; Buehler, *Ep. Ind.*, II, 467; Hultzsch, *JRAS.*, 1911, 785 ff.; 1913, 651 ff.; D.R. Bhandarkar, *IA.*, XLII, 25, De la Vallée Poussin, *Les Mauryas*, p. 100 ff.; Wickremasinghe, *BSOS.*, VI, 545 f.; Mookerji, *Aśoka*, p. 136.

2. Cp. Johansson, *Shāhbāzgarhi*, I, 32.

3. Quite recently repeated by M. de la Vallée Poussin.

4. This drum is sounded to announce great spectacles or festivals; it is the *chaṇabheri* of which we hear in *Jātaka*, vol. VI, p. 465, 8 ff.: *"atha rājā nagare chaṇabheriñ carāpetvā sattāhaṃ chaṇaṃ karontu*, etc...........*Imaṃ atthaṃ pakāsento Satthā āha: āhaññantu sabbavīṇā bheriyo deṇḍimāni ca/ nadantu māgadhā saṃkhā vaggu vadatu dundubhī//.*

the sounds, and the king upon hearing his words cancels the sacrifice and commands the *māghātabheri* to be sounded all through the town.[1] It seems to me that the passage in the Edict may perhaps get its most easy explanation by means of this parallel from the Jātakas.

Curiously enough no scholar so far seems to have noticed the necessity of putting a full stop after *dhaṃmaghoso*. That this must be done will be made obvious by our translation which will follow presently.

We now, however, come to the most crucial passage of the inscription viz., the words: *vimānadasaṇā ca hastidasdaṇā ca agikhaṃdhāni ca aññāni ca divyāni rūpāni dasayitpa janaṃ*. The construction of the sentence is wholly clear; the main question is, however, in what way to translate the words *vimāna, hastin,* and *agniskandha* in this connection, and there the opinions of very prominent scholars differ widely.[2] Thus, to quote only a few examples, Burnouf translated the two first expressions[3] by "des promenades de chars de parade, des promenades d'éléphants", while Kern has (quite correctly): "apparitions of chariots of the gods, and apparitions of celestial elephants"; about the same suggestions are found in the translations of Buehler and Hultzsch.[4] Senart's translation of *vimāna* by 'reliquaries' is, of course, out of the question. There is, however, no need to continue this enumeration as I shall take it for granted that the translation 'representations of aerial chariots' and 'representations of (celestial) elephants' are as nearly correct as they can possibly be.

The *vimānas*, of course, are celestial chariots, celestial mansions of the *devatās* moving about in the sky and described in the *Vimānavatthu* and cognate texts in the most exuberat expressions. In Jātaka 541 king Nimi, after having visited in the company of Mātali the lurid and terrifying abodes of the denizens of Hell, finally arrives at the *devaloka*. There he sees one *vimāna* after another, with pillars of gold and jewels, surrounded by lotus ponds and trees of paradise, built from gold, crystal, jewel etc. and described in a most fanciful way.[5] The representations of these *vimānas* are apparently meant to

1. Cp. also the *dhaṃmabherī* mentioned in *Jātaka*, IV, 269, 15f: (*Rājā*)........ *nagaraṃ gantvā "ito paṭṭhāya sakalaroṭṭhavāsino pañcasilāni rakkhant" ti dhammabheriñ çarāpesi*.

2. Their different opinions are mostly to be found in the literature referred to above.

3. For reasons that will obvious presently we leave *agniskandha* aside here.

4. *JRAS.*, XLII, 26 f.

5. In the verses describing these vimānas there often appears a word *vyamha* 'mansion, palace,' the derivation of which does not seem clear. *Vyamha*, however, is derivod from °*vémha* < °*vesma* < °*véman*, and is simply a materical form like *vyamhita: vimhita, vyasanna: visanna*.

give an idea of the bliss of the heavenly world, in which men of meritorious *karman* dwelt for periods that might to a human being seem strongly to approach to eternity. As for the (celestial) elephants Professor Bhandarkar[1] has suggested that the scenes may be representations of the Buddha when in the shape of a white elephant he descended into the womb of his mother. Although this idea was apparently familiar to Aśoka as is proved by the [*sa*] *rvasveto hasti sarvalokasukhāharo nāma* of Girmār and by the *gajatame* of Kālsī[2] the suggestion of Professor Bhandarkar is for obvious reasons an impossible one. Professor Hultzsch suggests the elephants of the Mahārājas or Lokapālas which seems far more acceptable. But above all we have propably to think of the elephant of Indra[3]; for Indra, the ruler of the *devatās,* is the most prominent being in the world of bliss, his position being the highest one to which a man might rise according to the belief of Aśoka's subjects.

But if so far we are on fairly safe ground we seem to be getting into deep waters when trying to deal with *agniskandha.* There, if anywhere, the suggestions of the authorities differ very widely. Thus Prinsep,[4] quoting *Mahāvaṃsa*, XII, 34, found here an allusion to the *Aggikkhandhasutta* of the *Aṅguttara Nikāya* (vol. IV, p. 128 ff.). This suggestion was correctly refuted by Burnouf, *Introduction*, p. 628, who pointed out that the word must mean something like 'a mass' of fire'. Burnouf himself (*Lotus*, p. 731) translates it by 'feux d'artifice' (fireworks) while Kern and Hultzsch[5] preferred to interpret it by 'fiery balls of fire, meteors.' In an earlier publication Hultzsch[6] approved of the interpretation of Buehler[7] who suggested that 'fire-trees' should be the correct mode of rendering the puzzling word.[8] Later on Hultzsch,[9] apparently misled by certain passages in the Pāli Canon,

---

1. *JA.*, XLII, 26f.
2. Of. Kern, *Jaartelling*, p. 44; Buehler, ZDMG., XXXIX, 490L Windisch, *Buddhas Geburt*, p. 6.f.; Hultzsch, CIII., I, p. 27 n. 2.
3. *Airāvata, Airāvaṇa (Erāvaṇa).* In the Pāli texts there seems to be no trace of his female counterpart Abhramu, which is perhaps first mentioned in *Śiśup.*, 1, 52: *Salīlayātāni na bhartur Abhramor na citram Uccaiḥ-śravasaḥ padakramam/ anudrutaḥ saṃyati yeana hevalaṃ Balosya śatruḥ praśaśaṃsa sīghratām //*
4. *JASB.*, VII, 266.
5. *JRAS.*, 1911, 788.
6. *ZDMG.*, XXXVII, 555.
7. *ZDMG.*, XXXVII, 260; *El.*, II, 467.
8. Such a suggestion has to a certain degree been supported by Professor S.K. Aiyangar,. *JRAS.*, 1915, 521 ff., who points to the South Indian custom of igniting a tree on the full-moon of Kārttika (the day of Viṣṇu's victory over Bali).
9. *JRAS.*, 1914, 394 ff.

translated it by 'radiant beings of another world', which has later on been altered into the more general expression 'masses of fire'. Professor Bhandarkar again thought that the *agniskandha* might refer to the fiery pit mentioned in the Jātaka 40 (*Khandiraṅgārajātaka*, vol. I, p. 226 ff.), a suggestion which, though by no means plausible in itself, still contains a hint in the true direction as will be seen presently. Finally Professor Thomas pointing to certain passages in the literature[1] arrives at the conclusion that the word must here mean "bonfire". Unfortunately this ingenious suggestion is hardly disputable as it is quite obvious that *agnīskandha* must here allude to some supernatural phenomenon.

In order to try to settle this disputed question let us first of all throw a glance at the eschatology of the Aśoka Edicts.

It has repeatedly been pointed out that a central point of the Buddhist doctrine, viz., the idea of *nirvāṇa* is never mentioned in the Edicts of Aśoka.[2] The historical Buddha undoubtedly preached the doctrine of Nirvāṇa, but only to the initiated; and it would certainly have been somewhat unpractical to preach to the common layman a doctrine which did either mean that the highest bliss consisted in complete annihilation or rather in an eternal existence not to be qualified by any attributes intelligible to the human mind. And it is the typical Buddhism of the layman that is proclaimed in the rescripts of Aśoka. To the layman meritorious actions performed during one or several existences led to a blissful life in Heaven (*svarga*). This is proved by several passages in the Edicts (such as VI, L Girnār):

*yaṃ ca kiṃci parākramāmī ahaṃ kiṃti bhūtānaṃ ānaṃṇaṃ gaccheyaṃ idha ca nāni sukhāpayāmi paratrā ca svagaṃ ārādhayaṃtu; IX, K.L. (Girnār) ta tu kho mitrena va suhadayena vā ñatikena va sahāyana va ovāditavyaṃ tamhi pakaraṇe idaṃ kacaṃ idaṃ sādha iti iminā saka svagaṃ ārādhetu iti.*[3] *Kiṃca iminā katavyataraṃ yathā svagāradhī;* Dhauli sep. *1. S, U*: *vipaṭipādayamīne hi etaṃ nathi svagasa āladhi na lājāladhi.........saṃpaṭipadyamīne cu etaṃ svagaṃ ālādhayitha mama ca ānaniyaṃ ehatha.*

Cp. further the passages, Sahasrām, Bairāṭ *G* and Brahmagiri-Siddāpura *H*.[4] Nothing more need be said about this here as the idea

---

1. *Saddharmapuṇḍarīka*, p. 72f. where *agniskandha* is translated by 'conflagration' but may as well simply mean 'mass of fire'. Cf. also *SBE.*, XXII, 238 (Triśalā dreams of a great fire).
2. Cp. e.g., Hultzsch, *CII*,[2] I, p. liii.
3. i.e. *sahāyena*.
4. The passage is also found in the recently discovered Gavīmaṭh inscr. *G*: *ṇo hi iyaṃ mahateṇeva cakiye pāpotave khuḍakona pi pakamamiṇena vipule pi cakiye svage ārādhayitave.* Cp. Professor Turner in *Hyderabad Arch. Series*, No. 10, p. 15 f.

of *svarga* as the ultimate goal of a meritorious existence is wholly clear as far as these inscriptions are concerned.

But if the remuneration of the just and pious man is the attainment of *svarga* then the simple and easy law of retribution—familiar to the adherents of nearly every religion—craves that the wicked and sinful one should get his ample share of tortures and punishments in Hell. It is quite true that Buddhism does not, at least in its developed form, know anything like an eternal Hell—just as little as an eternal Heaven. Time comes when its denizens are again sent back to earth to struggle, if possible with greater success with the problems of ethics and morality. However, the periods allotted to the existence in various Heavens and Hells are of such an immense duration that to the common man they may well appear to be equal to eternity.

As far as I am aware there is no direct mention of Hell in the Edicts of Aśoka. But there is, on the other side, ample mention of those sins that were sure to land the sinners in the very abyss. First among them stands the killing of animals. There are, within the Buddhist literature, so many horrid descriptions of the tortures awaiting the butcher, the hunter, the fisherman in the other world that no example need be adduced here.[1] Aśoka also mentions other serious sins such as discourtesy and disobedience to parents and relatives and discourtesy to Brahmins and ascetics.[2] No doubt these heinous crimes would all, according to common belief in the time of Aśoka, lead to an existence in the abode of damnation.

Keeping in mind what has now been said we may perhaps ask ourselves whether this might not throw some light upon the mysterious *agniskandhāḥ* of Rock Edict IV.

It seems tolerably clear that the representations of *vimānas* and elephants were meant to afford the spectators a view of the splendours of the celestial world; they were an exhortation to the pious, holding out to their eyes the rejoicings that were in store for them in the Heavens inhabited by the *devatās* and ruled over by Indra. But if such were the case then a contrast to these brilliant things was also wanted, viz., a picture bringing into the minds of the spectators the horrible

1. Cp. e.g. *Jātaka,* VI, 109, 4 ff.; 111, 4 ff. where fowlers are getting their throats split and are scalded in boiling water while butchers are cut in slices etc. Cp. also *Jātaka*, V, 270, 3 ff.

2. Impudent behaviour against Brahmins will be punished in Hell according to *AV.*, V, 19, 3 and other Vedic texts. The terrible fate awaiting the *paribhāsakā samaṇabrāhmaṇānaṃ* is described e.g. in *Jātaka,* V, 266, 23 ff. and in VI, 106, 21 ff.; 108, 23 ff. (where those *ye sīlavaṃ samaṇaṃ brāhmaṇaṃ ca hiṃsanti rosenti supāpadhammino* are plunged headlong into a giant blazing iron cauldron).

places of torture whether led the path of the sinner. No exhortation to virtue and piety could be a more effective one.

The Indian hells, however, are mainly abodes of fire; burnt, brazed, boiled in giant cauldrons, torn to pieces with glowing pincers, racked on beds of molten iron, running through caverns where the floor, the walls, and the ceiling are plates of blazing metal are the denizens of these torture-chambers.[1] It is quite true that to the Jains—just as to Dante—the deepest pits were a desert of ice and snow pervaded by a most horrid cold; but I know of no correspondence to this amongst the Buddhists. Even *Avīcī*, the very lowest hell, is to them a blazing furnace.[2] And I may say that I believe the *agniskandhāḥ* of Aśoka to have been meant as respresentations of the hellish flames.

Now it is quite true that *agniskandha* does sometimes denote persons or supernatural beings of extreme brilliancy and splendour. It is an old idea that a fiery light emanates from a pious and liberal man;[3] we see pictures of the Buddha with flames radiating from his shoulders etc. And such persons are sometimes compared to an *agniskandha*. Professor Hultzsch, in order to support his interpretation of the word, speaks of 'radiant beings of the other world.' To the quotations adduced by Childers Hultzsch himself has added *Mahāvagga* (I, 16, 1; 17, 1; 18, 1) where the four Mahārājas, Śakka, and Brahmā, Sahaṃpati stand in front of the Buddha like huge piles of fire (*seyyathāpi mahantā aggikkhandhā, s. mahā aggikkhandho*). To these examples may be added a few other ones such as *Jātaka,* IV, 125, 21; *mayhaṃ dve puttā aggikkhandhā viya jalanti,* "my two sons blaze like masses of fire";[4] *Jātaka,* VI, 372, 7f.: *mahā aggikkhandhasadiso Mahosadho paññāya jalati,* "Mahosadha because of his wit shines brilliantly like a great pile of fire" etc. However in all these passages great persons are only compared to *agniskanddhāḥ;* there is no example of the word having exactly the sense attributed to it by the late Professor Hultzsch.

In all passages known to me, however, the sense of the word is simply 'a mass, a pile of fire', perhaps even 'a bonfire'. Thus let us take at random some examples from the Pāli texts:

1. Without giving here any extensive quotations I simply point to the descriptions of the hells given in the Jātakas 530 and 541 and in *Mahāvastu,* I, p. 4 ff.; III, p. 454 ff. Cp. the literature quoted by myself in *Paccekabuddhageichichten* (1908), p. 11 n. 1.
2. Cp. e.g. *Jātaka,* I, 232, 16 ff.: *(:aṅgārakāsu) khadiraṅgārapuṇṇā sampajjalitā sajotibhūtā Avīcimahānirayo viya rhūyittha....* On the etymology of *Avīcī* cp. Johansson, *Monde Or.*, II, 97 ff.
3. Cp. e.g. Jānaśruti Pautrāyaṇa in *Chānd. Up.*, IV, 2, 1 ff.
4. Daśaratha is speaking of Rāma and Lakṣmaṇa.

*Jātaka*, IV, 139 , 25 ff.:

"*Nāvā taṃ samuddham atikkamitvā parato Aggimālaṃ nāma gatā. So pajjalita-aggikkhandho viya inajjhantikasuriyo viya ca obhāsaṃ muñcanto aṭṭhāsi.*" (Like a blazing pile of fire).

*Jātaka,* V, 269, 13 ff.:

> *Ayomayā simbaliyo soḷasaṅgulakaṇṭakā*
> *dubhato-m-abhilambanti duggaṃ Vetaraṇiṃ nadiṃ.*
> *Te accimanto tiṭṭhanti aggikkhandhā va ārakā*
> *ādittā jātavedena uddhaṃ yojanaṃ uggatā.*

Here the *Śālmali*-trees growing on both banks of the Vaitaraṇī river are compared to piles of fire.

*Jātaka,* VI, 330, 6 ff.:

*rājaṅgaṇe catūsu kaṇṇesu cattāro aggikkhandhā mahāpākārappamāṇen' uṭṭhāya jalanti* ("four bonfires").

Cp. further *Mil. P.*, p. 304, 7 (*mahatimahā aggikkhandho*); *Therīg.*, 351 (*amittā vadhakā kāmā aggik (k)handhūpamā dukkhā); Saṃy. Nik.*, II, 85 f. (a huge pile of fire consuming even forty wagon-loads of fuel); *Paṭis.*, I, 125; *Dīpav.*, VI, 37 etc.

The simple *khandha,* meaning 'a bulk, the trunk of a tree' is sometimes used in a sense which does not very much differ from that is sometimes used in a sense which does not very much differ from that of *aggikkhandha*. Thus in *Jātaka*, VI, 107, 14f; we hear about the sinners in Hell that:

> *Sajotibhūtā paṭhaviṃ kamanti*
> *tattehi khandhehi ca pothayanti, etc.*

The commentary to the second line runs thus:

"*Khandhehi ca pothayantī* ti nirayapālehi anubandhitvā tātappamāṇehi jalita-ayakhandhehi jaṅghāsu paharitvā patitā teh'eva khandhehi pothayanti cuṇṇavicuṇṇaṃ karonti."

In *Jātaka,* VI, 113, 35 the *'khandhā sajotibhūtā'* are explained in the commentary to be great masses of flaming mountains; literally we can only translate it by 'bulks flaming with fire'. Further examples could perhaps be adduced but these may be sufficient for our present purpose.

If then *aggikkhandha* means nothing but 'a mass, a pile of fire', and if it is even used in at least one passage[1] of the trees in Hell

---

1. *Jātaka*, V, 269, 15.

it may not seem too hazardous to suggest that in the Rock Edict IV it also means 'piles of fire' meant to symbolize the tortures to be suffered in the hellish fire-pits.[1]

My translation of Rock Edict IV, A-C, would then run as follows:

A. "In times gone by, for many hundreds of years, there had ever been increasing the killing of living beings, the hurting (of living beings), discourtesy to relatives and discourtesy to Brahmins and ascetics.

B. Now, however, because of the observance of the Buddhist doctrine on the part of the Beloved of the gods, the king of auspicious countenance, the sound of drums has become the announcement of the true religion (Buddhism). Showing the people representations of celestial mansions and of (celestial) elephants, piles of (hell-) fire and other supernatural apparitions.

C. These are now promoted by the Beloved of the gods, the king of auspicious countenance,[2] through instruction in the Buddhist doctrine, abstention from killing and hurting all living beings, courtesy to relatives, courtesy to Brāhmins and ascetics, obedience to mother and father, obedience to the aged such as they had not existed formerly for many a century.

I am well aware that my interpretation is no more than a hypothesis; still I venture to think that it may solve the difficulties of the passage in question in a somewhat easier way than some previous efforts.

---

1. An old and well known tradition tells us that Aśoka before his conversion was a very cruel ruler, who had amongst other things constructed a 'Hell' where people were subjected to the most fiendish tortures (cp. on this 'Hell' Senart, *Inscriptions de Piyadasi*, II, 300; *Divyāvadāna*, 374 ff.; *Fa-hien* (Giles, 1923), p. 56 ff.; *Yuan Chwang* (Watters), II, 89; *Tāranātha*, p. 28 ff. etc.). May not the legend of this torture-chamber contain a misrepresented tradition of the spectacles presented by Aśoka to his subjects as described in this Edict?

2. *Devānampriyasa Priyadasino rāño* does not directly rule *anusaṭiyā* but must be taken together with *vaḍhite*.

# Chapter - 17

# Asoka's Rock Edicts I, VIII, IX and XI[1]

## Manindra Mohan Bose

### Rock Edict I

1. In the first sentence the terms *Khapiṃgalasi pavatasi* occur in the *Jaugaḍa* version. As we have pointed out before (vide "The *Kaliṅga Edict*" in the I. H.Q., vol. iii, pp. 73-88, 336-55), this shows that the text of *Jaugaḍa* was specially prepared for that place only. The *Dhauli* version has only...*si* left to it. This may be the name of the rock on which the inscription was engraved there (vide Hultzsch's *Corpus*, p. 84, fn. 3). This also shows special preparation of the text for this place. The justification of such a statement, as we have pointed out, is found in leaving out from these two series the Rock Edicts XI, XII and XIII, and introducing two *Kaliṅga* edicts for making up this omission, besides changing the texts of the Rock Edict IX towards the end for a perfect counterpoise. The use of these two additional terms in these two places is thus justified.

2. *Hida no kichi jivaṃ ālabhitu pajohitaviye no pi ca samāje Kaṭviye* (*Jau.*). The word *hida* has been used in other edicts also, and it has been variously interpreted by scholars. In the Rock Edict XIII, *idha* (or *hida*) *rājavisayamhi*, is quite clear, meaning "in this (my) territory." But in the terms like *hida-loka* (M. XI. 14), *hida-likika* (S.V. 12), and *hidataṃ* (DS. IV. 7), *hida* undoubtedly signifies "in this world." In these places there is little difficulty in grasping the significance of *hida*, because of the explanatory words that have been

---

1. From the internal evidences of the edicts we find that these four edicts are connected with one another, and so, they should be taken together. In dealing with them we shall make a careful survey of some of the important points only, taking the edicts one after another, and refer mostly to the latest publications on the subject, such as Hultzsch's *Corpus*, A.C. Woolner's *Asoka*, Bhandarkar's *Asoka* and V.A. Smith's *Asoka* (third edition), etc.

used after it. In the Rock Edict V also, the use of the term *Pāṭalipute* in the *Girnār* version (G.V. 7) has cleared up the significance of *hida* (or *hidaṃ* etc.) used in the other versions. But in places where *hida* has been used alone, as in the sentence under review here, its significance is to be ascertained by other considerations. The object of Asoka in engraving the edicts on rocks and pillars is to acquaint his subjects with his wishes. Now, an edict inscribed at *Kālsī* with *hida* must significantly refer to that place only, otherwise it becomes a useless undertaking. Thus the local applications of Girnār, Kālsī, Dhauli, Jaugaḍa, Shāhbāz-garhi, Mānsehrā and Sopārā practically cover almost the whole of Asoka's empire; so, by the use of *hida* Asoka has circulated the prohibition throughout the whole of his dominion. It may be that the original order was meant for his capital only, but with the circulation of the edict it had acquired extensive application. We, therefore, cannot say that "the word 'here' (*hida* or *idha*, G.) is ambiguous" (V.A. Smith's *Asoka*, p. 159) or that "it is by no means clear that this prohibition was meant to be universal and not confined merely to his royal household" (Bhandarkar's *Asoka*, p. 131).

3. In the interpretation of the term *Samāja* (in its various spellings in the edicts) we need not trouble ourselves with literary evidences, for the subject has already been exhaustively dealt with by other scholars (vide *JBBRAS.*, 21, 395ff.; *IA.*, 1913, 255 ff.; *JRAS.*, 1914, 392 ff.; 1918, 221 ff., etc.). In all these discussions attempts have been made to find out

(i) what is meant by *Samāja*,

(ii) the nature of those disapproved by the king, and

(iii) that of the one approved by him.

We, however, find that all these matters have been left sufficiently explained in the edicts, so that all difficulties can be satisfactorily cleared up without even going to the evidences of literature. In the first place, it should be observed that Asoka is not a disapprover of every kind of ceremonies; for in the Rock Edict IX he says,—"*Katayvameva tu maṃgalaṃ*" (ceremonies should certainly be practised), and then he says that certain ceremonies "bear little fruit" while the *dhamma-maṃgala* "bears much fruit." We now turn to the Rock Edict I. Hultzsch has divided the sentence, we have taken up, into two parts, but some scholars are of opinion that the two clauses are connected by the conjunctions *api ca*. The word *Samāja*, as used here, particularly refers to that sort of festival gathering which is usually held in connection with animal sacrifice; otherwise, the last clause separated from the first takes the nature of a prohibition of every kind of *samāja*, which is not the object of Asoka, as we have pointed out by a quotation from the Rock Edict IX. The sense is somewhat like this—"In India no widow should be burnt with the dead body of her husband; and an assembly in that connection is declared unlawful." In this way both the act and the public demonstration are prohibited. In law such a declaration serves the purpose of holding persons responsible both individually and collectively, in order to alienate even a private act from public sympathy. The second clause is, therefore, a necessary adjunct to the first, and the two should form a single sentence. It is thus quite clear that the word *Samāja* in this sentence means that kind of festival gathering which is usually held at the time of a sacrifice. The aim of Asoka is to prohibit a demonstration of this kind.

4. *Bahukaṃ hi dosaṃ Samājamhi pasati etc.* Here *Samājamhi* is evidently in locative singular; so it does not allow itself to be translated as "in festival meetings" (vide Hultzsch's *Corpus*, p. 2), or "in merry-makings" (vide Smith's *Asoka*, p. 158). When in the text we get a word in the singular number, it should be our first concern to stick to the singular signification in the translation, but this has not been strictly followed in the translations noted above. This sentence, closely following the one we have discussed in section 2, simply gives the cause of prohibition mentioned there, so the word *Samāja* used in this sentence should reasonably mean that sort of gathering which is usually held on the occasion of a sacrifice. Bhandarkar's rendering "in a *Samāja*" (*Asoka*, p. 273) is also not up to the mark; for then it takes the nature of a general statement only: but the object of Asoka is not to point out the defects of all sorts of *Samājas*; for in the next sentence he speaks about the excellence of a kind of *Samāja* which was considered *Sadhumata*. We are, therefore, left with no other alternative but to render it thus—"For, the king finds many defects in a *Samāja* (of that kind)." Among numerous defects mentioned here, the text supplies us with one of sacrificing living creatures. About other defects, we shall see when we come to the Rock Edicts VIII and IX.

5. *Asti pi cu ekatiya samāja sadhumata devana priyasa etc.* (*Mans.*) It is to be noted in this connection that though *asti* is sometimes used in the Buddhist literature in the plural number, there is not a

single instance in the edicts where it has been so used in any other place. We do, therefore, conclude that in this version as well as in the Shāhbāzgarhi version at least, *Samaja* (*Samaye* of Sh.) can be taken as a form in the nominative singular (like *Samāja, Samājo* etc. of the sentence noted in section 2) with *asli*, a finite verb in the singular after it. So, *ekatiya samaja* must mean *Samaja* of a particular kind. Even *ekacā* (G.[1]) *Samāja* cannot be interpreted as "*certain Samājas*"; for we shall presently see in the Rock Edicts VIII and IX that only a particular kind of *Samāja* was held by Asoka, but not more of varied nature. The best rendering of this phrase would be, "certain kind of *Samājas*", the plurality indicating not varieties but repetitions of the same kind. We may note here that this sentence should not be lightly translated as "there are, however, certain *Samājas* which are considered excellent by Priyadarsin" etc. (Bhandarkar's *Asoka*, p. 273). Other scholars have translated it in a similar manner. The most appropriate sense is—There is a kind of *Samāja* of Priyadarsin, which is considered excellent. *Rāño* in the genitive case is connected with *Samāja*; instead of taking the sentence in the sense of a mere expression of theoretical opinion, we take it to be a definite statement about Asoka's holding a kind of *Samāja* which was considered excellent. That this is supported by the evidences of the Rock Edicts VIII and IX we shall presently see.

## Rock Edicts VIII, IX and XI

*Atikaṃtaṃ aṃtalaṃ lājāne vihālayātaṃ nāma nikhamisu* (Dhauli). In this sentence the word *Vihālayātāṃ* (Vihārayātāṃ, G.) has been translated by all scholars as "pleasure tours" or "tours of pleasure" (Hultzsch's *Corpus*, p. 14; Bhandarkar's *Asoka*, p. 293; V.A. Smith's *Asoka*, p. 176 etc.), perhaps for the presence of *yātā* (*yātrā*) as the second member of the compound. In this edict we have two words ending in *yātrā*, (i) *Vihārayātā* mentioned above and (ii) *Dhaṃmayātā* which occurs further below. It now remains to be seen what are possibly the best renderings of these two terms as used in this edict. Any dictionary will show that words ending in *yātrā* admit of various interpretations, such as journey, livelihood, festival, etc. What do, then, *Vihārayātrā* and *Dharmayātrā* signify here? Let us take the words one after another. Dr. Bhandarkar (*Asoka*, pp. 17 ff.) says "We cannot have any clear idea of this *vihāra-yātrā* as Asoka gives us no details, and as no account of it it also forthcoming from any work of

1. *Ekatiyā* of other versions.

literature." We are, however, of opinion that Asoka has given quite satisfactory account of this *Vihārayātrā*, and that full details of similar undertakings can also be found in literature. We refer to the *Mahābhārata* (Vanaparva, chap. 235-250), in which the *Ghoṣayātrā* of Duryodhana is described in details. It is worthwhile to quote a few typical passages from that place by way of illustration. The permission of the father of Duryodhana for going on *Ghoṣayātrā* was sought in the following manner—"O monarch, this also is an excellent season for thy son to go ahunting" (chap. 238, śloka 5), and it was said—"Indeed, we desire very much to go on a hunting expedition and will avail of that opportunity for supervising the tale of our cattle" (chap. 238, śloka 20). Some of the things actually done on this occasion are—"The citizens and the soldiers by thousands sported in that forest as best pleased them like the celestials (chap. 239, śloka 7), and the herdsmen well-skilled in singing and dancing and playing on musical instruments, and maidens adorned with ornaments, ministered to the pleasures of Dhṛtarāṣtra's son" (chap. 239, śloka 8); also, "attended by all his followers, the king killed many bisons, buffaloes, deer, gavayas, bears and boars. Pierced by his arrows animals by thousands died in that deep forest" (Ibid., ślokas 10-11). It is thus quite evident that on that occasion hunting and other pleasant festivities were held, and when we find that Asoka refers to similar functions in this edict in connection with *Vihārayātrā*, the conclusion is irresistible that he had in his mind's eye the observances of this nature when he caused this edict to be written down. So, *magavyā añāni ca etārisani abhiramakāni* clearly explains the nature of this *Vihārayātrā*, and from our quotations above, it will be seen that the *Ghoṣayātrā* is illustrative of the *Vihārayātrā*.

Dr. Bhandarkar has also referred to many other instances of this nature, such as, the pleasure trip of Dhṛtarāṣṭra, condemnation of chase by Piśuna, praise bestowed on it by Kauṭilya, the account of Megasthenes, the hunting excursion of king Duṣyanta mentioned in the *Śakuntalā* of Kālidāsa (*Asoka*, pp. 17 ff.). As an illustration of the significance of the word *vihāra*, we can aptly refer to the *Divāvihāra* of king Udāna mentioned in the *Mataṅga-Jātaka* (vide Fausböll's *Jātaka*, vol. iv, p. 375). All these references now give us the clue to the right interpretation of the word *Vihārayātrā*. In the first place, we object to the use of the word "tour" in the explanation of this term. Tour has the idea of continued journey from place to place, but in the undertakings like the *Vihārayātrās* the aim is to go to a particular place only, where hunting and other pleasant ceremonies are held, at the conclusion of which the persons taking part in the function return to their usual abodes. So, "pleasure trips or excursions" should be the most appropriate renderings in such cases. The element of pleasure preponderates on these occasions, and the journey is simply incidental. We do, therefore, find that the idea of touring is entirely absent even from the mind of those who take part in these amusements. So the word "tour" cannot be used to express the sense of *Vihārayātrā*. That the principal aim of these *Vihārayātrās* is the enjoyment of pleasure is also quite evident from the written text of this edict. *Eta magavyā añāni ca etārisani abhīramakāṇi ahuṃsu* (Here hunting and other such pleasures were enjoyed) clearly shows that the undertaking was meant for amusements, among which hunting only was definitely mentioned. In the last sentence also the word *rati* shows that Asoka viewed these *Vihārayātrās* from the standpoint of pleasure only. But we find that scholars have generally given prominence to the idea of tour in *Vihārayātā* (as well as in *Dhāṃmayāta*). This is wholly unwarranted. The sentence we have taken up can best be rendered as—"In times past the kings used to go out on what is called the excursions of pleasure." The significance of *Vihārayātrā* can never go beyond this limit. Then about *Dhaṃmayātā*. The word has been interpreted as "tours of morality" (Hult. *Corpus,* p. 15), "touring for Dhamma" or "religious tour" (Bhand. *Asoka*, pp. 81, 294), "tours of piety" (V.A. Smith's *Asoka*, p. 176) etc. We are, however, of opinion that the word here means nothing more than a kind of socio-religious festival that Asoka used to hold for the propagation of his *Dhamma*. Compound words ending in *yātrā* in the sense of festivals are undoubtedly very common in India In the first Act of the *Uttararāmacarita*, the Sūtradhāra introduces the play by saying that it was going to be acted on the occasion of a festival (*yātrā*) in honour of Kālapriyanātha. We may also refer to the celebrated *Indrayātrā* festival of Nepal which is annually held there even up to the present day. Moreover, the names of almost all the Vaiṣṇava festivals have the word *yātrā* affixed to them, such as, *Rathayātrā, Candanayātrā, Jhulanyātrā, Dolayātrā, Rāsayātrā, Snānayatrā,* etc. There can, therefore, be no objection to the interpretation of *Dhaṃmayātā* in the sense of festival. An objector will perhaps like to know why in *Dhaṃmayātā* we stick to the sense of festival but not of tour. Our answer is that the text of the edict does not allow us to take up any other sense and that the author of the edict has left clue for the correct interpretation of this term. Here, we turn to the concluding phrase *bhāge aṃñe*. All scholars have taken this phrase with the preceding sentence, but they have invariably found it difficult to accommodate it there, and to bring out a reasonable meaning with that arrangement, in which, however, there is also difference of opinion. Lüders (*SPAW.*, 1914, p. 845) and Hultzsch (*Corpus*, p. 14) begin the last sentence of the edict with *erā*, but other scholars begin it with the previous word *tadopayā*, as the text of the edict naturally suggests itself. Senart takes *bhāge aṃñe* as a locative singular masculine form, but Lüders (*SPAW.*, 1913, p. 990) objects to this interpretation on the ground that in the eastern dialects of Dhauli and Jaugaḍa at least, the locatives would have ended in *asi*. So he suggests nominative singular forms in those two versions, while retaining the locative sense in Girnār. Hultzsch has adopted the sense of a nominative in *bhāge* even in the Dhauli and Jaugaḍa versions and has taken *esā* as a nominative singular form connected with *bhāge* (*Corpus*, p. 15, n. 7).

About interpretations. Bühler renders the phrase as "in exchange for past pleasures"; Senart, "in the period following"; Lüders, "in his second period"; Hultzsch, "second period"; Laddu suggests aṃñe=only, exclusive, and *bhāge*=king's share of source of revenue; V.A. Smith, "a different portion"; Bhandarkar "in another sphere"; and so on. It is not possible to comment on all these interpretations, but it is quite evident that utmost difficulty was experienced in accommodating these two words in the sentence, and the renderings have been very complicated; for without further explanatory notes no one can understand what is meant by the expressions like "in exchange for past pleasures," "a different portion," "in another sphere" etc. In all these renderings attention has been mostly centred on the mode of life led by Asoka. But A.C. Woolner has deviated from this standpoint, and he is the only scholar who has come up almost to the right point. In his *Asoka Glossary* (p. 119), he writes—"Could it be 'second portion', i.e., 'Part 2,' a clerk's note? It is very nearly half way through the series." So, being dissatisfied with the previous interpretations, he has looked to the series for the explanation of *bhāge aṃñe* and has rightly separated the phrase from the preceding sentence taking it as a clerk's note.

Let us now offer our own explanations. The phrase literally means, as has already been suggested, *apara bhāge*, i.e., in the other part, and we are of opinion that it is an elliptical expression meaning, "(continued) in the other part," that is, "in the part following."

That the fourteen Rock Edicts forming this series were each treated as separate from one another is quite evident from the manner in which they have been engraved on rocks; in Girnār specially there is a line of demarcation between any two consecutive edicts. *Bhāge aṃñe* should, therefore, reasonably mean the edict following, thus referring the Rock Edict VIII to the Rock Edict IX for further explanation. In this arrangement the previous sentence should end in *rāño* (or *lājine* etc.), and we find that in the edicts there are many sentences of similar construction. *Tadopayā esā bhuya rati bhavati Devānaṃpiyasa Priyadasino rāño* of the Rock Edict VIII is almost similar in construction to *bahukaṃ hi dosaṃ samājamhi pasati Devānaṃpriyo Priyadasi rājā* and *asti pi tu ekacā sāmājā sādhumatā Devānaṃpriyasa Priyadasino rāño* of the Rock Edict I. There is, therefore, no necessity of grafting the phrase *bhāge aṃñe* to this sentence, when it gives out a complete sense even without it.

Let us now see why the Rock Edict VIII has referred to the Rock Edict IX. The latter is properly speaking a sermon on various *maṅgalas* delivered for the purpose of establishing the superiority of *dhaṃmamaṃgala* which ws observed by Asoka. The sentence *Ayaṃ tu mahāphale maṃgale ya dhaṃmamaṃgale* (this *dhaṃmamaṃgale* bears great fruit) of the Rock Edict IX clearly shows that Asoka was here speaking in favour of a particular ceremony that he actually observed, and when we have in the Rock Edict VIII the sentence *Tenesā dhaṃmayātā* (Then arose this *Dhaṃmayātā*), we are led to believe that this *Dhaṃmayātā* of the Rock Edict VIII is the *dhaṃmamaṃgala* of the Edict IX. For verification let us now look to the details of each performance. In the Rock Edict VIII, the word *dhaṃmayātā* is followed by the assertion *etayaṃ hoti* and in the Rock Edict IX the word *dhaṃmamaṃgale* by *hetāā iyaṃ* (Kālsi). Both these expressions are almost similar in sense and introduce what was being actually done in those two ceremonies. Then, coming to the details, we find that *bamhaṇa-samaṇānaṃ dānaṃ* is common to the two functions, but in the Rock Edict VIII we have *vudhānaṃ dasane ca hilaṃnapaṭ ividhāne cā* (visiting the aged and supporting them with money), while in the Rock Edict IX we have *gulūnaṃ apaciti* (reverence to elders), which are also almost similar in signification. Then "visiting the people of the country, instructing and questioning them about *dhaṃma*" of the Rock Edict VIII may be included in "these and other similar items are indeed the *dhaṃmamaṃgala*" of the Rock Edict IX, which we find to be more elaborate in respect of detailed descriptions than the Rock Edict VIII. It is not, therefore, unreasonable to believe that the functions of the *Dhaṃmayātā* and of the *dhaṃmamaṃgala* are of identical nature.

The author of the edicts was quite aware of the fact that *Dhaṃmayātā* can be interpreted in various ways, and hence he left the clue in *bhāge aṃñe* for proper interpretation of the sense in which the word was used in the Rock Edict VIII, and this is quite sufficient to convince the readers of the edicts about its true significance here. A proof more satisfactory there cannot be. Lüder's objection can also be satisfactorily answered. In every language, phrases like *bhāge aṃñe* suffer no change under any circumstances and hence the locatives did not end in *asi* even in the Dhauli and Jaugaḍa versions.

Moreover, we find that the Rock Edict IX is also a commentary of the R.E.I. In that edict we have "*Asti pi tu ekacā samājā sādhumatā Devānampriyasa Priyadasino rāño*. From this sentence, as we have said before, we know about the existence of a particular kind of *Samaja* that Asoka used to hold, and when in the Rock Edict VIII we find that *dhaṃmayātā* is followed by *etayaṃ hoti*, and then begins the narration of works done in this ceremony, and similarly in the Rock Edict IX *dhaṃmamaṃgala* is followed by *heta iyaṃ* (Kālsi) before such narration, the conclusion is irresistible that a kind of socio-religious ceremony was actually held by Asoka, and that it has been designated by the term *samāja* in the Rock Edict I, by *dhaṃmayātā* in the R.E. VIII, by *dhaṃmamaṃgala* in the Rock Edict IX.

The word *sādhumatā* also requires explanation. In the Rock Edict IX we have *ta vatavyaṃ pitā va putena vā bhātrā vā svāmikena vā idaṃ sādhu idaṃ katavyaṃ* etc. From this we know that the ceremony is to be considered meritorious by men of all classes, and hence the sentence instead of being rendered as "There are also some festival meetings which are considered meritorious by the king" (vide Hultzsch's *Corpus*, p. 2), may be more acurately interpretated as "There is a kind of *Samāja* of the king which is considered meritorious by all." In this way we can satisfactorily account for the use of *asti* in the singular, and even *ekacā Samājā* (*ektiyā samājā* etc.) also seem to have been used with a singular signification, like *esā dhaṃmayātā*, and *vihārayātaṃ* of the Rock Edict VIII, (as noted in Hultzsch's *Corpus*, p. 15 no. 2). Sticking to the sense of touring these words have been unnecessarily given a plural signification which is not at all supported by the text.

Now, to return to the topic of *Samājā* of the Rock Edict I. Asoka saw much evil in a *Samāja* (*bahukaṃ hi dosaṃ* etc.). From the Rock Edict I we can find, as Bhandarkar has observed (*Asoka,* p. 21), that "he naturally tabooed those where animals were slain." But another defect of such performances is narrated in the Rock Edict IX. The ceremonies performed in sickness, at the weddings of sons and daughters, and those of trivial and worthless nature which the women peform, are properly speaking ceremonials of this world, for they are performed with expectation of wordly benefits only. What is done in India even at the present day is this—A man falls sick, he offers a lamb to a god, hoping to be cured of the malady thereby. At weddings, animals are sacrificed for propitiating gods for the welfare of the couple. It is well-known that on each occasion a kind of socio-religious festivity is held. Asoka says that these things are of doubtful efficacy. Suppose, a man sacrifices an animal for the cure of a malady. If he is not cured, the sacrifice goes in vain, but if he is cured, the performance having attained its object remains also a thing of this world only, for the work being undertaken for worldly benefit has attained its finality in the fulfilment of its object, and hence it cannot have any effect thereafter. But the ceremony of *dhaṃmamaṃgala* is not of this nature. If any worldly object is attained thereby, it is well and good; if not, it is sure to earn endless merit in the other world. Herein lies the superiority of *dhaṃmamaṃgala.* So, we find that the Rock Edict I has also been explained in the Rock Edict IX. But this idea of the superiority of the functions of *dhaṃmamaṃgala* has also been clearly set forth in the Rock Edict XI, which is entirely devoted to this purpose. This edict practically begins with the following statement—"There is no such gift as the gift of *dhaṃma* (*nāsti etārisaṃ dānaṃ yārisaṃ dhaṃmadānaṃ*), acquaintance with *dhaṃma* (*dhaṃma-saṃstavo*), participation in *dhaṃma* (*dhaṃma-saṃvibhāgo*) and kinship with *dhaṃma* (*dhaṃma-saṃbadho*). This is an authoritative statement like "that rite, however, bears great fruit, which is *dhaṃmamaṃgala* (*ayaṃ tu māhāphale maṅgale ya dhaṃma-maṃgale*) of the Rock Edict IX. This is again followed by the clause *tata idaṃ bhavati* in the R.E. XI, like *hetā iyaṃ, atra iyaṃ* etc. of the R.E. IX, and *tenatā, tenadaṃ*, etc. of the R.E. VIII. All these definitely show that something was being actually held by Asoka.

Then, as regards details *dāsa-bhatakamhi samya-pralipatī* is common to the Rock Edicts IX and XI, so is *bamhaṇa-samaṇānaṃ sādhu dānam* with slight variations. *Prāṇānaṃ anārambho sādhu* of the R.E. XI. echoes the sense of *pāṇesu sayamo sādhu* of the R.E. IX. Do not these similarities speak of the same kind of ceremony that was being held? The statements about the excellence of the functions are almost of the same kind in Rock Edicts IX and XI, and explain that the sense of *Sādhumatā* used in the R.E.I. We do, therefore, hold that the Rock Edicts I, VIII, IX and XI are intimately connected with one another, and so, in *dhaṃmayātā* we cannot entertain the idea of touring.

It will now be clear that by *Samāja* Asoka refers to ceremonies that were usually performed in sickness, weddings of sons and daughters, on the birth of children, at the time of going on journeys, and similar festivities of trivial nature that are held by men and women. The Rock Edict IX is quite clear in this respect, and every Indian knows how they are performed in his own household throughout the whole year. These are common occurrences of our daily life and we are accustomed to them. The discussions about *raṅga or prekṣāgāra* may be extremely scholarly, but not necessary here for understanding the significance of the term *Samāja* for we know from Asoka's own explanation in the R.E. IX, what he really means by the term.

These ceremonies were disapproved by the king, because (i) animals were sacrificed on such occasions, (ii) they were things of this world only and (iii) did not produce merit in the world beyond, and (iv) are of trivial and worthless nature. Asoka has not spoken about other defects simply because the narration of those noted above was quite sufficient for him to establish the superiority of *dhaṃmayātā*. We may now guess about the rest in various ways, but that will not affect the issue in any appreciable manner. In the absence of the idea of tour in *dhaṃmayātā*, the interpretation of *Saṃbodhi* takes a different complexion. Bhandarkar's rendering of going to "the place where Buddha attained perfect intelligence" i.e. the Bodhi Tree or Mahābodhi, at Bodh-Gayā (IA., 1913, pp. 159ff.), is too physical to require justification. Bühler's "true knowledge," Senart's "perfect knowledge" are almost near to the mark. What is meant here is that Asoka "went forth towards enlightenment" i.e. he took to the right path of enlightenment when he had been consecrated ten years. We know from the Minor Rock Edict I that Asoka passed more than two years and a half in the *Upāsaka* stage. Counting from the eighth year of his reign when his mind turned to religious matters, the *Upāsaka* stage commences after the tenth year and some odd months. Then began his enlightenment, so that the Minor Rock Edict I and the Rock Edict VIII support each other so far as this statement is concerned. From this standpoint also we find no necessity of adopting the idea of going to the *Bodhi* tree here.

Now, taking into consideration the representations of processions in the Rock Edict IV, we are in a position to state what was actually done in the ceremony of *dhaṃmayātā*.

1. Interview with the Brāhmaṇas and Śramaṇas and gifts made to them (R.E. VIII, IX, XI).
2. Interview with the aged and distribution of gold to them (R.E. VIII, IX).
3. Interview with the people of the country, instructing them about *dhaṃma* and discussion with them about *dhaṃma* (R.E. VIII).
4. Proper treatment of slaves and servants (R.E. IX and XI).
5. Obedience to father and mother and giving prizes to friends, comrades and relatives (R.E. XI).
6. Abstention from the slaughter of animals (R.E. I, IX and XI).

   Further the functions consisted of :
7. Spectacles of aerial chariots, of elephants, masses of fire and other divine representations.

This was the nature of the *Samāja* approved by the king, and no speculation is required to find it out.

That these spectacles were part of the *Samāja* ceremony has also been admitted by other scholars (vide Hultzsch's *Asoka*, p. 2., No. 5; Bhandarkar's *Asoka*, pp. 21, 135 etc.). It is more probable that these were shown to the people of the town as well as the country assembled during the festival in the capital than that Asoka toured from place to place like a gipsy king with the whole paraphernalia of such representations. What is thus true of *Samāja* is also true of *Dhaṃmayātā or Dhaṃmamaṃgala*. From this standpoint also the idea of touring in *Dharmayātrā* cannot be obtained. But in the Rummindei and Nigliva pillar inscriptions there are evidences of Asoka's tour. How can that have any relation with the idea of religious tour? During the long rule of Asoka over a vast empire, it was not unnatural for the defender of all faiths, as he styled himself, to visit the birth-place of Buddha. We also often find the Christian Governor visiting the sacred places of the Hindus, but that cannot be interpreted as an act of pilgrimage. The contributions they make towards worship and the attention they pay for the preservation of mutilated monuments are not proofs of their embracing Hinduism. Who knows if the action of Asoka was not of this nature!

The sense of the Rock Edict I and VIII as modified in this manner stands as follows:

**Rock Edict I**

This *dhaṃma-lipi* was caused to be written by king Devānaṃpriya Priyadarsin. Here no animal should be killed and offered as a sacrifice; nor should any *Samāja* be held (in that connection); for king Devānaṃ-priya Priyadarsin sees much defects in a *Samāja* (of that kind). There is, however, a kind of *Samāja* of (held by) king Devānaṃpriya Priyadarsin which is considered excellent (by all).

**Rock Edict VIII**

In times past the kings used to go out on what is called the excursion of pleasure, in which hunting and other similar amusements were indulged. But king Devanaṃpriya Priyadarsin achieved *Sambodhi* (enlightenment) ten years after his consecration. Hence arose the festival of *Dharmayātrā*. Since then this (festival of) *Dharmayātrā* has become the object of much pleasure to the king Devānaṃpriya Priyadarsin.

In the Rock Edict I Asoka has prohibited the sacrificial slaughter of animals, (and the holding of Samāja of various kinds) and this has been taken as denunciation of the Brahmanical usage (*Hultzsch's Corpus*, Intro., p. I). Bhandarkar says that the conversion of Asoka took place in the eighth year of his reign (*Asoka*, p. 76), but Hultzsch places the incident in the eleventh year (*Corpus*. Intro., pp. xliii-xlvii). The Minor Rock Edict I is "considered the earliest of all the Asoka inscriptions" (*Ibid.*, p. xliv) and is said to have been issued in the thirteenth year of his reign (*Ibid.*, p. xlvi). The Rock Edict I must, therefore, be of a later date, but it says that when that edict was issued Asoka could not stop killing animals for meals even in the royal household. This has been a knotty problem to all scholars who found it difficult to reconcile this statement with the fact of Asoka's being a *Upāsaka* and joining the *Saṃgha* earlier, as stated in the Minor Rock Edict I. Hultzsch has remarked that the animals were killed "evidently on behalf of some members of the royal household who refused to turn strict vegetarians" (*Corpus*, p. 2, No.

7). We are, however, of opinion that there is no necessity of speculations of this kind, and that the question of Asoka's conversion to Buddhism cannot arise in consideration of this edict. Towards the end of the edict the personal statement runs: "Formerly many animals were slaughtered for curries, but at the time of issuing the edict only three used to be killed for the purpose." Then the king holds out a promise that no animal would be killed in future. This statement is simply a record of the gradual evolution of Asoka's sentiment. By prohibiting the sacrificial slaughter of animals he considered himself liable to the people for an explanation of his own conduct. In order that the people may not misinterpret his action as an attack on their religion on account of any religious bias, Asoka has taken care to state in the next few sentences the reason of such prohibition, by referring to his own conduct, so that the people might clearly see that the prohibition was issued as a result of the perfection of his feeling, Asoka does not say that it was due to the Buddhistic bias, and we are not authorised to interpret the edict in that light. In the Pillar Edict IV also there is nothing to show that Asoka was acting under Buddhistic influence. We have also shown in dealing with the Rock Edict IX why the *maṅgalas* were considered to be of little use by Asoka. In both these cases, Asoka has clearly set forth his own reasons. We fail to understand how all these facts can be ignored, and controversial speculations indulged in for the solution of apparently contradictory statements.

# *Chapter - 18*

# MISCELLANY

## Aśoka's Minor Rock Edict: the Yerraguḍi Copy

B.M. BARUA

### [Revised Reading]

A tentative reading of the Yerraguḍi version of Aśoka's Minor Rock Edict was published by me in this journal in March 1933, vol. IX, no. I, pp. 133f. on the basis of a poor photo-reproduction. There were a few places where I could not be quite sure of the readings then suggested by me. But now with the aid of a more accurate photo-reproduction of the copy in the *Archaeological Survey Report* for 1928-29, Pl. LXII, I have succeeded in deciphering the indistinct letters. Thus the text as offered here below may be regarded as a revised reading of the Yerraguḍi copy of the edict in question.

**A. The Text as Found Inscribed**

**1.** (D)evānaṃpiye hevaṃ **1a** haā[1] **1b** Sādhikāni . . . tekapa rachavasaṃ kaṃe[2] **2a**

kho tu no kesapāu kaṃha yaṃ **2**

**3.** husa sātirekaṃ tu kho savachare

yaṃ mayā saghe upayi-

-a nalekā ca nāmii tekapa me ca ḍhabā te[3] **4**

5. -misā muni-

sā devehi te dāni misibhūtā pakamasa hi

-khu yekisa vanetpahama n(a)[4] **6**

**7.** -dakena pi paka- **7a** dhetave e

1-4 Written from right to left.

**8.** -mamīnena sakiye vipule svage ārā——tāya ca arthāya iyaṃ

**9.** (s)āvane sāvite athā kh(u)daka-mahadhanā imaṃ parākamevū aṃca kātiṭhiraci vunejā me ca tā-[1] **10**

**11.** iyaṃ pakame hotu vipule pi ca vaḍhasitā aparadhiyā diyaḍhiyaṃ -sā nevasā ca yaṃ(i)[2] **12**

**13.** -vāpite vyūṭhena 200 50 6 hevaṃ Devānaṃ[3] Devānaṃpiye āha yathā Devāna(ṃ).[4]

yavitaka thāta hāā yepi[5] **14**

**15.** rājūke ānapetaviye

-naā dapanajā nāribhe[2] **16**

**17.** -payisati raṭhikāni ca mātāpitūsū s(su)-

**18.** -sifaviye hemeva garūsu sususitaviye prānesu dayitaviye saca vataviya[6]

**19.** susuma dhaṃmagunā pavatitaviyā hevaṃ tuphe änapayātha Devānaṃpiyasa[8] vacanena he-

pana'ā vame[9] **20**

**21.** -yatha hathiyārohāni kāranakāni yūgyacariyāni baṃbhanäni ca tuphe hevaṃ nivesayā-

**22.** -tha atevasīni yārisā porānā pakiti iyaṃ sususitaviye apacāyanā ya vā sava me

**22a** ācari-

**23.** -yasa yathācārina ācariyasa nātikāni yathāraha nātikesu pavatitaviye hesāpi

**24.** aṃtevāsīsu yathāraha pavatitaviye yārisā porānā pakiti yathāraha yathā iyaṃ

**25.** āroke siyā heva tuphe ānapayātha nivesayātha

**26.** ca aṃtevāsīni hevaṃ de-

tiyapanaā yepinaṃvā[10] **27**

---

1-2 Written from right to left.

3. Repeated by mistake on the part of the scribe.

4. The letter *vā* appears as the first letter of line 14, and the letter *naṃ* as the last letter of line 18, though it is actually not so.

5-6. Written from right to left.

7. The letter *ta* is placed in between and a little below *ye* and *pi* of line 14.

8. The letter *sa* is placed in between *va* and *vi* of line 18 and a little above line 19.

9-10. Written from right to left.

## B. The Text as Made Out

1. Devānaṃpiye hevaṃ **1a** āha[:] **1b** sādhikāni . . .
2. yaṃ hakaṃ upāsake no tu kho ekaṃ saṃvachara pakate
3. husa [,] sātirekaṃ tu kho savachare yaṃ mayā saṃghe upayi-
4. te bāḍha ca me pakate [.] Iminā ca kālena a-
5. misā munisā devehi[1] te dāni misibhūtā[2] [.] Pakamasa hi[3]
6. n(a) mahatpaneva sakiye [,] khu-
7. dakena pi paka-
8. mamīnena sakiye vipule svage ārā- **7a** dhetave [.] Etāya va aṭ hāya iyaṃ
9. sāvane sāvite athā kh(u)daka-mahadhanā imaṃ parakamevū [,] Aṃ-
10. tā ca me jānevu ciraṭhitikā ca
11. iyaṃ pakame hotu [,] vipule pi ca vaḍhasitā aparadhiyā diyaḍhiyaṃ[4] [.]
12. Iyaṃ ca sāvane sa-
13. vāpite vyūṭhena 200 50 6 [.] Hevaṃ Devānaṃ Devānaṃpiye āha [:] yarthā De-
14. vānaṃpiye āhā tathā kaṭaviya [,]
15. Rājūke ānapetaviye [,]
16. bherinā jānapada āna-
17. payisati raṭhikāni ca [:][5] mātāpitūsu su(su)-
18. sitaviye [,] hemeva garūsu sususitaviye [,] prānesu dayitaviye [,] saca vataviya [,]
19. susuma[6] dhaṃmagunā pavatitaviyā [.] Hevaṃ tuphe ānapayātha Devānaṃpirasa vacanena [.] He-
20. meva ānapa-
21. yatha hathiyārohāni kāranakāni yūgyacariyāni baṃbhanāni ca[7] [.] tuphe hevaṃ nivesayā -

---

1. Here *Jaṃbudipasi* is wanted after *devehi*.
2. Cf. Maski text.
3. Other texts have after *hi* either *tyaṃ phale* or *esa phale.*
4. The texts other than Maski have a longer reading.
5. From *yathā* to *raṭhikāni ca* is not to be found elsewhere.
6. In M.R.E. II (Siddāpur, etc.), one has *se ime* or simply *ime,* but here the reading distinctly is *susuma.*
7. From *Hemeva* to *baṃbhanāni ca* is not to be found elsewhere.

**22.** tha atevāsini yārisā porānā pakiti [:] iyaṃ sususitaviye [:] apacāyanā ya vā sava me

**22a.** ācari-

**23.** yasa yathācārina ācariyasa[1] [,] nātikāni yathāraha nātikesu pavatitaviye [,] hesāpi

**24.** aṃtevāsīsu yathāraha pavatitaviye yārisa porānā pakiti [,] yathāraha yathā iyaṃ

**25.** āroke siyā heva tuphe ānapayātha nivesayātha

**26.** ca aṃtevāsīni [.] Hevaṃ De-

**27.** vānaṃpiye ānapayati[2] [.]

## C. Translation

Thus verily has His Gifted Majesty[3] said: During . .. or more when 1 (first became) a (Buddhist) lay worshipper, for one year I had not been exerting myself, but (subsequently) in one year or more when the Sangha (Buddhist holy order) was approached[4] by me, I exerted much, and by this time men who had not mingled with gods[5] have now been intermingled. Verily, of exertion the greater man[6] alone is not capable, even the lesser man[7] exerting is capable of obtaining heavenly joy.[8] For this very purpose this message[9] has been caused to be proclaimed so that the lesser and the greater man will exert for it, and the Antas (people of the neighbouring territories)[10] will

---

1. The Siddāpur and another copy of M.R.E. II have *Hemeva aṃtevāsinā ācariye apacāyitaviye.*
2. From *hesāpi* to *ānapayati* is not to be found in other copies.
3. The 'Beloved of the gods' is only a verbal English rendering of *Devānaṃpiya.* Mookerjee adopts 'His Sacred Majesty' as an English equivalent of the royal style. But a *Devānaṃpiya* is rather one who is worthy of favour from the gods than whose person is sacred.
4. It is evident from Asoka's own statement that he had not entered the Sangha as a monk. He remained a lay worshipper for the whole period of time referred to in the edict.
5. See Bhandarkar's note in his *Asoka*, 2nd edition.
6. *i.e.*, a man of high position.
7. *i.e.*, a man of inferior position. The reference does not seem to have been to Asoka's own officials.
8. *Svaga* stands for a brighter prospect of existence hereafter.
9. *Sāvana* is a happy royal message conveyed to the people at large for their information.
10. For the *Aśokan* meaning of *Antas* or *Paccantas*, see R.E. II and R.E. XIII.

come to know it,[1] and may this tradition of exertion be long-enduring, and even it may be increased immensely, at least one-and-a-half times more. And when this message was proclaimed 256[2] (has to be taken) as passed.[3] Thus has His Gifted Majesty said: "As His Gifted Majesty has said so should it be done. The Rājūka[4] shall be ordered to announce, he by the beat of drum[5] shall announce to the people of the districts[6] and those of distinct realms,[7] (inculcating:) the parents[8] must be hearkened to, likewise the teachers; the living creatures should be treated with tender regard, truth should be spoken, (one should have the heart) to hear[9] the qualities of the *dharma* to be propounded. Thus indeed you must instruct by command of His Gifted Majesty. Likewise you must instruct the elephant-riders, the *kāranakas*,[10] the chariot-trainers, and the Brahmins[11]: 'You should thus establish your pupils according to the good old rule:[12] This is to be hearkened to: Whatever is estimable (in me), all that is due to my teacher, the teacher acting properly as teacher. The neighbours are to propound it to the neighbours as far as practicable. This should be propounded also among the pupils as far as practicable according to the good old rule. As it may remain unimpaired as far as practicable so should you instruct and establish the pupils." Thus indeed communicates[13] His Gifted Majesty.

---

1. Presumably through the *dūtas* (envoys) who had access, acc. to R.E. XIII, to those territories.
2. The question still remains open whether the figure refers to the number of nights or a regnal year counted in terms of a current era.
3. Acc. to the *Arthaśāstra*, the word *vyūṭha (Aśokan vyūṭha)* means a date stated in terms of a regnal year, month, etc.
4. Here the word is used in a singular form. The *Rājūka* is certainly the high official through whom the message was to be conveyed.
5. This may be taken to throw some light on Aśoka's enigmatic statement *bherighoso aho dhaṃmaghoso* in R.E. IV. The present statement clearly proves that *bherighosa* (the beat of drum) was used as a means of propagation of the Law (*dhammasāvana*).

6-7 The *jānapadas* are distinguished from the *antas* on the one hand, and from the *raṭhikas* on the other. See *raṭṭhiya-puttā* in *Sumaṅgalavilāsinī*, I, p. 148.

8. Literally, mother and father.
9. Literally, 'we will hear' (susuma).
10. They were probably the trying magistrates.
11. The elephant-riders, the *kāranakas*, the chariot-trainers, and the Brahmins are mentioned as the main agents employed for broadcasting the message. Cf. *Dhammapada-Comy.*, vol. III, pp. 81-82, which shows how the horses, the chariots, and the elephants were useful to *dhammaghosakakamma* (the work of a person engaged in calling attention of the people to the norm of conduct).
12. *i.e.*, according to the time-honoured custom or practice.
13. Of course, to his officials.

# *Chapter - 19*

# Asoka's mission to Ceylon and some connected problems

**Jyotirmay Sen**

There is yet considerable difference of opinion regarding the date and the process of the conversion of Ceylon to Buddhism, and scholars are not wanting who hold that although Ceylonese Buddhism is an undeniable fact it is difficult to believe that it was the work of Aśoka, and that Mahendra and Saṅghamitrā were ever historical persons entrusted with the mission. V.A. Smith[1] cites the authority of Oldenberg[2] to show that the entire account as given in the Ceylon chronicles is a myth and that the inscriptions of Aśoka are silent about Ceylon. Buddhism certainly was introduced into Ceylon at an early date, but the process was much slower than it is generally represented to have been.

Subsequently this opinion seems to have been modified when, in the Early History of India (4th Ed., 1924, pp. 193, 195), it is admitted that Aśoka is responsible for the conversion of Ceylon, but it took place late in his reign. This conclusion is apparently based on the following assumptions:—

(1) Aśoka's inscriptions, particularly R.E., II and XIII, while mentioning the foreign missions of the great Buddhist Emperor of India, are absolutely silent about Ceylon and Mahendra and Saṅghamitrā.

(2) Aśoka mentions *Tāmraparṇi* in the above two Rock Edicts, but it is to be taken as meaning the river of that name which flows through the Tinnevelli district in the extreme south of the peninsula.[3]

---

1. Ind. Ant. 1918, pp 48-9; Aśoka (R. I. Series, 1919), pp. 47-8.
2. Intro. to the Vinayapiṭakam, by Oldenberg, vol. I, pp. lii-lv.
3. Imp. Gaz. of India (1908), sub. voc. Tambraparni, pp. 215-16; Hultzsch, JRAS. (1910), p. 1310, n. 4. Hultzschh, Corpus Ins. Ind. (vol. I), p. xxxix; p. 3, n. 10. Although he revises his opinion and takes Tāmraparṇi to mean Ceylon, he still maintains that it was the name of a river in S. India. Apparently he keeps the problem open.

(3) It is difficult to believe that Mahendra came flying through the air, "as flies the king of swans," and that his first discourse converted the king and forty thousand of his subjects.[1] It is rather more natural to suppose that as Aśoka's mission to the Tamil countries was quite successful, as testified by the Chinese travellers of the 5th and 7th centuries. Mahendra took ship at some port in southern India and adopted steps for the conversion of Ceylon.[2]

The fact that we do not find in the inscriptions of Aśoka any mention of Mahendra and Saṅghamitrā is in no way surprising. Aśoka's inscriptions are very terse; they do not give us any names, either of the prince governors or officers or the Buddhist sages who found favour with him, and even the Emperor's name occurs in only one inscription (Maski). In R.E., XIII where the foreign missions are mentioned, they are not associated with any names save that of Piyadasi, and therefore it is but natural that even if they include the Ceylonese mission it would not give us the names of persons who conducted the movement. An *argumentum silentio* is no argument, and we cannot infer from it the non-existence of Mahendra and the impossibility of the Ceylonese mission. Moreover, the names of Mahendra and Saṅghamitrā were certainly more important and venerable to the monks of Ceylon than to Aśoka himself, and while R.E., XIII speaks only of the foreign missions and not of the missioners, the monkish chronicles give a detailed account of these missions and of the missioners associated with them.[3]

Regarding the contention whether the inscriptions of Aśoka refer to Ceylon, it is easier to be precise. The pivot of controversy is the word 'Tambapanni' occurring in R.E., XIII in connection with the foreign missions. 'Tambapanni,' no doubt, may mean the Tinnevelli district in the extreme south. But it is a modern identification,[4] and we are not sure if that was the name of the river in the Aśokan age. If we are to arrive at a proper identification, we must know what country in the days of Aśoka was called by that name. Here both indigenous and foreign sources come to our aid.

1. V. Smith, Aśoka, p. 50.
2. V. Smith, Aśoka, pp. 48-50.
3. Geiger, Mahāvaṃśa, p. 82.
4. Imp. Gaz. of Ind. (1908), pp. 215-16.

'The Tamils 1800 years ago' by V. Kanaka Sabhai, p. 23. The river Tāmraparṇi became important in later times. Its old name, in Tamil, was 'Sembil.'

In the Beginnings of S. Ind. Hist. by S.K. Aiyangar, pp. 62-3 a passage is quoted from the Rāmāyaṇa to prove the existence of the river in S. India; but as the author admits, the passage in question may be comparatively modern.

In the chronicles of Ceylon we get a full account of the names by which the island was known. In the days of the three former Buddhas the island had the names of Ojadīpa, Varadīpa and Maṇḍadīpa.[1] At the time of Buddha, and consequently of Vijaya, the port of landing and the city founded near it, was called Tambapanni.[2] At the time of Vijaya's successor Pāṇḍuvāsadeva the port was called 'Tammena'.[3] It was also called Tammapanni in the days of Mahendra and consequently of Aśoka, and the island was so called because the dust of the place which stuck to the hands and knees of Mahendra and his followers was copper-coloured.[4] The name, therefore, was that of the port and the city originally, but afterwards it covered the whole island.

Foreign writers also speak of Ceylon under the name of 'Taprobane'. In the Ist century A.C. Ptolemy wrote: "Opposite Cape Kory, which is in India, is the projecting point of the island of Taprobane, which was called formerly Simoundou, and now Salike."[5] We may remark here that Simoundou probably stands for Maṇḍadīpa mentioned in the Ceylon chronicles. The author of the Periplus,[6] belonging to the same country as Ptolemy, says that the old name of the island was 'Taprobane'.

These foreign accounts of the post-Aśokan period are also confirmed by an almost contemporary account, that of Megasthenes. Megasthenes says that "Taprobane is separated *from the mainland* by a river; that the inhabitants are called Palaiogonoi, and that their country is more productive of gold and large pearls *than India.*"[7] It is therefore reasonable to hold that Tambapanni referred to in Aśoka's R.E. II and XIII stands for Ceylon and not for the Tāmraparṇi river in Southern India (which is a comparatively modern name) or the adjoining country.

The Ceylonese story of Mahendra's aerial flight to the island may be a little over-done, but it is quite of a piece with other stories

---

1. Dīp., I, 73; IX, 20; Mahā., XV, 59, 93, 127.
2. Dīp., IX, 31; Rājāvali, p. 16 (Gunasekara) where it is called Tammanna-Tota.
3. Rājāvali, p. 20.
4. Dīp., IX, 30, 31.
5. M'Crindle's Ancient India as described by Ptolemy, p. 247.
6. Schoff, p. 47.
7. M'Crindle's Ancient India as described by Megasthenes and Arrian, p. 62.

The reference to Tāmraparṇika as a kind of gem in Kauṭilya's Arthaśāstra (Book II, ch. XI) is not relevant to our enquiry, as the problem of the age of the treatise is still an open question.

connected with the foreign missions. Almost all the missioners are said to have possessed "great magical powers," and many of them, besides Mahendra, pass through the air and perform other miracles.[1] The point, therefore, is taken out of the argument of V.A. Smith that it was from a southern port, and not directly, that Mahendra went over to the island. On the other hand, there are undeniable facts to show that Mahendra went straight to Ceylon and that the Tāmil country had very little to impose, in matters of religion at least, upon the neighbouring island. The arrival of Mahendra was not, as Smith holds, synchronous with the first intrusion of Buddhistic ideas, nor is it tenable as Cunningham[2] supposes, that there was no intercourse between India and Ceylon before Mahendra. In spite of their legendary character, the Ceylon chronicles enable us to arrive regarding the matter under enquiry at some general truths, which only stiff scepticism can deny. In the Dīpavaṃśa, mention is made of the visits of the previous Buddhas, Kakusandha, Koṇā-gamana and Kassapa. This may be a pure fiction. But the account that Vijaya landed in Ceylon and established the historical dynasty of the island, that Pāṇḍuvāsadeva came from India to succeed Vijaya, that he married a Śākya princess brought over from India, that Pāṇḍukābhaya built religious edifices for Nirgranthas, Brāhmaṇas, Parivrājakas and Ājīvikas, and that Devānampiya Tissa sent a mission to Aśoka who was Tissa's "dear alley" has a value of its own when taken together, and it points unmistakably to the conclusion that from the time of Vijaya onwards there was a constant intercourse between India and Ceylon, which might have influenced the socio-religious ideas of the islanders so as to make them afterwards amenable to the teachings of Aśoka.[3] That the way was gradually prepared for the introduction of Buddhism is also borne out by the inscriptions of Aśoka. In R.E. II, Aśoka says that everywhere in his dominions and in the frontier kingdoms of the Colas, Pāṇḍyas Keralaputras, Satiya-putras, and of Tāmraparṇi, as well as in those of king Antiochus and his neighbours he had established medical treatment of two kinds, that for men and that for animals. We are fully aware of the existence of diplomatic relations between the Maurya sovereigns and the kings of Syria which might have facilitated Aśoka's philanthropic measures. Is it too much to hold, in a similar strain, that in the case of Ceylon also there had

1. Dīp., VIII, 5-12; Mahā., XII, 11, 31.
2. Anc. Geo. of India, p. 561.
3. Eliot, Hinduism and Buddhism, vol. III, pp. 13, 14.

been, from an earlier time, relations of some sort with the Magadha house? Aśoka's R.E. II does not mean the introduction of Buddhism, but of the Buddhistic idea of kindness and non-killing, which paved the way for the introduction, later on, of Buddhism proper, as recorded in a subsequent edict, R.E., XIII.

Nor, in the absence of any positive proof, can it be maintained that it was from the Tāmil country that Mahendra went over to the island. In fact, there are traditions which cannot be altogether neglected, pointing to the conclusion that Aśoka's missions were not as successful in the Tāmil country as in Ceylon, that Ceylon maintained a cultural integrity of its own and to some extent influenced, rather than being itself influenced by, the religion of the mainland.

The story of the famine of 12 years in the time of Candragupta Maurya, during which a section of the Jaina community under Bhadrabāhu migrated to Southern India, is associated with the abdication of Candragupta Maurya and his death at Śrāvaṇa-Belgoḷā in Beloḷa in Mysore.[1]

It shows that Jainism in Southern India was older than the Buddhism of Aśoka by at least half a century. In the days of Aśoka, the older religion might have been pushed back by Buddhism, but that the latter was not a popular cult and did not have a permanent hold on the country is evident from the subsequent history of the South. In Hemacandra's Pariśiṣṭaparvan (XI, 89-102) it is related that Samprati, the successor of Aśoka and a zealous convert to the Jaina faith, sent missionaries to the Andhras and the Dramilas, brought the uncivilised nations under the influence of Jainism and made the southern country fit for the settlement of Jaina monks. That this story is not a pure fiction but has a substratum of truth is amply borne out by the fact that notwithstanding Aśoka's Buddhistic propaganda the southern nations ultimately gave up Buddhism and came to cherish the Digambara Jainas and the Śaiva religion.[2] At the time of Hiuen Tsang, in the Cola country and the country round about Madura the

1. Lewis Rice, Mysore and Coorg from the Inscriptions, pp. 4 ff. V. Smith, Early History of India, 4th Edition, pp. 154, 458.

2. S.K. Aiyanger, Beginnings of South Indian History, pp. 99, 100. The Mauryas were in hostile occupation of forts on the northern border of the Tāmil land, and hostility between Southern Hinduism and Northern Buddhism led to the expulsion of the northerners when the paramount power weakened.

few Buddhist monasteries were in a ruinous condition;[1] in the Pāṇḍya and Pallava countries there were numerous Hindu gods and Jaina temples and ascetics. Not only this, the Buddhism of Southern India owed a great deal to Ceylon, and Conjeeveram was long a Buddhist centre which kept up intercourse with both Ceylon and Burma.[2]

Having established the hypothesis[3] that 'Tambapanni' of the Aśokan edicts is no other than Ceylon, and that Ceylonese Buddhism was not a graft from the Southern Indian stock but a direct import from the north, it would be well for us now to attempt to find out the date of the conversion of Ceylon.

References to Tambapanni are found only in R.E.s II and XIII. Of these, as we have seen, R.E. II concerns itself with the provision of medical treatment in the foreign countries, and not with the introduction of Buddhism. The conversion of these countries was a later achievement for which the way was prepared by Aśoka's philanthropic activities in these regions. Hence it follows that R.E. XIII was later in date than R.E. II, and in fact, it is more reasonable to hold that the edicts of Aśoka are not complete sets, as Senart indicates,[4] but rescripts incised at different times, either singly or in groups as occasions arose.[5] This conclusion is strengthened by the following facts among others :

(1) Referring to the Kalsi rock, Hultzsch (Corpus, XI) admits that as the last portion of the inscription is written in a bolder type and a separate face of the rock is utilised, this last portion probably was of a later date.

(2) Portions of the 13th Edict of the Shahbazgarhi group were traced out on the back of the main rock (Corpus, XII).

(3) The Dhauli rock does not contain Edicts XI to XIII of the Girnar version, but compensates for them by two separate edicts (Corpus, XIII).

---

1. Watters, Yuan Chwang, vol. II, pp. 224, 228.
2. Eliot, Hinduism and Buddhism, vol. I, p. xxv.
3. My conclusions have been confirmed, although in an indirect way, by Soma Sundara Desikar's article, the Mauryan Invasion of Tamilakam (IHQ., vol. IV, no. I, pp. 135 ff.).
4. Ind. Ant., 1891, pp. 236ff.
5. H.K. Dev quoted in D.R. Bhandarkar's Aśoka, pp. 47, 47 n.1 266ff. Prof. Bhandarkar began with a correct assumption but ended with the conclusion that the dates in the different Rock Edicts refer to the events narrated and not to the actual engraving, and that the whole set was engraved as one document late in his reign.

(4) The Mansera group is engraved on three boulders; the 13th and the 14th are incised on the third boulder (Corpus, XII, XIII).

(5) At Jaugaḍa the main set is inscribed in two tablets, and a third tablet contains the two additional edicts and are enclosed in a separate frame (Corpus, XIV).

(6) The Delhi-Topra pillar is unique of its kind, because it alone gives the seventh and the most important edict. But the concluding portion of this last edict runs all round the pillar (Corpus, XVI). This shows that probably it was incised last, at a later date, and therefore, for want of space, which was originally calculated to contain six and not seven edicts, the last one was made to run round the whole shaft.

(7) The three Minor Rock Inscriptions of the Mysore State (Siddhapura, Brahmagiri and Jatinga-Rāmeśvara) contain an extra edict which is not found in the northern versions.

(8) The Girnar R.E.s are all separately engraved and separated by horizontal lines. The reason probably is that as each edict was written, it was thought fit by the engraver to mark off the preceding one by a line.

(9) Each edict begins with the word 'Devānampiya' and gives a separate sentiment. It is a self-contained whole, and the connection between the edicts in one inscription is more accidental than real. It is quite possible that there should not be any incongruity in the edicts being placed together, as the ideas of Aśoka are everywhere almost the same, all pertaining to the Dhamma he inculcated.

(10) The edicts of Aśoka give different dates in one and the same inscription. Nowhere is a date given which may be regarded as the date of the entire inscription. Either a single edict or a group of edicts is dated out of the whole set, and therefore there were different engravings at different times with dates.

If we assume, therefore, that the edicts in each inscription were not inscribed as a complete set, but at different dates on different occasions, we shall not be wrong if we assign the R.E.s specially to different dates. Some of them were engraved in the 13th, and some in the 14th year after Aśoka's coronation. But the real difficulty lies with the dating of the 13th R.E. which gives an account of the foreign missions. Senart and others who have taken the series as one document have unhesitatingly assigned the edict in question to the 14th year—the latest date in the inscription. Others,[1] while regarding

1. Cf. Bhandarkar's Aśoka, pp. 47 n. 1, 267-8.

the entire series as one single document, are of opinion that the actual engraving could not have been done before the 28th regnal year, the year in which Pillar Edict VII was issued. This sort of argument raises three difficulties.

(1) It is difficult to understand why Aśoka, *contrary to his usual practice,* should postpone the actual engraving of this set of edicts till at least 14 years had elapsed after the occurrence of events described by a majority of them.

(2) Granting that the date of the engraving was not earlier than the 28th year, it does not follow that R.E. XIII particularly, records events which took place in that year or a little later. They might have occurred very much later. In short, we are again in a chronological difficulty, and it is impossible to fix a date for the events discussed within a reasonably short period. Again, the sponsors of the above argument have been forced to take up this position because they have taken R.E. II and XIII to refer to the same events, and have hence come to the conclusion that the entire series was engraved at one and the same time, and that not earlier than the 28th regnal year. They found it difficult to explain the dates as given in R.E. III, IV and V. But as I have pointed out, R.E. II is differert from R.E. XIII in its content, and, therefore, even assuming that R.E. II was inscribed in the 13th year, we shall not be wrong if we assign a later date to R.E. XIII.

(3) Moreover, their argument rests on the assumption that Pillar Edict VII is a resumé of the acts of Dhamma performed by Aśoka till his 28th year. This assumption, which is that of almost all scholars who have dealt authoritatively with the subject, is, I think, erroneous, and even if not wholly so, it is dangerous to build chronological conclusions on an uncertain piece of evidence.

(a) Rhys David's position is untenable. Unable to account for the stūpas and monasteries and the missions to the Greek countries, which he regards as "mere royal rhodomontade,"[1] he says that Pillar Edict VII sums up all the *other measures* he had taken for the propagation of the Dhamma.[2] Granting the Ceylonese version of the missions to be correct, is it reasonable to hold that Aśoka himself should omit the foreign missions which he mentions twice in R.E. II and XIII?

1. Rhys Davids, Buddhist India (1916), p. 298.
2. Ibid., p. 304.

Even the Ceylonese mission is left out, which, according to Rhys Davids, is a reality.

(b) V. Smith regards Pillar Edict VII as a resumé of measures taken by Aśoka "within his empire."[1] This interpretation is not warranted by the edict, and is presumably set up to explain the omission of foreign missions. He also contradicts himself when he says that in Section III of his analysis[2] there may be an allusion to the foreign missions. If, again, the edict in question deals with internal measures only, why does it omit altogether the erection of the innumerable stūpas and monasteries which certainly formed an integral part of Aśoka's work in the line?

(c) Again, Pillar Edict VII need not be regarded as a *summary* of Aśoka's achievements in the propagation of the Dhamma. If a summary was at all in his contemplation, it should have been firstly exhaustive, secondly written towards the close of his reign and not about ten years earlier, thus omitting some of the most important achievements with which he is credited. That it is not exhaustive is clear from the fact that it omits the erection of innumerable stūpas and monasteries which, according to the Ceylon chronicles, were erected soon after his conversion.[3] Hiuen Tsang mentions more than eighty stūpas and monasteries ascribed to Aśoka, without counting the legendary five hundred convents in Kashmir and other large indefinite groups in other countries.[4] If the number of these structures is credible, we cannot by any stretch of imagination confine them to the last ten years of Aśoka. We should, on the contrary, regard the erection of these stūpas and monasteries as covering the whole reign, and even V.A. Smith believes that the Aśokārāma or Kukkuṭārāma was the first fruits of the emperor's zeal as a convert.[5]

The foregoing considerations tend to show that R.E. XIII need not necessarily belong to the 14th year of Aśoka's reign, nor should it be referred to the last ten years on the basis of a wrong interpretation of Pillar Edict VII. The date of the foreign missions

---

1. V.A. Smith, Aśoka, p. 212.
2. Ibid., p. 209.
3. Dīp., vi, 99; Mahā., v, 79-80; also Divyāvadāna (tr. Cowell and Neill), p. 379. This was also the tradition current in Yuan Chwang's time. Watters, Yuan Chwang, vol. II, pp. 91, 158.
4. V. Smith, Aśoka, p. 109.
5. Smith's Aśoka; JRAS., 1901, p. 846 apparently on the authority of Hiuen Tsang (Beal, Buddhist Records of the Westen World, vol. II, p. 95).

of Aśoka, or properly speaking that of R.E. XIII, is, therefore, to be found out in other ways.

Here we are on uncertain ground, and we are compelled to take some accounts and some arguments on trust. The foreign missions figure prominently in the Aśokan edicts and the monkish chronicles of Ceylon, and however prejudiced we may be regarding the authenticity of the chronicles when they speak of events prior to Aśoka's time, we are perfectly justified in regarding as facts of history the account from the time of Aśoka downwards, rejecting, however, the embellishments tending to make the whole thing unreal. From henceforward we are strengthened in our convictions by the concurrent testimony of the Aśokan monuments and the relic caskets of the Sanchi Topes.[1] In the Ceylon chronicles these missions are associated with the council of Pāṭaliputra where the resolve was made to make Buddhism, purged of its impurities and heresies, a world religion. The accounts of the Buddhist councils have been examined threadbare by orientalists, and whatever doubt there may be regarding the first two councils, there is perfect unanimity regarding the historicity of the Council of Pāṭaliputra. The only systematic account of this Council is given in the southern Buddhist works. The Dīp. (VII, 37, 44) states that the Council took place in 236 A.B.; according to the Mahā. (V, 280) it was held in the 17th year of Aśoka. The date of this Council has long been a subject of controversy. Rhys Davids[2] and Kern[3] take for granted the traditional date (18th year). A more sceptical but, nevertheless, logical attitude is that of V. Smith who says that it rests on tradition only, and took place "at some undetermined date."[4] But in the present case, as we shall see, there is a substratum of truth underlying the Ceylonese account.

Candragupta Maurya came to the throne in 325 B.C.[5] He reigned, according to the unanimous testimony of the Purāṇas and the Ceylonese and Burmese traditions, for 24 years. Bindusāra

1. Copleston, Buddhism, pp. 179-180.
2. Buddhism, p. 224.
3. Manual of Indian Buddhism, p. 112.
4. JRAS., 1901, p. 853.
5. I adhere to the view of Senart (Inscriptions of Piyadasi, Ind. Ant., 1891, pp. 236ff.), Jayaswal (JASB., vol. IX, 1913, pp. 317ff.) and S. Pradhan (Chronology of Ancient India, pp. 238-9), and I shall adduce other arguments in favour of this date in a subsequent paper.

reigned for 25 years.[1] Therefore the year of Aśoka's accession is 276 B.C.[2] Now the set of dates of the Hellenistic kings in R.E. XIII as given by Senart[3] places them all between B.C. 260 and 258.[4] Therefore the date of R.E. XIII, and consequently of the foreign missions of Aśoka, falls between the 16th and the 18th year of his reign. And this is in perfect agreement with the Ceylonese date of the Council of Pāṭaliputra and the conversion of Ceylon by Mahinda.

My chronological argument leaves the pre-sacramental years of Aśoka altogether out of account, as I believe all kinds of testimony run counter to the Ceylonese tradition. In addition to the arguments advanced by Prof. D.R. Bhandarkar,[5] it may be remarked that Aśoka, although full of remorse for the Kaliṅga war and solicitous for the preservation of human life, never alludes in any of his edicts to the slaughter of his brothers before he came to the throne. Moreover, there are gross inaccuracies in the southern tradition tending to make the whole story unreal. In the Mahā the brothers of Aśoka are numbered 90 at one time and 99 at another,[6] and in the Burmese account we find Bindusāra having 101 sons.[7]

1. I take the unanimous testimony of the Purāṇas, as there is some difference in other accounts. The Dīp. ignores it; in the Mahā. (V. 18) it is 28 years, whereas in the Burmese tradition it is 27 (Bigandet, The Life or Legend of Gautama, vol. II, p. 128).

2. This is also the date arrived at on other grounds by Jayaswal, JASB. (1913), pp. 317ff.

3. Ind. Ant., 1891, pp. 236ff.

4. Beloch's dates, as given in 'Griechische Geschichte' and accepted by D.R. Bhandarkar in his Aśoka, p. 48, differ from Senart's mainly on account of Alexander of Corinth superseding Alexander of Epirus; and this identification has been broached apparently to suit a different chronological solution.

5. Aśoka, pp. 9ff.

6. Turnour's Intro. to the Mahā., pp. xlvi, xlvii.

7. Bigandet., vol. II, pp. 128.

## Chapter - 20

# Notes on Asoka Rescripts

### Sailendranath Mitra

**Alam Capalam Samādapavitave.**—P.E. I. *Capalaṃ* has been taken to mean "fickle (person)" by Hultzsch (*Corpus*, p. 120) and "the fickle-minded" by Bhandarkar (*Aśoka*, 1925, p. 306). There is, however, nothing in the context to warrant this sense. In the Pali canon we meet with a verb *samādapeti* in the sense of inducing or urging *others* to a particular course, in contra-distinction to one's following it *oneself*. Thus, in Aṅg. II, pp. 253-256, we have a series of expressions, such as *attanā ca pāṇātipātī hoti parañ ca pāṇātipāte samādapeti* side by side with *attanā ca pīṇātipātā paṭivirato hoti parañ ca pāṇātipātā veramaṇiyā samādapeti*, and so forth. Buddha himself is known in the canon as a *samādapetā*, 'arouser,' 'instructor' of people, and it seems that Asoka had become another such in his own time. The same force is present again in the Pali expression *ekacce attanā deti parañ ca samādapeti* (DhA., III, p. 17), which means 'some not only themselves bestow gifts but urge others to do the same.' Wishing others to perform meritorious deeds is an attitude of mind which appeals also to Asoka, as is evident from the general tenour of his Rescripts, e.g., R.E.v : *tathaṃ ca me praja anuvaṭ-atu* (Mansehra). See also the concluding portion of R.E.VI. The idea of *para-samādapana* or *janasamādapana* is also latent in what is known in Pāli literature as "dhammaghosakakamma," e.g., DhA. III, pp. 81-82 "*mahājanaṃ samādapetvā puññāni karomi, uposathadivasesu uposathaṃ samādiyāmi, dānaṃ demi, dhammaṃ suṇāmi,* Buddharatanādīhi sadisaṃ ratanaṃ nāma ṇ'atthi tiṇṇaṃ ratanānaṃ sakkāraṃ karothā ti ugghosento carāmi." It is interesting to note that Asoka also speaks of 'dhaṃmaghoso' in R.E. IV., and when we find that the deeds implied by the Pali quotation, especially those contemplated in the italicised expressions, have also been recommended and, in some cases, actually performed by Asoka himself, it becomes easy to understand the sort of *dhammaghosa* which was his. *Mahājana-samādapana*, if we may be allowed to call it so, was, therefore, one of the sacred tasks Asoka had set for himself. If that is so, then we had better read *Alaṃ ca palaṃ samādapayitave* instead of combining *ca* and *palaṃ* into *capalaṃ* as has been done hitherto, and translate the expression "And (my *pulisās* are) able to urge others (to do it," viz., to conform to and practise morality).

**Eyadathā.**—P.E. VII. 1. 24. Hultzsch (*Corpus*, p. 135, n. 5) equates *athā* with *athāya* and refers for comparison to the expression *etāya athā* in R.E. XII (Girnar), II. 8-9, where *athā* is dative, and also to a parallel (*bhojanatthā*) in Müller's Pali Grammar, p. 67. Although in the Asoka Rescripts we come across such separate words as *etāya athāya* (R.E. IV, V, VI, XII, XIII), *etāye athāye* (R.E. III, IV, V, IX, XIII, etc.), or such *sandhi*-joined expressions as *etāyāṭhāye* (R.E. XII, Kālsi), *e[t]āyaṭhāya* (M.R.E.I, Brahmagiri), *etā[y]eṭhāye* (R.E. VI, Kālsi), nowhere do we find the *samāsa*-formed word *etadathā* except in the present instance, *viz.*, P.E. VII, 1. 24. Of such a *samāsa* form I have met with an exact counterpart in Aṅg. I, p. 198, from which I would quote at some length:

"Kathāsampayogena bhikkhave puggalo veditabbo yadi vā sa-upaniso yadi vā anupaniso ti.

Anohitasoto bhikkhave anupaniso hoti ohitasoto sa-upaniso hoti. So sa-upaniso samāno abhijānāti ekaṃ dhammaṃ parijānāti ekaṃ dhammaṃ pajahati ekaṃ dhammaṃ sacchi-karoti ekaṇ dhammaṃ. So abhijānanto ekaṃ dhammaṃ......... sammāvimuttiṃ phusati. *Etadatthā* bhikkhave kathā *etadatthā* mantanā *etadatthā* upanisā *etadatthaṃ* sotāvadhānaṃ yadidaṃ anupādā cittassa vimokho."

And the gloss on the italicised words is as follows:

"Bhikkhave yā esā 'kathāsampayogenā' ti kathā dassitā sā *etadatthā*, ayaṃ tassā kathāya bhūmi, ayaṃ patiṭṭhā, idam vatthuṃ, yadidaṃ anupādā cittassa vimokho ti evaṃ sabbapadesu yojanā veditabbā" (Manorathapūranī, Siamese edition), which may be rendered: 'O bhikkhus, what has been said here in the words "Kathāsampayogena etc." (of the text) *has this for its root purpose*, namely, complete emancipation of the citta, that is to say, it is the plane, the basis, the ground of that saying.'

It is clear that *etadatthā* or *etadatthaṃ* of the Aṅguttara passage is an adjective, a compound of *eta* and *attha*, meaning 'fraught with this intent,' which is not different from the sense 'for this purpose' or 'on this account,' hitherto read into the inscriptional term *etadathā*, taken as dative substantive by Hultzsch. But however justified and acceptable Hultzsch's interpretation may be, may not the term, on account of its close rapprochement, be derived in the same way as its Pali counterpart 'etadatthā,' being regarded as an adjective qualifying *esa* in "esa kaṭe"? If so, the final *ā* of of *etadáthā* will have to be regarded as due to the usual lengthening of finals in Topra, as Woolner points out (*Asoka Glossary*, p. 75, sub voce). The whole expression—*Imaṃ cu dhaṃmānupaṭīpati anupaṭīpajaṃtu ti etadathā me esa kaṭe* of P.E. VII, may thus be rendered "By me this has been instilled with this purpose viz., that people might also conform to this consistent practice of Dhaṃma." As a matter of fact, we find Asoka extremely anxious for "anulupā dhaṃmavaḍhi" towards the commencement of P.E. VII, and this was the foundational purpose for which he inaugurated his 'dhaṃmānusathini' (to which end he instituted the 'dhaṃmathaṃbhāni,' which were to bear his moral instructions, and the 'dhaṃma-mahāmātā,' who were to give effect to them) and 'dhaṃmasāvanāni' (the moral instructions themselves and proclamation thereof), a purpose which could only be fulfilled through 'dhaṃmāpadāna' (inculcation of morals, admonition) on his own part and 'dhaṃmānupaṭipati' (conforming to it) on that of the people for whom it was meant.

# *Chapter - 21*
# Notes on Aśoka Rescripts
## Sailendranath Mitra

*Dusampaṭipādaye* (P.E.I.)—Hitherto the form and the meaning of this term have not been clearly understood. The passage that contains the word runs as follows:—

*Hidata-pālate dusampaṭipādaye amnata agāya dhamma-kāmatāya agāya palīkhāya* etc. etc.—[Hultzsch, *Inscriptions of Aśoka*, p. 146,—Nandangarh P.E.I., section C].

Hultzsch has interpreted the expression *hidata-pālate dusam-paṭ ipādaye* as "(Happiness) in this (world) and in the other (world) is difficult to secure" (p. 119). The term *dusampaṭipādaye* was long understood to be equivalent to a Sk. *-pādyaḥ,* a future participle form, by Aśokan scholars, and Professor D.R. Bhandarkar also explained it in the same way in the first edition of his *Aśoka.* The latter has, however, changed his view as he now thinks that "this is philologically impossible, as remarked by Michelson" (see his *Aśoka*, second edition, p. 336, n. 1). He prefers to take *sampaṭ ipādaye*=sampratipādayet'; that is to say, he wants to make *dusampaṭ ipādaye* equivalent to a finite verb (Optative) prefixed by *du-*, as is shown also by his rendering 'One *may* with difficulty promote.' But such a procedure would make the construction extremely unidiomatic. He has not adduced any instance of such a use of a finite verb with the prefix *du-*, meaning 'difficult.' At any rate, it is not warranted by the dialect of the Aśoka rescripts. For instance, see R.E.V. section C, where occurs the expression *so dukaram karoti*, instead of *so dukaroti* as the Professor's interpretation would require.

I think that *dusampaṭipādaye* is neither a regular future participle nor an optative verbal form. I should like to point out that the term admits of a striking equivalence with such derivative adjectival forms in Pāli as are made up of the prefix *du-* or *su-* and the stem or formative part of a verb. Compare the italicized words in the following instances, where the final *-aya* represents neither an optative termination nor the future participle suffix *-ya*, but is only a part of the verbal stem:—

(i) "Pañc' ime bhikkhave uppannā *duppaṭivinodayā*:......... uppanno rāgo *duppaṭirinodayo*, uppanno moho *duppaṭivinodayo*, uppannaṃ paṭibhānaṃ *duppaṭivinodayaṃ*, uppannaṃ gamikaeittaṃ *duppaṭivinodayaṃ*."— (*Aṅguttara*, III, pp. 184-85).

(ii) "Phandanaṃ capalaṃ cittaṃ darakkhaṃ *dunnirārayaṃ*."—(*Dhammapada*, verse 33).

(iii) "Yo *duddamayo* damena danto."—(*Theragāthā*, verses 3, 8).

(iv) "*Vutti* susamud*ānayā*"='a living easy to procure.'— (*Jātaka*, III. p. 313, 1. 24).

(v) "*Dussaṇṭhāpayo* gharāvāso"='domestic life is difficult to settle down to.'—(Faushöll, *Dhammapada with commentary*, p. 199, II. 10-11=Norman, *Commentary on the Dhammapada* vol. 2, pt. 1, p. 302, n. 4).

Instances of such adjectival forms can be multiplied from the Pāli literature. Again, the Aśoka rescripts themselves contain analogous forms, which, though apparently somewhat different, are really cases of derivative adjective formed from du+some formative part of a verb. For instance, cf. R.E. VI (section N of Hultzsch, p. 196):—

Gir. *Dukaraṃ* tu idaṃ añatra agena parākramena.

Kāl. *Dukale* chu iyam anatā agenā palakamenā.

Shāh. *Dukara* tu kho imaṃ añatra agrena parakramena.

Mān. *Dukare* cha kho añatra agrena parakramena.

Dhau. *Dukale* chu iyaṃ aṃnata agena palakamena.

Jau. *Dukale* chu iyaṃ aṃnata agena palakamena.

It is evident from the table that *dukale* and *dukare* are not finite verbs in the optative, but adjective forms, as their variants *dukaraṃ* and *dukara* show. It is also noteworthy that the passages quoted are, in respect of constructin, exactly on a part with the passage of P.E.I. which contains the term *dusaṃpaṭipādaye*. For another parallel construction with *dukale, dukare* and *dukaraṃ*, see R.E. X, section E. Compare also the analogous forms *dupaṭirekhe* (P.E. III, section D) and *duāhale* (Sep. R.E.I., and my notes in *IHQ*., June, 1932, pp.

377-9). All these instances show that *dusaṃpaṭipādaye* cannot be regarded as a finite verb in the optative, as Prof. Bhandarkar would have it.

As regards the meaning of the term, different suggestions have been made by different scholars, e.g. Senart='difficult to provide,' Bühler='difficult to gain,' Smith='difficult to secure' (See Bhandarkar, *Aśoka*, second edition, pp. 336-7, n. 1). Hultzsch agrees with Smith, and the latest explanation, offered by Prof. Bhandarkar, is 'One may with difficulty promote' (*loc. cit.*). The latter also suggests that in order to ensure uniformity of meaning, *saṃpaṭipad*, as it refers to Aśoka's officers and not to his people, "must be taken to mean 'cause (people) to attain to'."

But such a causal sense of *saṃpaṭipad* is not uniform in the rescripts, even though it may refer to Aśoka's officers. For instance, we have in Sep. R.E.I. the non-causal form *saṃpaṭ-ipajamīne* (Dhau. 1. 16) side by side with the causal *vipaṭ-ipādayamīne* (Dhau. 1. 15) and in the same context, and both in the non-causal sense, the only difference being that while the former is affirmative, the latter — negative. It seems, therefore, better to take *saṃpaṭipādaya* in general sense, and, if causal at all, then as causal by "svârtha." If so, it very aptly suggests the meaning 'to duly give effect to,' 'to bring to perfection,' 'to fulfil,' 'to execute properly,' that is to say, 'to consummate.' Thus, in the same pillar edict the expression "anuvidhīyaṃti *saṃpaṭipādayaṃti* cha, alaṃ cha palaṃ samādapayitave (1. 8.)" would mean "(my officers) are conforming to (my anusaṭhi) and consummating it (lit. bringing it to perfection), and (they are) capable of initiating others." The same idea of 'consistent and successful management or execution' i.e. 'consummation' also runs through the term *saṃpaṭipādayitave* at Sep. R.E. II, last line: "Hevaṃ kalaṃtaṃ tuphe chaghatha *saṃpaṭ-ipādayitave*"—'acting thus (i.e. according to Aśoka's instruction or anusaṭhi), you (i.e. his officers) will be able to consummate it (i.e. justify the anusaṭhi).'

Accordingly, the expression *hidata-pālate dusaṃpaṭipādaye* signifies 'the here-and-the-hereafter is difficult to consummate (i.e. to work out perfectly)'—whether the consummation be through the agency of the officers or through that of the people, or Aśoka's own offspring. The fact is that Aśoka was anxious to ensure the bliss of *hidata-pālata* not only to his people (as in R.E. VI, IX, XI; P.E. III, IV; M.R.E. I), but also to his offspring (as in R.E. XIII; P.E. VII), his officers (as in Sep. R.E. I and II) and his Borderers (as in Sep. R.E. II), and all of them were expected by him, as these edicts show, to work out their salvation by conforming to his moral instructions (anusaṭ-hi) in theory and practice, whereby alone the course of *hidata-pālata* could be perfected. Compare also: *Hevaṃ hi anupaṭīpajaṃtaṃ hidata-pālate āladhe hoti* (P.E. VII. 1. 31) where the worker and winner of the bliss is Aśoka's offspring and not his officers.

Thus, the term *dusaṃpaṭipādaye* does not refer only to the officials' difficulty in causing people to attain to 'hidata-pālata,' but it is used in a general way at the beginning of the rescript to signify the general difficulty with which any toiler is faced in having to work for 'hidata-pālata;' and it is only when Aśoka particularly refers to the activity of his officers in that behalf in any particular context that the term may assume a bearing that will connect the officers alone with the act. But no such specification is present in the expression *Hidata-pālate dusaṃpaṭipādaye*.

## *Chapter - 22*

# Notes on Aśoka Rescripts

**Sailendranath Mitra**

**Etadathā***—We have seen that although there is a close rapprochement of form between *etadathā* of P.E. VII and *etadatthā* at Ang. i. 198, the construction of the P.E. passage becomes rather clumsy with *etadathā* as adjective. A better use of the word is at Mil. 31, in an adverbial sense, which also appears to be the sense expressed by *etadathā* of the inscription. In the Pāli passage the word occurs as a correlative, or rather, complement of *kinti* ('how', 'in order that') and necessarily means 'to that end', being, therefore, equivalent to *etadatthāya*, as the following quotation from the Milinda will show:—

> "Rājā āha: 'Kimatthiyā bhante Nāgasena tumhākaṃ pabbajjā, ko ca tumhākaṃ paramattho' ti. Thera āha: '*Kinti* mahārāja idaṃ dukkhaṃ nirujjheyya aññañ ca dukkhaṃ na uppajjeyyā ti *etadatthā* mahārāja amhākaṃ pabbajjā, anupādā' parinibbānaṃ kho pana amhākaṃ paramattho' ti.———'Kim pana bhante Nāgasena sabbe *etadatthāya* pabbajantī, ti" etc. etc. [pp. 31 (=65-'6)—2].

[For the correlation of the terms, cf. also R.E. XIII. 1. II : *etaye ca aṭhaye* ayo dhramadipi nipista *kiti* putra papotra me....... (*Shahbaz-garhi*)].

The theme of P.E. VII is 'anulupā dhaṃma-vaḍhi.' When Aśoka says *etadathā me esa kaṭe* ('to this end has it been done by me'), the end or intent is 'that men may conform to this befitting pursuit of Dhaṃma' (*Imaṃ ca dhaṃmānupaṭīpati anupatīpajaṃtu ti*. Cf. the concluding portion: *se etāye aṭhāye iyaṃ kaṭe.......tathā ca anupaṭ īpajaṃtu ti*. Cf. also P.E. II). And this conforming to the befitting

* Continued from the March number, 1931.

pursuit of Dhaṃma is, as the context in P.E. VII shows, calculated to ensure 'anulupā dhaṃma-vaḍhi.' The idea of 'vaḍhi' or spiritual thriving also runs through *etadatthā* of the Pāli passage quoted above (cf. also Pāli *pitu-atthā*, J. iii, 518, which the scholiast explains as 'pitu *vaḍḍhi*-atthāya').

Thus it appears that *etadattha*ā at Mil. 31 is a better parallel than *etadatthā* at Aṅg. i. 198; and it is infinitely better than Hultzsch's *bhojanatthā*, for the simple reason that besides being strikingly similar in form, it agrees with the P.E. term in inner meaning, namely, 'vaḍhi', 'furtherance', 'increase of merit'.

# Chapter - 23

# Notes on Aśoka Rescripts

**Sailendranath Mitra**

*Duāhale hi... ................atileke* (Dhauli and Jaugaḍa Sep. R.E.I.)—This is a very difficult passage and has hitherto defined explanation. The full text occurs in Hultzsch's *Inscriptions of Asoka* as follows:

P. 94. *Dhau* :— duā[ha]le hi i[ma]sa kaṃm[asa] m[e] kute man[o]-atileke—(1. 16).

P. 113. *Jau* :— du[ā]hale etasa [kaṃ]masa sa me k[u]t[ema]n[o-ati]le[ke]—(1. 8).

Hultzsch has admitted the difficulty of the passage (p. 96 n. 13) and followed Franke and clumsily rendered it: "For how (could my mind be pleased if one badly fulfils this duty'?" He has taken *duāhale* as a nominative absolute and, without justification, twisted the expression "*kute.........atileke*" to impart the sense "How could my mind be pleased," with no clear evidence adduced of a similar use of *atileke* either in the Aśoka rescripts or in literature. Indeed, the whole expression has been so loosely tried to be understood by scholars that the sense of the passage, has, at times, become mercilessly free. For instance, compare the rendering of Professor D.R. Bhandarkar (*Aśoka*, p. 324): "This duty (imposed) by me has thus a *two-fold consequence* ('duāhale'). Why *any doubt in your mind* ('mane atileke')."

I think that the difficulty has been due to a rather careless reading of the Jaugaḍa text (which contains the clue), ignoring the tiny little thing *sa* after *kaṃmasa*, perhaps as a faulty repetition of the scribe, which certainly it is not. If we make use of this *sa*, joining it to the next letter *me*, and read—*duāhale etasa kaṃmasa same*, the result we obtain is striking. For if one knows the relation between the terms *sama* ('like,' 'equal,' 'parallel') and *atireka* ('greater,' 'better,' 'more') in Pāli phraseology, the whole passage—*duāhale*...........*atileke*—at once becomes easy of interpretation. There is a very interesting expression in the *Theragāthā*, p. 45 (first line of verse 424), which reads:

"Nâttano *samakaṃ* kañci *atirekaṃ* ca maññisaṃ."

It means 'none would I regard as my *equal* or *superior*.' Now, the terms *same* and *atileke* of the inscription offer the same sense as do the italicized words in the Pāli quotation, and they forthwith suggest the following construction:—

1. Etasa kammasa same duāhale—the like of this duty is difficult to find.

2. Kute man [-] atileke—not to speak of a better.

What Aśoka means is that the course of conduct he is recommending to the Nagalaviyohālaka-mahāmātras of Tosalī and Samāpā for the good governance of his subjects is *the best* that one can think of or take upon oneself and that there can be *no better*. In the same strain does he speak in other edicts too. Compare:

(a) Esa hi *seṭhe kaṃme* yā dhaṃmānusāsanā—(Dhau. R.E. IV.1. 6) and (b) Nathi hi *kaṃmatalā* savalokahitena—(Jau. R.E. VI. 1. 5).

To complete the interpretation, a word is perhaps necessary about *duāhale* and *man* [-].

It is evident from what has been said above that there is no necessity for explaining *duāhale* as a nominative absolute, as Hultzsch has done. The word is a complementary adjective to *same*, and in respect of grammatical form it is on a par with such terms as *dukale* (Dhau. R.E. V) and *dupaṭivekhe* (P.E. III), the hiatus remaining as in *mahā-apāye* (Dhau. Sep. I. 1. 15) and *pasu-opagāni* (Dhau. and Jau. R.E. II). It goes back to ā+hṛ, 'to fetch,' 'to procure,' 'to bring upon oneself' [cf. Sk. ud+ā+hṛ, 'to cite a parallel,' and Pāli atītam āhari, 'he related (lit. 'conveyed') the past']. Hence, by extension *duāhale* = 'difficult to find.'

As regards *man*[-], occurring after *kute*, I almost felt tempted to explain it as a counterpart of Pāli *pana* occurring in such idiomatic expressions as (1) "Nābhijānāmi sāmikaṃ manasā pi aticarittā, *kuto pana* kāyena." (Aṅguttara IV. p. 66.—'I am not aware of having transgressed my husband even in my thoughts, much less with the body'); and (2) "*Kuto vā pana tassa* uttaritaraṃ" ('How, indeed, can there be a greater?—Childers, s.v. *kuto*). Although this latter quotation offers a close parallel to our *kute man* [-] *atileke*, I refrain from equating *man*[-] with *pana* for the simple reason that *pana* is not used here, although it is known to Aśokan Māgadhī, e.g. at Dhau. R.E. VI. 5 and Jau. R.E. VI. 5. Moreover, the change of *p* into *m* is not yet met with in the Dhauli and Jaugaḍa rescripts, although the opposite process is noticeable, e.g. in *aphe, tuphe* (=Prākṛit *amhe, tumhe*) in Sep. R.E. I and II.—In the circumstance of the final *o* of *man*[*o*] being problematical, let me try and examine the reading *mane* given in Bhandarkar and Majumdar's *Inscriptions* of *Aśoka*, p. 85. The term *mane* would admit of a two-fold explanation:

(1) *mane=manye*, 'methinks.' For the correspondence *n=ny*, one will have to refer to Kālsi R.E. X 27, where occurs the word *manati*, at the same time not ignoring the fact that such a correspondence cannot be fully established from Dhauli or Jaugaḍa orthography; and

(2) *kute-m-ane*=Sanskrit *kutaḥ anyaḥ*=Pāli *kuto-m-añño*, with *m* as euphonic, preventing the hiatus as in *bhaṭi*[*m-ayesu*] at Dhau. R.E. V. 4. For the correspondence *n=ny*, one will have to look, though not very confidently, to the end of P.E. III, where occurs a form *iyaṃmana*, which Hultzsch has doubtfully equated with Sk. *idaṃ anyat* (p. 122. n. 5).

It appears that these explanations of *man-* are far from satisfactory. In the alternative, I am driven to the Pāli *manam* (=Sk. *manāk*), 'a little,' 'somewhat,' 'almost' (See P.T.S. Dictionary, s.v.), and read—*kute mana atileke*—with the meaning 'how can there be one, the any better?'

Thus, the whole passage becomes rightly understood in the following way: 'The like of this duty is, indeed, difficult to find; how can there be one, any the better?'

## *Chapter - 24*

# Harṣa: A Buddhist

### Dasharatha Sharma

Harṣa has generally been regarded as a Buddhist. But of late this view has been questioned by some writers, notably by Dr. R.C. Majumdar who cannot believe that Harṣa ever "formally gave up his old faith", i.e., his devotion to Śiva, and regarded other religions as distinctly inferior.[1]

That Harṣa originally was a Śaiva and remained so up to the twenty-fifth year of his reign is well known to most students of history.[2] His Bānskheṛā and Madhuban Copper-plate Grants of the regnal years 22 and 25 respectively call him a *Parama-Māheśvara*, i.e., a worshipper of Maheśvara or Śiva. His seals similarly mention him as a Śaiva, while referring to his brother. Rājyavardhana as a *Parama-Saugata,* i.e., a Buddhist, and to his father, Prabhākaravardhana, as a *Paramādityabhakta,* i.e., worshipper of the Sun. Bāṇa speaks of Harṣa's offering worship to Nīlalohita, i.e., Śiva, before he started on his *digvijaya.*[3] His Sonepat seal bears the figure of Nāndī, the vehicle of Śiva.

To conclude, however, from this evidence that he continued as a Śaiva to the end of his life does not seem reasonable, not only in view of Yuan Chawāng's testimony which shows that by 643 A.D. Śiva had gone to the third place in Harṣa's estimation, but also on account of the testimony from Harṣa's own works and his biography by the court historiographer and poet, Bāṇa. Harṣa's two plays, *Priyadarśikā* and *Ratnāvalī* show no influence of Buddhism. They, obviously, are the works of a young author who enjoyed and liked people to enjoy life. But we have just to turn to *Nāgānanda,* the last and maturest of his plays, to see the great change in his religious attitude. It begins

---

1. *Classical Age,* Bhāratīya Vidyā Bhavan Series, pp. 119-120.
2. See R.S. Tripathi's *History of Kanauj*, p. 163.
3. *Harṣcarita*, Nirṇayasāgar Edition, p. 202.

with salutation to the Buddha, deals with the life of a Bodhisattva and preaches in uncompromising terms, the noble doctrine of Ahiṁsā.[1] It contains veiled references perhaps also to his *Mokṣa-pariṣads* and determination, in c. 643 A.D., to fight no more.[2]

We have to notice also a passage in the *Harṣacarita*, which has so far escaped the attention of practically all writers on Harṣa's religion. When maddened by grief at the death of her husband, Harṣa's sister, Rājyaśrī, desires to become a Buddhist nun. Harṣa, while dissuading her from adopting this course, not only arranges for her instruction in the philosophy of the Tathāgata "which brings all misery to an end",[3] *but promises also to don along with her the red robes of a bhikṣu,—as soon as he had finished his self-appointed task of punishing his brother's murderer, Śaśāṅka,* the ruler of Gauḍa.[4] Time, no doubt, never permitted him to implement this resolution. He died rather prematurely. But there is no reason to doubt his sincerity. An orthodox Brāhmaṇa like Bāṇa could hardly have put this statement in Harṣa's mouth, unless Harṣa had actually in his subsequent life become a very devout Buddhist and his conduct given a clear indication that someday he would renounce the world and retire to a Buddhist monastery.

1. See Acts IV and V and the final portion of Act III.
2. See Canto I, verse 8 which speaks of the grant of *kalpadruma* to suppliants.
3. *Harṣacarita*, p. 256.
4. *"Iyam tu grahīṣyati mayaiva samaṁ samāptakṛtyena kāṣāyāṇi"*

# Chapter - 25

# The Sea and Land Travels of a Buddhist Sādhu in the Sixteenth Century

**Guiseppe Tucci**

Modern researches have shown that Mahāyāna Buddhism continued to exist in India up to quite recent times. Mr. N.N. Vasu, Mm. Hara-prasāda Śāstrī and others have pointed out the existence of Buddhist schools in Orissa and Bengal up to the XVIIIth century; the *dharma*-worship in some parts of Bengal and Behar betrays even now its Buddhist origin. The Bengali literature of the XVth and XVIth centuries contains a large number of texts which testify to the existence at that time of various, more or less degenerated, Buddhist centres in Bengali countries. Caitanya himself is said to have converted large communities of Buddhists. If the authenticity of the *Karcā* of Govinda Dās was beyond any doubt, we could prove the existence of Buddhist schools and paṇḍits in South India at the time of the great Bengali Vaiṣṇava mystic. His discussion with the Buddhist paṇḍit Rāmagiri and the latter's conversion is in fact reported there.[1] It will not appear out of place to have recourse to a Tibetan source of the XVIth century which brings in some new information about these later periods of Mahāyāna Buddhism and at the same time gives us an idea of the geographical knowledge of Indian and extra-Indian countries as it circulated among the Tibetan monks. I refer here to the biography of Buddhagupta (*Saṅs rgyas sbas pa*) the *guru* of Tāranātha. Tāranātha himself collected the materials for his book from his master during the latter's travels to Tibet, and embodied them in a short biographical note called: *Grub c'en bu-ddha-gu-ptaḥi rnam t'ar rje brtsun ñid zal nas gzan du raṅ rtog gi dri mas*

1. Cf. *Karcā* ed. by D.C. Sen (new edition), p. 27. In the Annual Report on South Indian Epigraphy ending March 1927 an inscription of 1580 mentions the erection of a Buddhist temple by the Nāyaks of Tanjore.

*ma spags paḥi yi ge yaṅ dag pa,* the importance of which is chiefly geographical.

Buddhagupta was, as many of the Indian sādhus always have been, a great traveller. He visited many places in India and even outside India in far away countries in order to find traces of Buddhism and of Buddhist remains. We cannot say that his information is always exact; in this kind of writings we cannot expect to find everywhere that historical preciseness of detail which we demand from modern authors. These Indian and Tibetan saints lived in a kind of mythical atmosphere which gives a peculiar colour to all their experiences; the truth for them is not about external facts but rather about the meaning that they have for them or the ideal significance that they attach to them. Anyhow this biography is the first Tibetan document that we came across up to now in which information is found about a large number of countries outside India proper, and in a certain way it sheds some side-light upon the geographical knowledge and the trade routes of India in the XVIth century.

The importance of our text for the history of the geographical notions of the Tibetans seems therefore to be of no little moment. It is perhaps the only Tibetan treatise, at least to our knowledge, in which we find a great deal of direct information about some places in India and chiefly outside India proper which are not usually connected with Buddhist canonical tradition. This explains why Blo bzaṅ dpal ldan ye śes, while writing his *Śam-bha-laḥi lam yig*, practically copies from our text when he mentions countries as a rule not registered in the canonical literature, proving indirectly that he considered the little book of Tāranātha as the most complete and reliable treatise on the subject. I must also add that the readings of our text are generally more correct than those of the *Śam-bha-laḥi lam yig*, which are therefore to be accordingly modified.[1] Our

1. The geographical literature of Tibet concerned with India and foreign countries has not yet been studied chiefly on account of the scarce materials available in European libraries. Many of the *gsuṅ ḥbum* or collected writings of the Tibetan polygraphs contain some sections geographically very interesting, e.g., the very important chapters on China included in the writings of the fifth Dalai Lama, the *Śam-bha-laḥi lam yig* edited by Grünwedel and included in the works of the great Paṅ-c'en blo bzaṅ dpal ldan ye śes. Gloṅ c'en is said to have written a general description of India, which I have not been able to see as yet and which anyhow must be a compliation because the author never went to India. Geographical information is also contained in the astrological works such as the *Vai dūr-ya dkar po* and the *Vaidūrya gya' sel.* Nor must we forget the various *rnam t'ar*-s or biographical accounts, chiefly, of the locāvas or translators who came down to India. Some of them contain real itineraries such as the *rnam t'ar* of Ur gyen pa

source moreover shows that at the time of Buddhagupta India had not yet forgotten those great links of cultural relations which Buddhism had established between her and far away countries from Africa to Java.

The Buddhist culture of Buddhagupta was exclusively Tantric; no mention of a śāstra whatever is to be found in his biography. We must reasonably expect that at a later date, as that of Buddhagupta, the inter-connection between the Buddhist and Śaiva sects was even greater than it had been before. It must have been very difficult to draw a line of distinction between the followers of the two schools. The *Siddha-sampradāya* is common to the Buddhists as well as to the Śaivas, and Gorakṣa is even now a great saints for both the communities. Characteristically Hindu gods and ideas were creeping into declining Buddhism. This fact is worthy of notice because it will help us very much when we want to ascertain the peculiarities of the system of Tāranātha, in as much as there is no doubt that, whatever might have been the further developments of his school, he meant to reform and impart a new life to Tibetan Buddhism. It is quite certain that his meeting with Buddhagupta exercised a great influence upon the formation of his mind. The learning and the experience of his Indian *guru,* and his explanation of some of the most sacred rituals and a great deal of the exoteric literature of Mahāyāna as expounded in India, impressed the young lama and gave the first impulse to a new line of thoughts. It seems to me that his coming across Buddhagupta represents a moment of the foremost importance in the mental and religious evolution of Tāranātha. Blo bzaṅ dpal ldan ye śes also calls him the disciple of the Indian yogin (*Śam-bha-laḥi lam yig,* pp. 29, 49). Tāranātha himself begins his *Bkaḥ babs bdun ldan* by invoking with great reverence his great guru (*Edelsteinmine,* p. 9, cf. p. 116) of whom mention is also to be found in another work by the same author, viz., the *Gsaṅ baḥi rnam t'ar* in which the dream is narrated that foretold his imminent meeting with Buddhagupta. There can hardly be any doubt that many an

---

or of Stag tsaṅ ras pa. Many a useful information can be gathered from the guides for pilgrims such as the *Jam bu gliṅ spyi bśad* (on which see Waddell, *Lamaism,* p. 307 and *Proceedings,* Asiatic Society of Bengal, 1893) or the other one for the visitors of Nepal: *bal yul mc'od rten ḥp'ags pa śin kun daṅ deḥi gnas gzan rnams kyi sa dkar c'ag mdor sdus.*

I must add to the list the grographical dictionary in six languages printed in China by order of K'ien lung called *K'in-ting si yu t'ung wen chi* upon which see Von Zach, *Lexicographische Beiträge,* I, p. 83 and 111, p. 108 and Laufer, *Loan words in Tibetan,* p. 434.

information embodied in the *Bkaḥ babs bdun ldan* is directly derived from the teachings of Buddhagupta who is there considered as belonging to the Gorakṣasampradāya. This connection between Tāranātha and the Nāthapanthins, though of a specific Buddhist branch, is worthy of notice. Through Buddhagupta, one of the last if not the last of the Buddhist apostles into Tibet, Śaivaism more than Buddhism was finding its way into the "country of the snows." I shall not translate the entire text but shall give its résumé rendering into English those portions only which have a larger interest for us.

Buddhagupta was born in Indraliṅga near Rāmeśvara in South India, in the family of a rich merchant, whose name was Kṛṣṇa. He was initiated into the yoga by an ascetic called in our text Tīrthinātha, a name which must be corrected into Tīrthanātha as evidenced by its Tibetan translation *ḥbab stegs mgon po* to be found in the *Bkaḥ babs bdun ldan*, p. 16. This Sādhu is said to have been a contemporary of king Rāmarāja, who may be identified with Rāmarāja of Vijayanagara (1542-1565) of Talikoṭa fame or rather with his cousin Rāmarāja Viṭṭ-hala, who was Viceroy in the South and a contemporary of Viśvanātha, the Nāyak of Madura. It was Tīrthanātha who initiated him into the doctrines of the Siddha Gorakṣ anātha together with two other nāthas, Brahmanātha mentioned also in the *Bkaḥ babs bdun ldan* (p. 116) and Kṛṣṇanātha whom he met in North India during his pilgrimage to Delhi (ṭi li) VikramaHaridwār (Ha ri dhā ra=Haridvāra).[1] He learned and practised the *mahābaddhā* and the *svasambaddhā* mudrā (see *Gorakṣa-saṃhitā,* I, 66, 67 and *Haṭhayoga-pradīpikā*, Bengali ed., III, p. III) that is those special methos of prāṇāyāma, which were expounded in the Haṭha-yoga and those Tantras, Śaiva as well as Buddhist, which are connected with the same order of ideas. I refer chiefly to the *Sahaja-siddhi* class of Tantras which were specially followed by the Siddha-sampradāya and through this and its texts exercised a great influence upon Lamaism. At the time of Buddhagupta it seems that the school of Gorakṣa was greatly flourishing in India, though it was divided into a series of sub-sects, the peculiarities of which we are not yet in a position to determine. Their names are preserved in our text, and so far as I know some of them have not yet been met with in other sources:

---

1. The spelling Haridhāra shows that Tāranātha followed the spoken pronunciation and that even Sanskrit names were reproduced as they sounded in the vernaculars. Cf. also *dīpa* often used in our text for *dvīpa, bheragī* for *vairāgin*; *naṭesori* for *naṭeśvarī* suggests a Bengali pronunciation.

(a) Nāthapanthin which has many followers in India even now.

(b) Bakṣapanthin.

(c) Gopālapanthin.

(d) Pāgalapanthin (pa ga la) from *pāgal* (mad man) which may have been suggested by the strange ways of these yogins, cf. the Bāuls of Bengal perhaps from *vātula*.

(e) Āyi-panthin.

(f) Colipanthin (tso li), viz., Coliyāpanthin (vide Akṣaya Kumar Datta, *Bhāratavarṣīya-upāsaka-sampradāya*, p. 119).

(g) Hodupanthin (ho du).

(h) Dhvajapanthin (dva za).

(i) Veragipanthin (bhe ra gi) from Vairāgin, ascetic. Cf. the name of Vairāginātha given in the list of the Siddhas up to Āryadeva.

(l) Maṅgalanāthapanthin.

(m) Pathopanthin (pa tho).

(n) Sattanāthapanthin (from *sapta*?).

There was also another rather dissident sect more strictly Buddhist called Naṭeśvarīyogins (nā. ṭe so ri) to which Tīrthanātha, Brahmanātha and Kṛṣṇanātha, the gurus of Buddhagupta belonged, and which must therefore also be connected with Tāranātha.

Then the account of the travel begins. From the Himālaya, where, as we saw, he had been on pilgrimage, he went down to Māru (Rājputana) and spent some time in Rāṭhor (ra ṭhor). Then we find him in Nagaratata, and in Mūlasthāna (mo la tā na, Multān) and to the north up to Kābul (ka bhe la), Khorāsān (kho ra sā na) and a place called in our text ba. ja. sa. na, Goṣa,[1] Urgyan, which corres-ponds, as is known, to Uḍḍīyāna of the Sanskrit sources. The question concerning the localization of this country has been recently summarized by Dr. Bagchi in an article which gives the actual state of our knowledge about this province which played such an important part in the history of Buddhism and Tāntrism.[2] Without anticipating the results of my further investigation of the problem in the light of

1. Goṣa is perhaps Khost, kuo.si.to, of Yuan Chwang. Bajasān, which might also be a clerical mistake of the copyist for Bajastān, suggests Bagistān a town in the province of Khorāsān in Persia. It is difficult to understand how these countries are in the north while Urgyan is said to be in the west. Did Buddhagupta go to Persia before and then, after returning to India, proceed to Urgyan? We should expect otherwise, east instead of west of Khorāsān.

2. *Indian Historical Quarterly*, vol. VI, no. 3, pp. 580ff.

very important Tibetan itineraries recently found by me in some Western Tibetan monasteries I shall only say that Buddhagupta locates Urgyan, Uḍḍīyāna in Ghaznī. Then he went to Urgyan in the west. The Sanskrit name of the country is Au ṭi ya ṇa, but in the original language is Or gyen; since the pronunciation of *ṭa* and *ra* is similar it becomes like Or-ya-na. Now in the country itself in the language of the Muhammadans (kla klo) it is known to every body as Ghaznī (ga dsa ni). He went to all the great places such as the cave of Kambala-pā, the ruins of the palace of Indrabhūti,[1] the mountain Ilo.[2] Then he stopped for one month in the town of Dhūmasthira—in Tibetan, the place of the smoke (du baḥi gnas) in the very centre of the country. Generally speaking, the surface of this valley in the centre of Orgyan which is surrounded by the ravines and the woods of the mountains is large enough for two days' march from west to east and for four days' march from south to north. This country is surrounded by three lakes in the east, south and north.[3] Then he proceeded to the north to Balkh (Bha. lag. kha), Kashmir (Kha che) where he visited some sacred places of pilgrimage for the heretics such as Śāradātīrtha and Nāradatīrtha (na ra dha),[4] then he travelled up to Dā ra ta bo ṭa, viz., Dard-Tibetan country and to Kas kā ra, i.e., Kashgar. The Dard-Tibetan country must be the district of Kargil (Purig) and Ladak. It is therefore evident that Buddhagupta crossed the Zojila, visited the district of Purig which quite possibly was not yet at that time completely converted to Islamism as it is now, went westwards to Leh, a purely Buddhist country and through the Kardog Pass and Nubra reached Kashgar. The Sanskritic name for Purig and

---

1. The story of Kambala and Indrabhūti is narrated in the life of the eighty-four Siddhas (translated by Grünwedel, *Geschichten der vier und achtzig Zauberer* and in the *Bkaḥ babs bdun ldan* translated by the same author.
2. The form Ilora parvata found in the *Sam-bha-laḥi lam yig* is manifestly wrong and is not supported by any source. Cf. *Edelsteinmine*, p. 58.
3. The central lake is called Dhanakoṣa in other sources.—de nas nub phyogs Orgyen du phebs/ sans kri taḥi skad du Au ṭi ya ṇa/ raṅ bzin skad du Orgyan zer/ ṭa daṅ ra ḥdon tshul ḥdra min yod pas/ (I think that 'min' is out of place here) or ya ṇa zer ba ḥdra cig yod . . . da lta de phyogs raṅ na Kla kloḥi skad du grags pa kun gyi go ba la/ yul ga dza ni zer ro/ grub chen lva baḥi na bzaḥ can gyi phyug pa daṅ/ rgyal po yin ta bhu taḥi pho braṅ gyi sul daṅ/ ilo par ba ta zes bya baḥi gnas chen rnams su phebs/ Ur gyan gyi gnas mthil dhu ma sthi ra ste du bai gnas zes bya baḥi groṇ khyer zig zla geig tsam bzugs/ spyir Orgyen gyi gnas mthil der roṅ daṅ nags ḥthug pos skor baḥi dbus na thaṅ khor tsam śar nub du ñin lam gñis tsam/ lho byaṅ du bzi tsam/ . . . gnas ḥdi śar daṅ lho daṅ nub rnams mtsho gsum gyis bskor.
4. On Śāradātīrtha cf. *Rājātaraṅgiṇī* translated by Stein, 11, pp. 280, 486 and passim. Naradatīrtha is unknown to me.

Ladak shows that even when referring to countries well-known to Tibetans, Tāranātha strictly followed the information of his *guru*, preserving the Indian name of provinces which were under the direct influence of Tibet. The name for Ladak is, as is known, either Mar yul, or in recent sources, Maṅ yul.

Back to India he met his *guru* and passing through Delhi he proceeded to Bhīmeśvara where he stopped for some time in a ruined temple of Īśvara (dbaṅ phyug). After having visited some other small places in the south he started again for Rājputāna (Māru) where he saw the temple of Hevajra founded by Padmavajra; then we find him in Ābu, Saurāṣṭra, Kaccha (ka tsa), then back again to Saurāṣṭra and properly in Somanātha where he visited the Śiva-liṅga and a statue of Virūpa. Then he turned his steps towards the south and peregrinated through Marāṭhā, Khāndesh (khā na de sa), Tam pa la, Vijayanagara (very often in India itself written Vidyānagara), Karṇāṭa, Triliṅga, Trimalla, Kāñcī (tsan tsi), Malabar (ma lyar), Koṅkaṇa, tsā ri dra, Marvār, tsai va la, (corr: *ra* for *va*: Ceraḷam, Kerala), ni tsa ma sa (but *Śam bha-laḥi lam yig*: Nicambara, ni tsa mbra ha), tsan dra du ra, Pañcabhratāra (pañca-bhatā ra) that is Pañcadrāviḍa, Cola-maṇḍala (tsa ra maṇ ṭa la), (Mora maṇṭala) Moliyār maṇḍala, Jalamaṇḍala, Talamaṇḍala, Toṇḍaimaṇḍala (tunṭa man ṭa la), Bhogamalabar, Kaliṅga.

"Then in Koṅkaṇa he embarked and went to the west up to an island called *ḥgro ling* in Sanskrit *Dramiladvīpa*. In the language of the Muhammadans, the barbarians, and [the inhabitants] of the small island, it is called *la sam lo ra na so* (in *Śambh*: sam lo ra na so). In that island the teachings of the *guhyamantras* are largely diffused. He heard these from a paṇḍit called Sumati who had acquired the mystic realizations (abhijñā), the mystic power of the Saṃvara (tantra) and of the Hevajra (tantra) and then he learnt the detailed explanation of the Hevajratantra. This Hevajratantra belongs to the system of the Ācārya Padmasambhava. Generally speaking, the tradition of the fourfold tantras is still uninterrupted in that island, and if we except the sublime and largely diffused Kālacakratantra, whatever is in India is also there such as the (Vajra-) kīlatantra and the Tantra of the daśakrodhas, many Heruka-tantras, Vajrapāṇi, mkhaḥ ldiṅ (Garuḍa), Māmākī, Mahākāla, etc. Then the sublime order of Hayagrīva which is largely spread in India is to be found there. Moreover there are many sacred teachings (chos) belonging to the Tantras expounded by Padmasambhava. Though the community is numerous, the rules of the discipline are not so pure.

The monks wear black garments and usually drink intoxicating liquors . . . Then he embarked again with some merchants and went to Śaṅkhadvīpa (in Tibetan, duṅ gliṅ, the island of the conch-shell). There he remained some time in a mountain, rich in medicinal herbs and called bde ḥbyuṅ gi gnas (Śambhusthāna). There he saw many men with human face and the nose [big] as that of the elephant coming from an island called *Gajanāsa.*

Then he went to the south to the island Pa la ta, and from there sailing again towards the east, he reached Siṃhaladvīpa (Ceylon) where he remained five years. In a plateau in the country called Kan ṭa la (kandi) in the middle of a thick forest there is a cave in a rock. There the great ācārya Śāntipā, when he went to Siṃhaladvīpa, practised the mystic exercises.[1] His name is Yaṣākāraśānti which in Tibetan means glory-mine-peace.

Where Buddhagupta embarked is not mentioned in our text; perhaps it was in Goa or in Choul or in Dabul which are known to have been harbours on the mercantile route on the Koṅkaṇa shore. Nor can the islands that he touched be easily identified for the simple reason that their names are not to be met with in other sources known to us.

Our difficulty is increased by the fact that the distance is not given nor the days he spent in the sea are recorded. But if we consider

1. de na koṅku na nas rgy mts'o la nub p'yogs su gru btaṅ nas byon pas / 'gro gliṅ ste / ryya skad du ta mi ḍo dvipa zes par p'ebs / 'di la kla klo yaṅ yul mt'ai mi daṅ gliṅ p'ran rnams kyi skad du lam lo ra na so zer gyin gda / gliṅ de na gsaṅ sṅags kyi bstan pa c'es dar ba yod/mṅon śes daṅ ldan pai slob dpon su ma ti zes bya bai paṇḍita gcing la bde mc'og daṅ / dgyes rdor gyi dbaṅ gsan nas/ dgyes rdor gyi rgyud la bśad pa 'ṅ zil rgyas su gsan / dgyes rdor 'di slob dpon padma 'byuṅ gnas kyi lugs yin ciṅ / spyir gliṅ de nas rgyud sde bzi kai bka' ma c'ad pa daṅ / k'yad par bla med c'es dar dus 'k'or ma gtogs rgya gar na yod pa p'an c'er de na yod / p'ur bu daṅ k'ro lo bcui rgyud daṅ he ru kai rgyud maṅ po daṅ p'yag na rdo rje daṅ mk'a ldiṅ daṅ / ma mo daṅ nag po c'en sogs daṅ rtan mgrin bla med kyi rigs rgya gar na maṅ ba maṅ po yaṅ de na yod pa daṅ / slob dpon pad ma abyuṅ gnas nas brgyud pai c'os kyaṅ maṅ bar yod 'dug / rnams gos nag gyon pa p'al c'er c'an t'un ba sogs / par dge 'dun maṅ po yod kyaṅ 'dul bai lag len dog po med de / dge sloṅ adug go/. . . de na (read de nas) slar ts'oṅ pa daṅ lhan gcig gyur bzugs nas śaṅ k'a dvi pa ste / duṅ gi gliṅ du p'ebs / de nas bde adyuṅ gi gnas śes bya ba ri bo sman sna ts'ogs skye ba zig 'dug / der t'og cig bzugs gliṅ de na ga dza nā sa zes bya bai gliṅ nas 'oṅs pai mi la sna glaṅ po c'e lta bur yod pa maṅ po gzigs / de nas lho re byon pa la pa la ta zes bya bai gliṅ du p'ebs / de nas śar p'yogt su gru btaṅ bas siṅga / lai glin du p'ebs te der lo lṅa tsam bzugs / . . . kan ṭa la zes bya bai yul zig gi p'u / nags t'ug po zig gi dbus na brag p'ug 'dug / de na slob dpon c'en po śanti pas singalii yul du p'ebs pai dus kyi dṅos slob / yaśṅ ka ra śanti bod kad du grags pai 'byuṅ gnas zi ba zes bya ba.

that he sailed in Koṅkaṇa and that he landed at Ceylon we have a line of navigation which either went along the coast or passed through the Laccadives; but I think that this second alternative is less probable, because it would imply a rather long deviation.[1]

Nor can I suggest any definite identification as regards the first islands alluded to in our text, called Dramiladvīpa, the island of the Dravidians or Samloranaso; we must not necessarily think that this island is in the middle of the ocean and far away from the coast. It may as well be one of the small islands along the Koṅkaṇa country. One may think of Goa itself where traces of Buddhism are to be found up to recent times and which was known to Arab sailors under the name of Sindabūr or Sandabūr.[2] The mention of Muhammadan inhabitants of the country does not contradict this identification because we know that even before the time of Buddhagupta they had settled there. What on the other hand we know from Ibn Batuta about Islamism in the Laccadives seems also to exclude a *priori* that we have to search there for the island Samloronaso spoken of by Buddhagupta as a good centre of Buddhist studies. All these facts seem therefore to point out that the islands visited by our Sādhu are to be searched for along the coast from Goa to Cape Comorin. From there [Ceylon] he went to a small island called Uliṅga[3] and then joining some merchants of this place he proceeded to another small island called Amuga at a distance taking about one month of navigation from Ceylon. There he

---

1. Śaṅkadvīpa.

The Laccadives and the Maldives were known to Chinese sources as "the islands of the ocean of the streams." They were not rarely touched by the ships of foreign traders. Cf. also Ibn Batuta who speaks of the goods exported from these islands to China, India and Arabia.

2. I am afraid that the followers of Padmasambhava in black dress have no connection whatever with Buddhist sects. There is in fact no trace of such a black colour being used by Buddhist priests. It is perhaps not impossible that some Christian monks, probably Portuguese, were mistaken by Buddhagupta for Buddhist śramaṇas. It is to be noted in this connection that even Buddhagupta does not fail to remark a great discrepancy in the monastic rules between the usual Buddhist monks and the so-called disciples of Padmasambhava. Moreover they are clearly said to belong to an order. Drinking of wine, if now common among the rñim ma pas in Tibet seems, so far as we know, to have been not practised in India except for ritual purposes.

3. For Uliṅga Śambhalai Pam yig reads Umāliṅga. Buddhagupta adds that he was the only Indian to be there; anyhow, it seems to me that these two islands, we do not know (in what direction from Ceylon), must have possessed rather big harbours and been on the trade route if Buddhagupta was able to embark there on a big ship.

embarked on a big boat having five thousand men on board; this is at least the number we read in the text, but it is evident that we are confronted either with an exaggeration of the narrator of the writer or with a clerical error. No vessel was able to carry more than some hundred men. After about four months of navigation to the south he reached a country called Dzha mi gi ri (Jhāmigiri).

There are two towns, one in the north and one in the south, the distance between them being of about seven days for a traveller. Between these two towns there are three mountains and on the top of one of them there is a golden cave which spreads light at night. He remained there one year. In that island there is the throne of ācārya Nāgārjuna said to have been used by him when he went there. There are also many images of the Blessed One and many temples.[1]

"Thence he joined some merchants going to some small islands to the east and after one month of navigation he reached an island in which there was Potala, the king of the mountains. According to some this is the small Potala. Anyhow it is evidently the Potala on the land accessible to men. There he visited a rock-crystal cave, the place sacred to Maṇibhadrakumārā, then the place sacred to Bhrūkuṭ ī, the cave of the golden face of the Asura, the place sacred to Tārā and the places sacred to Brahmā, Viṣṇu, Mahendra, each one with a self-created temple in the mountain. Moreover he visited the place where it was possible to have the vision (of the god). He also made the *pradakṣiṇa* of the mountain. There was the celestial wood famous as the place of Mañjuśrī and the water falling down from that was really running there. He bathed in this water and made the *pradakṣiṇa* of the various places round the top and the neck of the mountain. There are also one hundred mountains with rock-crystal peaks and caves of diamond the height of which cannot be imagined. When one comes to this island all impurities are so to say purified. The people of this island have no Buddhist or non-Buddhist religion nor are they Muhammadan. With the exception of the little ones there are no towns. There is a temple of Buddha which was made in former times. For protecting the boundary of the houses there are many *yantras* made by magical art which do not exist in India. In this island he saw men whose body was covered by their ears. They came

---

1. Groṅ K'yer c'en po lho byaṅ gñis snaṅ ziṅ / de gñis re rei sraṅ bar lam ñi ma bdun tsam re'gro dgos pai lam yod pa / groṅ k'yer gñis kyi par na ri lho byaṅ du gsum tsam zig 'dug pai gcig gi rtse mo na mts 'an mo 'od 'p'ro bai gser gyi brag c'uṅ du zig kyaṅ snaṅ gsuṅ / der lo gcig lhag tsam bzugs śiṅ gliṅ de na slob dpon klu sgrub p' ebs pai bzugs k'ri daṅ bcom ldan 'das kyi rdo sku c'en po maṅ po daṅ lha k'aṅ maṅ du yod/

from other islands."[1] *Jhāmigiri* is one of those adaptations of foreign names to Sanskrit or pseudo-Sanskrit forms which are so common in the geographical terminology of India. If we do not take into consideration the word, *giri*, mountain, which, just as *kūṭa*, generally means a hilly country and cannot therefore be considered as an essential part of the word, the element Jhāmi is left. If we remember the direction of the travel of Buddhagupta and the duration of his navigation we are bound to admit that the place where he landed and was called Jhāmi must be somewhere in the African shore or near to it. The name *Jhāmigiri* points out unmistakably to the country of the Zanj, that is, Zanzibar known, also to Chinese sources as Ts'ong pa, which played a prominent part in the commercial communications of the period with which our source is concerned; but we must not forget that the "country of the Zanj" was generally called the eastern African shore.[2] One may object that even the people of Madagascar are in some Arabian writings referred to under the general designation of Zanj, the common name for "the black people"; but Zanj is nowhere given as the name peculiar to the island as is the case with Zanzibar or Eastern Africa. Moreover the country of Jhāmi is here described as being rather small, its length not exceeding seven days' journey. On the contrary, the next island on the south of Zanzibar where Buddhagupta proceeded and which is described as being very great seems to correspond even in its geographical position with Madagascar. If this identification is, as I think, correct, it will be interesting to note that at the time of

---

1. de nas śar p'yogs kyi gliṅ p'ran 'gar 'gro bai ts' oṅ pa rnams daṅ lhan gcig gru śar draṅ t'aṅ du btaṅ ste/ zla Jcig tsam p'ebs pa na/ rii rgyal po ṭa la ka yod pai gliṅ dup'ebs/ k'a cig 'di po ṭa la c'uṅ ba yin zer ba'ṅ yod/ gaṅ na'ṅ mii 'gro bai spyod yul gyi po ṭa la ste 'di k'o nar mṅon no/ nor bzaṅ gzon nui gnas śel gyi p'ug pa daṅ/ k'ro gñer can mai gnas daṅ/ lha ma yin gyi sgo gser gyi p'ug pa daṅ/ sgrol ma gnas daṅ/ ts'aṅs pa daṅ/ K'yab ajug daṇ dbaṅ c'en poi gnas ri bo raṅ abyuṅ gi lha k'aṅ dari bcas pa re re/ gzan yaṅ mjal du btub pai gnas p'al c'er mjal/ri po ṭa la ñid la'ṅ skor ba zig mdzad/ apags pa ajam dpal gyi gnas su grags pa nam mk'ai ṅos la nugs ts'al daṅ/ de nas abab pai c'u dṅos su abab pa yod de/ de la k'rus kyaṅ mdzad gsuṅ/ po ṭa lai ri c'en poi mgul t'ug par nagas sna ts'ogs 'dug pa bskor bar p'ebs/ rtze mo śel ma rdo rjei brag ri rgya dpaṅs tsam bsam gyis mi k'yab pa yod pa gliṅ dei mi kun la da lta p'yi naṅ kla klo sogs grub mt'u' gaṅ yaṅ med/ mi groṅ yaṅ t'an t'un ma gtogs mi 'dug/sṅon dus bzeṅs pai saṅs rgyas pai lha k'aṅ yod 'jam bu gliṅ na med pa la/ las la grub pai 'k'rul 'k'or maṅ pos k'yim gyi mt 'a' bsruṅ ba 'ba' zig 'dug/ gliṅ 'dir gliṅ gzan nas 'oṅs mi rna bas lus t'ams cad gyog t'ub pa maṅ po gzigs/

2. On Madagascur and its relation to India and Insulindia cf. Gabriel Ferrand *les K'ouen louen et les anciennes navigations,* in Journal Asiatique 1929. cf. also Journal Asiatique 1924, p. 240 and *Enciclopedie de l'Islam,* Madagascar, pp. 64ff.

Buddhagupta, Madagascar was known in India as Potala, though its being considered as the abode of Avalokiteśvara and heard of as a kind of a fairy-land seems to show that the intercourse between that island and India was indirect and very rare. It will not, in this connection, appear out of place to remember that the researches of Ferrand have shown that Indian culture left its traces in Madagascar and that even Sanskrit elements were introduced into Malgash language through the intercourse of sailors and settlers from Java. This means that for some time the island was within the reach, direct or indirect, of Indian culture. It also supposes that some information of the country reached India. It is quite possible that in the course of the centuries Potala as the seat of Avalokiteśvara shifted to this or that place, according to the beliefs of the various communities and the spreading of the geographical knowledge; but we cannot *a priori* exclude that Potala of the Buddhist tradition was originally connected with some real island, even if afterwards the legendary character of the country took the upperhand. In the present case we are not in a position to establish how an island known to India through sailors and semi-Indian colonies turned into the abode of the god. Anyhow we find even in our text mention of some features which in various and independent traditions are connected with Potala and Madagascar at the same time. The rock-crystal cave in the centre of the island may perhaps be connected with the story told to Yuan Chwang by some Ceylonese monks, and according to which some thousand *li* to the west of Ceylon, there was the "great-precious-substance-island" where there is a bright shining mountain; but we have seen that our text knows of a similar mountain in the country of Zanzibar already alluded to. As we saw, Potala is the name of the country, but chiefly of the mountain which is the abode of the god; now according to the Arabic sources in Madagascar there is the famous mountain of Komr which gives the island its name and from which the Nilus was supposed to spring forth. We find the same mention of a holy river running down from Potala in our text as well as in the description of Potala as we read it in Yuan Chwang. The existence of a sacred mountain and a sacred river seems therefore to be intimately connected with Potala, or rather the various Potala. In Potala Buddhagupta embarked again and after a very long navigation he reached Javadvīpa whose name is translated in our text as "the island of the barley" (*nas*). This means that the two places were connected by usual sea-routes and therefore proves once more the proposed identification of Potala of Buddhagupta with Madagascar, because we know the regular intercourse which took place between the two islands through the medium of Malasian sailors. There existed a permanent sea-trading intensified by the Portuguese linking Java, Madagascar and Zanzibar.

In Javadvīpa he found the followers of the Śrāvaka Sendhapa and then he proceeded to a small island in the middle of the sea called Vanadīpa (Baṅka?) where he saw the cave of Padmavajra and found traces of many Tantras. Then he sailed to the north for Ceylon and afterwards to Konkan.

"There is (in Koṅkaṇa) a self-created image of Mañjuśrī in the middle of a pond. It is called Jñānakāya. The measure of the body is like a small hill and it represents the god in the reclining position. Then he saw also the *bimbakāya* which looks like a rainbow raising the stūpa of the accumulated vapour beyond touch," "Then he embarked again and went to the south to Malabar and to a country near to it called Śambhudatta where he heard the Buddha-sancāra-tantra and the Saṃvaravikrīḍita Haridarisaṅgīti and the Sahajatattva from the king Hariprabha (p'rog byed 'od) who had forded the ocean of the Vajrayāna and possessed all of the vidyās of the usual *siddhas*."[1] He met again his gurus since he wanted the *abhiṣeka* in some other Tantric systems, but as money was required for that, he undertook a collecting tour in Triliṅga, Trimalla and Karṇāṭaka, gathering a good amount of donations.

"Then he stated again with the purpose of visiting the small islands of the east; so through Jārikhaṇḍa and Jagannātha he went to Khasarpana in Buntavarta (sic) where he spent in prayer about twenty days . . . Then he went to Tipura and to the highland of Tipura where there is Kasaraṅga or Devīkoṭa. For some days he remained in the temple erected by the Mahāsiddha Kṛṣṇācārya. Thence he proceeded to Ra k'an and to its places Haribhañja, Bu k'an and Bal gu. In all these countries there is a great community of monks and the Buddhist teaching is widely spread. He stopped there for a long time and heard many treatises of the sūtra class and as far as possible

---

1. de nu koṅka nai gliṅ du p'ebs te/ dzṅa na kāya zes bye ba mts'oi naṅ na 'jam dpal gyi sku raṅ 'byuṅ sku ts'ad ri c'uṅ tsam yod po ñal stabs su gnas pa daṅ/ bimba kā ya zes bya ba nam mk'a' la 'ja' ts' on śar ba lta bu mc' od rten gyi gzugs brñan śin tu c'e ba ziṅ gsal ba dpal du ba 'k'rigs pa reg pa med pai mc'od rten du grags pa de yin te/ . . . slar gru btaṅ nas lho p'yogs su ma lyār p'ebs 'di daṅ ñe bai yul p'ran śam bhu datta zes bya ba ni rdo rje t'eg pa rgya mts'o p'a rol soṅ ba/ t'un moṅ gi grub pai rtags ci rigs pa daṅ ldan pai rgyal po p'rog byed 'od zes bya ba la saṅs rgyas mñan 'byor gyi rgyud daṅ sdom pa rnam par rtsen pa/ daṅ lhan gcig skges pai de ñid daṅ hari darii glu dbyaṅs la sogs pa c'os maṅ du gsan/

the law of the secret mantras from paṇḍita Dharmākṣaghoṣa of the big stūpas in the temple of Haribhañja and equally from the lay paṇḍit Parhetanandaghoṣa in the country of Bal gu. Those gurus were the followers of the Mahāsiddha Śāntipāda. Then he embarked again and went to the island of Dhanaśrī. In this island also there are very many monks. There is a great stūpa of immense proportion which is called Śrīmad-dhanyakaṭaka or the stūpa with the offering or *astukakāya*. Its basement has the same shape as the stūpa itself, it is surrounded by two rails in stone. It takes about one day for its *pradakṣiṇa*. On the east there is a very big town where there is enormous assemblage of merchants coming from different countries such as China, Europe (p'ren gi) and India. When he visited the *asparśa pratibimbastūpa* he saw the maṇḍala of the five kulas with Vairocana as their central essence, in the Jñāna-kāyastūpa the maṇḍala of the five *kulas* with Amitābha as the central essence, and in Śrīmad-dhanyakaṭaka the maṇḍala of the five *kulas* with Akṣobhya as the central essence. Then together with some merchants he visited some very small islands such as another island in the middle of the sea called Potala, the island Paigu, an island occupied by the Europeans in which many medicinal herbs such as *jāti* and *lesi* are produced. Sadhadīpa the great Suvarṇadvīpa, the small Suvarṇadvīpa, Sūryadvīpa, Candradvīpa, Sarvadvīpa."[1] Sāgara-dvīpa is further

---

1. de na (read de nas) sar po'yogs kyi gliṅ p'ran rnams gzigs par bzeṅ nas dsā ri k'anta daṅ dsa gaṅ nā tha rgyud nas bhaṅga lar p'ebs/ yul bu ṇṭa bharta ru k'a sarba na mjal/ zag ñi śu tsam gsol la adebs kyin zugs/ . . . de nas Ti pu rar p'ebs/ ti pu rai yul gyi p'u ka sa ram ga'm devi koṭai gnas yod pa mjal bar mdzad ciṅ/ grub c'en po spyod pas bzaṅs pai gtsug lag k'aṅ du zag śas bzugs/ de nas ra k'aṅ gi yul gyi naṅ mts'an ha ri paṅja daṅ bu k'an daṅ sal gu rnams su p'ebs/ yul

'di rnams na dge sloṅ gi dge 'dun c'es maṅ ziṅ/ bstan pa lhag par dar ba yod pas/ yun riṅ rab re bzugs siṅ/ ha ri bhañ jai gtsug lag k'aṅ mc'od rten c'en po zes bya ba zig nas dharmā kśa gho śa zes bya bai paṇḍita c'en po zig daṅ de bzin du bal gui yul du bzugs pai par he ta nanda gho śa zes bya ba dge sñen paṇḍita c'en po zig la gsaṅ sṅags kyi c'os kyaṅ ci rigs pa gsan mdo lugs kyi gzun maṅ po zon ñan du mdad bla ma 'di kun yaṅ grub c'en bzi bai zabs kyi slob ma 'ba' zig yin gsuṅ de nas gru btaṅ ste dha nṅ śrī gliṅ du p'ebs gliṅ 'di na'n dge 'dun śiṅ du maṅ si zin dpal dan abras spuṅ ṅam mc'od rten dpal yon can zes kyaṅ bya ast ka kā ya zes bya ba mc'od rten c'en po ṅo bo śin tu rgya k'yon c'e bai brag ri mc'od rten gyi dbyibs can/ p'yi la rdo yi leags ri brag ri adra ba ñis rim kyis bskor ba/ ñi ma goig la bskor ba t'ebs tsam/ śar du groṅ k'yer śin tu c'e ba/ rgya nag daṅ p'reṅ gi daṅ rgya gar la sogs pai yul t'a dad pai ts'oṅ pa śin to maṅ bai ts'oṅ 'dus c'en po 'dug gsuṅ/ daṅ po rig pa med pa gzugs brñan gyi mc'od rten mjal bar mdsad dus/ rnam sṅaṅ gtso bor gyur bai rigs lnai dkyil 'k'or daṅ dsa na kā ya ni 'od dpag med gtso bor gyur pai rigs lnai nkyil 'k'or daṅ srī dha nya kaṭaka ni mi bskyod pa gtso bor byas pai rgyal ba rigs lṅai dkyil 'k'or du gzigs/ gzan yaṅ tśoṅ pa rnams daṅ lhan cig tu byon pas/ po ṭa la zer bai rgya

mentioned in connection with the younger Kṛṣṇācārya Bhubaripa and Bhubamati (bhu ba blo-ldan). We find him again in India studying Vajrayāna at the school of various Siddhas such as Gambhīmati, Ghanatapā, Siddhigarbha, Betatikṣaṇa, Vīrabandha, Gaṅgāpā. After having spent some time in Bodh-Gaya, Banda (bam dva) where he met the king Kumārapālabhadra, and Prayāga where he saw the great yogin Śubharakṣita, he proceeded to Jagannātha, Tipura and Bhīmeśvara. "He went again to Bhaṅgala or Tipura and Ra k'an and he spent in Assam (Kāmarūpa) about one year.

Afterwards he proceeded to Tibet and went to Lhasa passing through the monastery of bSam yas; then he visited the province of gTsan where he met Tāranātha. Having explained to him various Tantric texts and rituals, he took leave from his pupil and returned back to India passing via Kirong (skyid groṅ) on the Nepalese Himalayan range. From Nepal he came down to Bhanśyaya (Bhainsi-duhan near Bhinyashedi) in Champaram (Bettiah, tsam bā ra ṇa), the hill Khagendra and then through Magadha to Bengal and Tipura. While Tāranātha was writing his biography he heard that his guru was still living in Devīkoṭa or in some other place near it.

These long travels towards the east are not less important than the previous ones in so far as they not only show a strong survival of Mahāyāna Buddhism but also seem to indicate that the sea-relations with Insulindia were at the time of Buddhagupta not yet interrupted.

We can quite easily follow the itinerary of the Indian *sādhu* from South India to Orissa where Jārikhaṇḍa or Jarākhaṇḍa and Jagannātha are located. Buntavarta is evidently a corruptiou for Puṇḍra-vardhana corresponding to the districts of Bogra and Rājshahi. Khasarpaṇa cannot be exactly located, but its name seems to suggest that it is a high mountain. In fact Khasarpaṇa is known also to Tāranātha who takes it to be the seat of Avalokiteśvara but locates it in South India perhaps wrongly identifying it with Potalaka. The fact that Puṇḍravardhana indicates the country bordering on the sub-Himalayan range seems to point out that Khasarpaṇa was a general designation for the mountains bordering on the north Bengal. The identification of Tipura with Tipperah is self-evident. Kasaraṅga betrays in its Sanskrit form the name of the Khasi tribes populating the Khasi hills. Devīkoṭa is the temple of Kāmākhyā near Gauhāṭī

---

mts'oi rdo ri gzan cig daṅ pai gui gliṅ daṅ ja ti daṅ le śi sogs maṅ po skye ba p'ien gis adsin pai gliṅ zig daṅ sādha dhī pa daṅ gser gliṅ c'en po daṅ gser gliṅ gi min can c'uṅ ba gñis surjadhipa candradhīpa sarvadhīpa.

one of the greatest centres of Tantrism in India usually included among the four foremost pīṭhas and connected in the Buddhist tradition with the Mahāsiddha Kṛṣṇācārya. Buddhist images on the road leading to the temple are visible up to now.

Ra k'an is, as known, the general designation for Burma while Haribhañja is evidently a corruption for Haripuñjaya, north of Menam near Lamphūn, Bu k'an, which can also be Pu k'an (because in the manuscript at my disposal the two letters are often interchanged). Pu k'an corresponds to Pagan, Pukam, in the Cam inscriptions, P'u kan of the Chinese travellers and writers. It is at the same time the name of a district and of a town, the ruins of which are still to be seen on the left side of Irrawaddy. Bal gu, or Pal gu is Pegu in Burma. The information which Buddhagupta gives about Burmese Buddhism is of some interest because it is a new proof that even after the conversion of King Anuruddha of Pagan, the conqueror of Pegu, Mahāyāna flourished for long time in Pagaṇ.

Dhanaśrī corresponds to Tenasserim, Dahnasari of the Āin-i-Ākbarī. It belonged, as is known, to Siam up to the middle of the XVIIIth century and it was one of the most important trade centres in the Far East. It had a Protuguese settlement till 1641.[1] The name of the pagoda or stūpa which was seen by Buddhagupta near the town, is worthy of notice; in fact Śrīdhānyakaṭaka was the name, as it is known, of a famous Buddhist place in Orissa which was held in a very high estimation by Mahāyana schools. It was after that place that one of the most famous monasteries of Tibet was called, I mean the dPal ldan ḥbras spuṅs (Mt. Debung) near Lhasa. On the other side modern research seems to show that the influence of Orissa was specially felt in Siam. Nor is it out of place to notice that even our text points out the existence of a land route connecting Kāmarūpa or northern Assam with Burma. Unfortunately we find no mention as regards the itinerary followed by Buddhagupta from Gauhāṭī to

---

1. *p'ren gi*=later Sanskrit: *phiraṅga*, Hindī : *pharaṅgī* is not given in our dictionaries (the usual forms being *p'e ran, p'i lin, p'a raṅ, p'o raṅ*, on which see Laufer, *Loan words in Tibetan* n. 141). Its mention here has some importance in so far as it seems to us that the form was probably introduced into Tibet from India rather than from Persia. As regards the form *p'i liṅ*, which is now very common in Tibetan for "foreign country" or "Europe," I fully agree with Laufer that it cannot be considered as the popular pronunciation of *p'yi gliṅ*, but it is quite possible that it took the place of the original *p'reṅ gi* under the influence of that form. *P'vi gliṅ pa* is not only a foreigner but also is opposed to *naṅ pa*, "the man of the inside" "the believer," it implies therefore not only a geographical difference but also a spiritual demarcation. Cf, in Chinese Buddhist texts *nei* and *wei*.

Pagan, but it seems to me that the road must have passed between the Mikir and the Jaintia hills and then reached Upper Burma through Manipur. This appears to have been the shortest and the safest since it avoided the violent rivers of the Lushai hills and the head-hunting tribes of the Nāgās. Of the remaining islands only Suvarṇadvīpa may be identified with Sumatra though the problems connected with this identification are complicated by the fact that Buddhagupta knows two Suvarṇadvīpas, a small one and a big one. The mention of bSam yas is interesting in so far as it shows that Buddhagupta went into Tibet *via* Bhutān. This is suggested by the previous mention of Assam and by our knowledge of the roads between Tibet and India. It is generally believed that the usual intercourse between these two countries took place along the route, Darjeeling (rdo rje gling) and Gyantze (rgyan tshe). But this is wrong. This route is a new one as it was regularly opened in quite recent times and acquired its importance after the last Anglo-Tibetan war. But in former times there is no mention of it. There are good reasons for its being unknown in older texts. This road passes through Sikkim, and this country, populated chiefly by Lepchas, was converted to Buddhism by Lha brtsum c'enpo in the XVIIth century. The wild people of the country, the thick jungle which covered the hills and the absence of any Buddhist centre are the main reasons why the Sikkimmese road, though the shortest, was not used up to the end of the XVIIth century when Buddhism was firmly established in the country In former times the usual route of the Indian paṇḍits to Tibet or of the Tibetan locāvas to India was through Nepal (Kirong and Kuti) where Marpa, Ras ḥbyun, Rva locāva travelled or through the Sutlej and Kulu as in the case of Ur gyan pa and Stag gtsan ras pa. Eventually even the Ladak route through the Zojila was followed, though, it appears to me, not so common as the other routes. But in all *rnam thars* and other Tibetan sources accessible to me no mention whatever is to be found of the Sikkimese route. On the other hand, the fact, that in our text mention of bSam yas is made, excludes the probability that Buddhagupta went into Tibet *via* Nepal, that is, along the route which he followed when coming back to India as it is expressly stated in our text. If he had gone to Lha sa by this way he could not have reached bSam yas without deviating from his road, since we know that bSam yas is on the road to Bhutan, a country very early converted to Buddhism and a great centre of Tibetan learning. It was in fact there that one of the most important branches of the Bkaḥ ḥgyur ba sects, that of the ḥBrug pa, had its origin and wide diffusion. Anyhow, as stated before, the mention of Assam without referring to any further movement of Buddhagupta to other places makes us believe that he started just from there. We know that there was such a route from Bhutan to Assam through Devaṅgiri and that this route was largely followed by the Tibetans coming down to India to visit the place of the Mahāparinirvāṇa of Buddha. It is in fact well established that according to some Tibetan traditions, accepted also by the author of the *Śam bḥa laḥi lam yig* (but the origin of which we are not yet in a position to trace), Kuśinagara was in Assam. The place seems to be, as pointed out by Waddel, the village Salkusa some nine miles north-west from Gauhāṭī on the northern bank of the Brahmaputra. Unfortunately no mention of Kuśinagara is in our text, so we cannot say whether the location of Kuśinagara, the place of the Mahāparinirvāṇa, in Assam was current among the Indian Buddhists of the 16th century.

# Chapter - 26

# India's oversea Trade as Known from the Buddhist Canons

**Madan Mohan Singh**

There are some references in the Buddhist literature to show that people of Northern India, specially of the eastern region were interested in maritime activities and that they sailed to foreign lands for transacting business. Illustrations cited by the Buddha whose activities were mainly confined to Eastern Uttar Pradesh and Bihar, of sailing on the ocean for six months,[1] going to the ocean with direction-showing birds (*disākāka*),[2] merchants crossing the ocean[3] and so on would suggest that the people of the Buddha's time were acquainted with sea-faring. When the *Theragāthā* speaks of merchants sailing on the sea with the hope of earning wealth,[4] and when the popular stories tell us of ship-wrecks,[5] spacious ships,[6] ship-building activities,[7] and of sea-farers from Vārāṇasī, Videha and Campā sailing to foreign lands like Suvaṇṇadīpa[8] and Tambapaṇṇi and so on, they furnish us with the evidence of oversea trade. The description in the Ceylonese chronicles of prince Vijaya's voyage to Ceylon from Bengal with his 700 followers[8] presupposes a regular sea-trade and intercourse. It is true that Baudhāyana[9] and Manu[10] place the profession of sea-faring under prohibited practices, but the former's own statement that navigation was peculiar to the people of the North[11]

---

1. *SN.*, III, 155; V. 51; *AN.*, IV. 127.
2. *DN.*, I. 222.
3. *DN.*, II. 89.
4. Theragāthā, 530.
5. *Jātaka,* III. 127-29; V. 75.
6. *Jātaka*, Nos. 466, 539.
7. *Jāatka*, IV, 159; VI. 427.
8. *Dīpavaṃsa*, IX. 10-28; *Mahāvaṃsa*, VI.
9. *Bau. Dh. S.*, II. 1 41.
10. *Manu.*, III. 158.
11. *Bau, Dh. S.*, I. 1. 20.

shows that it was not given up. According to the Law-Givers, as sea-faring was taken up mainly by the Vaiśya community, it was not recommended for the Brāhmaṇas. It was probably the uncertainty of life and low estimation of the career from the orthodox point of view that some of the Dharmaśāstra writers prohibited the Brāhmaṇa community from resorting to sea-faring. But when we refer to the Sūtras of Pāṇini, the mention of various terms connected with navigation leave no doubt as regards the practice of sea-faring during this period.[1] Pāṇini refers to *samudra* (ocean)[2] and two kinds of islands, viz., near the sea-coast (*anusamudra*) and in the main ocean. Goods imported from the former type of islands are called *dvaipya*; whereas those from the latter *dvaipa* or *dvaipaka*.[3] Boat-ferry is called *nāvya*.[4] Merchants are valued in terms of the number of ship-loads of merchandise possessed by them, such as *dvināva-dhana* (one having two cargo-boats) or *pañcanāvapriya* (one sailing with five ship-loads)[5] and the like.

The merchants are also referred to as either owning the whole cargo-boat or sharing a part of its merchandise.[6] Pāṇini further makes mention of various types of boats, e.g. *Utsaṅga*,[7] *Udūpa* (*ḍongī*, it is described as shaped like the half-moon), *Utpate* (probably a longish fishing boat) and *Piṭaka* (a basket like cavacle).[8] The *Arthaśāstra* of Kauṭilya makes it quite clear that during the days of Candragupta Maurya, Indian navigation was in an advanced stage. The state had instituted an officer known as the *nāvadhyakṣa* as the Superintendent of ships.[9] We can assume that Pāṭaliputra was a great centre of navigation in Northern India during the Pre-Mauryan and Mauryan period.

Our sources reveal that sea-faring was well developed and proper training was given in the science of navigation, which was

---

1. Agrawala: *India as known to Pāṇini*, pp. 155-56.
2. *Pāṇini*, IV. 4. 118.
3. *Pāṇinī*, IV. 3. 10.
4. *Pāṇini*, IV. 4. 9.
5. Agrawala: India as known to *Pāṇini*, p. 155.
6. *Ibid.*, p. 156.
7. *Ibid.*, There is also reference to Bhastra (raft of inflated skins), and Bharata (float of wood). The former is used in Punjab, N.W.F.P. and Afghanistan.
8. *Pāṇini*, IV. 4. 15. It was originally made out of the hollow of a tree. It is known as *Dhang* in Sindh and was similar to Roman *Cumba*, (*India as known to Pāṇini*, p. 156). The boatmen of Chotanagpur construct their *dongis* by carving the hollow of a tree; they are unfamiliar with the practice of making boat as in the north. It seems that *Pāṇini* refers to such boats which must have been used for crossing small rivers, as is the case in Chotanagpur today.
9. *Kau.*, II. 28.

known as the *niyāmakasippa.*[1] We do not know exactly the nature of training imparted to the young sea-farers. Probably the mariners were trained in the knowledge of various trade-routes, directions of winds, how to train and utilise the *disākākas*, how to escape ship-wrecks and so on. While sailing on the waters, birds were of great help for the navigators. In every ship the mariners kept a direction-guiding-crow (*disākāka*), or other bird (*tīradassī sakuna*),[2] which would fly to the coast, if there was any visible, otherwise it would come back to the ship. Thus they were enabled to know if they were sailing near a land, or were still in a region where there was no trace of it. It seems that accomplished mariners had to possess a thorough knowledge of training and utilising birds for the purpose of knowing directions. Ship-wrecks were quite common and probably instructions were given how to escape from such accidents. Sea-trade was always precarious and life was never secure. Parents dissuaded their sons to take up this career. But the attraction of the adventure and thrill of navigation impelled many to choose this career.

The mariners (*niyāmakas*) had organised themselves into guilds, the head of which was known as the *niyāmakajeṭṭhaka.* The term *jeṭṭ-haka* was used to denote the head or the Alderman of a guild, and almost all the crafts of this period had formed their guilds, under their respective *jeṭṭhakas*. Probably the *niyāmakajeṭṭhaka* was the captain, the owner of the ship and the leader of the traders travelling with him. Decidedly, his responsibilities were heavy, as the lives of his fellow travellers might not be saved, if due to his negligence the ship lost its route.

The *Jātaka* stories tell us that traders from ports on the Gaṅgā sailed to the eastern lands. The *Saṅkha Jātaka* describes the journey of the Brāhmaṇa Saṅkha from Vārāṇasī to Suvaṇṇabhūmi[3] (Burma and portions of Indo-Chinese Peninsula). The *Sīlānisaṃsa Jātaka* refers to a sea-faring nymph as bringing ship-wrecked people to Vārāṇasī from the far off sea.[4] References are made to voyages from Videha to Suvaṇṇabhūmi. King Mahājanaka is said to have travelled in a ship with 700 caravans and reached there.[5] Campā to Suvaṇṇabhūmi voyage was quite common.[6] Traders from Vaiśālī and

1. *Jātaka*, IV. 137.
2. *D.N*, 1. 222; *Jātaka*, III. 126, 267.
3. *Jātaka*, IV. 15. 17.
4. *Jātaka*, II. 112.
5. *Jātaka* No. 539.
6. *Jātaka*, VI. 34.

the Arakan.[1] The *Valāhassa Jātaka* speaks of trade between Vārāṇasī and Tamba-paṇṇidīpa.[2] All these suggest that vessels from the ports on the Gaṅgā sailed to lands beyond the Bay of Bengal. The vessels starting from Vārāṇasī must have been anchoring at Pāṭaliputra and Campā, both being important river ports. At these ports traders most probably bartered their goods, loaded their vessels with local products and then proceeded further to the foreign market. It is not unlikely that traders from Pāṭaliputra and Campā sailed for the eastern lands with their ships carrying locally manufactured goods. These cities must have been busy centres of trade and commerce. Though only Suvaṇṇabhūmi and Tambapaṇṇidīpa are mentioned, it can be assumed that trade was carried on with all the islands of the East Indies. The *Mahāniddesa* tells us that India's trade to the east existed with Kālamukha, Suvaṇṇabhūmi, Vessuṅga, Verāpatha, Takkola, Tamali, Tambapaṇṇi and Java. First two of these places can be identified with Arakan coast and lower Burma.[3] Next three correspond to Ptolemy's Besyngeitai, Borbai, and Takkala.[4] Tamali has been identified by Sylvain Levi with Tāmralinga in the Malaya Peninsula.[5] The *Apadāna* states that traders from Malaya and China visited India.[6]

Thus we find that from the sea-ports on the Gaṅgā, traders of the eastern regions of India went to the eastern lands across the sea. During the earlier period Campā and Vārāṇasī were the most important ports, but when Pāṭaliputra rose to imperial status, it became the biggest and the most busy centre of trade in Eastern India.

The *Baveru Jātaka* speaks of trade with *Baveruraṭṭha*,[7] a birdless country, which appears to be Babylonia. There are evidences both foreign and indigenous to establish India's trade relation with Babylonia and the countries on the Mediterranean during the 6th

---

1. Vaiśālī was the name of a famous city in Arakan, and according to local chronicles it was built in 789 A.D. by a king of the Candra dynasty. Eor two centuries the city retained its position as a strong hold of Indian culture, specially Buddhism. At present it is a small village of 80 houses. Its relation with Vaiśālī is difficult to ascertain, but Burmese tradition is acquainted with Indian Vaiśālī and shows that Burmese people had great respect for Vaiśālī. (R.C. Majumdar in *Vaiśāli Abhinandan Grantha*, pp. 43-44).
2. *Jātaka*, II. 127-29.
3. R.C. Majumdar: *Suvaṇṇadvīpa*, p. 57; S. Levi: *Ētudes Asiatiques*, vol. II. Ch. II.
4. B.C. Law: *India as described in Early Texts of Buddhism and Jainism*, p. 188.
5. *Ibid.*
6. *Apadāna*, I. p. 2.
7. *Jātaka*, III. 126; Buhler: *Origin of Indian Alphabet*, p. 84.

cen. B.C.[1] Mr. Kennedy who worked on this subject concluded that 'maritime commerce between India and Babylonia flourished in the 7th and the 6th, but more specially in the 6th century B.C.[2] Another scholar Mr. A.M.T. Jackson writing on India's ancient trade has observed that the Buddhist *Jātakas* and some of the Sanskrit Law Books tell us that ships from Broach and Supārā traded with Babylonia from the 8th to the 6th century B.C.[3] The *Suppāraka Jātaka* says that a band of travellers sailed from the port of Bharukaccha and passed through six seas under the leadership of a blind, but skilled mariner.[4] The seas thus mentioned are the Khuramāla, the Aggimāla, the Dadhimāla, the Nīlakusamāla, the Nalamāla, and the Valabhamukha.[5] These seas have been identified with the Persian gulf, the Arabian coast, Nubia on the North-East corner of Africa, the canal joining the Red sea and the Mediterranean.[6] If this identification be correct, it can be established that Indians possessed the knowledge of a sea-route from the Western coast to the Mediterranean. During the 5th cen. B.C. certain Indian commodities, e.g. rice, sandalwood, and peacocks were known by Indian names to the Greeks and others.[7] It cannot be denied at the present knowledge of the subject that during this period Indians traded with the countries on the Mediterranean. This trade was probably not shared by the people of Eastern India; because in that case traders from the east would have to travel through land upto Bharukaccha or Suppāraka for sailing to the West. There are references of caravans regularly going to the port of Bharukaccha from the trade centres of the east. Hence, it is very likely that traders from the prosperous trade centres of Eastern India used to travel with their caravans upto the port of Bharukaccha, so that their merchandise might be exported for being sold in the markets of the foreign lands which had trade relations with India through her sea-ports on the Western Coast.

1. R.K. Mukherjee: *Indian Shipping*, Chap. I.
2. *JRAS.*, 1898.
3. Jackson, quoted by Mukherjee, *Indian Shipping*, p. 90.
4. *Jātaka*, IV. 138-43.
5. *Ibid.*
6. *JBORS.*, VI, 195 (Dr. Jayaswal's Article); Mukherjee: *Indian Shipping*, Chap. I; R.L. Mehta, *Pre-Buddhist India*, p. 228.
7. Mukherjee, *Indian Shipping*, p. 88.

# Chapter - 27

# Pre-Buddhistic Rajgīr

**Adris Banerji**

Rājagṛha, vulgo made it Rajgir, has immemorial traditions behind it. The wind which every day bellows through the gorge made between the Vaibhāra and Vipula, seems to pass through the empty corridors of dead memories, which mute stones, the silent spectators to the most gorgeous pageantries of Indian history, have no means to testify. Countless centuries ago, kingdoms and empires had raised themselves over its dust hoary with age, to disappear into eternity, leaving no trace behind, which we their descendants, would give so much to resurrect. It raises its head, from a misty unknown past, when primitive man first inhabited the secluded valley, girt by five picturesque hills; and oriental mysticism gave it a sacred colour, which repeated conquests, mass conversion, pillage, loot and plunder, have never been able to snatch away from it. The animists, the Vedic-Brahminism, Jainism, Hinduism and Buddhism have all given it their stamp of approval. Its eternal hot springs bubbling out its healing waters are gifts of mother earth to the suffering humanity. The later accretions have enveloped its principal charms, its primitive faith, arts, crafts and culture, in obscurity.

It had received dozens of names in different epochs of our national history. According to the *Mañjuśrī-mūla-kalpa*, (Kalpa lxii) and Jina-prabhā Surī's *Tīrthakalpa* (Vaibhāragiri-Kalpa, v. 4) its earlist name was Kuśāgrapura 'the city of the fragrant reed grass,' so sacred to modern Hindus, which survived till the time of Hiuen-Tsang.[1] Its another name was Girivraja, which is explained by the *Mahābhārata* and *Suttanipāta* as being situated within five hills.[2] The other names

---

1. *Yuan Chwang*, vol. ii, p. 149.
2. *Mbh. Sabhāparvan*, xxi, viii; *Suttanipāta*, vol. ii, p. 82; *Sāratthapakāsini* vol. ii, p. 159.

were Caṇakapura, Ṛṣabhapura, Vasumatī, Bṛhadrathapura. The name Rājagaha of Pali and Rājagṛha of Sanskrit literature is explained as being the abode of mythical kings like Māndhātā etc., as well as the place having been used as a prison house of conquered kings, according to the *Sumaṅgala Vilāsinī* by Buddhaghosa,[1] which is re-echoed by the tradition recorded in the *Bhāgavat Purāṇa* (X. 7). Our first peep into the primitive religious condition of this ancient metropolis of eastern India is received from the *Mahābhārata*, where two Nāgas, Maṇi and Svastikā, are mentioned, testifying that worship of the serpents was a feature of the religious practices of the citizens of Rajgir. The worship of the Serpents, a non-Aryan ritual, was incorporated in later Brāhmaṇical pantheon, and became a widely prevalent practice in eastern India and middle country. Originally, the snake itself or its replicas in wood, stone, ivory; or modelled or moulded in clay were worshipped, to propitiate this wriggling death-god. Gradually, myths and legends grew around snakes and ultimately, they were given anthropomorphic form, the survival of which is to be found in Hindu 'Manasā' and later Buddhist 'Jāṅgulī'. A race of people called the Nāgas inhabited a populous area in the modern Basti district, whom a king of Kośala is said to have exterminated.[2] The identity of Rāmagrāma remains a moot point; but probably the extensive remains in the neighbourhood of Bhuila Dih in Basti represents the ruins of the city. Hiuen-Tsang tells us of a fable, that on visiting Rāmagrāma, he was told of *kinnaras*, wild animals worshipping the deserted *stūpa* containing Buddha's relics.[3] The story is indeed of ancient origin, as an architrave of buff sandstone of Chunar, found in the excavations of Sarnath, represent the worship of the relic *stūpa* at Rāmagrāma by an wild elephant, *kinnara* etc. That it was the *stūpa* erected by the Nāgas at Rāmagrāma is proved by the snakes carved on the body of the *stūpa*. The piece belongs to *circa* 1st century B.C. Since the story is found depicted in such an early fragment, it is evident that Hiuen Tsang's account (c. 600-664 A.D.) has an earlier origin.[4]

## Snake-worship

The worship of snakes is even now prevalent in the peninsular India. In anthropomorphic form, it is worshipped in eastern Pakistan,

1. Vol. i, p. 232.
2. *DN.*, ii. 165; *Jāt.*, iv. 144; *Dhp. comm.* i. 344.
3. *Yuan Chwang*, vol. ii, p. 20.
4. D.R. Sahni, *Catalogue of Museum of Archæology*, Sarnath, p. 200, pl. xxiii.

West Bengal, Orissa and Bihar, while a celebration called Nāga *Pañcamī* is held annually in U.P. A relief of Manasā of about c. 600 A.D. has been found in the excavations at Sarnath. Maṇi Nāga, we learn from a verse in the *Mahābhārata* (2. xix. 9ff.)[1] used to reside on one of the peaks surrounding Girivraja, and was worshipped in the Magadha country to induce rain in the draught years. The location of the ancient temple of Maṇi Nāga has been made easier by the finds made in the ruins of Maniyāra *maṭha*, more correctly written as Maṇivāra *maṭha* situated almost at the centre of the old city. The place was first excavated by Mr. A.M. Broadley then S.D.O., Bihar sub division.[2] Almost a decade later it was dug by the late Theodore Bloch, in the working season of 1905-06, when the whole Rajgir valley was surveyed by Sir John Marshall. Bloch found a deserted Jaina shrine, on the top of what had then formed into a conical mound. Dismantling it, he found traces of snake worship at the site as late as V.S. 1547 (1490-91 A.D.). The excavations at the lower levels revealed the existence of a structural complex, with a hollow tower as the *piece d'resistance*. The outer wall of the hollow *stūpa* was decorated with a series of stucco figurines, within niches, and the style recalled the perfect poise in calm repose, remarkable for balance, the characteristic features of the Gupta art at its climax and having analogy with the Benares school of sculptures. None of these figures by any stretch of imagination can be regarded as Buddhistic, but Brāhmaṇical; a fact, which is often lost sight of, in hasty generalisations about the religious character of the site.[3]

Till Gupta times therefore, there are enough evidences to believe that the hollow circular *stūpa* at Maṇivāta *maṭha*, in Rajgir, was connected with snake worship, a primitive belief of the earliest inhabitants of Rajgir, inspite of ceaseless assaults by Brahmanism, Jainism and Buddhism. Brāhmaṇical and Jaina ritual, as evident from Śālibhadra *caraṇa* had adopted this alien cult into their pantheon. The cult of the *stūpa* was not original to Buddhism. In *Mahāparinibbāna-sutta* Gautama gives good ground for believing that in his time such monuments were raised over the mortal remains of *rāja-cakravartins*. The Buddhists added to it a new scope by making it a commemorative structure. The Jainas too erected *stūpas*, as is evident

1. I am indebted for this reference to Mr. M.V. Vaidya of the Bhandarkar Oriental Research Institute, Poona. According to him Adi. I. xxxi. also mention Maṇi Nāga.
2. A.M. Broadley, *The Antiquities of Bihar, in Patna,* Calcutta, 1872. p. 20.
3. *ARASI.*, 1905-06, p. 104, plates xxxix-xl.

from the *disjecta membra* found in the Kankali Tila, at Mathura. The *Śatapatha Brāhmaṇa* refers to *tumulis* or mounds of earth raised by members of the Brāhmaṇical faith.[1] It is rational therefore to conclude that the hollow *stūpa* decorated with beautiful stucco sculptures, within the amphitheatre of Girivraja, was neither a Buddhist *stūpa* nor a Hindu phallus, but represented the temple of Maṇi Nāga which vulgo had transformed from Maṇivāra *maṭha* to Maniyāta *maṭha*.[2] Later tradition converted the hollow *stūpa* into an well, in which were hidden the wealth of a mythical king. Maṇi Nāga the rain inducing divinity of primitive Rajgir was transformed into Manikāra, the fictitious treasurer of a mythical hoard of treasure, deposited by an imaginary king, which still survives in popular memory to our day, and enthusiastic sub-ordinates of our department some time point to the Son-Bhandar Cave, dedicated and utilised by the Jains, and decorated with the figures of their *tīrthaṅkaras* as the alleged treasure house.

Further excavations at this place in 1935-36, yielded valuable materials. The spade this time was carried to a depth of 12' below the circular structure. This year's work established that the hollow *stūpa* was erected in Gupta times on two earlier buildings which had no intervening layers of debris between them. The lowest structure has been assigned to the century preceding the birth of Christ, in view of the size of bricks found in the building. But my studies carried out at the instance of Dr. R.E. Mortimer Wheeler, and painstaking investigation carried out by Mr. A. Ghosh, at Arikamedu, a place in the neighbourhood of Pondicherry, have established that the size of bricks is no sure criterion for their antiquity.[3] According to the excavator, a large assortment of pottery was found in this enclosure. Most of these were spouted. One specimen contained about thirty four spouts, in shape of snake hoods, sieves, etc.[4] In another type of vessel, lamps were fixed. All the pottery was hand made, but dabbers were used. The other finds of clay, make the character of the site, as well as the ritual connected with it, very clear, being hoods of snake, etc. The utility of the offertory vessels was correctly interpreted by Mr. G.C. Chandra; "vessels with multiple channels

1. *Śat. Brāh. S.B.E.*, vol. xli pp. 423-24.
2. A. Ghosh, *A Guide to Rajgir*, p. 16. An inscribed image of Maṇināga with a companion who is probably Svastikā Nāga has been found at Maṇivāra *maṭha*.
3. *Ancient India*, No. 2, pp. 18-124.
4. *ARASI.*, 1935-36, plate xvi, (d).

simulating showers were used by the distressed people of Rajgir, praying for rain."[1]

## Cult of Yakṣas

The cult of the *yakṣas* was an important trait of the culture of Rajgir people in early times. This belief in inherent in Pre-Aryan customs, for whom the Brāhmaṇical religion made place of an inferior order. The late Dr. A.K. Coomaraswamy, late Raibahadur R. Chanda and Dr. V.S. Agrawall have studied the question thoroughly. The large colossai, remarkable for volume and mass, found at Patna (now in the Indian Museum, Calcutta), Besnagar, Mathura, Gwalior etc. amply testify to the popularity of this cult throughout eastern India and Brahmāvartta.[2] At Rajgir, the *Saṁyutta Nikāya* tells us, there was a *yakṣa* named Sivaka or Sivāka who was the guardian of Sītavana, often mentioned in the Buddhist religious literature. He was alleged to have been endowed with supernatural powers and was capable of producing supernatural phenomena.[3] Indaka or Indraka was another *yakṣa* who dwelt on a peak called Indrakūṭa.[4] Sakka or Śakra was a *yakṣa* of Gṛdhakuṭa hill.[5] The Vipula mountain was the dwelling place of another powerful *yakṣa* named Kumbhīra or Gambhīra.[6]

## Customs of the Dead

The name of Sītavana is very familiar to the students of Indian history. But it has seldom been realised that it possessed a unique character. The Siamese edition of the *Sāraṭṭhapakāsinī* as pointed out by Dr. B.C. Law, makes it *susāsanavana*, or the grove, which was utilised to throw human bodies after death, to undergo natural processes of decomposition, decay and to be eaten up by worms, dogs, birds, and other animals. The custom of cremation is indeed very ancient in India, but Harappa has supplied us two cemetries establishing the custom of burial in chalcolithic India. But the practice of the ancient people of Rajgir has no parallel except with the Zoroastrians of Iran, which is even now observed by the Parsis in modern India. This important trait of the culture of Magadha before the rise of Buddhism has seldom been appreciated. Sītavana is

1. *Ibid.*, pp. 52-54.
2. *Yakṣa,* in the Bulletins of the Smithsonian Institute.
3. Vol. iii, p. 17.
4. *Ibid.*, vol. i, p. 206.
5. *Ibid.*
6. *Digha Nikāya*, vol. ii, p. 257.

mentioned in the *Mahāparinibbānasutta*, as pointed out by Principal D.N. Sen.[1] But for precise location we are indebted to Dr. B.C. Law. It was situated near the north face of the Vaibhāra hill beyond Venuvana. Its location therefore must be beyond Jarasandhkā-Baiṭhak near the modern village.[2]

In my paper on 'Non Buddhistic Elements in Buddhism,'[3] I had occasion to point out the absorption of early beliefs and cults, or places and objects, venerated in folk traditions, by the Buddhists. Gautama preached in the language of the people, which was *ardha-māgadhi* Pra-*krit* and not Pali. He probably had a far greater knowledge of the mass psychology, than we credit him with. This mass of ancient Magadha was heterogeneous in racial composition. Magadha, according to tradition, had its name, from one of the five sons of *asūra* queen Sudeṣṇā, by the alleged Aryan sage Dīrghatamas, according to the *Kṣetraja* custom. Gautama seeks at Gaya, a tree to whose benevolent spirit, Sujātā, the daughter of the *grāma-mukhyā* of Uruvelā, had prayed the previous year for a child. Gautama goes to Mṛgadāva leaving Benares, the stronghold of Brahminism, Jainism and finds a protected 'Deer Park,' where Deers might have been sacred like the peacocks on the banks of Sumagadhā, at Rajgir, near Gṛdhrakūṭa. The city of Rajgir he adored, with its ancient lore and primitive beliefs.

## Tree Worship

Trees formed, and still continues to be the greatest object of veneration with the Indian masses. Its antiquity, after the discovery of the Harappa culture, is undoubted, as well as the custom of encircling trees or sacred objects with railings etc. In Magadha the most sacred trees were *Pippala* and *Nyāgrodhas*. The most well known of these at Rajgir was the *Gotama-nyāgrodha* (*ramanīyo Gotamo-nyāgrodha*).[4] The second class of evidence is furnished by several reference to *caityas*. Of late this term has often been misinterpreted. At Nalanda excavations, *vihāra* sites are generally designated *caitya* sites, by people claiming special knowledge of Indian art and architecture. A *caitya* implies and will always imply a place of tree worship. It was in almost all cases, and exceptions proved

1. *Rajgir and its neighbourhood,* p. 2.
2. *MASI.*, no. 58, pp. 10-11.
3. This is to appear in *New Indian Antiquary.*
4. *DN.*, vol. ii, pp. 116-17.

the rule, a roofless structure or a railing surrounding a tree. Such temples are often found depicted at Barhut, Sañci and Bodh Gaya. *Caitya-vṛkṣas* are referred to in the Epics; and Hopkins has defined them as places of tree worship.[1] The belief in the existence of beneficent and evil divinities or spirits residing in certain trees was widely prevalent since chalcolithic times, as the Mohenjodaro and Harappa seals have proved. The *Jātakas* which depict the social, religious and political life of India, of at least c. 600 B.C., give us a good deal of information. Referring to Guṇaśilā-caitya, Hemacandra Surī tells us that it was *caitya vṛkṣopaśobhitam.*[2] *Bahuputta-caitya* was another sylvan divinity about whom details are lacking. Another place of this kind, was *Nyāgrodhārāma*. An *ārāma* in Pali literature implies an abode. Thus the abodes of monks were known as *saṅghārāmas*.

Another famous place of tree worship was the Guṇaśilā-*caitya.*[3] It was at this place that Mahāvīra, the 24th *tīrthaṅkara*,[4] resided several seasons while at Rajgir.

1. E.W. Hopkins, *Epic Mythology*, pp. 6-8.
2. *Tri-ṣaṣṭhi-śalākā-puruṣa-caritra*, x. 6363.
3. The whole question has been discussed in my paper 'The Jaina Antiquities of Rajgir.'
4. Most of these references I owe to the late Prof. Dhammananda Kosambī, when I resided at Sarnath. Some of these have also been discussed by Dr. B.C. Law, in the *Memoirs of the Archæological Survey of India*, no. 58.

## *Chapter - 28*

# Pātaliputra: Its Importance in the History of Buddhism

**Binayendranath Chaudhuri**

*Name and Location*—Pāṭaliputra, the later capital of the Magadhan empire, was recognised as one of the six great cities of ancient India. The various forms of the name Pāṭaliputra are Pāṭaliputta (Pāli); Pāḍaliputta (Prakrit), Palibothra[1] or Palimbothra;[2] Palienfu (Chinese).[3] The city was otherwise known as Puṣpapura or Kusumapura.[4]

All the sources of information about the city of Pāṭaliputra suggest its location to the southern bank of the Ganges near the ancient site of modern Patna. The village Pāṭaliputra suggest its location to the southern bank of the Ganges near the ancient site of modern Patna. The village Pāṭaligāma (earlier name of the place) lay opposite to Koṭigāma on the northern bank of the Ganges which formed the boundary between Magadha and the territory of the Licchavis of Vaiśālī.[5]

According to the Jaina *Vividha-tīrthakalpa* the city was built on the bank of the Ganges near the confluence of the great rivers of Mid-India, the Ganges, the Sone and the Gaṇḍak. Patañjali locates the city just on the bank of the Sone (*anuśonaṃ Pāṭaliputram*)[6] while in *Mudrārākṣasa* (IV. 16) Malayaketu is said to have crossed the river Sone to reach Pāṭaliputra. These accounts indicate that

---

1. McCrindle, *Ancient India as described by Megasthanes and Arrian,* p. 65.
2. McCrindle, *Ancient India as described by Ptolemy* (N.G. Mazumdar edition), p. 169.
3. Beal, *Records of the Western World,* I, iv.
4. *Allahabad Stone Pillar Inscription of Samudragupta* (C.I.I.); *Mahāvaṁsa,* ch. 18, 5; *Mahāvastu,* III, p. 231.
5. *Digha Nikāya,* II, p. 89.
6. *Mahābhāṣya,* 2. 1. 2. p. 510.

formerly the river Sone met the Ganges at the ancient site of Pāṭ aliputra but later receded westwards.

Fa-Hien coming from Vaiśālī crossed the river Ganges and walked southwards for a *yojana* along the river and reached Pāṭ-aliputta.[1] Prolonged excavations carried out by the Archaeological Department have led to the exact location of the city of Pāṭaliputra, the remains of which have been found in the villages of Kumrāhār, Bulandi-Bāgh and other outskirts of the city of Patna.[2]

## Buddhist Heritages of the City

**Pre-Maurya Period**: At the time of Buddha, Pāṭaliputra was merely a village named Pāṭaligama (*op. cit.*). During his last visit to the village while he was passing from Rājagṛha to Vaiśālī, shortly before his death, Buddha prophesied about the future greatness of the village and its ultimate destruction by fire, innundation and internal dissensions. At this time King Ajātaśatru employed two brāhmin ministers Vassakāra and Sunīdha to build a fortress at Pāṭ aligāma as a precaution against the Vajjian attack. In honour of Buddha the people of Pāṭaliputra called the gate, Gotamadvāra, through which he left the city and the ferry ghat, Gotamatittha, at which he crossed the Ganges.[3]

The *Udāna*[4] relates that a large hall was constructed in the middle of the village of Pāṭāli for the officers of Ajātaśatru. At the request of the villagers, Buddha passed a night in the hall. On the following day, he delivered a sermon to the people on the five kinds of reward of observance of precepts and the five kinds of disadvantages of an evil doer.[5] At a later date a brāhmin householder of Aṅga built an assembly hall for the Saṅgha of Pāṭaliputra.[6]

After the demise of Buddha, the waterpot and the girdle used by him were deposited in the city of Pāṭaliputra.[7]

According to the Buddhist traditions Ajātaśatru in his later life became an earnest and enthusiastic devotee of Buddha. After Ajātasātru, his son, Udāyībhadra reigned for 16 years. Udāyībhadra was succeeded by Anuruddha and then by Muṇḍa. Muṇḍa, it seems,

---

1. Legge, p. 77, *Northern India According to the Shui-Ching-Chu* by L. Petech, p. 42.
2. *Annual Reports* (A.S.I.) 1912-13, pp. 54-59.
3. *Vinaya*, I, pp. 226-230; *Dīgha*, II, 86 ff.
4. *Udāna*, VIII. 6; *Ud. A.*, 407 ff.
5. *Dīgha*, II, pp. 85-86.
6. *Majjhima*, II, 57 ff.
7. *Buddhavaṁsa*, ch. XXVIII.

had leanings towards Buddhism, because, just after the death of his queen Bhadrā he approached Bhikkhu Nārada at Pāṭaliputra and listened to a discourse on the impermanence of worldly objects.[1]

One hundred years after the demise of Buddha, the Second Buddhist Council was held for the purpose of settling disputes over certain Vinaya rules. Due to the difference of opinions, the Buddhist Church was split into two and afterwards into more than eighteen schools. The seceders were known as the Mahāsāṅghikas and the orthodox party as the Theravādins.

According to Hiuen Tsang, Khujjasobhita, a prominent member of the Second Council belonged to Pāṭaliputra.[2]

The Mahāsāṅghikas had great influence at Pāṭaliputra and though the Theravādins lived side by side with the other school they could not live with the Mahāsāṅghikas and finally receded westwards.[3]

After Kālāśoka and his descendants another new dynasty headed by Nanda came to the throne of Magadha. According to the *Mañjuśrīmūlakalpa*, a Sanskrit Buddhist text, Nanda was a great patron of Buddhism. King Nanda, at the advice of his spiritual teacher, offered several gifts to the Caityas which were built on the deposited relics of Buddha.[4] Mahāpadma Nanda, son and successor of Nanda, was also devoted to Buddhism and provided the monks at Kusumapura with all their requisites.[5]

Bu-ston quotes from the *Mahākaruṇāpuṇḍarika* Buddha's prediction of a list of successive guardians of his doctrine after his death and cites the names of two monks Aśvagupta and Uttara, both of whom belonged to Pāṭaliputra.[6]

All the facts stated above show that within a century after Buddha's demise the main centre of Buddhism along with the capital of Magadha was shifted from Rājagṛha to Pāṭaliputra, which also became the stronghold of the Mahāsāṅghikas.[7]

**Maurya Period**: Pātaliputra attained pre-eminence during the rule of the Mauryas. The first two emperors of this dynasty Candragupta and Bindusāra, were not so much in favour of Buddhism

1. *Aṅguttara Nikāya*, III, pp. 57 ff.
2. Dutt, *Early Monastic Buddhism*, vol. II, p. 28.
3. *Buddhist Sects* by N. Dutt, in B.C. Law Volume I, pp. 285-286.
4. *Mañjuśrīmūlakalpa*, pp. 611-612.
5. *Tāranātha's Geschichte des Buddhismus* by Scheifner, p. 55.
6. Bu-ston's *History of Buddhism*, vol. 2, p. 109.
7. *Early Monastic Buddhism*, vol. II, p. 30.

as were their remote ancestors, the Moriyas of Pipphalivana, who took a share of the relics of Buddha and erected a stūpa over them.[1]

Aśoka surpassed all of his ancestors by his outstanding system of administration and by his broad religious outlook. Though Aśoka showed sympathy and favour to all religious creeds, there are clear evidences which reveal his strong faith and leanings towards the doctrine of Buddha and his Order.

As the accounts of the Chinese travellers testify, Pāṭaliputra was the first place where Aśoka commenced his activities for the benefit of Buddhism. He took out the relics preserved in the seven stūpas (vide *Mahāparinibbāna Sutta*), distributed them all over his dominion and erected on them stūpas of which the very first was constructed at Pāṭaliputra.[2] Aśoka it is said did this pious act at the advice of Upagupta, the spiritual teacher of the emperor.[3]

Hiuen Tsang furnishes us with the information that there was a miraculous stone with Buddha's foot-print, placed in a temple near the relic tope at Pāṭaliputra. Buddha stood on this stone before his departure from Magadha towards Kuśīnagara.[4] Near that temple there was an Aśokan pillar, more than thirty feet in height with an inscription recording Aśoka's deep faith and his offer of the whole of Jambudvīpa (his empire) to the Buddhist Saṅgha.[5]

About two hundred years north from the stūpa Aśoka built a new palace called Ne-le and erected another stone pillar known by the same name with a lion capital on the top of it and an inscription.

Both Dr. Spooner and Col. Waddell, who carried on excavations at the ancient site of Pāṭaliputra, support the statements of the Chinese travellers that Aśoka erected two pillars, some fragments of polished sandstone of which were traced by Col. Waddell.[6]

During the excavations at the site, a well, known as Agam Kuāñ (unfathomable well) was discovered. It was a large circular well (20 feet and 2 inches in diameter), the walls of which were raised about 10 feet above the ground level and had eight windows. Huen Tsang perhaps witnessed this well and identified it with Aśoka's

---

1. *Mahāparinibbāna Suttanta of the Dīgha Nikāya.*
2. Watters, *On Yuan Chwang*, vol. II, p. 91; Legge, *Travels of Fa-Hien*, p. 79; *Samanta-pāsādikā*, Introduction; *Sumaṅgalavilāsinī.*
3. Watters, vol. II, p. 91.
4. Watters, II p. 92, Legge p. 79.
5. Watters, II, p. 93, Legge p. 79.
6. *Ancient Monuments of Bihar and Orissa*, by H. Quereshi, A.S.I., 1931, p. 102. Henceforth shortened as *Ancient Monuments.*

Prison. He is supported by Waddell. The tradition about the prison is as follows:[1] Aśoka, when he was very cruel (before his conversion to Buddhism) constructed a prison called 'Hell' which accommodated one thousand inhabitants within a walled city in order to punish the unruly citizens. But one day the king was overwhelmed at the sight of the magical power of a Buddhist Śramaṇa who was thrown into the Prison, and since then he destroyed the 'Prison' and made the penal code liberal.[2]

Among other objects noticed by Huen Tsang, there are, (i) a large stone vessel, which Aśoka said to have kept to hold the food for monks;[3] (ii) a large cave excavated at the instance of Aśoka at Pāṭ-aliputra for the use of Mahendra who joined the Buddhist order and attained the state of Arhathood;[4] (iii) caves for the use of Upagupta and other Arhats on a small hill to the south west of the city. By the hill side there were stone foundations of an old terrace and holy tanks[5] and (iv) five topes to the south-west of this very hill in a dilapidated condition. In later period some other smaller topes were built upon this main tope.

Col. Waddell identified the above cave-dwelling of Upagupta with the Chota-Pahari site of Pañch Pahari now known as Bara Pahari in the village of Nirandanpur Kharuma. The Panch Pahari was a group of five mounds containing five stūpas constructed by Aśoka. The Bara Pahari mound was the largest and highest of all in the area. Dr. Spooner discovered a few fragments of Chunar stone probably of the Mauryan period and remains of two brick stūpas. Dr. Spooner supposes that all the fives stūpas which Aśoka built were in this single mound. In one of the stūpas Dr. Spooner found an empty relic chamber and a small very early type of a Triratna symbol.[6]

## The Monastery of Kukkuṭārāma

Kukkuṭārāma was a park at Pāṭaliputra. The Kukkuṭārāma vihāra was situated in a garden named Upakaṇṭhakārāma on the right bank of the Ganges.[7] Originally the monastery was built by Kukkuṭaseṭṭhī.[8] It became an *āvāsa* of monks and a favourite resort

1. *Ancient Monuments,* p. 96.
2. Watters, vol. II. p. 88.
3. Watters, vol. II, p. 93.
4. *Ibid.*, p. 93.
5. *Ancient Monuments,* p. 96.
6. *Ibid.*, p. 98.
7. *Aśokāvadāna* in R.L. Mitra's *Sanskrit Buddhist Literature,* 6f. vide, N.L. De's *Dictionary,* p. 152.
8. *Majjhima Aṭṭhakatha,* II, 571; *Aṅguttara Aṭṭhakathā*, II, 866.

of Ānanda.[1] A monk named Bhadda, also a resident of the monastery, had conversation with Ānanda on the subjects of true religion, objects of recollection etc.[2] The Elders Nitavāsi, Sānavāsi, Gopaka, Bhagu, Phalikasandana lived here.[3] At a later date here resided Bhikkhu Nārada who delivered a discourse to king Muṇḍa.[4] Soṇaka, the preceptor of Siggava, Thera Caṇḍavajji, the teacher of Moggaliputta Tissa lived in this monastery.[5] Upagupta also resided in this monastery.[6]

According to Tāranātha and *Divyāvadāna*, Puṣyamitra made an attempt to destroy the monastery but was obstructed, as the legend goes, by the roar of a lion which appeared miraculously.[7]

Huen Tsang located the Kukkuṭārāma to the south-east of the old city of Pāṭaliputra. Perhaps the old shrine of Kukkuṭārāma fell into decay before Aśoka. Asoka built another monastery over the ruins of the old one which at a later date was known as Aśokārāma. Tissa, the younger brother of Aśoka, was ordained in this monastery and he lived here.

In the Pāli commentaries and Ceylonese Chronicles it is stated that the Third Buddhist Council of the Theravada School was convened in this monastery under the patronage of Aśoka. Huen Tsang also mentioned an assembly of one thousand Buddhist monks in this monastery.[8] In the *Divyāvadāna* the number of monks is given 30000 but they did not come to hold a council but only to attend Aśoka's first 'quinquennial festival of the holy priesthood.' The senior among them was the great Piṇḍola Bhāradvāja who had seen the Buddha.[9]

Aśoka used to provide daily food for all monks residing at the Aśokārāma.[10] A large number of monks from Aśokārāma headed by *Miṭṭhina* went to Anurādhapura of Ceylon to celebrate the foundations of the Mahāthūpa.[11] From this monastery Mahinda set out on his mission to Ceylon.[12]

---

1. *Aṅguttara*, v. 342; *Majjhima*, i. 349.
2. *Saṁyutta*, v. pp. 15-16; 171-172.
3. *Vinaya*, I. 300, vide, Malalaṣekara's *Dictionary of Pali Proper Names*, vol. I. p. 615.
4. *op. cit.*
5. *Mahavaṁsa*, v. 122; *Dictionary of Pali Proper Name*, by G.P. Malalasekara, I, p. 615.
6. *Svayambhū Purāṇa*, ch. I.
7. *Divya.*, pp. 381 ff; 430 ff.
8. Watters, vol. II, p. 98.
9. *Divyā.*, p. 398 ff. v. 80; 163, 174, 234, 276.
10. *Mahavaṁsa.*
11. *Ibid.*, xxix, 36.
12. *Samantapāsādikā*, I. 69.

Thera Dhammarakkhita, teacher of Nāgasena, lived in this monastery.[1] Indagutta Thera (date unknown) was appointed by the king of the country to superintend the building of the Vihāra of Aśokārāma.[2]

### The Āmalaka and the Gong Tope

Huen Tsang found a large tope called Āmalaka stūpa just by the side of Kukkuṭārāma. He records that when Samprati ascended the throne after Aśoka's retirement he stopped the Aśoka's largesses to the Buddhist church and reduced gradually his allowance which was given away by him to the Sangha. At last Samprati gave him half an *āmalaka* fruit in an earthen pot. Aśoka sent even this half to the bhikkhus of Kukkuṭārāma. Yaśa, the abbot of the monastery, had the fruit cooked "to keep the kernal and have a tope raised" over it.[3] This mound was situated to the east of modern Ranipura within the Kukkuṭārāma.[4]

Huen Tsang witnessed another tope called Gong-Call Tope in an old monastery to the north-west of the Āmalaka Tope. He narrates the legend of the foundation of this tope also. Formerly there were in the city about one hundred monasteries with the "Brethren of high character and the Tīrthikas (heretics) were silenced. The Buddhist clergy gradually died and there was a great falling off in their successors." The Tirthikas assembled in the city and defeated the Buddhists in discussion and as a result occupied the Buddhist monastery and gained royal favour. After twelve years Deva Pusa (Āryadeva) a disciple of Nāgārjuna (Pusa Bodhisattva) of South India came to Pāṭ-aliputra and defeated them in an open meeting. "The king and his minister's were greatly pleased and raised this sacred structure as a memorial." But according to Fang-Chih it was not Āryadeva but Nāgārjuna himself who defeated the Tīrthikas.[5]

### After Aśoka

The successors of Asoka were not in favour of Buddhism and so the traditions are silent on the condition of Buddhism in Pāṭaliputra during their reigns. But there is no doubt that Pāṭaliputra still continued to be a centre of Buddhist learning for several centuries.

---

1. *Milinda,* pp. 16-18.
2. *Samantapāsādikā*, i. pp. 48-49.
3. Watters, vol. II. pp. 99-100; *Divya.*, p. 430.
4. N.L. De, *Geographical Dictionary of Ancient and Mediaeval India,* p. 152.
5. *Watters,* vol., II, pp. 100-102.

Though Puṣyamitra Suṅga, the usurper of the Maurya throne was an adherent of Brahmanism, he was not so antagonistic towards Buddhist monks as stated in the *Divyāvadāna* and the *Aśokāvadāna.*[1] According to these texts, Puṣyamitra attempted to destroy the monastery of Pāṭaliputra[2] and declared the reward of one hundred dinaras to one who would bring the head of a Buddhist monk. Buddhism however was in flourishing condition within the boundary of the Magadhan empire under the Suṅgas. Besides the massive construction of the Sānchi Stūpa, archaeological antiquitics of this period have been traced from Pāṭaliputra.[3]

According to the *Petavatthu commentary* (pp. 244 ff) the general of King Piṅgala of Saurāṣṭra came to Pāṭaliputra and embraced Buddhism. King Paṇḍu of Pāṭaliputra (date not mentioned), his vassal Guhasiva and his subordinate King Cittāyana were converted to Buddhism.[4] Two Brahmins of Pāṭaliputra set out for Ceylon to meet Mahānāga Thera, a famous monk of the Island.[5]

Tāranātha relates that during the reign of Kaṇiṣka, a brahmin named Vidu was making one thousand copies of the sacred Buddhist texts at Pāṭaliputra, while Huen Tsang states that the great Buddhist poet Aśvaghoṣa lived in a house at Pāṭaliputra.[6]

As archaeological evidence of the presence of Buddhism, a large Bodhisattva image of Mathurā school of the Kuṣāṇa period, was found at the site of Pāṭaliputra.[7]

**Period of the Guptas and Kanauj King Harṣavardhana**

Fa-Hien (or Fa-hsien) visited the city during the reign of Candragupta II. At the time of his visit there resided in the city a great learned Brāhmaṇa named Rādhasvāmi, a professor of Mahāyāna doctrine. The king of the country honoured and showed reverence to him. He might be more than fifty years old and all the kingdom looked up to him as a great teacher.[8]

According to the traveller,[9] the cities and towns of Magadha were the greatest of all in the Middle Kingdom (Central India). The

---

1. *Early Monastic Buddhism,* vol. 2. p. 256.
2. *Op. cit.*
3. A beautiful Triratna slab of high artistic value of the Suṅga period was found in Paṭaliputra.—Annual Reports of 1912-13, *A.S. 1* (1916), p. 77.
4. *Dāṭhāvaṁsa,* by B.C. Law, pp. XII-XIV.
5. *Aṅguttara Nikāya Aṭṭhakathā,* i. 384.
6. Watters, vol. 2. p. 102. p. 107.
7. *Ancient Monuments.*
8. Legge, p. 78.
9. *Ibid.*, pp. 78-79.

inhabitants were rich and prosperous and vied with each other in the practice of benevolence and religious ceremonies. every year on the eighth day of the second month they used to take out a procession of images.

By the side of the tope of Aśoka there was a Mahāyāna monastery, a very grand and beautiful structure and there was also a Hīnayāna one, two together containing six or seven hundred monks. A brāhmin teacher, Mañjuśrī of the greatest virtue to whom the Samaṇas and the Mahāyāna Bhikṣus in the country showed honour, lived in this monastery.

A Bodhisattva image brought from Mathurā of early Gupta period was found in the ruins of a building at Pāṭaliputra.[1]

Dr. Spooner discovered a maze of ruined brick walls of the late Gupta period extending over the entire area of excavations.

Numerous clay sealings of which one or two were old but the majority belonged to the Gupta period had been found at the site.[2] Buddhism had already begun to decline before the visit of Huen Tsang who travelled over this country for 16 years during the reign of Kanauj King Harṣavardhana. Huen Tsang witnessed Buddhism in a gradually decaying condition in many places of India. In the places like Malava, Mahārāṣṭra, Kanauj and Jalandhara where once Buddhism overshadowed all other religions, the traveller found Buddhists and non-Buddhists in equal number. But still in Pāṭaliputra along with Ayodhyā and Sind, Buddhist establishments and the monks of both the Vehicles were of far greater number in comparison to the Devas and the Heretics.[3] In the view of the traveller there were fifty monasteries with ten thousands monks but only ten Deva temples in Pāṭaliputra.[4]

Ou-Kong, who came after Huen Tsang, found Buddhism in a flourishing condition in Magadha. He stayed in a monastery of the Chinese which was probably situated at Pāṭaliputra. This was a rich monastery frequented by the monks and their disciples.[5]

Our history of Buddhism in Pāṭaliputra ends here on account of the final destruction of the city. Though the exact causes and the time of destruction are hithereto unknown to us yet the discovery of

1. *Annual Reports*, op. cit., p. 26.
2. *Ancient Monuments*, p. 102.
3. Vide *Decline of Buddhism in India*, by R.C. Mitra, p. 3.
4. Watters, II. pp. 86, 165.
5. *Decline of Buddhism*, p. 18.

burnt wooden structures and the masses of alluvial soil over the site suggest that the first two of the three dangers if not the third one predicted by Buddha were the main catastrophes and it occurred long before the rise of the Pālas of Bengal. But the fame of Paṭaliputra lasted even at the time of Alberuni in the tenth or at the commencement of the eleventh century A.D.[1]

### Archeological finds

Archaeological finds which were discovered during the prolonged excavations testify that Pāṭaliputra was a great centre of Buddhism for more than one thousand years. Interesting discoveries bearing Buddhist antiquities (besides those which are mentioned above) found out by the Archaeological Survey of India are as follows:[2]

1. Fragment of sandstone polished on both sides and with one face decorated with very narrow flutings (Mauryan).
2. A smooth slab of stone bearing in low incision an admitable figure of the Triratna symbol, the conventional trident representing the Buddhist Trinity with the Wheel of Law underneath.
3. Inscribed stone fragment possibly from the Triratna slab (Maurya or Suṅga period).
4. A matrix bearing a trio of a very archaic symbols probably of 3rd century B.C.
5. Oval terracotta plaque bearing apparently, a picture of Bodh-Gayā temple in the centre with a figure of Buddha seated inside.
6. Head of a small Buddha figure in terracotta (probably from the plaque).
7. Matrix of baked clay bearing the legend ("seal of Buddha-rakṣ ita") in Brahmi character of the most primitive form.
8. Seal bearing the Buddhist creed in the lower half of a complete stūpa containing a figure of Buddha and flanked by two Bodhisattvas above.
9. A hoard of 52 Kuṣāṇa copper coins, containing coins of Kadphises II, Kaṇiṣka and Huviṣka.
10. Two gold coins of Kuṣāṇa type.

---

1. *Alberuni's India,* vol. I, p. 200 Vide N.L. De's *Dictionary of Geography of Ancient India*, p. 151.
2. *Ancient Monument,* pp. 107-110.

# Chapter - 29

# Kashmir's Contribution to the Expansion of Buddhism in the Far East

Jan Yün Hua

The expansion of Buddhism from India to mediaeval China and from there to other parts of the Far East is a great and glorious chapter in the history of mankind, because this event involved millions of people and influenced their culture and lives. In this connection, Kashmirians once took a leading part in transmission of the Buddhist literature and traditions to the Far East. During the fourth and fifth centuries of the Christian era. Kashmir sent to China a number of Buddhist Masters, whose works and virtues were not only appreciated by their Chinese followers, but also by the Buddhists of the Far East.

These Kashmirians worked with determination, overcame many difficulties and dangers, crossed deserts and oceans, climbed across

---

**Abbreviations:—**

| | | |
|---|---|---|
| CBC | = | *Le Canon Bouddhique en Chine.* 2 vols. by P.C. Bagchi, Paris & Calcutta, 1927 and 1938. |
| CSTCC | = | *Ch'u-san-tsang chi-chi* (A collection of the records of Translation of Tripiṭaka). By Monk Sêng-yu (445-518), Taisho edition, No. 2145. |
| HJAS | = | *Harvard Journal of Asiatic Studies.* |
| FTTC | = | *Fo-tsu-t'ung-chi* (A General Record on Buddha and Patriarchs). By Monk Chih-p'an (13th century A.D.) Taisho edition No. 2035. |
| Hob. | = | *Hobogirin,* Fascicule Annexe, *Tables du Taisho Issaikyo.* Ed. by Maison Franco-japonaise, (Chief Editor—Paul Demiéville). Tokyo, 1931. |
| KSC | = | *Kao-sêng-chuan* (Biographies of the Eminent Monks). By Monk Hui-chiao (497-554). Taisho edition No. 2059. |
| Nj | = | *A Catalogue of Chinese Translation of the Buddhist Tripiṭaka.* By B. Nanjio. Oxford 1883; Rep. Tokyo, 1929. |
| T | = | *Taisho Issaikyo* (Taisho edition of Tripiṭaka in Chinese). Ed. by J. Takakusu; K. Watanabe and others. Tokyo, 1924-29. |
| TP | = | *T'oung Pao.* |

snowy mountains and walked hundreds of miles towards the East. They served as the torch-bearers of Indian culture, preached Buddhism, translated Buddhist canons into foreign languages, performed religious ceremonies and prayed for the good of those countries. For centuries, India had little knowledge about the achievements and activities of these noble Indian Masters. But as a result of modern scholarship and specially through the works of B. Nanjio, P.C. Bagchi and others, the story and works of these Indian Masters in China were gradually revealed to scholars throughout the world. Despite these past efforts, there are still some materials and other related problems in the field, which are worthy of further study. In this article, our attempt is concentrated on reaching two objectives: (i) To give an outline but factually complete survey of activities of Kashmirian Buddhist monks who worked in mediaeval China. (ii) To analyse and evaluate their contribution to Buddhism in the Far East. This is only for the convenience of discussion, because sending missionaries to foreign countries itself is a great contribution.

Before we start the survey, it is necessary to have a clear concept of the geographical term, Kashmir as mentioned in Chinese texts. Scholars agree that the name of *Ki-pin* or *Chi-pin* mentioned in the pre-T'ang documents (i.e. before 618 A.D.) is broadly identified with the present Kashmir.[1] From the time of Hsüan-tsang onwards, Chinese historians and scholars correctly knew the name to be *Kia-shih-mi-lo* or Kashmira.[2] From this nomenclature, we can regard all the monks of *Ki-pin* or *Chipin* mentioned in early Chinese documents and those of Kashmira in later records as Kashmirian monks.

## Survey

When we start the survey, the first question is, who was the earliest Kashmirian monk to work in China. According to P.C. Bagchi and others, Saṅghabhūti was "The first Kashmirian scholar to go to China.[3]" This Saṅghabhūti arrived at the Northern capital (Ch'ang-

---

1. A good and concise résumé of views by E. Chavannes, S. Lévi and P. Pelliot on this identification has been given by P.C. Bagchi: "Ki-pin and Kashmir," *Sino-Indian Studies,* II, 1946-47, pp.42-53. Also see L. Petech: "Chi-pin"—in *Northern India According to Shui-ching-chu*, Roma, 1950 and Hatnai Ryotei: "Buddhism in Western Region," (Chinese translation byHo Ch'ang-ch'ün under the title *Hsi-yü chih fo-chiao*), pp. 313ff.
2. Cf. Watters "On Yuan-chwang's Travel to India," p. 257 and for Chinese documents, see *Hsin-t' ang-shu* and other later records.
3. See "India and China," p. 35-36; Nj. p. 404 No. 54 but Mr. B. Nanjio had wrongly identified Saṅghabhūti as a monk from Kabul.

an) in 381 A.D. But after our investigation, we find that there was another Kashmirian who worked at Lo-yang about seventy years before Saṅghabhūti. In the text of *Pi-ch'iu-ni chuan* (Biography of Bhikṣunis) by Pao-ch'ang in sixth century A.D. it is recorded:—

"Chih-shan was originally a resident of Chi-pin. He was kind and wise. He was a great Master in meditation and recitation. During the later part of Yung-chia era (307-312 A.D.) of the Chin dynasty, he came to China. He maintained his life by begging (*Piṇḍapāta* in Skt.) and he always talked about the expansion of religion. At that time, the standard of attainment of people was still shallow, thus no one could appreciate him or learn from this Master. Therefore, he returned to his country during the first year of Chien-wu era (i.e. 317 A.D.). Later, when Fo-t'u-t'eng returned from West to China, he talked about the virtue and attainment of that Master, which made others regret..."[1]

Literally, Chih-shan means 'Mountain of Wisdom,' which can be restored as Prajñā-kūṭa. From the above quotation, we may rightly say that so far as our knowledge is concerned, Chih-shan was the earliest Kashmirian who went to China. Unfortunately, his mission was unsuccessful due to uncongenial circumstances and could not achieve any substantial result. On the other hand, his determination and sincerity was undeniable.

Decades after the mission of Chih-shan, Buddhist studies and understanding in China showed much progress. Therefore, the later Kashmirians could work showing results where Chih-shan failed. Amongst these later Kashmirian Masters, we find the name of Saṅghabhūti, Gautama Saṅghadeva, Dharmapriya, Saṅgharakṣa, Dharmayaśas, Puṇyatārā (—404 A.D.), Vimalākṣa (—413 A.D.), Buddhayaśas, Buddhajīva, Dharma-mitra (356-442 A.D.), Guṇavarman (367-431 A.D.), Shih-hsien (460 A.D. his Chinese name might be a translation of Skt. Guru-bhadra or Upadhyāya-bhadra) and so forth.

Saṅghabhūti specialized in *Abhidharmavibhāṣā.* He arrived in China during 381 and worked till 384. There are three works said to have been translated by him.[2] Gautama Saṅghadeva arrived at Ch'ang-an in 384. He worked there for a few years for translation and revision of Buddhist canons. Six years later, he joined the famous centre of Buddhist studies Lu-shan, translated two works at the request

1. Original text of this quotation is contained in T 50, p. 934c. Translation is mine.

2. Details about the life and works of Saṅghabhūti, see *CBC.*, vol. 1, p. 160.

of Master Hui-yüan (334-416). He then went to Nanking where he translated important scriptures along with his Chinese colleagues.[1]

Besides these two eminent translators, there were two other monks from Kashmir. They were Dharmapriya and Dharmarakṣa. Identification of native place of these two monks were recorded in the books by Seng-yu and Hui-chiao respectively. They were undoubtedly Kashmirians. Dharmarakṣa was the collaborator of Saṅghadeva in his translation of *Madhyamāgama* (*Chung-a-han-ching*).[2]

When Kumārajīva (344-413) was working at Ch'ang-an, there were quite a number of scholars who worked with that celebrated Master of Tripiṭaka. Of his associates, Puṇyatārā, Dharmayaśas, Buddhayaśas, and Vimalākṣa were the outstanding figures. Puṇyatārā collaborated with Kumārajīva in translation of Vinaya texts[3]; Dharmayaśas also worked in co-operation with other Indian and Chinese monks. He worked both in Northern and Southern China for a number of years and translated three works into Chinese.[4] Vimalākṣa was an expert in Vinaya. He was also a teacher of Kumārajīva. When his disciple secured a distinguished position in Ch'ang-an, he went and joined the latter in 406. He revised Kumārajīva's translation of *Sarvāstivādavinaya* (*Shih-sung-lü*) and also wrote a commentary on it.[5] Buddhayaśas was an old friend of Kumārajīva. He joined and worked with his friend at Ch'ang-an for some years. He was one of the few who could return to their homeland after completing their mission in the East.[6]

During the first half of the fifth century A.D. there were many eminent Kashmirian monks who worked in China. In the Southern kingdoms, Buddhajīva, a Master of Discipline, translated three works at Yang-chou.[7] Another Kashmirian monk called Dharmamitra, reached Nanking via a special route, i.e. Kashmir-Central Asia-Tun Huang-Szu Ch'uan and from the last place he sailed along the Yang-tse River to Nanking in 420. Dharmamitra was a master of many subjects, his translations covered both Hinayāna and Mahāyāna works.[8] Guṇavarman went to China via Celyon and Java. He arrived

1. *Ibid.*, p. 161.
2. Original evidence on this identification is in Chinese, which is contained in T 55, p. 73c and T 50, 329b.
3. Cf. *CBC.*, I. 176 ff.
4. *Ibid.*, p. 174 ff.
5. *Ibid.*, p. 338.
6. *Ibid.*, p. 200.
7. *Ibid.*, p. 363.
8. *Ibid.*, p. 338.

at Nanking in 431, translated ten works mainly on Vinaya into Chinese.[1]

In North China, there was a five-men Kashmirian mission led by Shih-hsien. They arrived at the capital of the N. Wei kingdom sometime between 446 and 450 when Buddhism was suppressed by the Toba Wei rulers. In the circumstances, these Kashmirians appeared as laymen and lived there as medical practitioners. In 452, when Buddhism was re-established in that kingdom, Shih-hsien re-entered clergy and was appointed. "The Superintendent of Monks" (*Tao-jên-t'ung*). He was the only foreign monk who held such a high Government post in the history of Chinese Buddhist religion.[2]

After an interruption of about two hundred years, Kashmirian Masters again appeared in Chinese records. Buddhapāla went to China in 676. He translated one Tantric text along with his Chinese co-translator. He probably remained in China till his death, because a later record informs us that this Kashmirian monk was enshrined and worshipped in a district of Ho-nan province.[3] Ratnacintā went and translated three works at Ch'ang-an in 693-706. Another Kasmirian monk Arjuna who was mentioned in Chinese records as a prince of Kashmir worked as a colleague of Yi-tsing (635-713).[4]

During the eighth and ninth centuries, we find another break in Kashmir Buddhist mission to the East, till the year 980, when a Kashmir Master T'ien-hsi-tsai (1000) went to K'ai-feng, the capital of the Sung empire. Following this, another Kasmirian monk Dharma-pāla (963-1058) went to China from Nālandā and worked there in 1003-1058. This T'ien-hsi-tsai translated one hundred and odd canons into Chinese, he was much honoured by the ruler of the Sung dynasty. He was renamed by Chinese king but his new name Dharma-bhadra was wrongly identified with another Indian called Dharma-deva. Similarly, the name of Dharma-pāla was also wrongly restored as Dharmarakṣa and he was mentioned as a monk of Northern or Western India. It is very likely that they were natives of Kashmir, which is also proved by contemporary documents about them.[5]

1. *Ibid.*, p. 370.
2. See "Wei Shou on Buddhism," tr. by J.R. Ware, *TP.*, vol. XXX, p. 145.
3. About his life and works, see *CBC.*, vol. II, p. 513. For the story mentioned in later record, see *FTTC.*, 46. T. 49, p. 417c.
4. For Ratnakinta, see *Hob.*, p. 139a; for Arjuna, see *CBC.*, II; 528.
5. Early evidences on the identifications of these two Kashmirian Masters are contained in "An Inscription of The Bureau of the Transmission of Dharma," Fragments of Hsiang-fu and Ching-yu catalogues. All of them are in Chinese. Detailed discussion about these problems will appear in another article by the author entitled "Ch'üab-fa-yüan Pei and its New Light on Buddhist Translators of the Northern Sung Empire."

Another Kashmir monk called Mu-lo-shih-chi went and presented Sanskrit manuscripts and the leaf of Bodhi-tree to China in 1005.[1]

We should not forget that besides these Kashmirian Masters, there were also other Indian and Central Asian monks who although natives of other places, did spend some years in Kashmir where they studied Buddhism. For example, Fo-t'u-teng "Had gone twice to Chi-pin (Kashmir) and had there received instructions from famous Masters." Others who learnt Buddhism from Kashmir and worked in China were Dharmakṣema (385-443 A.D.), Buddha-bhadra (359-429), Prajñā and others. Similarly, there were also a good number of Chinese monks who visited and learnt Buddhism in Kashmir.[2]

### Contribution

The direct contribution of Kashmirian Masters to Buddhism in China and Far Eastern countries embraces both works in translations and religious practices.

Their contribution as regards translations of Buddhist canons into Chinese is very important. The sections on *Āgamas, Madhyamāgama* and *Ekottarāgama* were translated by Gautama Saṅghadeva[3] and *Dīrghāgama* by another Kashmirian Buddhayaśas.[4] This means that out of four comprehensive collections of *Āgamas*, three were done by Kashmirian Masters. Besides this, there are also other references about *Āgama* studies which flourished in Kashmir. For instance, in the biography of Kumārajīva, it is recorded that he went to Kashmir in 352, studied *Madhyamāgama, Dīrghāgama* and other miscellaneous canons which belonged to the Hīnayāna school under the famous Kashmirian Master Bandhudatta.[5]

Translations of *Abhidharma* is another important Kashmirian contribution to *Tripiṭaka in Chinese*. It was Saṅghabhūti who translated *Vibhāṣā-śāstra*;[6] Saṅghadeva translated *Abhidharmajñānaprasthāna-śāstra* and *Abhidharmahṛdayaśāstra*;

---

1. See *FTTC.*, 44, T. 49, p. 402c.
2. For Fo-t'u-teng, see Arthur F. Wright: "Fo-t'u-teng," *HJAS.*, vol. XI, p. 337. About the others, see *CBC.*, vol. I or P.C. Bagchi's "India and China" which have a good account of Indian Masters in China. About the Chinese pilgrims to India, there are two recent résumés on the subject by Paul Lévy: "Les Pèlerins chinois en Inde"; and K.A. Nilakanta Sastri: "The Chinese pilgrims" both published in *France Asie, Présence du Bouddhisme,* (Nos. 153-157, 1959), pp. 375ff. and 437 ff.
3. *Hob.*, Nos. 2F, 125 and Nj. Nos. 542 and 543.
4. *Hob.*, No. 1 and Nj. No. 545.
5. *KSC.*, II, T 50, p. 330b.
6. *Hob.*, No. 1547 and Nj. No. 1279.

Dharmayaśas translated *Śāriputrābhidharma* along with another Indian monk Dharma-gupta.[1] Similarly, in *The Life of Hsüan-tsang*, it is clearly mentioned that after the Chinese Pilgrim arrived at Srinagar, he stayed at Jayendra monastery, studied *Abhidharma-kośa* and *Abhidharma-nyāyānusāra-śāstra* and other canons under the celebrated teacher Saṅghakīrti.[2] It is well-known that Hsüan-tsang contributed a large number of works in the translations of *Abhidharma* section after he returned to China from India. In the biography of Gautama Prajñā, it is also stated that this Master once went to Kashmir and studied nearly 40,000 *gāthās* of *Mūlasarvstivāda Vinaya*, 28,000 *gāthās* of *Abhidharma-kośa*, and also mastered *Mahavibhāṣā*.[3] From these facts, we can realise how important was Kashmirian Masters' contribution directly and indirectly to the *Abhidharma* section of *Tripiṭaka in Chinese*.

Besides their contribution on *Āgama* and *Abhidharma*, the Kashmirian Masters also did important and extensive works in the section of the Vinaya texts. In Chinese translation of Buddhist canons, there are five different Vinaya-piṭakas, viz, (i) *Mahāsāṅghika Vinaya*, (ii) *Sarvāstivāda-vinaya*, (iii) *Dharmaguptaka-vinaya*, (iv) *Mahīśāsaka-vinaya* and (v) *Mūlasarvāstivāda-vinaya*. In this connection, Buddhajīva translated two works one in thirty and another in one fascicle which belonged to Mahīśāsaka school.[4] In the collection of *Dharmaguptaka-vinaya* Buddhayaśas translated four works, of which one consisted of sixty fascicles.[5] In the section of *Sarvāstivāda-vinaya*, Puṇyatārā and Kumārajīva's translation was in fifty-eight fascicles. This work was enlarged to sixty one fascicles by another Kashmirian Vimalākṣa whom we have referred to in previous paragraphs.[6] Guṇavarman also did works in Vinaya section.[7] Yi-tsing, another celebrated Chinese Pilgrim to India, did not visit Kashmir. He however translated *Mūlasarvāstivāda vinaya* which definitely developed in Kashmir and other centres in India. On the point, the discovery of Gilgit Manuscripts on Vinaya and its correspondance

1. *Hob.*, Nos. 1543 and 1550; Nj. Nos. 1273 and 1288.
2. *Hob.*, No. 1548 and Nj. No. 1268.
3. Cf. "The Life of Hsüan-tsang." Tr. by Li Yung-hsi, Peking, 1959, p. 70. *CBC.*, vol. II, p. 582 and my article "On Chinese Translation of Avataṁsaka-sūtra," *Orissa Historical Research Journal*, vol. VII, p. 125 ff, 1959.
4. *Hob.*, Nos. 1421, 1422 and Nj. Nos. 1122, 1157.
5. *Ibid.*, Nos. 1428-1431 and Nos. 1117, 1154, 1155, 1156.
6. *Hob.*, Nos. 1435 and 1115. About Vimalakṣa, see *CBC.*, I. 338.
7. *Hob.*, Nos. 1434, 1466, 1472, 1476 and 1487.

with Yi-tsing's translation is very significant.[1] P.C. Bagchi said: "As a whole the Vinaya-piṭaka in Chinese is the richest collection of the Vinaya literature that ever existed . . ."[2]

As regards religious practices, Kashmirian contribution to Buddhism in mediaeval China are mainly in two directions: one is on the exposition of the Vinaya texts and another on the teaching of Ch'an (Dhyāna or meditation).

Besides Kashmirian's translation of Vinaya texts, they also did good works in explaining the texts and implementing monastic disciplines. In the biography of Vimalākṣa, it is stated that he had great achievements in preaching Vinaya rules at Shou-ch'ün and Yang-chou, both in eastern China.[3] Guṇavarman was described as "A profound scholar in Vinaya" and he also gave practical advice to Chinese Saṅghas. Others like Buddhayaśas and Buddhajīva possessed high virtues in observance of monastic discipline, thus they set examples to their followers to imitate. Their conduct was respected and appreciated by Chinese Saṅghas. In fact, Hui-chiao a most eminent Buddhist historian of the sixth century wrote: "Chi-pin turned out more sages."[4] In this regard, we should not forget another Kashmirian Shih-hsien, since he held the post of "Superintendent of Monks," which was usually occupied by the Masters of Discipline. Unless he possessed high virtue and good knowledge of Vinaya, it was impossible for him to hold that high post.

Kashmir was also a famous place where Buddhist meditation once flourished. In the biography of Kashmirian Masters, it was frequently mentioned that these Masters had a complete mastery of Dhyāna. For instance, Chih-shan was mentioned as "A great Master in meditation"; Dharmayaśas, Dharma-mitra and Guṇavarman were all well-known for their power of Meditation. In a preface to a translation relating to meditation, a Chinese monk Hui-kuan (433 A.D.) mentioned a genealogy of Dhyāna Masters of Kashmir. According to that Chinese source, Dhyāna Buddhism had a long

---

1. *Hob.*, Nos. 1442-1457. About the relation between Yi-tsing's translation and Gilgit MSS, see Prof. Chi Hsien-lin's comparative study: "*Chi kêng-pên-shuo-yi-ch'ieh-yu-pu-lü fan-wên-yüan-pên tê fa-hsien*" (The Discovery of Sanskrit Original text of Mūlasarvāstivāda-vinayavastu), in *Chung-yin wên-hua kuan-hsi-shih-lun-ts'ung* (Essays on Sino-Indian Cultural and Historical Relations), Peking, 1957, pp. 95 ff.
2. *India and China*, p. 131.
3. Cf. note No. 10.
4. The original version of this passage is "*Chi-pin to ch'u shêng-jên*" which is existing in T 50, p. 342, line 10.

tradition in Kashmir. Puṇyamitra was respected as the first Patriarch of the Dhyāna Buddhist school in Kashmir. He was succeeded by his disciple Puṇyatārā and later, two of Puṇyatārā's disciples namely Dharmatrāta and Buddhasena were jointly respected as the third Patriarchs. Dharmatrāta's method of Dhyāna was introduced in China by Buddhabhadra and it occupied an important place amongst the canons of Meditation. There is also the reference concerning Dhyāna tradition of Buddhasena in Chinese translations. Buddhabhadra though a native of Central India, resided in Kashmir for some time before he proceeded further East. His translation of *Ch'an-ching* which was originally written by Dharmatrāta proves his appreciation of Dhyāna Buddhism of Kashmir.[1] Similarly, some of the Chinese pilgrims visited Kashmir in order to learn the methods of Dhyāna. Chih-yên and Hui-lan are good examples.

According to a postscript appended to the end of *Hsiu-hsing-tao-ti-ching* (Chinese translation of *Yogācārabhūmi*), the original text of that canon was brought to Tun-huang, the celebrated ancient Buddhist centre in N.W. China frontier by a Chi-pin scholar (*Wên-shih*) named Chu Hou chêng (or Chêng-jo). The text was then translated by Dharmarakṣa (Chu Fa-hu) with collaboration of that Kashmirian, which was completed on the 26th March, 284 A.D. (See T. XV, 230c, foot note 19).

From this reference, we may further push back the date of the earliest Kashmirian who went and worked in China to the later part of the third century A.D. This reference has also further proved the prevalence of *Dhyāna* Buddhism in Kashmir. (Cf. Demiéville, Paul: "Le Yogācārabhūmi de Saṅgharakṣa," *Bulletin de l'Ecole française d'Extrême-Orient,* XLIV, (1954). About the name of this Kashmirian, see p. 348 note I).

From the above discussions and evidences, we may conclude that the activities of Kashmirian Buddhist Masters in China flourished during the fourth and fifth centuries of the Christian era. Their mission was once again revived in the seventh and early decades of the eighth century. After another interruption of two hundred and odd years, their activities once again came into the picture during the last quarter of the tenth and first half of the eleventh century.

Their contribution on translation of Buddhist canons was mainly in the fields of *Āgama*. They were also responsible for transmission of Buddhist metaphysical philosophy as found in

1. *Hob.*, No. 618 and Nj. No. 1341.

*Abhidharma* collection to China and the Far East. Their contribution in translation of Vinaya-piṭaka was outstanding. Besides these, they also translated other works of different categories. Their translations of Tantric texts during the tenth and eleventh centuries are very significant. Their contribution on religious practices was mainly concentrated on monastic discipline and on Buddhist meditation. Their works and virtue were respected by the Buddhists in China and in the Far East. These were recorded in various biographies, catalogues as well as other documents.

# *Chapter - 30*

# Hidden Traces of Buddhism in Assam

**Sarat Chandra Goswami**

1. I desire to state at the outset that in a paper dealing with social and religious customs it is well nigh impossible to give exact facts which go to make scientific history. Conclusions therefore have to be drawn from observed facts of a later day, which take the colour of personal opinions and are always subject to correction or verification in the light of other and more abundant materials, which may be available afterwards. The observations which I make later on in this paper are necessarily of this character and may be accepted with this caution.

2. Mention of Kāmarūpa is easily traceable in the Epics. In the Rāmāyaṇa the name Dharmāraṇya appears to denote Kāmarūpa; while the name Prāg-jyotiṣa also occurs, which is said to be on the Barāha mountain on the sea-coast. The sea probably means the Brahmaputra, whose estuary at that distant date is thought to have been near the Garo-Hills.

In the Mahābhārata, the king Bhagadatta and his kingdom Prāg-jyotiṣa are so famous that they require hardly to be mentioned in this connection.

All the Purāṇas mention Kāmarūpa as a kingdom lying on the eastern side of India; and some of them contain long and detailed description of this country.

Kālidāsa has been held to have flourished in the middle of the 5th century A.D. at the latest. He describes his hero, Raghu, the great grand-father of Rāma, as a conqueror of Kāmarūpa. This at least proves that in the 5th century A.D. Kāmarūpa was a well-known kingdom.

And before that in the days of Candragupta Maurya (316-292 B.C.) "we learn from the famous Allahabad Pillar that Kāmarūpa was known then as a state lying away east of Nepal" (Col. Shakespeare).

3. Though thus through a long period, the name of Kāmarūpa is to be found in what may be called the Hindu records, it is strange that we do not come across this name in the voluminous records of Buddhism till the time of Hieun-Tsiang. It cannot be that the kingdom of Kāmarūpa sank into such insignificance that it was not known to the Buddhists. For other records contemporary with the hey-day of Buddhism (i.e. from about 500 B.C. to 700 A.D.) mention the kingdom. We are therefore irresistibly led to the conclusion that to the Buddhist the country was known by some other name. And this seems all the more probable from two facts:

First, many places and tribes of India are known by different names in the Buddhistic literature.

Secondly, it appears that each religion at that period regarded the other with hostility, and as far as it was possible, refrained from making references to the others' activities, e.g., even such of the Purāṇas, as are thought by competent authorities to have been written in the Buddhistic period, speak only meagrely or indirectly of the great Buddha and the social upheaval which his teachings led to.

4. Even if Kāmarūpa was known by a different name to the Buddhists, it is very difficult to known what this name really was. There is a tradition in Burma, Bhutan and Tibet that the name of Kāmarūpa at that time was Wesali-Long or Vaisālī, and that the Second Synod of the Buddhists was held here in the early part of the 4th century B.C. Col. Shakespeare also states these facts in his History, but does not mention the source of his information. In some of the Vaṃśāvalīs of Assam, the ancient name of the place has been stated to have been Vaiśālī. It may be borne in mind that the scholars have not agreed as to the exact location of Vaiśālī and very few of them have yet turned their eyes towards Assam.

There is however a general belief that Buddhism was never a prevalent religion in Kāmarūpa. I am inclined to think that Sir Edward Gait is mainly responsible for this theory. He based his conclusions solely on Hieun-Tsiang's description of Kāmarūpa in the 7th century A.D. and seems to have overlooked other facts.

What Hieun-Tsiang says, however, is—"though the people adored the Devas, there seemed to be little faith in the Buddha himself; and no place in which Buddhist Priests could assemble appears to exist. Such disciples, as there are, are certainly of pure faith, but pray more or less secretly" (Col. Shakespeare).

This, it would appear, simply means that the prevalent faith was not Buddhism though there were certainly disciples of the Buddha at the time. The Chinese Pilgrim also says that the king Kumāra Bhāskara Varman though not of the pure faith still respects the Buddhist Śramaṇas greatly. All these show that Buddhism was tolerated, and even regarded with certain respect, though the people generally might not have been professed Buddhists. It should be borne in mind that while the countries surrounding Kāmarūpa, namely Tibet, Bhutan, Burma, Pauṇḍra-vardhana (north Bengal) and Samataṭa (east Bengal), all came under the sway of Buddhism, it would be strange if the kingdom of Kāmarūpa could altogether escape from its influence—an influence which spread throughout the whole civilized world.

I have already related a few traditions, and in this connection I wish to quote from Col. Shakespeare: "Tibetans and Bhutanese believe that Buddha died in Kāmarūpa, while the learned Hungarian traveller, Csomo de Koros, claims that the Saint died in Gauhati under a pair of Sal Trees. The great Chinese Hieun-Tsiang had also the same idea."

This strikes us as a bit startling, specially when we have learned not to associate anything great with the degenerated eastern nook of India of the present day. But traditions are not valueless, because they happen to be traditions. Here is what Prof. Breasted, speaking of discoveries in the Tutankhamen Tomb, where a documentary reference to the Trojan War was traced, says:—

> "This contemporary reference to the Trojan War is an epoch-making revelation, which must re-act powerfully upon our treatment of early human traditions. It is at once demonstrable that such traditions must not be thrown on the scrap-heap, but rather carefully divested of gods, goddesses, prodigies and wonders, and then examined for the nucleus of sober truth upon which the legendary tale was built."

Materials at present available would not justify any definite conclusion; but such traditions are certainly indicative that the great religion of the Buddha had some hold on the people of this ancient kingdom.

5. Not only tradition, but history also gives some hints about prevalence of Buddhism in Kāmarūpa. During the reign of Mahārāja Naranārāyaṇa of Cooch Behar, one Ralph Fitch, a European, visited the country. Sir Edward Gait quotes the following in his History of Assam (p. 60) from the description left by this traveller:—

". . .There (in the Koch-kingdom) they be all gentiles, and they will kill nothing. They have hospitals for sheep, goats, dogs, cats, birds and for all living creatures. When they be old and lame, they keep them until they die. If a man catch or buy any quick thing in other places and bring it thither, they will give him money for it, or other victuals, and keep it in their hospitals or let it go. They will give meat to the ants."

But with the pre-conceived idea that Buddhism never flourished in Kāmarūpa, Sir Edward (*loc. cit.*) finds it "difficult to explain the statements made by this traveller regarding the great tenderness shown by the people for animal life" and presumes that "the state of things described was due solely to the personal action of Nara-nārāyaṇa himself."

Would it not, however, be the simpler theory and accord with facts, if it was frankly held that it appears that Buddhism flourished in Kāmarūpa during the days of the rise of Kocha power? A single man, powerful ruler though he be, cannot transform a people into such gentle creatures in the course of one generation.

In fact, we find many references to Buddhism in the ancient Assamese Literature. Sir Edward Gait says that there is no trace of this religion in the old records and inscriptions. But he forgets to mention that in one of the most well-known copper-plates, which he himself discovered and caused to be deciphered by Dr. Hornle, namely the copper-plates of Indra-Pāla (about 1050 A.D.), there is a clear mention of a Śāsana (or rock-cut edict) of the Tathāgata (Buddha), which was then existing, and which is given as a boundary mark of the land-grant forming the subject of this inscription. This land-grant was made in a village, then known as Makkhhi-yāna and now called Mākhi-bāhā near Tihu in Kāmrūpa. There is still a small mound in the neighbourhood, of which no one knows the history or the tradition. The people call it Banuwā Deul or the Jungle-mound. We will hear more of Indra Pāla later on.

6. Coming to Literature, we find mention of the Bauddhas and their excesses in the writings of Mādhava Kanadalī, Ananta Kandalī and Rāma Sarasvatī. The famous Kīrtan also contains such a passage. And in the life of Śrī Śaṅkara Deva, Daityāri mentions some Bauddhas coming to the Guru and having been driven away by his purifying force.

In the Dīpikā-cchandaḥ of Puruṣottama Gajapati, there are many passages referring to the Bauddhas and their excesses, and complaining that even the Brāhmaṇas were following the customs of the Buddhists ( বৌদ্ধাচাৰী ). It is true that the Dīpikā-cchandaḥ speaks of the Devī-pūjā which was characteristic of these impure people. But we must remember how Buddhism, in later days, gave rise to a form of religion which combined in its rituals Tāntric form of worship and sex worship. It is on this account that we find all the classical authors speaking of excesses of the votaries of Buddhism.

7. But there is a different kind of literature in ancient Assamese, which has up till now attracted very little attention. This may be called, for want of a better name, the Tract Literature, as distinguished from the classics of the more well known authors.

This literature has two distinct sides—the exoteric and the esoteric. The tracts are original, though some of the esoteric kind profess to have derived their views from Caitanyadeva or Śaṅkara Deva. The names of the authors are not generally mentioned in the tracts and the writers give in them free scope to their heterodox views or other opinions.

A few of the exoteric kind (which cover a wide range of subjects) have been published. But the esotric ones are kept in great secrecy; and he must consider himself fortunate who is allowed a glimpse even into the less important ones. They contain things, which to describe them mildly, are very extra-ordinary; and speak with approval of the excesses of which the classical writers complain. There will be no space to speak of them in any more detail: and this is hardly the place for it. But I shall mention one of them.

This pamphlet is called Dharmasambād and was written in the reign of king Śiva Siṃha (middle of the 18th century). It narrates the following story:

Yudhiṣṭhira once performed a Yajña extending over 12 years; and Bhīmasena was at the gate to receive the guests. On the last day of the sacrifice, when the Pūrṇāhuti ceremony was to be performed, a Caṇḍāla appeared at the gate. Bhīmasena refused him admission, because of his low caste. Thus a discussion ensues, as the result of which Bhīma goes to Yudhiṣṭhira and speaks of this Caṇḍāla. The King comes to see him at the gate and again a deeper discussion begins, towards the end of which the Caṇḍāla declares that he is unable to accept any gift from the king, because a king is the impure of the impure:

পশু মধ্যে অধম কুকুৰ বুলি যাক ।
দশ কুকুৰ সম কুমাৰৰ চাক ॥
দশ খান কুমাৰৰ চাকৰ সমান ।
হবে অপবিত্র ৰজকৰ পাট খান ।

দশ থান পাটৰ সমান বেশ্যা জাতি।
দশ বেশ্যা সমান নৃপতি হোবে আতি ॥

And when the Brāhmaṇas heard this from the Caṇḍāla, they were also afraid of accepting gifts from the king, and went away, leaving the 12 years' Yajña unfinished. But Yudhiṣṭhira does not in the least mind this; for he recognises in the Caṇḍāla Dharma himself and worships him.

The points to be noted in this extra-vagant story are: that the Dharma appears in the guise of a Caṇḍāla, that the Brāhmaṇas take his speech as more authoritative than the Śāstras and that a king like Yudhiṣṭhira does not mind the unfulfilment of a Yajña over which he spent 12 years.

That Dharma is the Buddha himself in another garb has been proved by scholars; and they in Bengal have been able to unearth a considerable literature on the Dharma-cult. A peculiar feature of this cult is that the Guru is generally a Caṇḍāla or of some such low caste. The respect for the Caṇḍāla in the story on the part of the Brāhmaṇas and the king is borne of this cause. What the Caṇḍāla says of the true nature of religion completely identifies his teachings with Buddhist tenets:

সত্য হন্তে ধর্ম উপজয় পুনু,
দয়াত বাঢ়য় আতি।
ক্ষমাতে সে ধর্ম সদাই থাকয়,
ক্রোধত বিনাশ যান্তি ॥

"Religion springs from Truth, increases in Charity, resides in Forgiveness, and is destroyed in Anger."

I believe any comment on this is unnecessary.

8. Another significant fact in this connection is the Cosmogony, as related in a considerable part of the esoteric literature above spoken of, and also in the Beulā-Lakhindar literature, that is, the works of Mānkar, Durgābar, and Nārāyaṇ Dev. They all derive the Universe from Śūnya (Nothingness) and speak of the Deity as Nirañjana. Now Śunya-vāda is a well-known philosophic doctrine of Buddhism. Nirañjana as a name of the Deity is widely employed in the Dharma-cult.

These are facts which show that the doctrines of Buddhism permeated throughout all the strata of social life in Kāmarūpa, and greatly influenced the thoughts of the time and were in vogue (in some form or other) even after the great Vaiṣṇavic revival of Śaṅkara Deva.

9. This brings me to that form of Vaiṣṇavism that had its revival and growth in Kamarūpa and its probable indebtedness to Buddhism. The Kāmarūpa-Vaiṣṇavism differs considerably from other schools of this great Indian form of worship. Its proper appreciation in relation to those other schools requires an amount of scholarship and research, which the present writer is unable to command. Here it is sufficient to touch upon its most salient features and to show how this school was greatly influenced by Buddhistic ideas.

The most note-worthy institutions of Kāmarūpa-Vaiṣṇavism are the Satra, the Nām-ghar, and the Śaraṇ.

The Satra is an institution which is not known, in the form existing in Assam, in any other part of India. It has many peculiar characteristics, e.g.,

A Satra is built in four Hatis or lines enclosing a big quadrangle; and an inner and an outer gate leads to it from the outside;

The Bhakatas are celebates in all the representative Satras; they live under the authority of an Adhikārin;

A Satra is essentially a democratic institution where the Samūha, as the Bhakats are collectively called, has more or less effective voice in the control of affairs; and

The Bhakats live, or had to live in former days, on alms, that is, doles received from the disciples of the Satra.

Now celebacy, living on alms, leadership of an erudite monk and control on democratic lines are essential features of a Buddhist Monastery. And it is also known that many monasteries, as also the Buddhist Universities, were built in four lines enclosing a huge quandrangle, and on the road leading to them from the outside were placed abodes for the Dvāra Paṇḍitas.

With our present knowledge it is useless to say definitely that our Vaiṣṇava-Satras are counterparts of Buddhist monasteries. But it must be borne in mind that the Satra must have had a history behind it; and I leave it to the learned to work out what this history is.

10. I shall now add a word about the Nām-ghar. This is also an institution at once peculiar to, and national of, the Assamese people.

Every Assamese village has a Nām-ghar. Free entrance is allowed into the prayer-hall, even to the people who are generally regarded as untouchable. In later time, however, this freedom has been restricted to that portion of the Hall which is known as the Top.

And this word Top appears to have kept in concealment within itself a whole history of a religion. The Top is that portion of a Nām-ghar which is covered by a rounded roof, this roof being added as a third roof to the western end of the other two roofs of the Hall. From the use to which it is put, viz., the accommodation of the lower class people, it is more than probable that the word comes from Stūpa the well-known Buddhist word. It is on this account, perhaps, that even to-day all sorts of people are allowed entrance to this part. The rotundity of the roof of the Top may also owe its origin to the rounded shape of the Buddhist Stūpa.

11. Lastly, I shall have to speak a word about the Saraṇa. The Kāmarūpa School of Vaiṣṇavism recognises four Śaraṇas, viz., (1) হৰিত শৰণ, (2) নামত শৰণ, (3) গুৰুত শৰণ, and (4) ভকতত শৰণ, i.e., a Vaiṣṇava must reverence the God, the Nāma or the Teaching, the Guru or the Teacher, and the Bhakata or the Order. The famous Tri-ratnas (three jewels) of Buddhism are the Dharma, the Buddha and the Saṅgha, that is, the Teaching (Dharma), the Teacher (Buddha) and the Order (Saṅgha).

It is striking that excepting the Śaraṇa in Hari or the God-head, the other three Śaraṇas are exactly identical in Buddhism and Kāmarūpa Vaiṣṇavism. Buddhism did not teach anything explicit of the God-head, so that Śaraṇa in Hari is a necessary addition in the Vaiṣṇavic cult. Now this very striking identity cannot be a matter of accident. It indicates some deeper connection between the two forms of worship.

There will be no space here to speak in detail of the Dissenters from the orthodox forms of Vaiṣṇavism and their teachings, which form the contents of the esoteric tract literature briefly noticed in a preceding paragraph; nor it will be possible to demostrate here how these teachings are similar to the doctrines of that form of Buddhism, which prevailed in a later age in the North, including Tibet and Bhutan.

But one particular sect cannot be overlooked. They are the Tamol-Nokhowas (তামোল-নোখোৱা). They are only a few hundred people and live in three or four villages of Upper Assam. They have their own priests and do not recognise Brāhmaṇas, and are so much freed from all ceremonials, that even their marriage is performed

freed from all ceremonials, that even their marriage is performed without any other ceremony than a formal intimation to their Order. They claim to be worshippers of the Buddha himself. They have got their own Kīrtan, Ghoṣa, and Bhāgavat; and these are entirely different from those we know. But the teachings of Śaṅkara Deva have had such a great hold on the people of Assam, that they think that the Buddha incarnation occurred after Śaṅkara Deva, and that the latter was a person superior to their Buddha. They derive their name from the extreme exclusiveness they maintain from other people, so much that they are forbidden to take even a Tamol from anyone outside their creed.

12. It will bear mention in this connection that almost till now (and in some places even now) many lower caste people used to take their priests from their own castes. These priests are not regarded as Brāhmaṇas and till a generation ago did not wear the sacred thread; but had a pair of Karias (ear ornament) as their distinctive mark.

Near the Sorbhog Railway Station on the E.B. Railway in Barpeta Sub-division, there is a Thān (or sacred place) called the Gorakhīyā Gosāi Thān (গোৰখীয়া গোঁসাই থান), the abode of the God of the common people. Here the priest belongs to the Koch caste, though the god is held in high reverence by all castes, including Brāhmaṇas. Similar Thāns are common all over Kāmarūpa, though without a priest. The word Gorakhīyā literally means cow-keeper; but by transference it now signifies common people.

All these do show clear and distinct Buddhistic influence in Assam, even to a over-critical mind.

13. Now from Vaiṣṇavism, I come to certain Viṣṇu images. Of the well-known and oft-discussed images, one is the Janārdana image at Gauhati, just on the Brahmaputra, below the Śukreśvara Hills. It is regarded as an image of a Dhyāni-Buddha by many; while others think that it might be a Viṣṇu Mūrti as well, though the position of the lower two hands are very significant. And to any one who has seen it with a scrutinising eye, it will appear that the upper two arms were cut out in after age rather clumsily.

And the other Mūrti is the Haya-grīva Mūrti at Hajo. Tibetans and Bhutanese still come to this shrine and worship the image with an amount of devotion which is extremely rare among us. They call the image Mahā-Muni, or the Great Saint. Sir Edward Gait cites Dr. Bloch as the authority who thinks the Mūrti as that of the Man-Lion, Narasiṃha. But the characteristic posture of the lower hands is that of a Dhyānī Buddha.

As to this image there is a secret; and at Hajo there is a family who keeps this secret, and is known on that account as Viśvāsī. The real secret is not known, perhaps even to this family; but it is known that the inner rock image is covered by a layer of plaster of special preparation; and repairs tc this layer are to be occasionally done by the members of this Visvāsī family. It is not improbable that under a layer of plaster which depicts the Haya-grīva (or the Man-Lion, as has been thought) there shine the beautifully composed features of a Dhyānī Buddha.

And, in connection with this shrine there is a deeper secret still, the existence of which even is known only to a few. In the innermost recesses of the temple, the true object of worship is contained in a series of gold caskets. Not even all the Dalais—chief preists—are allowed to see what these caskets conceal. Only a few, whose devotion and good faith are beyond suspicion, are allowed to see this mysterious object under the most terrible vows. In one generation only two or three persons become acquainted with this secret; and they would not divulge it even at the cost of their lives.

Other traditions about Hindu shrines having been built over Buddhist ones ascribe the Kāmakhyā and many other temples to Buddhism. No real proof, which could count in history, can however be produced at this stage of our knowledge. Major Hannay, who made extensive tours of the Sadiya country, is of opinion that he found many Buddhistic ruins in that part.

I have already spoken of Indra-Pāla and his copper plates. In that plate which has been already mentioned, Indra-Pāla is depicted to be a devotee of Śiva. But it appears that he embraced Buddhism later on, and turned himself into a monk. To test him, he was placed with a Dārikā, public woman. But he proved himself true; so he was taken into the monastic order and renamed Dārikā-Pāla and in this name the King of Kāmrūpa composed many songs on Buddhism.

There are many indications which go to show that Kāmarūpa has had many glories in the Buddhistic period and researches into this particular period are likely to yield startling results.[1]

1. I am indebted for this information to Maulvi Muhammad Sahidulla, M.A., B.L., of the Dacca University; and he tells me that it is from Tibetan sources.

# Chapter - 31

# Buddhism in Kāmarūpa

**Nalini Nath Das Gupta**

In Kāmarūpa, a land *par excellence* of Hinduism, religion had had in both early and mediaeval ages almost a uniform history, seldom perturbed by diversity. Our curiosity is by far intensified by its geographical position; it just borders to the west upon Bengal, where various religious systems played more or less a conspicuous part of its own in its early history. When in or about 637 A.D. Hiuen Tsang came to visit Bengal he found there all the three prominent religions of the day, *viz.* Brāhmanism, Buddhism and Jainism, flourishing side by side. But the same pilgrim noticed no trace of Jainism and very little of Buddhism in Kia mo-lu po. And even when from the middle of the eighth century right up to the twelfth, Buddhism was prospering in Bengal under the auspices of the great Pāla monarchs, producing a vast body of literature, a rich store of sculptures and a galaxy of notable Buddhist teachers and other celebrities, Buddhism still retained the meagreness of its history in Kāmarūpa.

It is characteristic of the Faith that it could not often gain ground upon any soil without royal ægis and royal patronage. Very often does the history of India bear witness to this characteristic of the religion which thrives or gets debilitated according to the amount of favour and security it derives or not from a king or a line of kings. And since the early kings of Kāmarūpa, all Brāhmaṇical Hindus, did not shore up the religion with their patronage, Kāmarūpa, although at the eastern fringe of Bengal, successfully demonstrated itself as a land where Buddhism failed to make any readable history of it.

Even in the earnestness and persistence with which Bhāskaravarman, the ally of Harṣavardhana, sought an interview with Hiuen Tsang in his own kingdom and his subsequent reluctance to part with him, there was the gesture, engendered by a genuine feeling, of personal respect for the foreign pilgrim, rather than any pro-Buddhistic sentiment on the part of Bhāskaravarman. Hiuen Tsang is frank enough to say that the people of Kāmarūpa adored and sacrificed to the Devas and had no faith in the Buddha, and if there were a few Buddhists in the country, they had to say their prayers or perform their devotional rites in secret, evidently in fear of persecution. This could not possibly have been the case if Bhāskaravarman would champion the cause of Buddhism, or in any way, countenance it in his dominion, by deviating from the ancestral path of religious orthodoxy, and it is idle to find, we must agree, in the adoration to Dharma in the invocatory portion of his Nidhānpur grant, just following the salutation to his tutelary deity, Śiva, a reference to the Law of the Buddha. Dharma described therein as "the sole friend of creation, the cause of prosperity in this and the next world whose form is the good of others and which is unseen but whose existence is inferred from the results" is anything but a Buddhist deity. In the later Buddhist conception Dharma was supposed to belong to the female sex and the goddess Dharma in the Buddhist trinity came to represent Ārya Tārā, Prajñāpāramitā, the mother of all Buddhas, and the like, and even when Dharma was sometimes regarded as a male symbolising the primordial energy, his conception is not such as to conform to the description of Dharma as is in the Nidhānpur grant.

Hiuen Tsang further states that from the time when the Buddha appeared in the world even down to his time there never was built one *Saṁghārāma* as a place for the priests to assemble. And what was true of a *Saṁghārāma* or *Vihāra* in Kāmarūpa till the days of Bhāskara-varman was also true of the same in all succeeding times. Neither during the rule of the Sālastambha dynasty nor during that of the Pālas of Kāmarūpa from Brahmapāla to Jayapāla, do we come across any evidence as to any established seat of Buddhistic learning and culture anywhere in Kāmarūpa. As regards Buddhist sculptures, too, we have, so far as is known, none from Kāmarūpa except the few, of probably the tenth-eleventh century, unearthed by the Gauhati excavations. One of them, in a thin stone slab, represents the Buddha in the *Abhaya mudrā*, and another, a terracotta plaque, delineates the same in the *Bhūmisparśa mudrā*, in which the Buddha, seated, touches with his finger the earth, indicating thereby that he asks the Earth goddess to bear witness to his attainment of *Sambodhi* against all Māra's temptations. The third sculpture, in stone, probably depicts a minor goddess of the Vajrayāna pantheon, Mahāpratisarā, seated, and with four faces, eight arms and a *caitya* symbol overhead.

Of Buddhist celebrities of the province, neither epigraphical nor authentic literary source affords us any definite information. The *Tanjur*, nevertheless, contains the Tibetan translation of a tract, entitled *Dhyāna-saḍ-dharma-vyavasthāna* by one Avadhūtipāda, who is, as we are told, probably identical with Ratnaśīla of Kāmarūpa. If the identification be tenable, we have herein perhaps the name of one Buddhist (rather than Śaivite) scholar who can with a degree of precision be attributed to Kāmarūpa. But in this case also, beyond his name we know nothing about his personal history, though we can only assume that he belonged to the eleventh or twelfth century A.D. Nowhere else, in the *Tanjur* the name of Kāmarūpa is known to occur to have been the native land of any other scholar, either as an author, or as a commentator, or as a translator.

In the first inscription of King Indrapāla from Gauhati, there is the mention of a *śāsana* or charter connected with the name of Tathāgata. This is, however, the name borne by a private individual who built a temple, and does not refer to the Buddha, as the late lamented Rai Bahadur Kanak Lal Baua conjectured.[1] That even the person with this Buddhistic name was not himself a Buddhist is vouched for by the fact that the temple he got constructed was dedicated not to any Buddhist divinity but to the holy Āditya or the Sun-god (*uttareṇa Tathāgata-kārit-Ādityabhaṭṭāraka satka-śāsana-bhaviṣā-bhūsīmni* . . .).[2] We have no reason, therefore, to see in this charter any trace of Buddhism or any Buddhist influence.

Late Tibetan tradition as embodied in the *Grub t'ob* and the *Bka'gbabs bdun ldan* makes Mīnanātha a fisherman from Kāmarūpa. The name *Mīnanātha* is sometimes synonymous with *Matsyendranātha*, or, in some lists, one is said to be the son of the other.[3] Professor Giuseppe Tucci tries to show that *Matsyendra* or its synonym is but a title or an appellative of some *siddhas* or those mystics who attempted to harmonise Mahāyāna Buddhism and Hinduism, and that the title was first given to Lui-pā,[4] who, as we know, was a native of Rāḍha or West Bengal. If we accept Prof. Tucci's theory, all that can be said of the above tradition, without questioning its truth, is that one *siddha* bearing the title or appellative of Mīna,

1. *Early History of Kāmarūpa*, p. 152.
2. *Kāmarūpa-Śāsanāvalī*, pp. 124 and 129.
3. Cf., for instance, Cordier, *Catalogue du Fonds Tibétain*, II, p. 237.
4. *JASB.*, 1930, pp. 133-134.

but other than Lui-pā, was a fisherman from Kāmarūpa. In case we do not, the genuineness of the tradition recorded by the two books has to be questioned in view of that Mīnapāda, *alias* Vajrapāda, *alias* Acintya, is claimed by other traditions to be of Bengal. Again, in the *Grub t'ob*, Rāhula, another Buddhist scholar, was a Śūdra from Kāmarūpa, but there also, as pointed out by Prof. Tucci, Rāhulabhadra is the name of Saraha, and, on the other hand, in the *bKa'babs bdun ldan*, Rāhulabhadra is a Brahmin of Oḍivisa,[1] while according to the *Pag Sam Jon Zang*, Saraha Chūṅ or Śavarīpā was a huntsman in the hills of Baṅgāla.[2] Nothing, therefore, ensures us that the *Grub t'ob* records a correct story about the homeland of Rāhula. As regards Mahīdhara and Dārika, the two other scholars claimed to be Kāmarūpa, the grounds are far more uncertain.

1. *Ibid.*, p. 141.
2. P. cxxi.

## *Chapter - 32*

# Buddhism in Kāmarūpa

### Maheswar Neog

In the Nidhanpur grant of Bhāskatavarman, king of Kāmarūpa of the seventh century A.D. (verse 3) occurs the word *dharma* and in the Gauhati grant of Indrapāla of the eleventh century A.D. is the description of a spot *tathāgatakāritādityabhaṭṭārakasatkaśāsanabhaviṣā*, "the Bhaviṣā with the still existing charter of holy Āditya (or Sun God) made by Tathāgata" (as rendered by Dr. Hoernle). In his Puṣpabhadrā grant (verse 7) Dharmapāla (eleventh century) reminds the future kings that *dharma* is not to be abandoned. The occurrence of these words in these royal grants has been taken by some scholars as indication of the existence of Buddhism in ancient Kāmarūpa. These are however extremely doubtful evidences (Dr. B.K. Barua: "Notices of Buddhism in Assam," *Mahamahopadhyaya Prof. D.V. Poddar Commemoration Volume,* 1950, p. 26). Archæology also does not bring forward any convincing proofs. Kanaklal Barua mentions some sculptured images on stones and terra-cotta plaques representing the Buddha which can be assigned to the tenth or eleventh century. Below the figure in a terra-cotta votive tablet found at Gauhati is inscribed the well-known Mahāyāna creed. But as he has pointed out, these images are of a portable nature and might easily have been imported from outside by itinerant Mahāyāna monks (*An Early History of Kāmarūpa*, pp. 155 f).

Hiuen Tsiang who visited Kāmarūpa in the first half of the seventh century remarks that there was no Buddhist monastery in the land, and that "whatever Buddhists there were in it performed their acts of devotion secretly" (Watters, *On Yuan Chwang,* vol. II, p. 186). This would show that though Buddhism did not prevail in the country on an organised scale nor was patronised by the king, traces of it were not absolutely found wanting. It could not be said if Hiuen

Tsiang's mention of secret performances of Buddhists is a reference to the existence of some esoteric type of the religion. It will however be wide of the mark to infer that the Buddhists of Kāmarūpa did their acts of devotion in secret "evidently in fear of persecution" by the ardently Śaivite king, as has been supposed (*Indian Historical Quarterly*, vol. XXVI, Dec., 1950, p. 333). The Bhāskarvarman invited the Chinese pilgrim to his court convinces us that a sort of religious toleration was the rule of his days.

An inscription discovered at Nāgārjunikoṇḍa in the ancient Andhra country of the fourteenth regnal year of king Māḍhariputa, probably identical with king Māḍhariputa Śrī Virapurisadata of the Ikṣvāku dynasty (third century A.D.), dedicated a shrine "for the benefit of the fraternities (of monks) of Taṃbapaṃna who had converted Kāśmīra, Gandhāra, Cīna, Cilāta, Tosali, Avaraṁta, Vaṁga, Vanavāsī, Yavana (?), Damila (?), Palura (?) and the Isle of Taṃbapaṃni" (*Ep. Ind.*, XX, pp. 22-23, Second Apsidal Temple, Insc. F. cited by Dr. N. Ray, *Theravāda Buddhism in Burma,* pp. 14-15). It is noteworthy that Cilāta is here mentioned along with Cīna. The Cīnas and the Kirātas together manned the army of Bhagadatta of Kāmarūpa led to the Kurukṣetra war. In the Buddhist *Mahāvaṁśa* and in the Kūrmavibhāga section of the *Bṛhatsaṃhitā*, the Cīnas and Kirātas (*Cīlāta* in the former text) are together mentioned (Dr. N. Ray, *op. cit.*, pp. 15, 17). Dr. Ray identifies Cīlāta of the inscription with Burma; but it may very well mean Kāmarūpa, with which the Kirātas have always been associated.

The later and degenerate form of Buddhism called Vajrayāna or Tāntric Buddhism, "a queer mixture of monistic philosophy, magic and erotics, with a small admixture of Buddhist ideas" (Winternitz, *History of Indian Literature,* vol. II, p. 388), is considered by scholars to have originated in the seventh century A.D. It propounded the theory of Mahāsukhavāda and admitted the five *m's* (*makāras*)—wine, woman, fish, meat and all kinds of exciting food as indispensable for the votary. The seekers of salvation should enjoy Prajñāpāramitā or perfect truth that resides in every woman, high or low, young or old, healthy or diseased (Dr. B. Bhattacharya, *Buddhist Esoterism*, pp. 32 ff). This religion, associated with magic and sorcery, at once became popular. It gained ground through the teachings and mystic songs of the eighty-four Siddhapuruṣas and their disciples. The names of some of these Siddhas have been connected with Kāmarūpa in old accounts of them. In the Vajrayāna scripture *Sādhanamālā* (pp. 453,

455), moreover, the four *pīṭhas* of the cult are enumerated as Kāmākhyā or Kāmarūpa, Sirihaṭṭa, Pūrṇagiri and Oḍiyāna (Uḍḍiyāna, Oḍḍiyāna or Oḍryan, *Sādhanamālā*, II, intro., p. xxxvii-n). While Kāmākhyā and Sirihaṭṭa are evidently in Kāmarūpa, Oḍiyāna also is supposed by some scholars to be in the western part of the country (Dr. B. Bhattacharya, *op. cit.*, pp. 45 f.). This view however has met with vehement criticism (Dr. P.C. Bagchi, *IHQ.*, vol. VI, pp. 580 f). Even Pūrṇagiri is said to be some Puṇyatīrtha (?) in Assam (Dr. B. Bhattacharya, *op. cit.*, p. 43-n). But there is no conclusive evidence to prove that this place was really in Kāmarūpa. It is sufficient that two out of these four places, which were possibly main centres of dissemination of Vajrayāna doctrines belonged to this country. In Sahajayāna the Siddhas likened the stations where the nerve-channels *laland, rasanā*, and *avadhūtī* combined in the body to Uḍḍiyāna, Jālandhara, Pūrṇagiri and Kamarūpa (Dr. P.C. Bagchi: "Some aspects of Buddhist mysticism of Bengal," *The Culture Heritage of India,* vol. I, pp. 312-13).

Kāmarūpa, Pūrṇagiri and Oḍḍiyāna seem to be also centres of Śākta Tāntricism. The *Kālikā Puraṇa* (18. 42-44) describes how during Śiva's wandering with the dead body of Satī on his shoulders, her feet, severed by divine magic, fell down at Devīkūṭa (in Bengal), the two thighs in Uḍḍiyāna, the genital organ on the mount Kāmagiri in Kāmarūpa, the navel a little east of that hill, the breasts at Jālandhara, the neck on Pūrṇagiri and the head beyond Kāmarūpa. In another place (68. 43-45) the same Purāṇa enumerates the four main *pīṭhas* as Oḍrapīṭha, Jālaśaila, Pūrṇapīṭha and Kāmarūpa. Oḍrapīṭha is in the west where the goddess resides in the form of Oḍreśvarī Kātyāyanī and her consort as Oḍreśa Jagannātha. It is therefore clear that Oḍḍiyāna at least here is a variation of Oḍra, modern Orissa. Pūrṇaśaila is described as situated in the south. Kāmākhyā or Kāmarūpa remains as one of the indisputable centres of Śānta and Buddhist Tāntricism.

According to *Pag Sam Jon Zan* (index, pp. xli, lv) Saraha or Rāhula-bhadra was a Buddhist sage born of a Brāhmaṇa and a Ḍākinī in the city of Rājñī in the Eastern country and flourished during the reign of Candanapāla of Prācya. Saraha or Sarahapā alias Sarahabhadra or Rāhula-bhadra was one of the early *ācāryas*, who propounded the Tantra doctrines and practices, and is said to be an adept both in Brāhmaṇical and Buddhist lores. His place of birth Rājñī is probably the small principality of Rāṇī in western Assam (Kanaklal Barua:

"Kāmarūpa and Vajrayāna," *Journ. of Assam Res. Soc.*, vol. II, p. 47; Dr. B.K. Barua: "Notices of sorcery and its practices in Assam," *Journ. of University of Gauhati*, vol. I, p. 51). Giuseppe Tucci points out that according to the Tibetan work *Grub to'b* Rāhula was a Śūdra from Kāmarūpa, although in another work b*Ka'babs bdun ldan* Rāhulabhadra is a Brāhmaṇa from Oḍivisa (*JASB.*, 1930, p. 141). Kanaklal Barua wishes to identify Candanapāla of Prācya with Ratnapāla (tenth-eleventh century A.D.) of the Brahmapāla dynasty of Kāmarūpa (*loc. cit.*) M. Shahidullah in his *Les Chants Mystiques de Kānhu et de Saraha* calls Saraha a man of Roli in Rājñī and a contemporary of Ratnapāla of Kāmarūpa (Kanaklal Barua: "The date of Saraha," *JARS.*, vol. II, p. 85).

Saraha's disciple is the famous Nāgārjuna. In the *Sādhanamālā* (pp. 193 f, 265 f) two *sādhanas* are ascribed to him, one for the worship of the goddess Vajratārā, the other for the worship of Ekajaṭ ā. The latter is said to have been rescued by Nāgārjuna from the country of Bhoṭa. Kanaklal Barua holds (*loc. cit.*, p. 48) that he was "well-known in Assam, Bhutan, Nepal and Tibet though he may or may not have been a native of Kāmarūpa." He moreover says that probably the temple of Ugratārā at Gauhati was built by king Ratnapāla or his successor Indrapāla after the worship of Ekajaṭā (Ugratārā) was introduced by Nāgārjuna. The temple is considered by Śāktas to be *nābhi-pīṭha*, the sacred place where Satī's navel dropped. In the *Ārya-mañju-śrī-mūla-kalpa* (verse 900) Kāmarūpa is mentioned as a place where the worship of Tārā led to easy *siddhi*.

Tucci points out also that in *Grub to'b* and *bKa'babs bdun ldan* the Siddha Mīnanātha was a fisherman from Kāmarūpa (*op. cit.*, p. 133). Tāranātha describes Siddha Mīna and his son Siddha Macchindra both as disciples of Carpati. Mīna was a fisherman in the east of India in Kāmarūpa (Dr. Bhupendranath Datta, *Mystic Tales of Lama Tārānātha* 1944, p. 56. Also see Grünwedel, *Baessler-Archiv*, Band V, p. 152 cited in *IHQ.*, vol. VI, p. 181). Jayārtha's commentary on the *Tantrāloka* of Abhinavagupta (Trivandrum Skt. Series, pp. 24-25) quotes a verse from an earlier Tantra to the effect that Kaula-jñāna was transmitted from Bhairava, the fearful god, to Bhairavī, the goddess, and from her the Siddha Mīna or Macchanda acquired it in the *mahāpīṭha* of Kāmarūpa (*IHQ.*, vol. VI, pp. 179, 181). Mīnanātha later became known as the propounder of the Yoginī-kaula doctrine, popular in Kāmarūpa (Dr. P.C. Bagchi, *Kaula-jñāna-nirṇaya*, Cal. Skt. Series, p. 55).

Another Buddhist teacher Padmavajra was the preceptor of Anaṅga-vajra, who was according to Tāranātha a son of 'king Gopāla of Eastern India.' Kanaklal Barua seeks to identify this king with the king of Kāmarūpa of the name, the great-grandson of Ratnapāla (*JARS.*, vol. II, p. 49). He also thinks that the Kāmarūpa kings were initiated to the Vajrayāna tenet and in that connection refers to the word *dharma* occurring in the Puṣpabhadrā grant of Dharmapāla as an indication of Buddhism. He further adduces that the adherents of the esoteric sect called Rātī-khowā (night-worshippers), which indulges in the five *m's* and seeks salvation through women, may have been influenced by Vajrayāna practices (*ibid.*, pp. 50-51).

In his history of Buddhism in India Tāranātha describes how in the time of the venerable Dhītika, who succeeded Upagupta to teachership, the Brāhmaṇa Siddha of Kāmarūpa brought offerings to the Sun god with a company of many thousands. Dhītika in a magical feat took the form of the Sun and preached the law of the Buddha to Siddha, who "perceived the truth, and living full of great faith, he built the Mahācaitya Vihāra, gave a great feast to the brethren of the four regions and spread the teachings of Buddha considerably in Kāmarūpa" (*IHQ.*, vol. V, p. 720).

In the Tibetan *Tanjur* is contained the translation of a tract called *Dhyāna-sad-dharma-vyavasthāna* by Avadhūtīpāda, identified with Ratnaśilā of Kāmarūpa (*IHQ.*, vol. XXVI, p. 334).

In the biographies of the Vaiṣṇava saint Śaṅkaradeva (1449-1568 A.D.) is described how he had encounters with Buddhist magicians (*Baudhamatīyā ṭāṭakīyā*). In his *Kīrtana-ghoṣā* he writes that the God Supreme incarnated as the Buddha only to destroy the way of the Vedas and confound people with *Vāmānaya śāstra* (left handed scriptures). This is clearly a reference to the excesses committed by the Tāntric Buddhists as Śaṅkaradeva himself saw them. He further adds that the Kalki incarnation will descend on earth towards the end of the Kali age and will massacre the Mlecchas, exterminate all the Bauddhas that there be, and establish the Truth.

Rāma Sarasvatī, a Brāhmaṇa contemporary and disciple of Śaṅkara-deva, in his *Vyāsāśrama* (MS., verses 294-350) described how the Brāhmanas of the Kali age would take to the left-handed rites and scriptures (*Vāmānaya vidhi śāstra*) and turn Bauddha. They would profess by the Bauddha śāstras and give up the duties of Brāhmaṇas. They would earn their living by performing magical feats with funny idols made of copper, bell-metal, wood and earth.

Vaṁśīgopāladeva (later sixteenth century), a disciple of Śaṅkaradeva's followers, Dāmodaradeva and Mādhavadeva, met with great opposition and bitter enmity of the Bauddhas when he tried to propagate the tenets of Vaiṣṇavism in Asama rājya, modern Upper Assam (M. Neog, ed., *Vaṁśīgopāladevar Caritra*, 1950, intro.).

It is curiously remarkable that the Hayagrīva Mādhava temple at Hājo at a distance of fifteen miles from Gauhati is visited by the Buddhists from Bhutan and Tibet and even from Ladakh and south-western China. They consider Hājo as the place of the Buddha's *mahāparinirvāṇa*. The present temple of Mādhava was built by the Koc king Raghudevanārāyaṇa of Kāmarūpa 1505 Śaka or 1583 A.D. on the ruins of an older shrine, supposed to have been destroyed by Kālāpāhār (Sir E.A. Gait, *A History of Assam*, 1926, p. 63). According to the Buddhist tradition, of Tibet and Bhutan, of course, the older shrine was the great Caitya erected over the cremated relics of the Tathāgata's body. The principal stone image of the shrine, called Mādhava by the Hindus, is considered by the Lāmās to be Mahāmuni or the Buddha. It may be mentioned here that the worship conducted in the temple of Bodh Gaya is that of Viṣṇu, but the deity is represented in an image of the Buddha and, curiously enough, Gait notes, the Mahant there is a Śaiva ascetic (*Census of India, 1901,* vol. I, pt. I, p. 361). In the Hājo temple the minor stone images of Lāl Kānāyā Vaṅkavihārī, Vāsudeva and Hayagrīva to the right of Mādhava, and that of Dvitīya Mādhava to the left are respectively called Dorje Dolo, Sakyā Thuba, Sencha Muni and Ugyar Guru by the Lāmā pilgrims. The rock, which is pointed out by the Buddhists as the place of death and cremation of the Lord and where there is the figure of a four-armed Viṣṇu, bears several roughly cut inscriptions in Tibetan characters of the mystic sentences *Om maṇipadme hum, Om ah hum, Om,* etc. The liṅga and yoni symbols enshrined on the bank of the Kamala lake on the Kedāranātha hillock are identified by the Lāmās as a mass of butter which was brought to the Buddha and set down by him there. The Lāmās have thus and thus found a Buddhistic name and interpretation for every spot in the locality. They have made copies of this spot supposedly of Buddha's passing away (called by them Sil-wa ts'al-gi tur do, 'the pyre of the cool grove') in at least four places in Tibet. They carry off scrapings of the rocks and soil in the locality and treasure them up in amulets to be placed beside their dead bodies as warrant against dire calamities here on earth and transmigration into lower animals hereafter. It is not definitely known if any Buddhist building here existed previous to the Lāmās' fixing on the site as the Kusanagara of the Buddha's *mahāparinirvāṇa*. Hiuen Tsiang in the seventh century remarked that from the time when the Buddha appeared in the world even down to his own time "there never as yet has been built one *Saṅghārāma* as a place for the priests to assemble." Tāranātha in the sixteenth century, on the other hand, refers to the great *stūpa* of Kusanagara as being situated in Kāmarūpa. Dr. L.A. Waddell suggests that any Caitya or other Buddhist building must be subsequent to the seventh century A.D. and can only mark a site visited by the great founder of Lāmāism, Padmasambhava, or one of his disciples (*The Buddhism of Tibet, or Lāmāism*, 1895, pp. 307-314). The Bhutanese Lāmās visit Hājo in the cold season and worship the Mahāmuni. Some of them even burn a thumb or finger of the hand as an offering to the deity. This is a general Tāntric mode of worship symbolic of self-immolation in the name of a deity. E. Tuite Dalton went so far as to make this remark about the image of Mādhava: "Its modern votaries have, to conceal mutiliation, given it a pair of silver goggle-eyes, and a hooked, gilt or silvered nose, and the form is concealed from view by cloths and chaplets of flowers: but remove these and there is no doubt of the image having been intended for the 'ruler of all, the propitious, the asylum of clemency, the all-wise, the lotus-eyed, the comprehensible Buddha'" ("Notes on Assam temple ruins," *JASB.*, 1855, LXXI, pp. 8ff.). The name Maṇikūṭa of the temple hillock also deserves some notice.

The Janārdana Viṣṇu image at Gauhati below the Śukreśvara hill is generally known as Bodh (Buddha) Janārdana. There is also a tradition that originally a Buddhist shrine stood where the temple of goddess Kāmākhyā now is (S.C. Goswami: "Hidden traces of Buddhism in Assam," *IHQ.*, vol. III, p. 755).

# Chapter - 33

# The Rise and Growth of Buddhism in Andhra

P.S. Sastri

Buddhism entered the Andhra area at a very early time. Most of the centres of Buddhist interest are at present to be found in the Guntur and Krishna districts, though there are a few at other places also. On both sides of the Krishna river we get the places Bhaṭṭiprolu, Śrīkākulam, Amarāvati, Dhānyakaṭaka, Nāgārjunakoṇḍa, Jaggayyapeṭa, Bezawala and the like. In the Interior, near Bahṭṭiprolu we have Cherukupalli with a mound, Chandolu (formerly Nandavolu, Dhanadavolu, Dhanadapuri and Nandapuri), and Buddām (or Buddhapuri). Most of these places are connected with one another by the river. Some places of Buddhist interest are also to be found in the Telugu speaking areas of the Hyderabad state. But when was Buddhism introduced into that part of the country?

### 1. During Buddha's time

First we note certain facts referring to the time of the Buddha. During the six years of his struggle Gotama had with him certain companions, to whom he gave his first sermon after his enlightenment. In the names of these original followers we have strange names like Koṇḍanna, Bappa and Bhaddiya.[1] Here at least the name of Koṇḍanna is most familiar till this day in the Andhra area. This cannot be a sheer accident.

The Nāga king Mucalinda was one of the few first persons to meet the Buddha after his enlightenment.[2] These Nāgas are associated with the sea and are said to be living in forests and in a hilly country.[3] The Nāgas are located at a variety of places. The Gaṇḍavyūha tells us

1. *Majjhima Nikāya,* 26th Sutta
2. See *SBE.*, 21. pp. 80, 119.
3. Jātaka, III, 82, V. 2.

that Mañjuśrī lived in the extensive forest at Dhānyakaṭaka and that he converted there many Nāgas to the Buddhist faith; and this is corroborated by the Saddharmapuṇḍarīka.[1] Nāgārjuna was supposed to have brought the Mahāyāna Sūtras from the Nāgas. Here we have two lines of approach to determine the exact place of the Nāgas referred to here. The first refers to the mention of Mucilipatana in the Mahāvaṃsa.[2] It is the same as the modern Mauslipatam, and it suggests that the place got that name from Mucalinda Nāga and his dynasty. Padmasambhava proceeds to the Asura cave where he learns that the Pāramitās were hidden in the realm of the Nāgas in Urgyan.[3] In the life of Padmasambhava we read that Dhānykaṭaka was in the northwestern corner of the country of Urgyan.[4] Yuan Chwang refers to the Asura palace as being not far from the south side of Dhānyakaṭka.[5]

Our second line of approach is from the word Nāga, which in the language of the times was Nāya, as can be seen from names like Nāyajjuna and Nayanikā. The word Nāya with the Telugu nominative suffix 'ḍu' gives us Nāyaḍu and its variants Nīḍu, Neḍu, Nāyuḍu and Naiḍu. This is the name by which a certain community in Andhra styles itself till this day. In this community particularly names having Nāga as a part are still frequent. It is a strong and powerful community in and around Masulipatam, and it has its branches elsewhere also. These considerations compel us to locate Mucalinda Nāga and his dynasty in and around Masulipatam which is not far away from Bhaṭṭiprolu. Mucalinda Nāga of this area was one of the few that met the Buddha after his enlightenment.

In the Andhaka territory, says the commentary on the Sutta Nipāta, there are Assaka and Mulaka.[6] There are Brāhmaṇas in Andhra calling themselves Mulaka-nāṭi, belonging to the Nāḍu or Maṇḍala called Mulaka. This is the areas comprising the south-east part of the present Hyderabad state with certain parts of Rayalasima. Godāvarī was said to flow through Assaka[7] and Mulaka. At the time of the Buddha, Assaka was ruled by the father of Prince Sujāta. The capital of Assaka was given as Potala, with its variants Potana, Potalaka, Podana, and so on. This name has now become Bodana and then Bodhan. The

1. Chapters 11 and 13.
2. Chapter 36, p. 144.
3. Evans-Wentz: *The Tibetan Book of Great Liberation,* pp. 123-129.
4. *Ibid.*, p. 105
5. Watters, II. 125
6. *Sutta-Nipāta,* verse 977
7. *Dīgha Nikāya*, Mahā-Govinda-Suttanta

Vimānavatthu commentary has the story of an Assaka king who was ordained by Mahā-Kātyāyana.[1] This Mahā-Kātyāyana was one of the foremost of Buddha's disciples. That the Buddha sent this important disciple to a part of the Andhra is enough to justify the close relationship between the founder of the new religion and the Andhra area.

Amarāvati and Dhānyakaṭaka also have been in direct touch with the Buddha. One of the previous births of the Buddha was placed in Amarāvati.[2] According to a Tibetan tradition we hear that Śākyamuni promulgated the Kālacakra system in Dhāyakaṭaka.[3] We have earlier noted that acccording to the life of Padmasambhava written by his disciple the Buddha was born as Padmasambhava in Dhānyakaṭaka to propound the Tantric Buddhism.[4] The Vajrayāna thinkers tell us that the Buddha turned the third wheel of the Law at Dhānyakaṭaka sixteen years after his enlightenment.[5] These traditional accounts cannot be brushed aside as fictions, though the available Pāli canon may not mention these activities of the Buddha.

On more evidence comes from the inscriptions obtained at Bhaṭṭiprolu.[6] Judging from the script and other factors the later V.R. Ramachandra Diskshitar has concluded that these inscriptions are definitely pre-Maurayan.[7] The first inscription speaks of the preparation of a casket and of a box of crystal to deposit some relics of the Buddha. Inscriptions 3, 5, 6, 8 and 9 speak of the various village communities and nigamas that have offered caskets, boxes of crystal and boxes of stone. The tenth tells us that even the women of Nandapura (modern Chandolu, near Bhaṭṭiprolu) and the sramaneras from Suvanamaha participated in this enterprise in memory of the Buddha who had departed. Why should even these women participate in this great task? They should evidently be Buddhists. But this alone will not explain all this eagerness and enthusiasm. These inscriptions clearly reveal that these preparations were made immediately after the nirvāṇa of the Buddha. And the enthusiam of even the women can be explained only on the ground that they have seen the Buddha at least once in their life. And a couple of miles near this Nandapura we have a village Buddām (Buddhapuri), evidently named after the Buddha in memory of his visit to these areas.

---

1. See pp. 259 ff
2. *Dhammapada Aṭṭhakathā*, 1. 83
3. See Sir Charles Eliot: *Hinduism and Buddhism,* III. 386.
4. See Evans-Wentz: *The Tibetan Book of the Great Liberation,* p. 105
5. *History of Buddhism* by Hbrug-pa-dma-dkar-po, pp. 14b-15a referred to by Mr. R. Sankrityayana in his *Introduction to Vigraha-Vyāvartanī.*
6. *Epigraphica Indica*, II, 323 ff.
7. See his paper in the B.C. Law Volume.

## 2. The Rise of the Mahāsaṅghikas

In the second Buddhist congregation at Vaiśali (c. 386 B.C.) the monks of Kauśāmbi, Pāṭheyya, Avanti, and other places came into conflict with those of Vaiśāli and Pāṭaliputra. These Vajjiputtakas under the leadership of Mahādeva convented another council called Mahāsaṅgīti and claimed Mahākassapa as their earliest expounder. But we hear of one Pūraṇa Dakkhinagiri in the Cullavagga who refused to accept the Law at the first council, because he wanted to stick to the Dhamma and the Vinaya as he himself heard from the Master.[1] It was a fact that there was a revolt. This revolt came from the Vajjiputtaka group which includes Ikṣākus. Earlier to the Sātavāhanas there were these Ikṣākus at Bhaṭṭiprolu, and later they moved to the area of Nāgārjunakoṇḍa also. The later prominence of the Mahāsaṅghikas in Andhra comples us to believe that the Ikṣākus who were among the Vajjiputtakas actually came from Andhra.

The Mahāsaṅghikās had also a saint called Sudarśana. They wrote a life of the Buddha in mixed Sanskrit; and this Mahāvastu represents the symbolic revolt against the language employed by the *sthaviras*. As the Dīpavaṃśa tells us, each sect with its rise changed the original texts, their arrangement, language and meaning.[2] Even the Prātimokṣa, says the Tibetan tradition, was written in a mixed dialect by the Mahāsaṅghikas. These changes are possible only in the area where Sanskrit was considered to be comparatively easier and better fitted than Pāli, because Pāli was not the mother tongue there, because the Brāhmaṇical writers were writing there in Sanskrit, and because these Brāhmaṇical writers of that region did not care to learn Pāli. These considerations point the source or birth-place of the Mahāsaṅghika movement as lying outside the area where Pāli was spoken or easily understood.

Among the Mahāsaṅghikas there is an important branch comprising of the Śaila schools. According to Vasumitra the Śaila schools are Caitya śaila, Apara śaila and Uttara śaila. The Kathāvatthu renders them as Caityaka, Aparśaila, and Uttarapathaka. The Uttaraśaila has become Uttarāpathaka, and an erroneous interpretation has crept in. They have nothing to do with northern India. The Uttara Śaila schools comprising of Pūrvaśaila, Aparaśaila, Uttaraśaila, Caityaka and Lokottaravādins are collectively treated as Andhakas, Andhras, among the Mahāsaṅghikas. The inscriptions at

1. See XI. i. 11.
2. See 5. 32 to 50.

Nāgārjunakoṇḍa and Amarāvati along with Yuan Chwang's statements place the Pūrvaśaila and Aparaśaila at Dhānyakaṭaka. The Mahācaitya at Nāgārjunakoṇḍa was the place of the Caityakas. The other two are to be sought in Nāgārjunakoṇḍa area and in places near it.

Some of the tenets of the Mahāsaṅghikas are available in the inscriptions at Nāgārjunakoṇḍa. Here we find that the Buddha is not only "jita-rāga-dveṣa-moha", but we find "sammā sambuddhasa dhātuvara parigahitasa mahā cetiya". Here is a reference to the dharmadhātu. The donors held that the merits of ordinary actions are transferrable, and that they long for the nirvāṇasampada not for themselves only. Words like "gahapati putasa dusakasa......" reveal that even householders belonged to the Āryasaṅgha. The extension of membership to householders is an important element in the Mahāsaṅghika ideology, and it ultimately led to the composition of Vimala-kīrti-sūtra. These schools not only had the Dīgha and Majjhima nikāyas, but had a Mātrikā of their own. This Mātrikā covers Vinaya and Abhidharma; and Yuan Chwang tells us that they had an Abhidharma-Piṭaka of their own.

From Vasumitra and from the Kathāvatthu we learn a good deal about the doctrines of the Andhra Mahāsaṅghikas. Only we should not regard the faulty Uttarāpathakas of Kathvatthu as north Indian Mahāsaṅghikas. They are a branch of the Andhra Mahāsaṅghikas. The Andhaka view that the Buddha's actions are lokottara, and that the Buddhas have both kṣaya-jñāna and anutpādajñāna refers to the sambhogakāya. The Uttaraśailyas held that the Buddhas can have no karuṇā; and this is basis of the conception of the Dharmakāya, of Śūnyatā. They also believed that even householders can become arhats. These and similar doctrines played a considerable part in the evolution of Mahāyāna which has to be traced to the Andhakas.

### 3. The Mahāyāna Texts

Coming to the texts accepted as authoritative by the Mahāyānist we find that a great many of these texts actually originated at the hands of the Andhra Mahāsaṅghikas. From various sources we gather that Nāgārjuna brought from the dynasty of Mucalinda Nāga the great texts like the Prajñā-Pāramitās, the Avataṃsaka and the Saddharma Puṇḍarīka; and that after Nāgārjuna there were no fresh Mahāyāna texts. We have found that these Nāgas were the inhabitants in and about modern Masulipatam. According to Taranatha, some of the śrāvakas actually attributed the composition of the Śatasāhasrikā to Nāgārjuna. The same Taranatha tells us that the Aṣṭasāhasrikā was composed after the time of Mahāpadma Nanda. The Tibetan tradition admits that the Śaila schools had a Prajñā-Pāramitā in Prakrit. This Prakrit can only refer to the language spoken near and around Masulipatam and Dhānyakaṭaka. Nāgārjuna we can understand brought forth these texts written or compiled by the Nāgas in their own language, and sanskritised them. In the Aṣṭasāhasrikā we actually read: "These Sūtrāntas, in which the six Pāramitās are taught, will originate in Dakṣiṇāpatha after the passing away of the Tathāgata; from the south they will go (Vartanyām) to the east and form the east to the north".[1] And Dr. Nalinaksha Dutt had to say: "Putting all these pieces of evidence together, we may conclude that Mahāyāna Buddhism originated about the first century B.C., in Andhra country where the Mahāsaṅghikas had their centre; it became a recognised form of Buddhism at the time of Kanishka; and then it spread all over northern India in the first or second century A.D., to blossom into its full glory under the care of Nāgārjuna, Āryadeva, Asaṅga and Vasubandhu".[2]

The basic texts of Mahāyāna, it is now clear, originated in Andhra Śaila schools. The Saddharmapuṇḍarīkā and its 24th chapter entitled Avalokiteśvara-Vikurvaṇa-Nirdeśa, Avataṃsaka-sūtra comprising of the Gaṇḍavayūha and Daśabhumika, and the Pāramitās have come from the Nāgas through Nāgārjuna. The Vimalakīrti-sūtra, we have seen, is foreshadowed in the admission of the householders to the Āryasaṅgha at Nāgārjunakoṇḍa. The Parinirvāṇa-sūtra is the logical outcome of the Andhaka emphasis on Bodhicitta. The Sukhāvatī-vyūha-sūtra with its faith in Amitābha, goes to the teacher of Nāgārjuna who lived at Dhānyakaṭaka as we will presently show. Here we have all the Mahāyāna texts except the Laṅkāvatāra, which begins with Rāvanādhyeṣaṇā and which had Mañjuśrī as its interlocutor. The introduction of the scene in the south and presence of Mañjuśrī will take this text also to the same locality.

### 4. The Bodhisattvas

With the rise of the Mahāsaṅghikas in Andhra there also arose a few Bodhisattvas, who were actually located in certain parts of the Andhra country. The vogue of the very presence of these Bodhisattvas was so great and compelling that a Brāhmaṇa left his home at Takṣaśilā, according to the Bhīmasena Jātaka, and came to the Andhra country to gain practical experience for becoming a Bodhisattva.

---

1. See pp. 225 ff.
2. *The Age of Imperial Unity*, p. 388.

The first Bodhisattva is Mañjuśrī, who is treated as Kumāra and Kumārabhūta. As Kumāra he remained in the Śaiva patheon, and as Kumārī he became Bālā, the original deity at Tirupathi and at the Durgā temple on the Bezawada hill called Indrakīla. In the Gaṇḍavayāha we learn Manjuśrī lives in a wide *vana* (forest) at Māla-dhvaja-vyūha-caitya lying to the east of Dhānyakaṭaka.[1] In the Māradamana-sūtra quoted in the Prasannapadā we hear of Mañjuśrī coming to the Indrakīla hill of Bezawada to kill Māra.[2] Having his permanent abode at the Mahāvana of Dhānyakaṭaka, Mañjuśrī came into prominence as a Bodhisattva, probably due to the labours of the Mahā-vana-śailīyas. Then as the Maradamana-sūtra tells us, he moved to Bezawada; and the so called image of Kanaka-Durgā goes back to Mañjuśri, who was credited with the conversion of the Nāgas.

The next Bodhisattva is Amitābha whose worship goes back to Saraha, the teacher of Tantric Nāgārjuna. This Saraha or Rāhulabhadra says Taranatha, "saw Amitābha in the land of Dhingkota and died with his face turned towards Sukhāvatī".[3] This Dhingkota is a corruption of Dharaṇikoṭa, the later name of Dhānyakaṭaka. In the life fo Padmasambhava we read that when there was a famine in Dhāyakaṭ-aka, Avalokiteśvara appealed to Amitābha who thought of taking birth in the Dhanakaṭaka lake. And from the heart of Amitābha there emerged a Vajra, of the Vajrayāna school in all certainly.[4] the same Dhānyakaṭ-aka gave both Amitābha and Sukhāvatī, besides the Vajra which is held to be a technical term for Śūnyatā. Here is also the origin of the Sukhāvatī-vyūha-sūtra.

The third Bodhisattva is Avalokiteśvara whose connections with Dhānyakaṭaka and Amitābha are apparent in the foregoing account. Avalokiteśvara is the spiritual son or reflex of Amitābha. The Buddhist tradition connects Avalokiteśvara with Potala or Potalaka. Yuan Chwang

---

1. "*Dhyanyākarasya mahā nagarasya pūrveṇa vicitra māla-dhvajavyūham nāma mahāvana khaṇḍam pūrva buddhādhyāsitam tathagatādhisṭhṭhitam......*" See also *Saddharma*, chapters 11 and 13.

2. *Buddhist Text Society of India Edition,* pp. 107-108: "*Ata evoktam arya Māra-damana-sūtre—"Atha Mañjuśriḥ Kumārabhūtaḥ tasyām velāyām tathā rūpam samanvāharam samanvāharati sma. Yan māra pāpiyāṇ Indrakila bandhana baddho dharaṇī tara......*"

3. See Sir Charles Eliot: *Hindusim and Buddhism,* III, 219. See also Schiefner's Taranatha, pp. 93, 105, 303.

4. See Evans-Wentz: *Tibetan Book of Great Liberation,* pp. 106-107.

in his hurry placed it in Malakūṭa which too he did not see.[1] That Potala was the capital of Assaka on Godāvarī, an Andhaka country, we have already seen. It has also been tentatively identified with modern Bodhan. This is the seat of Avalokiteśvara.

The fourth Bodhisattva is Samantabhadra who appears with his magnificent and sublime ten vows for the first time in the Avataṃsaka, a text brought forth by Nāgārjuna from the family of Mucalinda Nāga. These four Bodhisattvas constitute the front rank of the original Bodhisattvas that are introduced into the new canon by the Mahāsaṅghikas of the Śaila schools to revolutionise the old gospe

Potala was the capital of Assaka on Godāvarī, an Andhaka country, we have already seen. It has also been tentatively identified with modern Bodhan. This is the seat of Avalokiteśvara.

The fourth Bodhisattva is Samantabhadra who appears with his magnificent and sublime ten vows for the first time in the Avataṃsaka, a text brought forth by Nāgārjuna from the family of Mucalinda Nāga. These four Bodhisattvas constitute the front rank of the original Bodhisattvas that are introduced into the new canon by the Mahāsaṅghikas of the Śaila schools to revolutionise the old gospel.

---

1. However Yuan Chwang admits with I-Tsing that Buddhism flourished in Samataṭa; and I-Tsing mentions the images of Avalokiteśvara and the reading of the Pāramitās in Saṁataṭa. (See Eliot: *Hindusim and Buddhism*, III. 53). Samataṭa has variants Samanta and Samantamukha. The *Gaṇḍa-vayūha* clearly mentions Samantamukha or Samataṭa, and treats it as a city in Mulaka. We have to look for this city in the south-eastern parts of the present Hyderabad territory, which part was formerly the Mulākanāḍu.

# *Chapter - 34*

# Some Buddhist Thinker of Andhra

**P.S. Sastri**

A historical study of the Buddhist philosophical literature reveals the great contributions made by the ancient Andhra area to the growth of the various systems of Buddhist thought. In two earlier papers[1] an attempt has been made to trace the growth of Buddhism in Andhra from the time of the Buddha; and it was also shown that Nāgārjuna and Āryadeva came from the same area in Andhra. Here it is proposed to find out the place from which certain other Buddhist thinkers hailed. Sometimes these thinkers had their main field of activity in the Andhra area.

1. In a Chinese work (Shittanzo) Aśvaghoṣa was considered to belong to South India.[2] The Nāgārjunakoṇḍa bas-reliefs present in full the story of *Saundarananda*. The first of these shows the Buddha's conversation with Nanda and Sundarī; the second reveals Nanda after the shaving, with a figure holding his head-dress; the third is the visit to Indra's paradise. The dress of the Buddha and Nanda recalls the tenth canto of *Saundarananda*. Another figure shows Arhat Nanda going to preach almost reminding us of 18, 58, 62 of the poem. It is not possible to say whether these sculptural representations were based on the poem, or the poem itself was written to depict them. Johnston has ably argued that Aśvaghoṣa belonged to the Bahuśrutīya sect,[3] and this accords with the fact that an *āyaka* pillar at Nāgārjunakoṇḍa caitya mentions the existence of the Bahuśrutīyas in that locality.[4]

2. *Mañjuśri-mūla-tantra* assigns Āryadeva to Saihnika-pura,[5] and calls him a non-Aryan. Buston, following the lead of this text, puts him in

---

1. See *IHQ.*, 1955 on 'Rise and growth of Buddhism in Andhra' and on 'Nāgārjuna and Āryadeva'.
2. See B.C. Law's monograph on Aśvaghoṣa.
3. Johnston: *Buddhacarita,* Part 2, xxxiii-xxxv.
4. इवं विहरो स व जिन नियतो अचरियनं बहुसुतियनं पतिथपितो।
5. अपरः प्रव्रजिः श्रेष्ठः सैह्निकपुर वास्तवी।
अनार्या आर्य संज्ञो च सिंहलद्वीपवासिनः॥

Simhala, while other Tibetan chronicles observe that his father ruled over Seṅ-ga-gliṅ. Yuan Chwang speaks of Deva P'usa of Chi-shih-tzu-kho[1] which may be a transliteration or a rendering of Simahadharaputrapura. The *Bṛhatkathā* observes that Dīpakarṇi was fortunate enough to find, in accordance with a dream he had, a boy borne by a lioness. This boy was Simhadhara, otherwise known as Śāta-vāhana or the one who was carried by a lion. Āryadeva, then, belongs to the town ruled by the Śātavāhanas; and it is called Seṅ-ga-gliṅ, Sakāla or Sakāla which was later pronounced Singala.[2] This Sagāla is the same as the modern Śrī-kā-ku-lam which was, according to the traditional accounts, the original home of the Śātavāhanas. This Śrīkākulam lies due north east of Nāgārjunakoṇḍa and as such it justifies Candrakīrti's statement that Āryadeva came southwards to meet Nāgārjuna. Seṅ-ga-gliṅ, Sagāla and Śrīkākulam refer to one and the same place which now appears in the Krishna delta near Masulipatam; and it is not surprising to believe that a place on the banks of a river in the delta could be mistaken for an island.[3]

3. Maitreyanātha has been associated with Potala which has to be located near modern Bodhan in the Hyderabad territory.[4] Of his disciple Asaṅga, we are told that he belongs to Peshawar. Here we are asked to rely on the Chinese or on the Tibetan traditions. But as Prof. Demieville observes, Chinese tradition, for all the mass of documents on which it rests, hardly affords, at least for the early period, more positive historical information than Indian tradition with the complete absence of documents".[5] This applies to the Tibetan traditional dates as well. We find that Asaṅga was known as the sage of the Ajanta; and the caves of Ajanta in his day were known as Acinta-purī-vihāra,[6] probably named after the original name of Asaṅga which may have been Ajita.

4. Dinnāga, as per the Tibetan tradition, was born in Simha-vaktra near Kāñcī, lived in a cave on Bhoraśaila in Orissa, and sojourned in Nalanda. Fortunately enough, this misleading statement does not find a place in Yuan Chwang. Yuaṇ Chwang entered the An-to-lo (Andhra) country, saw its capital P'ing-k'i (Vengi), and found a hill 200 li further southwest of the town. On the ridge of this isolated hill, he observes, was a stone tope where Ch'en-na (Dinnāga) P'usa composed a treatise on logic. "Mañjuśrī summoned him to develop for the benefit of

---

1. Watters, II. 320. Modern Nellore was originally called Vikrama-Simha-pura.
2. Evans-Wentz: *The Tibetan Book of the Great Liberation*, pp. 113. 156-7.
3. *IHQ.*, 1955 on 'Nāgārjuna and Āryadeva'.
4. *IHQ.*, 1955 on ' The Rise and growth of Buddhism in Andhra'.
5. See Johnston: *Buddhacarita*, pt. 2, xvi.
6. Evans-Wentz, 158.

posterity the *Yogācāra-bhūmi-śāstra* originally delivered by Maitreya".[1] It was on this hill near Vengi in the West Godāvarī district that the *Pramāṇsamuccaya* was composed. He was born in Simhapura or Nellore.

5. Of the critics of Dinnāga's system of logic the most famous Buddhist thinkers appear to be Buddhapālita, Bhāvaviveka and Candrakīrti. Candrakīrti, the disciple of Buddhapālita, was born in Samanta; and according to the Gaṇḍavyūha, there was a Samanta-mukha in the Mulaka country. This Mulaka country comprises the area round about the Bhadrācalam hills on the banks of the Godāvarī. Samanta, Samataṭa, Samantamukha are one and the same.

Regarding Bhāvaviveka we have definite information from Yuan Chwang. The pilgrim writes, "Not far from the south side of the capital (Dhānyakaṭaka) was a mountain cliff in the Asura's palace in which the Śāstra-master P'o-p'i-fai-ka (Bhāvaviveka) waits to see Maitreya when he comes to be the Buddha. Then we have the story of this renowned dialectician, who externally displaying the Sāṅkhya grab, internally propogated the learning of Nāgārjuna".[2] Bhāvaviveka not only belongs to Dhānyakaṭaka, but was originally a follower of the Saṅkhya. That he was believed to be waiting for the second coming of Maitreya only proves that Maitreya originally belonged to the same place which was chosen by Bhāvaviveka.

Rahula-mitra, the *parama-guru* of Saṅgharakṣita, appears in one of the inscriptions found near Gollamūḍi in the Krishna district. Sthiramati, the student of Vasubandhu, is believed to have come from the Daṇḍaka which extends over a very wide area from the Marāthi speaking tract in the west to the Telugu speaking zone in the east.

6. Next we have the famous logician Dharmakīrti who has been accepted by tradition to be the relative (nephew) of Kumārila. The Jina-vijaya records:

आंध्रोत्कलानां संयोगे पवित्ते जय मंगले
ग्रामे तस्मिन् महानद्यां भट्टाचार्यः कुमारकः ।
आंध्र-जातिस्तित्तिरिको माता चंद्रगुणासतो
यज्ञेश्वरः पिता यस्य महावादिर्महान् घोरः ॥

Kumārila was an Āndhra hailing from a village called Jayamaṅgala on the banks of the Mahāndī. Dharmakīrti was supposed to be born in Trimalaya or Tirumalaya. The prefix Tri or Tiru is the

1. Watters, II, 209-210.
2. Watters, II. 215.

Dravidian cognate of Śrī; and the word malai means a mountain. Thus Tirumalaya is the Dravidian translation of Śrīśaila or Śrī-Parvata. In his Vāda-nyāya we read the interesting statement:[1]

यस्तु नक्कशब्दं मुक्कु शब्दमेव वा नासापर्यायं
वेत्ति न नासाशब्दं सकथमपशब्दात्...

Here Dharmakīrti is giving the words *nakka, mukku,* and *nāsika*. These three are from three different language, and all mean the nose. Of these the second word is *mukku*, a pure Telugu word meaning the nose. It is not an accident that made Dharmakīti use this term. It came direct from his mother tongue. Thus a few pages later he distinguishes his mother-tongue from the Dravidian language:[2]

तत् स्वभावस्य अन्यतोऽपि सिद्धेः प्राकृतापभ्रंश-द्रमिडांध्र-भाषावत्

Prākrita, Apabhramsa, Dramiḍa and Andhra are the languages he takes for examples in his discussion of the correct and incorrect words.

7. We have found reason to disbelieve the Tibetan tradition regarding the home of Dinnāga. Yuan Chwang placed him in Vengi. Jinendrabodhi was said to be the countryman of the venerable Bodhisattva Dinnāga. Nāgārjuna II and Āryadeva II belonged to Śrī Parvata. Likewise there was at the same place a Matrīnātha who, according to Tāranatha, died nine years after Nayapāla of Bengal (c 1040-1075).

8. Padmasambhava's chief disciple, the Tibetan lady Yeshey Tshogyal, gave an account of the life and teachings of her teacher. According to this biography, Buddha himself decided to take birth from a lotus blossom in the Dhanakoṣa (= Dhāyakaṭaka) lake in the country called Urgyan. This country was also called Udyana, Odiyana Ogyan and the like.[3] This is no other than the Andhra country. This country was ruled by Indrabodhi, who adopted Padmasambhava. Indrabodhi is the same as Indrābhūti, the disciple of Anangavajra. Padmavajra, the teacher of Ananagavajra, was the author of *Guhyasiddhi*. Indrabhūti was styled Oḍiyāna-siddha, Avadhūta, Mahācārya and the like. They were practically the pioneers in the Vajrayāna school of Buddhism. According to the Vajrayānists, the Buddha turned the third wheel of the law of Vajrayāna at Dhānyakaṭaka, sixteen years after his enlightenment.[4]

Padmasambhava married Mandaravā, the sister of Śāntarakṣita and Śāntarakṣita belonged to the city of Sahor in the north-western

1. *Vādanyāya,* pp. 103-104.
2. *Ibid.*, p. 107.
3. Evans-Wentz, 105.
4. See Rāhula Sankrityāyana's Preface to his edition of the *Vegraha-vyāvartanī.*

corner of the Andhra country.[1] It was at Śāntarakṣita's suggestion that the king of Tibet invited Padmasambhava to Tibet. Here we have definite evidence to refer Padmasambhava Śāntarakṣita and the Vajrayāna teachers to the Andhra country. It was in the same area again that the Buddhist thought and religion lingered till the thirteenth and fourteenth centuries, as the inscriptions during the times of the Velanāṭi-colas testify.

1. Evans-Wentz, 142-4.

## Chapter - 35

# A Buddhist Inscription from Bodh-Gaya of the Reign of Jayaccandradeva—V.S. 124x.

**Niradbandhu Sanyal**

This inscription was found at Bodh-Gaya some fifty years ago by Sir Alexander Cunningham. He placed it for decipherment at the disposal of Dr. Rajendralal Mitra, who published it with a translation and a facsimile in the *Proceedings of the Asiatic Society of Bengal*, 1880, pp.78-80, pl. VIII. It is noticed as No. 177 in Kielhorn's *List of the Inscriptions of Northern India*[1] and included by Messrs, Mehta and Diskalkar in their *List of Inscriptions of the Gāhaḍavāla Rulers of Kanauj*.[2] An excellent facsimile of the inscription (without, however, any transcript) appeared in Mr. R.D. Banerji's memoir on the *Pālas of Bengal*.[3] During my study of the Gāhaḍavāla records, I found that Dr. Mitra's readings and translation of this inscription required revision. I, therefore, re-edit the inscription from the two published facsimiles mentioned above. I had not the advantage of examining any estampage of the original inscription, which, I am told, is no longer available.

The inscription according to Dr. Mitra covers a space of 19" x 12" and consists of 17 lines of writing. A portion of the slab is broken away and eight letters are thus missing,—two in 1. 15, two in 1. 16, and four in 1. 17. A few others are also injured in lines 3, 4, 6, 8, 9, and 17. With the exception of these, the inscription appears to have been quite in a good condition.

1. *Ep. Ind.*, vol. V. App., p. 26.
2. *J.B.O.R.S.*, vol. XIII, p. 84.
3. *Mem. As. Soc. Beng.*, vol. V, no. 3, pl. xxxii.

The Characters are Nāgarī of the twelfth century A.C. and in type resemble those of the Sārnāth inscription of Kumāradevī,[1] the Śītalāghāṭa (Gaya) inscription of Yakṣapāla,[2] the Kṛṣṇa-dvārikā[3] and the Narasiṃha temple[4] (Gaya) inscriptions of Nayapāla, the Akṣayavaṭa (Gaya) inscription of Vigrahapāla III,[5] and the Silimpur inscription of Prahāsa.[6] Regarding the vowel signs attention may be drawn to the different forms of the medial *u,* viz. a comma-shaped curve annexed below, e.g. in *guru* (1, 2), a hook attached to the right, e.g. in *rucira* (1.1), and a wedge at the lower end, e.g. in *madhura* (1.7). In respect of consonants the final forms of *t* and *m* are noteworthy. Final *t* is written by a comma-shaped curve with a hook upon it and the sign of the *virāma* below, e.g. in *samantāt* (1.1). Final *m* has the form of the usual looped *m*, only smaller in size, the *virāma* stroke being shown below, e.g. in *citram* (1.7). Superscript *r* is indicated by a short slanting stroke starting from the middle of the left side of the following consonant, e.g. in *nirjara* (1.11). *Y* is distinguished from *p* in having the vertical straight line on the right continued below its junction with the curve on the left.

In respect of Orthography may be noted the use of the same sign both for *v* and *b*, the occasional substitution of *s* for *visarga* and the doubling of *c, ṇ* and *t* following a superscript *r.* Instances of errors of writing occur in *ākalpaśa,* (1.12) where the *visarga* at the end is omitted, and in *ghaṭunā* (1.7) miswritten for *paṭunā*.

The Language of the record is Sanskrit. With the exception of the introductory *Oṃ namo Buddhāya* the whole of the inscription is in verse, numbering 17 in all and composed in a variety of metres, viz. Sragdharā, Śārddūlavikrīḍita, Indravajrā, Vasantatilaka, Mālinī, Anuṣṭubh, Rathoddhatā and Āryā. As to the style of the composition Dr. Mitra observes, "The language of the large record is high-flown, and very much involved. Metaphors and similes are scattered in it with no niggard hand, and they are mostly very much overstrained, an difficult of reproduction in plain English."

---

1. *Ep. Ind.*, vol. IX, pp. 319ff., pl. facing p. 324.
2. *Ind. Ant.*, vol. XVI, pp. 64ff.; *Mem. As. Soc. Beng.*, vol. V, no. 3, pp. 96-97 and Pl.
3. *J.A.S.B.*, 1900, pt. 1, pp. 190-195; *Mem. As. Soc. Beng.*, vol. V, no. 3, pl. xxv.
4. *Mem. As Soc. Beng.*, vol. V, no. 3, p. 78 and pl.
5. *Ibid.*, pp. 81-82 and pl.
6. *Ep. Ind.*, vol. XIII, pp. 283-295 and pl.

The object of the inscription is to record the excavation by a Buddhist monk, named Śrīmitra, of a large cave at Jayapura, bearing in front one or two figures of Siṃhanāda[1] and in the courts images of three Tārās installed in separate shrines. Of these three Tārās two are mentioned by name, viz., Ugratārā[2] and Dattatārā,[3] while the third one is merely described as "wearing orange clothes."[4] The record opens with an obeisance to Buddha; the first three verses are addressed respectively to the Primordial Nature, known also as the Ādi-Buddha,[5] Bodhisattva Lokeśvara and Ekajaṭā (vs. 1-3). The inscription then proceeds to give an eulogistic account of the monk Śrīmitra who caused this cave to be made (vs. 4-9). His virtues are described, and it is stated that he converted to the Buddhist faith many kings who had formerly followed the 'wrong path' (v. 7). These royal disciples of Śrīmitra included Jayaccandradeva (v. 10), who is referred to in the following verse as the king of Kāśī (v. 11). It is also stated that he restored the discipline of Mahābodhi and recovered some scriptures and treatises of a like nature that had fallen into obscurity (v. 11). The cave is then described (vs. 12-14), the date of its excavation being noted in terms of a chronogram the year of king Vikramāṅka indicated by ... 'vedas', 'eyes' and 'moon', *i.e.*, the Vikrama year 124 x (vs. 14, 15). Finally, we are informed that this eulogy (*praśasti*) was composed by Manoratha, the son of Sīda, written by the *kāyastha* Purandara and engraved by the artisan Dhārādhara (vs. 16, 17).

As the first word of the chronogram is missing it is not possible to make an exact calculation of the date. It is evident, however, that the date falls somewhere within the period 1183-1192 A.C. Messrs.

---

1. It is of interest to note in this connection that at Patan in Nepal, all the more important Vihāras have two images of Siṃhanāda, either in stone or in bronze, on either side of the staircase leading to the sanctum; see Bhattacharya, *Indian Buddhist Iconography*, p. 36, similar method appears to have been adopted in the decoration of this cave, too, either with one or two figures of Siṃhanāda in front of the entrance.

2. This is a ferocious form of Blue Tārā, identified by Getty with Ekajaṭā, to whom an invocation is made in one of the introductory verses of the *praśasti*; see Getty, *Gods of Northern Buddhism*, p. 111. Bhattacharya takes her to be identical with Mahācīna Tārā. Both the varieties are, however, believed to be of Northern origin and belong to the same class of Blue Tārā. See Bhattacharya, *op. cit.*, pp. 76-81.

3. I could trace no mention of this variety of Tārā elsewhere.

4. This description is not, however, definite enough to identify this Tārā with any particular form.

5. He is also called Svayambhū or Svabhāva, see Getty, *op. cit.*, p. 3.

Mehta and Diskalkar assume the missing word to be equivalent to '5', and accordingly give the date as v. s. 1245. This is, however, a mere surmise.

The prelude to the *praśasti* that starts with a homage to Ādi-Buddha shows that the monk in honour of whom it was written was a follower of that system, which forms a special phase of the Mahāyāna Buddhism.[1] Once it was believed that this cult first sprang from Nepal in the eleventh century A.C. among the Aiśvarikas[2]; subsequent studies have however, shown that it originated during the rule of the Pālas in Eastern India, whence it found its way to the north.[3] The special feature of this system consists in tracing the origin of even the Dhyānī Buddhas to a Primordial Being, the Ādi-Buddha, who creates the former by the five acts of his contemplative power, i.e., the *dhyāna*. Invisible and inactive as he is in principle, he is nevertheless a god,[4] for whom the Iconography of the later Buddhist pantheon conceived a distinct representation. "The Ādi-Buddha," says Getty "is always represented as a 'crowned Buddha,' that is to say, that although he is a Buddha, he wears the five-leafed crown as well as the other traditional ornaments of a Dhyānī-Bodhisattva, and is dressed in princely garments."[5] In view of this observation an attempt has been made to identify him with a type of crowned figures of Buddha, decked also with other jewellery, found in Bihar and Bengal.[6] The Ādi-Buddha is also represented in Nepal in the shaped of a flame in accordance with the belief that at the creation of the world he manifested himself in the form of a flame issuing out of a lotus flower.[7] Sometimes this flame symbol is put in the centre of a crescent moon.[8] The invocatory stanza, referred to, is of interest not only as confirming the evidence of the existence of the cult of Ādi-Buddha

---

1. See N.G. Majumdar on "Ādi-Buddha in the Eastern School of Art," *Annual Report of the Varendra Research Society,* 1926-27, Museum Notes, p. 7; Louis de la Vallée Poussin on 'Mahāyāna' and 'Ādi-Buddha,' *Ency. Rel. Eth.*, vol. 8, pp. 380ff. and vol. I, pp. 93ff.
2. Getty, *op. cit.*, p. 2 and n. 2; Grünwedel, *Buddhist Art in India,* p. 198.
3. Cf. Majumdar, *op. cit.*, p. 8; *J.A.S.B.*, vol. II, pp. 57ff.; *J.B.O.R.S.*, vol. IX, p. 114, *et seq.*
4. See Poussin, *Ency. Rel. Eth.*, vol. I, p. 99.
5. Getty, *op. cit.*, p. 3.
6. Majumdar, *op. cit.*, p. 8.
7. Getty, *op. cit.*, p. 2; Bhattacharya, *op. cit.*, p. xxviii; Mitra, *Sanskrit Buddhist Literature of Nepal*, p. 250.
8. Getty, *op. cit.*, p. 2, n. 6 and pl. xix, fig. d.

A BUDDHIST INSCRIPTION OF THE REIGN OF JAYACCANDRADEVA

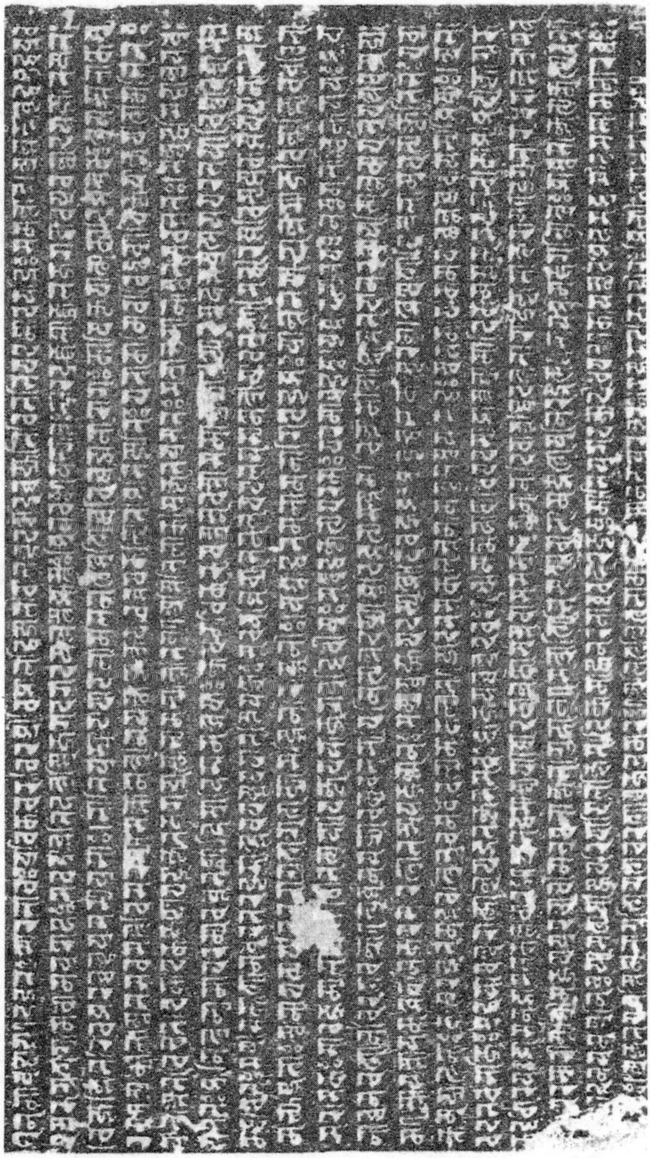

*Reproduced from the* Palas of Bengal *by the courtesy of the A.S.B.*

in Eastern India in the twelfth century A.C., but further, as revealing a conception of his symbolic representation, similar to that found to exist now only in Nepal.

The invocations to Bodhisattva Lokeśvara and Ekajaṭā in the two following verses seem also to be quite appropriate in the light of our knowledge that an image of the former in the form of Siṃhanāda was exhibited at the entrance of the cave and another of Ugratārā (who is identical with Ekajaṭā)[1] was set up inside. I could, however, find no mention of Dattatārā elsewhere. Dr. Benoytosh Bhattacharya, to whom I referred, suggests that she is identical with Dattā the Yakṣ-iṇī[2] whose *mantra* has to be uttered in propitiating Jambhala.

This document is also of importance a throwing a fresh light on the religion of the Gāhaḍavāla king Jayaccandradeva (1170-1194 A.C.), regarding whom it discloses that he was a disciple of this Buddhist monk. On the seals attached to the copper-plate grants of the Gāhaḍavāla rulers, there are, however, figures of Garuḍa, and a conch-shell, which is suggested by some to be a representation of the *pāñcajanya* conch.[3] In a copper-plate grant of Candra-deva, the founder of the dynasty, it is stated that he made gifts of certain villages in the presence of the image of Ādikeśava.[4] We are also informed by a Kamauli grant of Vijayacandra that Jayaccandra was initiated 'as a worshipper of the god Kṛṣṇa' on the day of his installation as Yuvarāja.[5] These circumstances indicate that the Gāha-ḍavāla kings were Vaiṣṇavas. Nevertheless, the significant epithet *paramamāheśvara* adopted by them attests to their devotion to Śiva.[6] Evidence is also available of their patronage shown to the Buddhist faith. Govindacandra (1114-1154 A.C.), the grand-father of Jayaccandra, assigned several villages for the support of the friars living in the 'great convent of the Holy Jetavana.'[7] It is also known that two of Govinda-candra's wives were Buddhists.[8] Of a more definite nature is the information furnished by the present inscription which states that Jayaccandra received initiation from a Buddhist teacher. All these

1. *Ibid.*, p. 111.
2. Bhattacharya, *op. cit.*, p. 114.
3. *J.A.S.B.*, vol. XLII, pt. I, p. 314.
4. *Ep. Ind.*, vol. XIV, p. 197.
5. *Ep. Ind.*, vol. IV, pp. 118ff.
6. Cf. *Ep. Ind.*, vol. IV, pp. 125ff.
7. *Ep. Ind.*, vol. XI, pp. 20ff.
8. *Ep. Ind.*, vol. IX, p. 321.

facts as noted above afford some clear indications of a catholic and eclectic spirit that characterised the religious beliefs of the Gāhaḍavāla princes.

The record under review describes Jayaccandradeva as the king of Kāśī. Under a similar style, he is also referred to by the Muhammadan historians.[1] In the Mādhāinagar grant,[2] Lakṣ-maṇasena is stated to have defeated a king of Kāśī. Although the latter's name is not mentioned there, there is hardly any room for doubt that he belonged to the well-known Gāhaḍavāla family. The fact of their being thus known as the kings of Benares combined with the evidence of their copper-plate grants, the bulk of which were issued from Benares, tends to show that the principal residence of the Gāhaḍavāla kings was at Benares. We are aware that the first king of the line made Kanauj[3] the capital of his dominions, the choice being probably due to the prestige which attached to this "Rome of mediæval India" in those days. But the insecurity of its position so close to the Ghaznavid dominions of the Punjab probably necessitated ere long the selection of a second capital in a more central situation. The danger was more evident because of the incessant hostilities of the Gāhaḍavālas with their Muhammadan neighbours.[4] The situation of Benares 'in the centre of the country of Hind' coupled with its holy associations doubtless marked it out as a suitable site for their purpose and Benares thus became the "sister capital" of the Gāhaḍavāla empire, which proud position it continued to hold till its occupation by the onrushing Muslim hordes after the battle of Chandrawar[5] in 1194 A.C.

## Translation

Om, Adoration to Buddha!

May that Smiling Nature, revealed through the mark of a cluster of high lustres rising from a crescent (lit. young) moon,[6] looking like rows of large teeth of fully-expanded and charm- ing beauty, the cause

---

1. Elliot, *History of India,* vol. II, pp. 223, 300.

2. *Jour. Proc. As. Soc. Beng.* (N.S.), vol. V, pp. 467ff.

3. *J.A.S.B.*, vol. XLII, pt. I, pp. 321ff.

4. *Ep. Ind.*, vol. IX, pp. 321ff.; *Ibid.*, vol. IV, pp. 118ff. Cf. also *Tabakāt-i-Nāsirī,* Raverty's trans., p. 107; Elliot, *History of India,* vol. IV, p. 526.

5. *Tabakāt-i-Nāsirī,* Raverty's transl., p. 470; Elliot, *History of India*, vol. II, p. 223.

6. For such symbolic representation of the Primæval Buddha (Ādi-Buddha) cf. Getty, *Gods of Northern Buddhism,* p. 2, n. 6 and pl. xix, fig. d.

of the emanation of Sarvajña,[1] with the scripture as a weapon,[2] freeing the three worlds of ills,[3] by the shoots,[4] manifest all around, of the light of a multitude of pure, noble and great virtues, growing within, confer prosperity upon you[5] (v. 1).

May that Lokeśvara, the lord with the lustre of the autumn moon, caused as if by theradiation of a mass of light springing from the flow of knowledge of the world,[6] gleaming bright in his heart, whose

---

1. See Hodgson, *Language, Literature and Religion of Nepal and Tibet,* p. 82. The Ādi-Buddha is supposed to have produced a Bodhi-sattva, "who having migrated through the three worlds, and through all six forms of animate existence........appeared at last as Śākyasiṃha to teach mankind the real sources of happiness and misery."

For the names of Gautama Buddha, see *Sanskrit-Tibetan-English Vocabulary, Mem. As. Soc. Beng.*, vol. IV, pp. 1-4.

2. *The Samāsa 'astra-śāstraḥ'* may be expounded as *astram iva śāstraṃ yasya saḥ* or "he who holds the scripture like a weapon," *i.e.*, "he who has the scripture as an attribute." The epithet is significant, describing the nature of Ādi-Buddha, who represents the ultimate source of supreme wisdom. As 'the king of the Prajñā' the same character was also ascribed to Mañjuśrī at a later age. See Poussin, *Ency. Rel. Eth.*, vol. I, pp. 95ff.; also Getty, *op. cit.*, pp. 3, 9.

Cf. "*Asti nāsti svarūpāya jñāna-rūpa-svarūpine*
*Śūnya-rūpa-svarūpāya nānā-rupāya te namaḥ*
*Svayambhū Purāṇa,* I. 3.

3. Cf. *Svayambhū Purāṇa* (Bib Ind.), I, 1-8. The Ādi-Buddha is believed to be universally propitious; see Poussin, *op. cit.*, p. 100. According to the tradition of Northern Buddhism the special function of curing diseases, is attributed to Manla, the 'Healing Buddha,' who is said to have obtained his power from Gautama Buddha, who, we know, was the spiritual son of the Ādi-Buddha, See Getty, *loc. cit.* pp. 23-24. The Śāntatīrtha near the shrine of the Ādi-Buddha at the Svayambhūkṣetra in Nepal is believed to possess the virtue of curing diseases by ablution in its waters; see Mitra, *Sanskrit Buddhist Literature of Nepal*, p. 253.

4. For *Praroha* used in a similar sense, cf. *Jyotiḥ-prarohair-uditaḥ śirastaḥ—Kumārasambhava,* III, 49.

5. "May he, who is of smiling nature, who is of delightfully expanded beauty, who is endowed with the radiance of the sprouts of his internal, thriving, noble and mighty mass of merits, made manifest by the light of young moons of the large rows of his teeth, who, for the sake of glory, has relieved the three spheres of all illness by bestowing on them the śāstra—may he be to your welfare."—Mitra.

6. Avalokiteśvara is said to be the Bodhisattva of the present cycle, namely Bhadrakalpa, covering the period between the disapearance of the Mortal Buddha, Śākyasiṃha and the advent of the Future Buddha, Maitreya.

Cf. *Karaṇḍavyūha*, pp. 21-22:

"*Yāvat Avalokiteśvarasya dṛḍhapratijñā na paripūritā bhavanti sarvasattvāḥ sarvaduḥkhebhyaḥ parimokṣitāḥ yāvat anuttarāyāṃ samyak sambodhau na pratiṣṭhāpitā bhavanti......yena yena rūpeṇa vaineyāḥ sattvāḥ tena tena rūpeṇa dharmaṃ deśayanti tathāgatavaineyānāṃ tathāgatarūpeṇa dharmaṃ deśayanti......maheśvara-vaineyānāṃ maheśvararūpeṇa dharmaṃ*

wonderful sympathy,[1] of which the essence is mercy, shines forth in the guise of the beauty of his bright, clean and rosy[2] nails, grant welfare unto you.[3] (v. 2).

May Ekajaṭā, who has made the world flourish,[4] who holds by her the uplifted sword of all-pervading mercy, like a flag of white lustre formed of the peculiar excellence of the mind consisting of the grace devoted to the multitude of dependent sentient beings,[5] bestow good fortune upon you (v. 3).

Here lived a great saint, Śrīmitra by name, who was the foremost of the class of enlightened Siddhas,[6] who was brought to being by

---

*deśayanti...... vāyuvaineyānaṃ vāyūrupeṇa dharmaṃ deśayanti......rājavaineyānāṃ sattvānāṃ rājarūpeṇa dharmaṃ deśayanti mātāpitṛvaineyānāṃ sattvānāṃ . . . mātṛpitṛrūpeṇa dharmaṃ désayanti yathāyathāvaineyānāṃ sattvānāṃ tathātathārūpeṇa dharmaṃ deśayanti.*"

1. There is a pun on the word *rāga,* which means both 'sympathy' and 'redness.' The idea implied, is that the sympathy exhibits itself in the redness of his nails.

Cf. "*Lokeśvaraṃ sarvāṅgamahārāgaraktaṃ ekamukhaṃ dvibhujaṃ trinetraṃ jaṭāmukuṭamaṇḍitaṃ vajrāṅkitapāśāṅkuśahastaṃ raktapadme vajraparyaṅkaniṣaṇṇaṃ divyābharaṇavastravibhūṣitam ātmānaṃ vicintya....*"

*Sādhanamālā* vol. I (G.O. Series), p. 80.

For varieties of Avalokiteśvara see Bhattacharyya, *op. cit.*, pp. 32ff.

2. The name of the colour *pāṭala* is evidently derived from the flower of the same name (Bignonia Suaveolens).

3. "May that lord of regions, the lord, the autumnal moon-light of whose heart is manifest by the resplendence of the glorious light of the world-enlightening moon of knowledge, whose benevolent mind appears lustrous under the guise of the resplendent row of his pure, rose-coloured nials—may he grant you blessings."—Mitra.

4. Cf. "*Tārā Mārabhayaṅkarī suravaraiḥ sampūjitā sarvvadā*
*Lokānāṃ hitakāriṇī jayati sā māteva yā rakṣati /*
*Kāruṇyena samāyutā bahuvidhān saṃsārabhīrūn janān*
*Trātrī bhaktimatāṃ bibhāti jagatāṃ nityaṃ*
* * * * *bhayadhvaṃsiṁ //*
*Devyā Ekajaṭayās tu mantrarājo mahābalaḥ /*
*Asya śravaṇmātreṇa nirvighno jāyate naraḥ //*
*Saubhāgyaṃ jāyate nityaṃ vilayaṃ yānti śatravaḥ /*
*Dharmaskandho bhaven nityaṃ Buddhatulyo na saṃśayaḥ //*
*Sādhanamālā,* vol. I, pp. 260-262."

For the *Dhyāna* see Bhattacharya, p. 80.

5. "May he of the one lock of matted hair, whose mind is engaged in friendship for those who depend on him, who holds up, like a standard, the white light of noble speech, who wields the beautiful scymitar of all-pervading mercy which has made the world fearless—may he promote your prosperity."—Mitra.

6. "The chief of the pure race of Sambuddha"—Mitra.

the merits of the three worlds and by whom all the sentient beings were invited for redemption (v. 4).

It is a wonder that at the benevolence[1] of him, who was the object of universal confidence, on account of his being inclined to affection, (*marked by*) his uplifted hands, all the animals delighted,—the ferocious shaking off their ferocity, the passionate their anger, and the timid their fear,—by sweet looks, embraces and the shower of nectar,[2] were representing their heart having been purged of the mass of impurities[3] (v. 5).

With a mind free from duality and delighting to sport in life with the maiden of emancipation, he disdainfully looked a little through the corner of his eyes at the eight charming Siddhis,[4] with a passion for virtues, who, in quest of a lord, went up to him, possessing excellence,[5] skilled (*as he was*) in leaving afflictions away, and lay at his feet[6] (v. 6).

Being free from all desires, yet in (*his*) compassion, intent on delivering the world and endowed with the highest vision, with the achievements of the Enlightened One as his highest aim,[7] who guided the rulers of earth addicted to the wrong path and ere long made them renowned for the worship of Śrīghana[8] (v. 7).

---

1. *Maitrī* is one of the four perfect states with Buddhist; see Monier Williams, *Sanskrit-English Dictionary,* s.v.
2. *I. e.*, their tears.
3. "By whose friendly aid the ferocious, giving up their needless ferocity, the passionate forsaking their superabundant anger, the timid abandoning their fear.—Relying on the friendship of him who is the asylum of radiance in this world, even (wild) animals, endowing themselves with love, conversed with each other with affection, diffusing the nectar of their delightful eyes. What a wonder!"—Mitra.
4. The eight Siddhis are enumerated in the following verse:

   *Aṇimā laghimā prāptiḥ prākāmyaṃ mahimā tathā /*
   *Īśitvaṃ ca vaśitvaṃ ca tathā kāmāvasāyitā //*
   see Monier-Williams' *Sanskrit-English Dictionary,* s.v.
5. *Sauṣṭhavaṃ syād-avaṣṭambho,* see Halāyudha *Abhidhānaratnamālā,* ed. Aufrecht, IV, 74.
6. "Enamoured by the maiden of emancipation in this life, that person of undeviating mind, did not by the corner of his eyes, cast even a reproachful glance at the eight Siddhis, who had achieved the exclusion of all created evils, who were devoted voluntarily to their husband, who delighted in the enjoyment of good qualities, and who lying at his feet."—Mitra.
7. "Looking up for his enterprise."—Mitra.
8. A name of Buddha.

He was always quickly giving away without any attachment even what did not cross the mind of the supplicant, wherefore the 'thought-gem' famous for yielding things desired became dull in shame[1] (v. 8).

Of (*his*) fame, of which the body was rising upwards, which was ever gaining prosperity in many ways and which even fully touched the abode of Brahmā, the wonderful and thriving whiteness, having bathed again and again from its birth in the waters of the river of countless immortals, was equalled in achievements with Śeṣa and (*thus*) proclaimed in the three worlds for as long as the cycle continues[2] (v. 9).

Of that emancipated being the illustrious Jayaccandradeva, the attainment of whose sovereignty was proclaimed all over the expanse of the Earth, who was of clear understanding and who was served by a hundred kings, became, out of reverence, himself the disciple with a pleasing heart and an indescribable hankering (v. 10).

The pilot of the Faith and the initiating preceptor of the king of Kāśī, he restored the discipline and recovered the numerous collection of lost scriptures and others of the same kind, belonging to the illustrious site of the Māhābodhi (v. 11).

It is this accomplished, all-knowing and illustrious friend of the world, free from impurities,[3] that made this large cave here in the auspicious *Jayapura*, with Siṃhanāda[4] in front and bearing therein (*images of*) Ugratārā, with her hand raised upwards, Dattatārā, adored in the morning (lit. in the van of the day) and (another Tārā) draped in orange clothes, fair as the evening clouds[5] and at the same time

---

1. The Cintā-maṇi could not cope with the monk, being entirely dependent for its gift on the suppliant's desire, while the latter did not even wait for it.

2. The poet implies that his fame traversed the three worlds in this way: it bathed in the Ganges in the land of mortals, it touched the abode of Brahmā in the world above, and was balanced with the achievements of Śeṣa in the world beneath.

"The work of him who, bathing over and over in the river of endless felicity, had, from the day of his birth, taken the lord proprietor of wealth and propriety for asylum, who,—having repeatedly touched the dignity of the highest Brahmā, had ultimately become unrivalled among wise men, and of thriving persons;—his work had attained a wonderful whiteness for ages."—Mitra.

3. "The wifeless."—Mitra. Cf. "Aṅgana," *J.R.A.S.*, 1898, pp. 171ff. and 461ff.

4. For Siṃhanāda, see Bhattacharya, op. cit. pp. 35ff.

5. "The three Bodhis—adorned in golden raiment, resplendent as the garlanded cloud of twilight—the adored of day with the forehead decked with a bright star. Bearing a refulgent star—this cave, in the auspicious Jayapura."—Mitra.

shrines[1] for these three in the courts, eternally to last, in the month of Jyaiṣṭha, in the year of king Vikramāṅka indicated by the arrangement of the number (composed) by the figures represented by . . 'vedas', 'eyes' and 'moon' (vs. 12-15).

Manoratha, son of the illustrious Sīda, the best of the Kāyastha race . . . . who was like a bee of the lotus-feet of the virtuous, composed this eulogium (v. 16).

The illustrious Purandara, the adored of scribes, copied it down (*on the slab*) and the patient artisan Dhārādhara engraved it with a chisel (v. 17).

1. "Sacrifices."—Mitra.

L.1. ॐ[1] नमो बुद्धाय।

[2]उद्भूतः समेरभावः प्रविकच–रुचिर–श्रीविशालहिजालौ–

बालेन्दूदञ्चदु[3]ञ्चद्युतिविततिपदेनोदयद्भिः समन्तात्।

अन्तस्संवृद्ध[4]–शुद्ध–प्रव–

L.2. र–गुरुगुणाग्रामधामप्ररोहैः

सर्वज्ञोद्भूतिहेतुस्त्रिजगदगदयन्त्रस्त्रशास्त्रः[5] श्रिये वः॥ [1]

[6]यस्यान्तःस्फुरदुज्ज्वलोज्ज्वलजगद्बोधप्रबन्धो[7]दय–

ज्योतिर्जाल–

L.3. विजृम्भितैरिव शरच्चन्द्रप्रभस्य प्रभोः।

भाति प्रस्फुटपाटलामलनखश्रेणौच्छविच्छद्मना

रागः कोपि कृपात्मको दिशतु वः श्रेयस्स लोकेश्वरः॥ [2]

L.4. [8]अध्यालम्बितसर्वसत्त्वविसर[9]व्यासक्तमैत्रीमय–

स्वान्तोत्[10]कर्षविशेषकल्पितशितिज्योतिःपताकामिव।

विश्वव्यापिकृपाकृपाणमभितः

L.5. प्रोत्तम्भितं[11] विभ्रती[12]

देयादेकजटा पटूकृतजगदुयुस्मभ्यमभ्युन्नतिम्॥ [3]

[13]अस्तित्रिलोकौसुकृतप्रसूतः[14]

संत्रातुमामन्त्रित[15] सर्वभूतः।

सम्बुद्धसिद्धान्वय धु–

L.6. र्य्यभूतः[16]

श्रीमित्रनामा परमावधूतः[17]॥ [4]

[18]हिंसा हिंसामशेषाः कुधमधिकरुषस्त्रस्त्रवस्त्रासमाशु

व्याधूयोदस्तहस्त[19] प्रणयपरतया विश्वविश्वासभू–

L.7. मेः।

चेतःसंप्रीयमाणा मधुरतरदृशा[20] श्लेषपेयूषपातै–

स्तिर्यञ्चः सूचयन्ति[21] च्युतमलपटलं यस्य मैत्रीषु चित्रम्॥ [5]

[22]सिद्धोरष्टविसृष्टकष्टघ( प टुना[23]वष्टम्भ–

L.8. मभ्युद्गता:

खेनोपेत्य पतिं(वरा)[24] गुणगणव्यासङ्गिनी रङ्गिनी:।

यश्चाद्वैतमना मनागि दृश: प्रान्तेन पादान्तगा

जीवन्मुक्तिवधुवला-

L.9. सरसिक: सावज्ञमालो[25] (कते)॥ [6]

[26]वीतस्पृहौपि क्रपया जमदुद्दिधीर्षु:

सम्बुद्धकृत्यपरम: परमोश्चदृश्वा॥

पृथ्वौपतौनपथ[27] निष्ठमतीन्विनीय

य: श्रीघ-

L.10. नार्च्चनचणानचिरेण चक्रे॥ [7]

[28]स्पृष्टं न यदुयाचकचेतमापि

नित्यन्तदप्याशु दिशत्यसङ्गम्॥

चिन्तामणिश्चिन्तितदानचुञ्चु[29]

र्यस्मिन्नवाप[30] त्रपयेव जाड्य[31]

L.11. म्॥ [8]

[31]स्नायं स्नायमशेषनिर्जरसरित्स्रोतस्सु य[33]ज्जन्मन:

सम्यग्ब्रह्मपदस्पृशोपि वहुश: श्रीवृद्धिभाजश्चिरम्[34]।

शेषेणापि तुलामुपेत्य कृतिभि[35] प्रव्य-

L.12. क्तमुद्यत्तनो:

कौर्त्तेरद्भुतमुद्भवत्रिभुवने धावल्यमाकल्पश[36](श:)॥ [9]

[37]उदितसकलभूमौमण्डलैश्वर्य[38] सिद्धि:

स्वयमपि किमपौच्छन्नच्छधीर्यस्य[39] शिष्य:।

अभ-

L.13. वदभवभाज: श्रद्धया बन्धुरात्मा

नृपशतकृतसेव: श्रीजयश्चन्द्रदेव:॥ [10]

[40]श्रीमन्महाबोधिपदस्य शास्त्र-

ग्रामादिकं मग्रमशेषमेव।

काशीशदौक्षागुरु-

L. 14. रुद्दधार

य: शासनं शासनकर्णाधार: ॥ [11]

[41]आनद्ध[42]सान्ध्यपाथोदकान्तकौमुम्भवाससम्।

वन्द्यमानां दिवामूर्द्धि दत्ततारा‌ङ्क्कतोत्कराम्॥ [12]

[43]उग्रताराधरान्तत सिंह[44]–

L. 15. (नाद ?)पुरस्सरौम्।

श्रीमज्जयपुरे चोर्वौमत्त[45] चैतां क्कतौ गुहाम्॥ [13]

[46]सन्त्राणि तिसृणां चासामङ्गणेषु निरङ्गण:।

सोयं श्रीमज्जगन्मित्त: शाश्वतौक्कत्य क्कत्स्त्रवित्[47] ॥ [14]

L. 16. [48]**वेदनयनेन्दुनिष्ठया संख्ययाङ्कपरिपाटिलक्षिते।

विक्रमाङ्कनरनाथवत्सरे ज्यैष्ठमासि युगपद्यदौधयत्॥ [15]

[49]कायस्थवंशहंसश्रीसीदसुतो मनोरथ:

L. 17. ....:।

अक्कत प्रशस्तिमेतां गुणिगणचरणाम्बुजभ्रमर: ॥ [16]

[50]अलिखल्लिखतामर्ज्ञा: (श्री)मनितां पुरन्दर:।

टडैरुदकिरद्धोर: शिल्पी धाराधराभिध: ॥ [17]

## Footnotes To The Text

1. Expressed by a symbol.
2. Metre: Sragdharā.
3. M (—Mitra) reads—*ūdgacchhad.*
4. M. reads *sambaddho.*
5. M. *reads nastaśāstraḥ.*
6. Metre: Śārddūlavikrīḍita.
7. M. reads *pracandra.*
8. Metre: Śārddūlavikrīḍita.
9. M. reads *viṣaya.*
10. M. reads-*mvārtto.*
11. M. reads *śrīnirmmitaṃ.*
12. M. reads *vibhrato.*
13. Metre: Indravajrā.
14. M. reads *trilokīṣu kṛtaprasūtaḥ.*
15. M. reads *satr—ottam—āmattrita.*
16. M. reads *dhīrabhūtaḥ.*
17. M. reads *paramovadhūtaḥ.*
18. Metre: Sragdharā.
19. M. reads *mvahantaḥ.*
20. M. reads *madhuratara-dṛsoḥ.*
21. M. reads-*sū(su)kavanti.*
22. Metre: Śārddūlavīkrīḍita.
23. M. reads *paṭalā.*
24. M. reads *ratā.*
25. M. reads *sāvarjjam.*
26. Metre: Vasantatilaka.
27. M. reads-apara.
28. Metre: Indravajrā.
29. M. reads *dāna-candro.*
30. M. reads *Yasminn-avāpa.*
31. M. reads *cad yām.*
32. Metre: Śārddūlavikrīḍita.
33. M. reads *srotaḥsra.*
34. M. reads *śrīvṛddhibhājīśvaram.*
35. M. reads *kṛtinaḥ.* The last *i-kāra* stroke was originally inadvertently omitted; only the curve on the top was supplied afterwards.
36. M. Reads *ākalpasaḥ.*
37. Metre: Mālinī.
38. M. reads *śvaryya.*
39. M. reads *acchadhīyasya.*
40. Metre Indravajrā.
41. Metre: Anuṣṭubh.

42. M. rads *sannaddha.*
43. Metre: Anuṣṭubh.
44. M. reads *siṃva*.
45. M. reads *bodhi.*
46. Metre: Anuṣṭubh.
47. The last six letters are omitted by M.
48. Metre: Rathoddhatā.
49. Metre: Āryyā.
50. Metre: Anuṣṭubh.

## Chapter - 36

# Buddhism in the Classical Age

**(*as revealed by archaeology*)**

**Sudha Sengupta**

The period under review, designated by scholars as "Classical Age," covers a period of about four centuries. It begins with the Gupta rulers in the administrative horizon of India, their glorious ascent like the midday sun, their temporary eclipse by the Huṇa invaders, and their gradual setting down. Then the twilight of various petty rulers and then the advent of the Moon in the form of Harṣavardhana with many other rulers scattered all over the country like stars in a nocturnal sky. Then with the disappearance of Harṣa, there is again a dark period, which ends with the azure with the glimpses of morning light just before the rise of another Sun in the horizon, the Pālas.

For the history of the Buddhist church in the classical period, there is a considerable number of inscriptions and archaeological remains in the form of images, shrines, *stūpas*, cave-temples, *caityas*, etc. which enable us to rebuild a complete structure of the history of the religion.

Though Buddhism was not a state religion in this period,—none of the main ruling families of this period having professed the religion of Sākya-Muni,—still, following the general Indian tradition of religious toleration which favoured the growth of diverse rival religious sects side by side in the Indian soil, most of the Indian kings patronised religions other than their own. A study of the archaeological remains reveal to us the fact that as on the one hand the Buddhist kings made religious grants to non-Buddhist communities, in the same manner the non-Buddhist kings also did not refrain from stretching their bounteous hands to the Buddhists. And this spirit of sympathetic co-operation stimulated the art, architecture and sculpture of this period to rise to such a level of perfection that it drew unstinted admiration of art-connoisseurs for many centuries. Though the Gupta kings held political supremacy up to the end of the 5th century A.D., the era of art which began with them lasted much longer up to the 7-8th centuries A.D. And the influence of Gupta art spread far beyond the historical and geographical boundaries of the Gupta empire.

The Buddhist monuments consist mainly of (1) Pillars, (2) *Stūpas* (3) Railings, (4) *Caityas* or prayer halls and (5) *Vihāras* or monastic abodes.[1] The images, which play a great part in the history of the development of the Buddhist church, were introduced at a later date. In the hilly tracts, the Buddhist establishments are hewn out of living rocks—splendid specimens of rock-architecture. In fact, the earliest and the major number of the cave-temples of India are Buddhist. In the Buddhist literature the mode of preparing *stūpas* was suggested by Buddha himself,[2] and the worship of *stūpas* commenced immediately after his demise. In the *Mahāparinibbāna-sutta* it is said that after the demise of the Buddha, a dispute arose among the Mallas, Koliyas, Śākyas and others for possession of the relics of Buddha's body, which were at last divided among eight chiefs, each of whom built a *stūpa* over them in their respective countries.[3] During the life-time of the Buddha, his religion was confined to Middle India. It was during the reign of the Emperor Aśoka that the religion gained a wide popularity. Aśoka erected several *stūpas* and pillars all over India, especially at the places associated with some memorable event in the life of Buddha. The fabulous number of eighty-four thousand *stūpas* erected by Aśoka in place of seven out of the eight *stūpas* erected over the relics of Buddha may be incredible, but that their number was quite large appears to be true. And the places around these *stūpas* must have been important centres of Buddhism for a few centuries upto about the fourth century A.D. when the building of new *stūpas* became less in number but there was enlargement or alteration of the older ones. Pillars became very rare and railings encircling *stūpas* in vogue from the earliest period of the Buddhist architecture—also became much rarer, and probably the only stone railing that may be ascribed to this period is one of the two sets found at Bodh-Gaya, the older one being of the time of Aśoka and made of the same kind of

1. Fergusson, *History of Ind. & Eastern Architecture*, Introduction.
2. *Mahāparinibbāna Sutta, Dighanikāya*, XVI. 5. 12-13.
3. *Ibid*, XVI. 6. 25.

polished sand-stone peculiar to all Aśokan monoliths. The more popular Buddhist architectures of this period are the *Vihāras* or a group of monastic abodes for the residence of monks, *caityas* or prayer halls enshrining *stūpas* and images of Buddha. Figures of Buddha were in some cases carved on the *stūpas* placed inside the *caityas*. These *Vihāras* and *Caityas* gained in popularity and increased in number. The *Vihāras* were used to be made by the Buddhists from the earliest period of its organisation—from the life-time of its Founder who himself lived in various *Vihāras*. *Caitya* halls were introduced somewhat later, the earliest form of paying homage by the Buddhists being the erection and worship of relic *stūpas*. With the rise and development of Mahāyāna, *Caitya* halls became more and more popular and the cultural atmosphere and the patronising spirit of the rulers encouraged the Buddhists of this age to revive their intellectual activities, particularly in the art and architecture of the *Caityas* and *Vihāras*. Lastly, with the growing popularity of Mahāyāna, and the gradual introduction of various gods and goddesses into its pantheon the family of Buddhist gods became enlarged to a considerable extent. This large pantheon gave inspiration and ample scope to the display of skill by the sculptors whose productions are really a treasure for all times. The archaeologists' spades have brought to light before us the long mute story of those forgotten far off days and we remain struck with wonder and admiration when we think of the men of that remote past who could build such magnificent structures with such delicate ornamentations and graceful and lovely figures with their hands and very meagre implements. We shall now begin our survey of the state of Buddhism during the Gupta period and commence with the extreme north-western part of India.

Buddhism reached the north-western region through the proselytising efforts of Aśoka. Three inscriptions found from Swat[1] corroborate the statement of the Chinese travellers that Buddhism lingered on this region upto the 7th century A.D. The characters of these inscriptions resemble the so-called north-western Gupta characters. These inscriptions, being quotations from the Sūtras, are very important from the literary standpoint.

It was Aśoka who was responsible for the introduction of Buddhism into the Gandhāra region. Here he built several *stūpas* which were seen by the Chinese pilgrims. After Aśoka, the region passed

---

1. *Ep. Ind.*, VI, 133-4.

into the hands of foreign rulers who could have the religion easily rooted out from the territory but they did not do so, and on the other hand the great Kushān king Kaṇiṣka helped it in its further development. Kaṇiṣka very probably repaired the older *stūpas* or built new ones in their places, and it is said that during his time Gandhāra became a popular centre of Buddhism. The rulers, who governed this place after Kaṇiṣka, did not show much interest in Buddhism, which therefore gradually faded out in the area. But that religion of Gautama did not totally disappear from these places at least upto the 7th century, is proved by the records of the Chinese travellers as well as by archaeological discoveries. The Dharmarājika Vihāra built by Kaṇiṣka was seen by Fa-Hian in the 5th century in a flourishing condition. Hwen-tsang, who came to India in the early 7th century, reports that he saw many *stūpas* and monasteries in this region, in a somewhat decayed condition but their glory and sancitity were not much diminished. The Buddhist establishments of Mohra-Moradu and Kalvan appear around the Dharmarājika *stūpa*. The Archaeological reports tell us that *stūpas* and other buildings continued to be erected around the Dharmarājika *stūpa* from the 4th to 7th centuries A.D. The Bhāmala monastery in Taxila was built about the 4th or 5th century A.D. On the tiled pavement in front of the western steps of the main *stūpa* at Bhāmala is depicted the *Dharmacakra* and various other symbols, like Swastikā, lotus, rosettes, concentric circles, quarter-foils of Pipal leaves, crosses, spirals and double-axes.[1] A few decades later, the whole of this region must have been set on fire, apparently by the formidable enemy of India, the Hūṇa invaders, Toramāna and Mihirakula as is proved by the traces of incendiarism on the sites like some half-burnt birch bark manuscripts written in upright Gupta characters of the 5th century A.D., found from Juliāñ.[2]

I. In Sind, the brick-built *stūpa* of Kahu-jo-daro near Mirpurkhās contains ornamentations and patterns resembling those at Sarnāth and at Mathurā. Clay tablets containing the well-known Buddhist formula "Ye dharma—" etc. in 7th-8th century characters go to prove that Buddhism still had its hold over this place. The *stūpa* named Sudharanjo-daro near Tando-Mohamed-Khan, of which unfortunately nothing but the square plinth is extant, is also assigned to about the 5th-6th century A.D., on the basis of the evidence furnished by its carved bricks lying scattered.

1-2 Marshall, *Taxila*, vol. I, (plates 119a, 119b).

II. That there was a net-work of Buddhist institutions with a considerable number of devotees in the Kabul valley and the Punjab region of India from the remotest period of its history is further proved by the inscriptions found in the neighbouring places. An inscription on a stone-slab from Kura in the salt-range records[1] the erection of a *Vihāra* "for the congregation of monks of Bhagavat Buddha by the lord of the Vihāra, Roṭṭa Siddha Vṛddhi, son of Roṭṭa Jaya Vṛddhi whose name was honoured by the lord of Naschira, for the benefit of the relatives of the donor and the queens, princes and princesses, of Mahārāja Toramāṇa Sāha Jauvala for the acceptance of the teachers (Ācāryas) of the Mahiśāsakas." The characters resemble the older Buddhist nail-headed inscriptions of the Gupta period with some peculiarities. The Toramāṇa mentioned in this inscription is certainly not the famous Huṇa king of the same name, who was rather a staunch antagonist to all Indian religions—not to speak of Buddhism—but might be some other independent king bearing similar name and ruling over some territory in North-Western India. Traces of Buddhism in Punjab are found in an inscribed brass image of Buddha found in Fatehpur (Kangra dist.) approximately of the 6th century A.D. which records[2] the pious gift of the Buddhist friar Dharmapriya together with his brother Dharmasiṃha and with his preceptor of the same name (viz. Dharmasiṃha), and "with all sentient beings."

III. Kashmir was a great centre of Buddhism of the Sarvāstivāda school of the Hinayāna sect from a very early period. Its later history is furnished by literary as well as architectural evidences. According to the *Mahāvaṁsa*, of the thirteen missionaries sent by Aśoka to preach Buddhism in different countries, one named Majjhantika was sent to Kashmir and Gandhāra. According to some opinion including that of Hwen Tsang, Kashmir was the venue of the Buddhist council held under the auspices of Kaṇiṣka. The *Rājataraṅginī*, the famous chronicle of Kashmir by Kalhaṇa, tells us that Buddhism and Hinduism flourished side by side in Kashmir during the reign of the great king Lalitāditya Muktāpiḍa (699-735) when the *Vihāras* and *Caitya* of Parihāspura (mod. Paraspur) and the Vihāra of Huviṣkapura (mod. Uskara) were built. The Vihāra of Uskara seems to have been built at least some time before that, because, Hwen Tsang, who visited

---

1. *Ep. Ind.*, I, p. 238.
2. *ASI. Ann., Rep.*, 1904-5, pp. 107-8.

Kashmir a few decades earlier and lived there for two years, is said to have spent a night in the Huṣkara Vihāra, which must be the same as that at Huviṣkapura. Another monastery mentioned by the pilgrim was the Jayendra-Vihāra. The Chinese pilgrim is said to have seen about 100 monasteries in Kashmir, but Wu-K'ung who lived at the same place about a century later, reports to have seen about 300 monasteries.[1] The most remarkable early Buddhist remains at Kashmir are unearthed at Harwan near Srinagar. It occupies a lovely situation on a slope facing the beautiful Dal lake, with a mountain range on its background. The remains reveal a large Buddhist establishment with a *stūpa* in its courtyard, a *Caitya* hall and some monastic abodes around them. The *Caitya* hall which occupies a prominent position on the highest part of the plateau is one of the rare specimens of the type in northern India, bearing remarkable affinity to those of the rock-cut *Caitya* halls in the southern parts of India. Numerous terracotta plaques found at the site are unique specimens of Indian art. As observed by Percy Brown, "the remains at Harwan indicate that the memorable impact of diverse historical cultures, which took place in this part of Asia in the early centuries of the first millennium, also had repurcussions on the arts of Kashmir."[2] And though we have hitherto found no inscription from Kashmir, the deficiency is more than made up by the monumental discovery of a number of Sanskrit manuscripts of various Buddhist texts from a *stūpa* at Gilgit, written in characters of 5-6th century A.D. These manuscripts are supposed to be the earliest manuscripts so far discovered in India, and were hitherto known to have existed only in their Tibetan translations.[3]

IV. For the region lying between the north-western countries and M a t h u r a, we have practically no archaeological materials to depict the story of the condition of Buddhism in these regions. Hwen Tsang reports to have seen a number of Buddhist institutions and also Buddhist devotees in this region. Mathura and its neighbourhood was a great centre of Jainism as well as of Buddhism from a very early date, the form of Buddhism being mainly the Sarvāstivāda as it is associated with the name of Upagupta, the religious teacher of Aśoka, who is said to have had great success as a missionary in this region and converted numerous people. An inscription of the time of

---

1. *Watters*, I, pp. 258ff; cf. *IA.*, 1895, p. 342ff.
2. P. Brown, *Indian Architecture,* p. 186.
3. *Gilgit Manuscripts,* ed. N. Dutt.

Kaṇiṣka records that the Sāmmitiyas also resided at this place. Hwen Tsang is said to have seen the followers of Mahāyāna also. The Chinese travellers saw here about twenty Buddhist monasteries and a large number of devotees. But unfortunately no remains of any monastery have so far been found out in this area, though numerous Buddhist figures, some of which are inscribed, prove that at one time the place was a flourishing centre of Buddhism. The sculptures of Mathura had a peculiar type of its own and its school of art, which developed almost immediately after that of Gandhara, is regarded as the connecting link between the Gandhara and the Gupta school of art. Some Buddhist figures of the early Gupta period hailing from Mathura clearly manifest the vestiges of the older form of art mingled with the glimpses of the advancing Gupta art.[1] The Boston Museum of America has in its collection some images of Buddha from Mathura belonging to the Gupta period.[2] Two inscriptions inscribed on the pedestals of two standing Buddha images from Mathura have been discovered. These, on paleographic grounds, are to be placed at an interval of about a century. These are regarded as the latest inscriptions so far found in this region. The earlier one, ascribed to the middle of the 5th century A.D., is inscribed on the pedestal of a broken image of standing Buddha and records the gift of the figure by some "Vihārasvāmini Devatā," most probably a "Mother Superior" of a nunnery, "for the acquisition of supreme knowledge by her parents and all sentient beings." The later one is the gift of another nun of the name of Jayabhaṭṭā to a monastery named Yaśovihāra.[3] Not only stone but bronze images also have been discovered from Mathura and other places which add to the glory of the artists of this period.

V. The city of Ś r ā v a s t ī is prominent in Buddhist literature for continued presence and activities of Buddha himself. It is identified with the modern ruined city of Saheth-Maheth in the Gonda and Bahraich districts of U.P. where Gen. Cunningham discovered a colossal image of Buddha with the name of Śrāvastī inscribed on it. Archaeological excavations have brought to light many of the sites mentioned by the Chinese pilgrims and those agree reasonably with their description. The Jetavana-vihāra with its eastern and northern gates, as described by Fa-Hian, has been brought to light by Gen. Cunningham at Saheth. The Aṅgulimāla-stūpa, the Gandha-kūṭī, and

---

1. *ASI.*, 1922-23, p. 169-69.
2. Cf. *Boston Museum Catalogue* by Coomaraswamy.
3. *CII.*, III, pp. 262ff, 273ff.

the Kosāmba-kūṭī have been identified by the excavators. Five brick built monasteries together with a shrine and a *stūpa* have been unearthed in this area and very likely these belong to our period of survey. There are some structural remains of the Gupta and subsequent periods, as also of the earlier period testifying that the site was occupied from the Kushān upto the 11-12th centuries A.D. The sculptures so far found at this site are anterior to the classical period, and it is strange enough that no sculpture of this period has hitherto been come to light. But there are many inscribed terracotta seals and sealings bearing the Buddhist creed in scripts of the 6th-7th century.

VI. P r a y ā g a or the district around Allahabad was the centre of Buddhism from the lifetime of Buddha. Kausāmbī, modern Kosam near Allahabad, where the Ghoṣ-itārāma monastery mentioned in the Buddhist literature has been unearthed together with an inscription of the earlier centuries mentioning the name of the monastery, was sanctified by the presence of the lord himself. The records of the Chinese pilgrims prove that this country continued to be a centre of Buddhism in subsequent periods also, at least upto the 7th century when Hwen Tsang visited India, and Harṣavardhana was ruling in this region. Though there is no inscription either of Harṣa or any other ruler, both Hwen Tsang and Harṣa's biographer Bāṇa depict the king as a great patron of Buddhism. The quinquennial religious assembly organised under the auspices of Harṣa is said to have taken place during the visit of the Chinese pilgrim at Allahabad. Hwen Tsang speaks eloquently of the assembly and the favour shown to Buddhism by its inaugarator, Harṣa. Two inscriptions belonging to periods earlier than Harṣa found in the neighbouring areas relate the continuation of the religion from its inception. Of the two inscriptions, the first, ascribed to the reign of the Gupta ruler Kumāragupta I, found at Mankuwar in the Allahabad district records the installation by a monk called Buddhamitra of the stone-figure of Buddha, on which appears the inscription.[1] An attempt has been made to identify this Buddhamitra with his namesake, the teacher of Vasubandhu.[2] The other inscription, found in a village named Deoriya in the same district though undated, is assigned to the 5th century on paleographic grounds, and records the gift of the image of Buddha by a Śākya monk Bodhivarman.[3]

---

1. *CII.*, III, p. 45ff.
2. *IA.*, 1912. also *Allan Cat. of Gupta Coins*, p. XLII.
3. *CII.* III, p. 271ff.

VII. K a s i a in the Gorakhpur district is the modern site of ancient Kuśīnagara, the site of hallowed memory in the history of Buddhism as the place of the *Mahāparinirvāṇa* of the Buddha, and as such one of the four great places of pilgrimage for the Buddhists. Kasia has yielded a large number of archaeological materials which show that the origin of the place goes back to a remote antiquity, even as early as the Mauryan age. Of the many Mahāparinirvāṇa *Caityas* found at this place, the main one, designated Māthā-kuvar-kā-koṭ, by the local people, is supposed to have been rebuilt at this period. A colossal recumbent stone image of Buddha in the pose of attaining *Mahāparinirvāṇa* has been unearthed at Kasia. It bears an inscription under its pedestal which records the gift of the same figure by an abbot (Mahāvihāra-svāmin) named Haribala.[1] Again, in the relic chamber of a large *stūpa* behind the Nirvāṇa temple at Kasia, was found a copper vessel—probably containing the relics, with an inscribed copper lid. The inscription contains the Buddhist *Nidāna Sūtra* and also the record of the gift (of the vessel) by the pious Haribala, obviously the same person as the donor of the image mentioned above. It is also stated in the inscription that the urn belonged to the Nirvāṇa-caitya, confirming the identity of Kasia with the ancient Kuśīnagara. Further evidence of the identity of Kasia with Kuśīnagara is supplied by a number of clay seals depicting Buddha in the attitude of attaining *Mahāparinirvāṇa*, with the *Dharmacakra* or the wheel of Law underneath, and the legend 'Mahāparinirvāṇa Bhikṣusaṅghasya' on it in Gupta characters, or 'Sri Mahāparinirvāṇa mahāvihāriyārya bhikshusaṅghasya' in 8th century characters. Some official sealings with legends in Gupta characters and fragmentary stone inscriptions have also been found in the area.[2]

VIII. S a r n a t h had the singular fortune of being the birth place of Buddhism as well as of the Buddhist Saṅgha, the two jewels of the Buddhist Trinity. The first monastic organisation formed at Sarnath continued to exist here in subsequent days. Aśoka, who is credited with building numerous Buddhist edifices, constructed the Dharmarājika *stūpa* here, and erected one of his edict pillars, the stump of which still remain in situ. Its inscription portion has been preserved in such excellent condition that it can be read quite easily even after such a long interval of time. The *stūpa* was seen by Hwen

1. *Ibid*, p. 272.
2. *ASI. Ann. Rep.*, 1911-12.

Tsang, and it remained extant even about two centuries ago, when a local chief of Benares, Jagat Singh by name, destroyed it for procuring stones. The lion capital crowning the pillar which has been adopted recently as the insignia of the Republic of India, is exhibited in the adjoining museum. In the Suṅga, Kānva, and Andhra periods, the arnath monastery continued to exist in an insignificant way, but it was revived again in the Kushan period, specially under Kaṇiṣka. The most notable statue of the period of Kaṇiṣka found at Sarnath is the colossal Bodhisattva figure with the umbrella dedicated by the monk Bala. The Buddhist art attained the summit of its glory at Sarnath during the Gupta period, and a considerable number of Buddhist images which have been unearthed from Sarnath during excavations as well as those of the same period found from Mathura, are regarded as the finest specimens of Indian art. The main shrine of Sarnath is supposed to have been erected during the Gupta period, but who was its patron, is not yet clear. The famous Dhāmekh *stūpa*, still extant at Sarnath, must have been rebuilt on an earlier nucleus during this period, and show a marked distinction in its formation compared with other *stūpas* of earlier date. A fair number of inscriptions found from Sarnath help us to ascertain the condition of Buddhism in this period. An inscription of the 4th century A.D., on the pedestal of a broken image of standing Buddha, records the gift of the statue by a Buddhist nun 'Dharmmade.' The inscription below a sandstone bas-relief representation of three scenes of the life of Buddha, belonging to the 5th century (now deposited in the Indian Museum, Calcutta) records that the sculpture was made by the order of a religious mendicant named Harigupta. An inscription on a figure of Buddha, assigned to the reign of Kumāragupta (II) records the gift of the image by a certain monk Abhayamitra. Another image contains the inscription 'Deya-dharmo-yam Kumāraguptasya' which suggests that the donor was perhaps the Gupta king Kumāragupta himself. Two other inscriptions of the monk Abhayamitra have been found at Sarnath on the pedestals of two similar beautiful Buddha images standing on lotus, assigned to a later period, to the reign of Budhagupta. There are also the 5th century inscription of the gift of the monk Śīlasena and the 6th century gift of the great lay-devotee Narnnana as well as the gift of a pillar used as a lamp-post in the main shrine by the devout worshipper Kīrti, belonging to the 5th century. A peculiar fact about the inscriptions of this period is that they seldom state the particular sect of Buddhism to which the donors or the donee belonged. And as such we are confronted with a difficulty to ascertain the form of religion prevalent in a certain locality. This difficulty is somewhat solved by two dedicatory inscriptions on a railing-stone at Sarnath, recording the paying of homage to the Sarvāstivādin teachers. Sten Konow remarks about these inscriptions: "the inscription consists of two distinct parts in different characters. The beginning belongs to the 3rd or 4th c. A.D. The final portion......is older by about four centuries. It appears that the first part of the earlier inscription has been erased and a different beginning substituted." From these, it becomes evident that the Sarvāstivādins were predominant in this region, and previously some rival sect had its centre in the same region. The later sects scratched the previous names and substituted that of their own.[1]

IX. The city of P ā ṭ a l i p u t r a, modern Patna, had no less importance in the history of Buddhism than its political one. It became the capital city as early as the time of the grandson of Bimbisāra. Aśoka too had his capital at this city, and this place must have been a centre of Buddhism from that very period. Fa-Hian in the early 5th-6 c. saw a large monastery with the adherents of the Mahāyāna sect, and another with those of the Hinayāna faith. Both the monasteries contained numerous priests and were great centres of learning. But Hwen Tsang, two centuries later, found the city almost deserted, with very few Buddhist and Brahmanic ruins scattered here and there. Archaeological excavations have brought to light what is supposed to be the palace of Aśoka, and recent excavations have unearthed some Buddhist establishments which, if further excavations are carried on, might, in the long run, be identified with those referred to by Fa-hian.

X. The illustrious institution of N ā l a n d ā did not rise into prominence till the later part of the Gupta rule. According to Tāra-nātha Nālandā was a flourishing centre of Buddhism as early as the time of Nāgārjuna (i.e. and c. A.D.), who is said to have passed his academic as well as teaching career in the monastery of Nālandā. But we have no archaeological or epigraphic record in support of the statement. All the Buddhist Vihāras, from their earliest history, provided educational facilities particularly of the Tripiṭaka. In the same manner, the Nālandā monastery with its educational activities might have existed in an insignificant position from an earlier period, till it gained the world-wide reputation as a University centre at the time

1. Sahni. *Guide to Sarnath.*

of the late Gupta rulers. Archaeological reports also do not prove its importance before that period. Probably it was not before the time of Kumāragupta that the Nālandā monastery came into prominence, as the coin of the king found on the site claims to prove; the inscribed copper-plate ascribed to Samudragupta is supposed by scholars as spurious; and Fa-Hian does not mention a single word about the monastery of Nālandā, though he speaks of the village Nalô and the Sāriputra tope. On the other hand, Hwen Tsang, two centuries later, speaks highly of the monastic establishment of Nālandā, of its patron kings, of the succession of teachers, the fame of whose vast knowledge and scholasticism spread all over Asia and attracted students from far off countries. Under one of them, viz., Śīlabhadra, he himself studied for a long period. The architectural remains of Nālandā disclose several strata which indicates that the buildings were built and re-built several times, and was in a flourishing condition upto the period of the Pālas. The majority of the inscriptions from Nālandā belongs to the age of the Pālas. For the period under review, we have very few inscriptions, one of which is quite interesting. This is the inscription of the time of Yaśovarmadeva, the characters of which resemble those of Ādityasena found at Āpsaḍ, and hence is placed in the 6th century A.D. It records certain gifts of Mālāda,[1] son of a minister of Yaśovarmadeva, to the temple of Buddha, erected by Bālāditya at Nālandā. Though some difference of opinion have occurred about the identity and date of the Yaśovarmadeva during whose reign the gift was made,[2] this inscription is of considerable value as it confirms the statement made by Hwen Tsang, that the Nālandā monastery was built by 'Bālāditya Rājā.' The inscription gives the description of the Nālandā monastery as follows: "Bālāditya, the great king of irresistible valour, erected a great and extraordinary temple of the illustrious son of Śuddhodana (i.e. Buddha) here at Nālandā. Nālandā had scholars well-known for their (knowledge of the) sacred texts and art, and (was full of the) heaps of the rays of *Caityas* shining and bright like white clouds. It had a row of Vihāras, the line of whose tops touched the clouds—Nālandā had temples which were brilliant on account of the net-work of the rays of the various jewels set in them and was the pleasant abode of the learned and virtuous Saṅgha"—From the record it seems probable that the donor Mālāda himself also took to the life of a monk and his sister Nirmalā mentioned in the inscription might

1. *Ep. Ind.*, XX p. 294ff.
2. *IHQ.*, VII, p. 664.

also have been a nun. Besides this and one or two other minor inscriptions, numerous votive, inscriptions—some of them bearing different Buddhist sūtras—and clay seals bearing the name of the organisation of the Bhikkhus of Nālandā ('sri Nālandā mahāvihāriya bhikkhusaṅghasya'), belonging to different periods, have been unearthed during excavations. Two of the carved bricks bear on them the complete *Pratītyasamutpādasūtra* and its exposition in Gupta characters, which is supposed to be unique of its kind.[1]

XI. The township of R ā j a g ṛ h a, modern Rajgir, where the Buddhistic monastic institution developed during the life time of Buddha was found by both the Chinese pilgrims as almost deserted, and archaeological reports also ascribe practically nothing to this period, except the *stūpa* of Giriyek near Rajgir, which has a shape quite different from the earlier ones.

XII. B o d h-G a y a is a place of perpetual interest not for the Buddhists only, but for everyone who is in the least interested in the religion of the Buddha, because it is here that Gautama Buddha attained his supreme knowledge, and as such, is being visited by numerous Buddhists as well as non-Buddhists from the earliest times. Aśoka made a pilgrimage to this place, in commemoration of which he constructed a railing around the Bodhi tree and the seat of the Buddha underneath it, and perhaps also erected a pillar as is supposed from some carvings of Bharhut, but this assumption does not find support from the Chinese pilgrims. Two sets of railings are to be found at Bodh-Gaya, one belonging to the time of Aśoka with the stories of Buddha's life carved on them, and the other belonging to the Gupta period, with the typical Gupta ornamentations pictured on them. A peculiar fact is that all the inscriptions, both old and new, are incised on the older set of railings.[2] The Bodh-Gaya temple shows marks of additions and alterations, and the nucleus of the present temple is supposed to have been originated in the Gupta period. Of the inscriptions of Bodh-Gaya pertaining to our period, the earliest is the one ascribed to the reign of Mahārāja Trikamala, possibly a feudatory of the Gupta monarchs. It records that two monks, both teachers of Vinaya, caused one Siṁharatha to dedicate the image of the Bodhisattva, evidently the one on which it is incised, with the help of two other persons, one of whom is a female lay devotee and the

1. *ASI.*, Memoir 66, p. 75.
2. Cf. Barua, *Gaya* and *Bodh-Gaya*, p. 11.

other an expounder of the holy text.[1] Then there are the two inscriptions of the Ceylonese monk Mahānāman, dated in the 6th century A.D., one recording the erection of a 'Maṇḍapa' for Buddha within the area of Bodh-Gaya, and the other recording the gift of a figure of Buddha, by the same person. This monk Mahānāman is recorded to be an inhabitant of Laṅkādvīpa or the island of Ceylon, and is doubtfully identified with the author of the well-known Pali chronicle of Ceylon, viz. the Mahāvaṁsa.[2] But whatever his identity might be, these two inscriptions testify to the fact that people from such a distant country like Ceylon retained their connection with this place (which began with the mission sent by Aśoka), even in this period, though it is evident from other inscriptions that these are not the first pilgrims from Ceylon to Bodh-Gaya.[3] That pilgrims from Ceylon continued their visit to this place in subsequent centuries also, is proved from a 6th or 7th century inscription in which it is stated that some scion of the ruling family of Lanka, Prakhyātakīrtī by name, caused some buildings to be made here ("at Triratna" as the expression runs).[4] Another fragmentary inscription from the same place and the same period records the pious gift of an unknown devotee for the plastering, regular repairing, maintenance of lamps in the shrine of Buddha, and in the monastery, as well as the excavation of a well or pond for the use of monks.[5] Another inscription of the 6th century on the pedestal of a Buddha image (now in the Indian Museum, Calcutta), records the gift of the image by two Śākya monks, Dharmagupta and Daṃṣṭrāsena, natives of an unidentified place called Tiṣyāmratīrtha.[6]

XIII. Buddhism must have penetrated into B e n g a l at least in the early years of the Christian era, as referred to in the Nāgārjuni-koṇḍa inscription, even if we leave out of consideration the Mahāsthān inscription written in Maurya characters, which mentions the Chabbaggiya bhikkhus, i.e. the party of six men headed by Devadatta, and as such an anti-party of the organisation of Buddha. Of the Chinese pilgrims, Fa-Hian did not visit North Bengal, but he went to the adjacent countries like Campā in the Bhāgalpur district, and

---

1. *ASI., An. Rep.*, 1922-23, p. 169.
2. For details see *CII.*, III, p. 274ff.
3. *ASI., An. Rep.*, 1908-09; Bloch's *Report on Bodh-Gaya*, p. 156.
4. *ASI., An. Rep.*, 1908-09; Bloch's *Report on Bodh-Gaya*, p. 156.
5. *Ibid.*
6. *CII.*, III, p. 281.

Tāmralipti, where he himself stayed for two years and studied Buddhist scriptures, and found the religion flourishing with many *stūpas* and monasteries full of monks. Hwen Tsang travelled in Bengal and is said to have seen many *stūpas* and monasteries containing both Hinayānic and Mahāyānic monks. The establishments mentioned by Hwen Tsang and other Chinese pilgrims who visited subsequently, are not yet definitely located, but the numerous ruins scattered all over the length and breadth of Bengal,—the major portion of which is at present included within the area of Pakistan,—suggest that if systematic exploration is carried out, most of the places mentioned by them will ultimately be traced. The prosperous condition of Buddhism in Bengal in the Gupta period onwards is also attested by various documents. The Gunaighar copper-plate[1] of the reign of Mahārāja Vainyagupta, a scion of the Gupta family, dated in 506-7 A.D., records the grant of land by the king at the instance of his vassal Mahārāja Rudradatta in favour of the Buddhist Avaivartaka saṅgha of the Mahāyāna sect. The saṅgha founded by Ācārya Śāntideva was living in a monastery called Āśrama-vihāra, which was dedicated to Ārya Avalokiteśvara and had been established by the said Rudradatta. The plate also refers to two other Buddhist monasteries in the neighbouring area, one of which is designated Rajā-vihāra or the royal monastery. Śāntideva of the inscriptions is surely not the author of *Śikṣ-āsamuccaya*, who is supposed to have lived a century later[2] but some other teacher of the same name. And the name of the particular *saṅgha* viz. Avaivartaka, found for the first time in this plate, is not mentioned elsewhere. By way of explanation it may be stated that in the *Saddharmapuṇḍarīkasūtra* and other Mahāyāna texts, there are a number of references to a spiritual stage 'Avaivartika Bodhisattvasthānam' and also to 'Avivartika', 'Avaivartika teja', and 'Avaivartika' etc.[3] It seems that a sect which aimed at the Avaivartika or 'incapable of sliding back' stage, grew up in this locality, which took the name of Avaivartika or Avaivartika saṅgha. At any rate, this record is a positive evidence that Buddhism took a firm root in Bengal even in this period, under the royal patronage. The condition of Buddhism in the 7th century in Bengal, if not the whole of India, is

1. *IHQ.*, VI, p. 45f.
2. Winternitz, II, p. 365.
3. Cf. *Saddharmapundarika-sūtra*—Bib. Bud. X, p. 264; also the *Gilgit Mss.* of the text, ed. N. Dutt, pt. I, p. 70, verse 5; pt. II, p. 253 v. 130; pt. III, p. 465, v. 1126; also p. 510 (avaivartiko bhavisyatyanuttarāyām samyaksambodhau).

reflected in an inscription on a copper plate found from Kailan in the Tippera District of Bengal. It is the donation of an official of a certain king named Sridharana Rāta, to the Buddhist Triratna, as well as some other donations to a number of Brahmins for performing 'the five great sacrifices.'[1] The religious toleration which is the characteristic feature of the Indians, is once more manifested in this inscription. It supplies further evidence to the fact that Buddhism was tending towards merger with Brahmanism and devotees of the Buddha did not refrain from being respectful to Buddhism and Brahmanism in the same breath. Another inscription of a somewhat later date, found in Bengal, is also of a similar effect as the Kailan plate. It is the inscription on an image of Śarvāṇī[2] (a form of Dūrgā) dedicated by Prabhāvatī, queen of a Buddhist king named Devakhaḍga. Two copper-plates with inscriptions found from Asrafpur in Bengal[3] reveal that a number of rulers whose names ended with Khaḍga, and hence might be called the 'Khaḍga family,' ruled in Bengal during the earlier part of the 8th c. A.D. The plates are significant for the fact that Buddhism received royal recognition after a long period, as the royal records depict all of them as devout Buddhists. And further, though none of this line of Buddhist kings were as illustrious as any of the previous Buddhist rulers like Aśoka, Kaṇiṣka, or the Sātavāhana rulers, these Khaḍga rulers may be regarded as the predecessor and ancestors of a long and glorious line of Buddhist kings, viz., the Pālas. Numerous Buddhist figures have been found in Bengal, but the majority of them belong to the Pāla period. The earliest find is the standing image of Buddha from Biharail in Rajshahi district.[4] The image is to be dated from its style, not later than the 5th century A.D. and is now deposited in the Varendra Research Society Museum, Rajshahi. It bears such close affinity to those of Sarnath, that one may quite well infer that it was supplied from the place. Unfortunately the image is very badly damaged, but still it is a fine piece of sculpture. Another interesting Buddhist figure of the same period is the gold-plated image of Mañjuśrī, collected from the Balaidhāp mound near Mahāsthān, Bogra. This is undoubtedly one of the finest specimens of bronze or octo-alloy images so far found in Northern and Eastern India. The figure has the Dhyānī Buddha Akṣobhya, the spiritual father of

---

1. *IHQ.*, XXIII, p. 221ff.
2. *Ep. Ind.*, XVII, p. 357.
3. *MASB.*, I, no. 6, p. 65ff.
4. *History of Bengal,* Dacca, I, p. 523.

Mañjuśrī, according to the code of *Sādhanamālā*, placed on its crown. This image is also damaged, but the loveliness of the figure prove that it was also beautiful in its original state. The execution of the limbs and drapery leads us to assign it to the Gupta period. An important point to be noticed in connection with this image is that it has changed the earlier notion that gold-plated images were made for the first time by the Siamese artists in Siam only in the 8th c. A.D. In fact, this image shows that metal images were used to be gilt long before that period in India and perhaps the Siamese artists were indebted to India in this respect also.[1]

**XIV.** Orissa was one of the cradles of Buddhism when it tasted the religious fervour at the time of Aśoka. The religion again took its last shelter in this country before its final disappearance from Bengal and other parts of India after the Muhammadan invasion.[2] We do not hear of any activities of the Buddhists in this part of the country during the intervening period. That Buddhism existed in Orissa in the 6th-7th centuries A.D. is proved by the statement of Hwen Tsang who is said to have seen many Buddhist monasteries and numerous devotees in Wu-Tu (Odra or Orissa country,[3] and who was selected by Harṣ avardhana to be deputed with four other scholars from Nālandā to silence the Hīnayānist monks of Orissa who were becoming vehemently opposed to the Mahāyānists.[4] The group of Buddhist monasteries in the Jajpur hills, known as Udaygiri, Lalitagiri, and Ratnagiri, have produced a large number of sculptures and images datable to Gupta period. An image of the Bodhisattva Padmapāṇi belonging to the later Gupta period has been found out from a place named Śāntamādhava in Jajpur, and a life-size image of four-armed Avalokiteśvara on the Ratnagiri have the same pose common to the sculptures of the Gupta age. Many votive *stūpas* and architectural and sculptural fragments comprising heads of some colossal Buddha images have been found from this Ratnagiri hill. Sculptures belonging to later periods found in this place prove the continuance of this place as a Buddhist centre. At Lalitagiri there are also a large number of sculptures fixed in modern temples, which have inscriptions on them in 8th century characters, mostly containing the Buddhist creed. The sculptures represent the Buddhist gods and goddesses like

1. *N. Dasgupta, Bāṅglāy Bauddhadharma* (in Bengali) p. 46-47.
2. H.P. Sastri, *Bauddha Dharma* (in Bengali), p. 106-7.
3. Watters, II. p. 193.
4. Beal, *Life*, p. 160-61.

Avalokiteśvara, Tārā, and Maitreya. A number of images of Buddha, Avalokiteśvara, Prajñāpāramitā and other Buddhist gods have been found in Udayagiri hill also and these sculptures too contain inscriptions in scripts of 7th to 10 or 11th centuries. On the back of one such image of Avalokiteśvara, with the Dhyanī-Buddha Amitābha seated in its crest, is an inscription saying that it was the gift of a monk Śubhagupta, written in 7th or 8th century characters.[1] The extensive ruins in these three hills prove that this locality was a flourishing centre of Buddhism from the 7th century onwards, and the cult of Avalokiteśvara and Tārā was more prevalent. The Neulpur grant of the king Śubhakaradeva[2] reveals that a line of Buddhist kings was ruling in Orissa in the 8th century, and Buddhism must have been flourishing under their patronage. In the inscription, instead of the conventional epithet used by all Buddhist kings and devotees, viz. 'Parama Saugata,' the Kara kings of Orissa adopted a new designation for themselves, viz. 'Parama Tāthāgata' which, of course, carries the same meaning. The object of the grant is to register the gift of some villages to a number of Brāhmins by the king. Here again we are confronted with another example of the liberal character of Indian religions, as also to the fact that Buddhism and Brāhmanism were coming in closer relations with each other.

XV. The religion of Buddha was introduced into W e s t e r n I n d i a during the life time of its founder who is said to have deputed his disciple Mahākaccāyana, a native of Avantī, to preach his religion there. Again, during the time of Aśoka, Aparānta or the western country received the Yavana Dhammarakṣita as the missionary, despatched by the emperor. This country was fortunate enough in having the Sātavāhana rulers as great patrons of Buddhism under whom the religion flourished greatly and numerous cave-temples were excavated in the hilly tracts of Western India. The origin of these cave-temple belongs to further antiquity, perhaps to the time of Aṣoka, who incised one of his rock-edicts on the hill of Girnar, though the credit of constructing the majority of the cave-temples goes to the Sātavāhanas. The caves of Nāsik, Kārlê, Bhājā, Junnār, Kānherī etc. bear testimony to the palmy days of Buddhism. Though they lost their importance in subsequent periods, some of them at least were not altogether deserted and were occupied or frequented by the Buddhists

1. *ASI.*, Memoir, 44.
2. *Ep. Ind.*, XX, p. 1f.

who made gifts to them even upto the 10th-11th centuries. In the great caitya-cava at Kānherī, there is an inscription recording the gift by a Buddhist monk of the seated figure of Buddha under which it is carved. On the verandā of the same cave, there is under a standing image of Buddha an inscription which records that the image was dedicated by a mendicant Buddhaghoṣa, the disciple of a teacher named Dharmavatsa, who was well-versed in the three Piṭakas. In the veranda of cave no. 3 is the 'meritorious gift' of a Buddha figure by a monk Dharmagupta. Near the great pillar at the same place, on a small *caitya* in bas-relief, is incised the beginning of the well-known Buddhist creed and in a small chamber stands a figure of Buddha as the gift of a teacher Buddharakṣita. All these inscriptions belong to the 5th to 7th centuries A.D.[1] The original architecture of Kānherī is Simple but there are subsequent additions of sculpture with the development of Mahāyāna.

The Buddhist caves of Lonaḍ—a few miles off Kalyan in the Bombay presidency—seems to be an intermediate station on the long pilgrim and trade route which led from Sopara via Kānherī and other Buddhist monasteries on Salsette islands to the Nanaghat Pass and on to the higher Deccan. Due to absence of inscriptions the date of the caves cannot be ascertained definitely, but the beautiful and lively sculptures that are chiselled out in the caves bear such close affinity with those in the later caves of Ajanta, that they may be well ascribed to that period. The sculptures in these caves depict *Jātaka* stories, some of which cannot be identified. There are also scenes of the Buddha's subjugation of the furious elephant Nālagiri, court scenes, etc.[2] That Junagarh was a fairly large centre of Buddhism at least upto the 7th century A.D., is testified by the statement of Hwen Tsang who found about fifty convents with nearly 3000 monks, belonging to the Sthavira sect of the Mahāyāna, as also by the discovery of numerous Buddhist caves near modern monastery named Bawa Pyara's Math.[3]

XVI. The Maitraka rulers of V a l a b h ī began their career as the vassal (Sāmanta) of the Imperial Guptas. They threw off the Gupta suzerainty with the decline of the Gupta power and gradually changed their epithet from 'Sāmanta' to the glorious title of Mahārājādhirāja.[4]

---

1. *ASWI.*, V. & VI.
2. *JISOA.*, XV, p. 84ff.
3. *ASWI.*, II, p. 139.
4. For the gradual change in their epithet see Bhandarkar's List of Inscs. in *Ep. Ind.*, XX, appendix.

These Maitraka kings, though themselves not professed Buddhists, were great patrons of the religion, and a large number of inscriptions of the rulers of this dynasty record the bounteous gifts made by those kings to the Buddhist organisations of the country. Two lady members of this royal family were devout Buddhist nuns who established monasteries of their own. One of them, Duḍḍā was the niece of king Dhruvasena. She is also mentioned as a queen in some other inscriptions. The other lady of the royal family who embraced the life of a nun is Mimmā. From the inscriptions of the Maitraka rulers it becomes clear that during their rule, the region around modern Saurāṣ ṭra was a flourishing centre of Buddhism with no less than thirteen monasteries, names of which are: Bhaṭārka vihāra, Gôhaka vihāra, Ābhyantarika v., Kakka v., Buddhadāsa v., Vimalagupta v., Sthiramati v., Yakṣa-sūtra v., Pūrṇa-Bhaṭṭa v., Ajjita v., Bappapādiya v., Vaṁsataka v., and Yodhāvaka vihāra.[1] Hwen Tsang associates the two eminent Buddhist scholars Guṇamati and Sthiramati with Valabhi, and this is corroborated by the name of the Vihāra. In the inscriptions the mention of donations for buying books for the monasteries[2] also supports the tradition that the Valabhi monasteries were great centres of education not inferior to those of Nālandā.

XV. The missionary activities of Aśoka is best illustrated in the monuments of S ā ñ c i, the earliest strata of the main *stūpa* of which is ascribed to Aśoka. The remains of an edict pillar of the same emperor found in the vicinity lends support to this assumption. Incidentally it may be mentioned that in the Ceylonse chronicle *Mahāvaṁsa*, it is stated that Mahendra, son of Aśoka, who headed the Buddhist mission to Ceylon, visited his mother 'Devī' before his journey, at a monastery at Cetiyagiri near Vidiśā, where she was living as a nun, and stayed in that monastery for a short period. This Cetiyagiri is probably identical with the hillock of Sāñci, where the remains of the 'Devī's monastery' lie still extant. It is strange to note that none of the Chinese pilgrims seem to have visited Sāñci during their tour in India. For none of them make any mention of this centre of Buddhism, which, as is evident from the extensive ruins found at the site, was in a flourishing condition at the time of their visit to India. The main *stūpa* must have been dedicated to Buddha and the rest to the more distinguished disciples of the Master, as is proved

---

1. *ANC. Hist. of Saurāstra* by Vriji.
2. *IA.*, VII, p. 66.

from the discovery of the relics of Sāriputra and Moggalāna from the top of the *stūpa* no. 3. The original *stūpa* erected by Aśoka, having been damaged in course of time, was encased in a newer one and thus it became larger to a great extent than its former size. This system of constructing new *stūpas* over the older ones was not uncommon in those days. In subsequent centuries, when erection of votive *stūpas* became the custom of the day, numerous *stūpas* of different dimensions, pillars, and gateways continued to be erected on the site. Some of the very few pillars which exist in India, with the exception of those erected by Aśoka, are found at Sāñcī. One of them contain a fragmentary inscription in 5th c. characters recording the gift of the pillar by a Vihārasvāmin whose name ended in 'Rudra' and who was the son of 'Gosura-Siṁhabala.' The pillar was surmounted by the figure of Vajrapāṇi, which now remains in the Museum at Sāñci. An inscription of Āmrakardava, an officer of Candragupta II of the Imperial Gupta line, records the gifts of an allotment of land called Īśvaravāsaka, as also of some amount of money, to the Buddhist community of Kākanādabhoṭa (the name which was often mentioned in ancient inscriptions to designate Sāñcī) for the purpose of feeding the monks and maintaining lamps. Another inscription dated in the year 131 of the Gupta era, records the grant of a female lay-devotee Harisvāminī, wife of the lay devotee Sanasiddha, of certain amount of money to the same community and for the same purpose.[1] Some more inscriptions incised mostly on the pedestals of Buddhist figures and dating from the 4th-7th or 8th centuries, have been found at the site. Of course inscriptions belonging to earlier or later periods are not also lacking, but we are not concerned with them for the present. A fragmentary inscription in 7th c. characters has been found from the monastery no. 43 at Sāñcī which is devoted to the praise of Lokanātha, who is described as having lotus in his hand and bear Amitābha (on his head), and also of Vajrapāṇi...... It also mentions the lord of Mahāmālava (Malwa) and a certain ruler Vappaka Deva......a monastery with cells (*layana*) is stated to have been built. ...There seems to be further reference that the (above-mentioned) monastery belonging to a person named Tuṅga and that the benefaction recorded took place at Boṭa-Śrīparvata (i.e. Sāñci).[2] There are numerous sculptural and architectural remains on the site which bear

1. *CII.*, III, p. 29ff. and p. 260.
2. Marshall, *Monuments of Sañci*, insc. no. 842.

witness to the fact that the place was a flourishing centre of Buddhism during our period of review.[1]

XVIII. M a n d a s o r (ancient Daśapura) in the Gwalior district was known to have been a centre of Brāhmanism only. But a stone slab discovered at the place indicates that Buddhism had some place there also. The inscription on the slab records the construction of a well along with a '*stūpa*', a garden and a '*prapā*' (water stall) by Dattabhaṭa, commander-in-chief of king Prabhākara. The record is dated in the Mālava saṃvat 524 (467-68 A.D.). The inscription mentions the early Gupta king Candragupta II and his younger son Govindagupta, the donor Dattabhaṭṭa being a son of Govindagupta's general Vāyurakṣita.[2]

Though Mandasor did not produce many Buddhist remains, the prevalence of Buddhism in the Gwalior district is amply proved by a group of Buddhist caves at Bagh in the same district. These caves, though only four in number, form a very interesting group. They belong to the classical period of Indian history, and have some sculptured figures and the most charming paintings which can very well stand in comparison with those at Ajanta. One more interesting fact about these caves is that though the caves belonged to the Mahāyānists, and there are Buddha and Bodhisattva figures carved in the caves, the main object of worship in them is the plain and simple rock-cut *stūpa* and no figure of Buddha is carved on them, as is most natural for the Mahāyānists. The very soft nature of the hill on which the caves of Bagh are excavated cannot be durable and a few of them have already collapsed leaving the four surviving ones.[3]

XIX. The most illustrious examples of rock-cut caves of this period are those at A j a n t a and Ellora in Deccan. The caves of Ajanta had their beginning more than a century earlier than the Christian era, most probably under the patronage of the Sātavāhana rulers, whose dominions included this region. But in the earlier stage, the monastery of Ajanta did not prosper much. And though it continued for a period of more than three centuries, only five out of the present twenty-nine caves are said to have been used at that period. After that, the monastery of Ajanta must have been deserted for a long period of four centuries, when, about the fifth century A.D., the Mahāyānists

1. For details, see Marshall, *op. cit.*
2. *ASI., Ann. Rep.*, 1922-23 p. 189.
3. *The Bagh Caves*, Marshall also cf. *Mahabodhi*, June'55, pp. 246.

took charge of the hill resorts, and turned them to an important centre of Buddhism. Of the 24 caves belonging to the Mahāyāna sect, there are two *Caitya* halls enshrining *stūpas* with images of Buddha carved on them as a contrast to the corresponding two *Caitya* halls enshrining *stūpas* but without any kind of carving on them, out of the five earlier Hinayāna ones. The rste twenty-two caves belonging to the Mahāyāna sect are dormitories for the residence of monks with stone beds in them and the innermost central chamber of these cave-dwellings were used as shrines sheltering colossal figures of Buddha. These caves are decorated with fine sculptures representing Buddhist figures and in one of them is carved a colossal figure of recumbent Buddha with various Mahāyānic symbols underneath. But the far-reaching fame of Ajanta caves is not so much for its architecture and sculpture as it is for its fresco-paintings on the wall of the caves. These paintings are the living embodiment of grace and loveliness which have attracted admiration from the most scrupulous critics of the world. "The artists" remarks Lady Herringham, one of the premier admirers of Ajanta art, "had a complete command of posture. Their seated and floating poses especially are of great interest. Their knowledge of the types and positions, gestures and beauties of hands are amazing......the drawing of foliage and flowers is very beautiful......some of the schemes of colour and composition are most remarkable and interesting, and there is a great variety." Nothing need be added to this note of appreciation about the art of Ajanta. These paintings illustrate in addition to decorative designs, scenes from the life of Buddha and the Jātakas or the past lives of the Buddha, as also scenes from secular and court lives. The paintings are so mutilated in some places that identification of them becomes very difficult and sometimes impossible. That the religion of Buddha had travelled a long way from its primitive phase, is also well attested by the fact that among the paintings of Ajanta there are profuse scenes of dancing and music, which, though included among popular or court scenes, were even beyond imagination to have been painted in the dormitories of Buddhist monks, as dancing and music and some other things like toileting and garlanding (which also form the subject-matter of some scenes) were strictly prohibited for the recluses. The art of Ajanta influenced later artists not only of India proper, but also of its neighbours like Ceylon, China, Japan, and Eastern Islands. The paintings of Sigiriya at Ceylon, executed about the same period, bear a close affinity with those at Ajanta, and the 'Thousand-Buddha cave' of China, of some later days have gained world-wide reputation.

The patrons under whom the monastry of Ajanta flourished in its later phase were certainly the Vākāṭaka rulers of Deccan, in whose dominions this region was included. An inscription from the cave no. 16 at Ajanta lends further support to the assumption. Though the inscription is not preserved in full, it is interesting in that it records that the cave was excavated by order of Vīradeva, a minister of the Vākaṭaka king Hariṣeṇa. Vīradeva was a devout Buddhist. In cave no. 17, an inscription records that Acitya, a minister of Rabisāmba, a feudatory to the Vākāṭaka king Hariṣ-eṇa, caused to excavate the 'monolithic, gem-like hall' with a *Caitya*, a reservoir, with cool refreshing water, and a Gandhakūṭi.' Another important inscription is that in cave no. 26. According to this inscription, it was the monk Buddhabhadra who was responsible for this cave to be excavated, and provided funds for the work. His own disciple Bhadrabandhu and another monk Dharmadatta were the supervisors of the work. The information about Buddhabhadra as are given in this inscription, suggests that he was not an ordinary roving recluse, but must have been an abbot of a great institution,—might be that of the Ajanta monastery itself, and possessed a considerable amount of wealth. Possession of a large amount of wealth by an abbot was no more an unnatural occurrence in this period, though in primitive Buddhism, a monk was debarred from having anything more than the four requisites prescribed by the Buddha, as his own. That the monk Budhabhadra also held an esteemed position is indicated by the mention of his friendship with the minister of the king of Asmaka, in whose name the cave was dedicated. Another name of importance which is mentioned in this inscription, is that of Sthavira Acala, who is described as one of the former builders of the Vihāras. This Sthavira Acala seems to be no other than the 'Arahat 'O-che-lo' mentioned by Hwen Tsang, who is credited to have built a convent in honour of his mother. Besides these important ones, there are other inscriptions, both painted and incised, recording gifts of ministers, noblemen, lay-devotees as well as monks. There are also explanatory titles of the Jatakas painted on the walls of the caves.[1]

A less known Vihāra-cave, 11 miles away from Ajanta, known as the Ghaṭotkaca cave, contains the fragments of a long inscription. It begins with invocation to the Buddha, Dharma, and Saṅgha and mentions about Hastibhoja, the minister of the Vākāṭaka king

1. *ASWI.*, p. 124ff. and p. 60 (vol. IV).

Devasena, father of Harișeṇa mentioned in the cave no. 16 at Ajanta. The Hastibhoja mentioned in this inscription was the father of Vīradeva, during whose ministry the Ajanta vihāra was excavated. From the fragmentary character of the inscription, it cannot be stated definitely whether Hastibhoja or his son Vīradeva was responsible for the excavation of the Ghaṭotkaca cave.[1]

XX. Situated about sixty miles away from Ajanta, the twelve Buddhist caves of E l l o r a are contemporary with the later phase of those at Ajanta. These caves are richer in sculpture but lack the paintings and inscriptions of Ajanta, the only inscription at Ellora being the Buddhist formula in the Caitya-cave called the Viśvakarmā cave. There are about 35 caves scattered over a vast table land, belonging to the three main Indian sects, viz. the Buddhist, the Brāhmins and the Jains, the Buddhist group of caves occupying the southern most part of the hill. Of the 12 Buddhist caves, all are Vihāras, except the Viśvakarmā, which is a *Caitya* hall enshrining a *stūpa* carved with a colossal seated figure of Buddha attended by two attendants on both sides. A number of colossal Buddha images are to be seen at Ellora also like those of Ajanta, but the difference between the two sets of caves lies in the fact that while at Ajanta the Buddhas are represented without or only with one or two attendants, at Ellora, he is most frequently attended by a large number of side-figures, mostly the Bodhisattvas, and the Śaktis or the female counterparts of the Bodhisattvas. Cave nos. 11 and 12, are designated Do-Thal and Tin-Thal respectively, though both of them are three-storied, and contain a large number of sculptures which include the seven human Buddhas, the five Dhyānī Buddhas, and their respective Bodhisattvas, in addition to Gandharvas and other decorative motifs. Some of the Brahmanic goddesses like Sarasvatī and Kālī were being gradually incorporated into the Mahāyāna pantheon in this period, but the figure of the goddess carved on one of the walls of these caves, with books in her hand and a peacock by her side, which had so far been identified as the goddess Sarasvatī, has of late been correctly identified by Dr. J.N. Banerjea, with the personified form of the *Dhāraṇī* or 'protecting spells' named *Mahā-Māyūrī*,[2] used to be recited by the Buddhists in order to cure diseases, particularly, snake-poisoning, as the peacock was regarded as the greatest enemy of the snakes. The sculptures of

---

1. *ASWI.*, p. 124ff. and p. 60 (vol. IV).
2. Paper read in the *Indian History Congress* at Waltair, 1953.

the caves of Ellora conform to the mythology of the Yogācāra school of Buddhism, and it is supposed that these caves were the resorts of the same sect also. The caves of Ellora were probably the last activity of the Buddhists in this region as we do not find any other works of importance in the subsequent period.[1]

XXI. A few miles distant from Ellora, are the rock-hewn Vihāras of A u r a n g a b a d, divided into three groups. The first and the second group are certainly Buddhist, while the incompleteness of the caves and as such the absence of sculptures in the third group renders it difficult to regard them definitely as Buddhist, though there is nothing as negative evidence against their being Buddhist. Among the whole set of caves there is one *caitya* hall and the rest are Vihāras. From their features it seems that the caves were in good condition from the third to the seventh century A.D. The sculptures in these caves are lovely and are imitations of those in Ajanta, particularly the 'vase and foliage' pattern. The Viharas nos. 3 and 7 of this group are the finest and the best preserved. The carvings of the images of Buddha and other gods and goddesses are on a massive proportion. These and the group of musicians and the set of devotees carved on the walls of the caves are of a very special type.[2]

XXII. Recent as well as previous finds prove that the ancient site of S o u t h K o ś a l a, comprising modern Bilaspur and Raipur districts, was a centre of Buddhism at least from the 5th century. Sirpur, in the Raipur district, was noticed and hinted as a site of archaeological interest by Cousens as early as 1903 in his report. The site has been recently excavated and has brought to light the remains of two large Buddhist monasteries and several other small structures including vihāras. A colossal image of seated Buddha and a life-size figure of Padmapāṇi has been found from one shrine, which, according to an inscription found at the same place, is stated to have been built by a monk Ānandaprabhu during the reign of Bālārjuna in about the first quarter of the 8th c. A.D. A considerable amount of antiquities of various kinds have been found at the site. These include a fine bronze statue of Buddha plated with gold witheyes set in silver. A number of seals with Buddhist texts, an exquisitely carved crystal *stūpa* and a gilt. Vajra have also been found at an adjacent site. Of the monasteries discovered at the site, one seems to be a nunnery, from the evidence

1. *ASWI.*, V, p. 2ff.
2. *ASWI.*, III, p. 59ff. also cf. *Ind. Art & Lett.*, IX, new Series.

of a large number of shell and glass bangles found at the site.[1] An inscription from Ratanpur in the Bilaspur dist. (now in the Nagpur museum), confirms the view that in the 7th-8th c. A.D. this place was a populous centre of Buddhism. The inscription in question is of Bhavadeva Raṇakeśarin. It opens with an invocation to Buddha, and relates that a certain illustrious king Sūryaghoṣa built a splendid temple or Vihāra for Buddha, in order to mitigate the sorrow incurred by the accidental death of his son. ......The inscription further records the restoration of the said temple after some time had elapsed after the king Sūryaghoṣa, under the supervision of Bhavadeva, who was in charge of the temple. The restoration work was done by two persons under Bhavadeva, one of whom is described as the favourite of the (then ruling) king, a Brāhmin well-versed in Buddhist scriptures, and the other, a novice in the Buddhist institution.[2] Another inscription, the Mallar plate of Mahāśivagupta of South Kośala, ascribed to the 7th c. A.D., records the grant of the said king, of a village to the Buddhist congregation of the monastery at Tāradaṁsaka. The king himself is stated to be a devout Śaiva.[3]

XXIII. Extensive ruins prove that A n d h r a and countries on further south were flourishing centres of Buddhism from the pre-Christian era. Though in our period, Buddhism had lost here its palmy days, it nevertheless lingered on in these countries. The Buddhist site of Salihundam is on the summit and slopes of a very fine hill in the Ganjam district. There are remains of a large and some smaller *stūpas*, fragments of Buddhist figures, a broken image of Buddha, a figure of Māricī, and such other antiquities, found on the hill-top and in the neighbouring village of the same name. The Boston Museum has in its collections a standing image of Buddha found in Buddhapād in Bezwada district. The place is not far from Amarāvatī, the most illustrious centre of Buddhism in Southern India from the 2nd-3rd centuries. The image in question belonged to the 6th c. A.D., and it is said that basketfuls of images and fragments were found at Buddhapād while excavating a canal.[4] That the region encircling the *stūpa* of Amarāvatī was a flourishing centre also is well proved by inscriptions as well as sculptures found there. The *stūpa* at Goḷi is ascribed to the 4th c. A.D. The great *stūpa* of Amarāvatī was

---

1. *ASI., Ann, Rep*, 1203-04; *Indian Archaeology*, 1954-55, pp. 24-25.
2. *JRAS.*, 1905, p. 618ff.
3. *EI.*, XXIII, p. 115.
4. Coomaraswamy, *Cat. Boston Museum*, II, p. 60ff.

frequented and kept in repairs even as late as the 12th century. The sculptures of Amarāvatī and its neighbourhood form a different school of art. The British Museum has a very good collection of the sculptures of Amarāvatī and of the places influenced by its art. One of them is a bas-relief carved with an image of Mañjuśrī which has a lotus in one of his hands, which hold a book, and a second lotus issuing out of the stem of the first. The figure is interesting because earlier images of Mañjuśrī found in N. India, have the Dhyanī Buddha Akṣobhya in their head-drėsses. The date of the image is supposed to be some time between 650 and 750 A.D.[1] The Pallava king Siṁhavarman II, who belonged to the last quarter of the 6th c. A.D., presented an image of Buddha to the *stūpa* of Amarāvati. The inscription recording the presentation, is incomplete and it records that on his return from an expedition to the North, Siṁhavarman came to a place sacred to the Buddha which was called Dhānyaghaṭa or Dhānyaghaṭaka (evidently identified with Dhānyakaṭaka, the well-known name of Amarāvatī). The lost part of the inscription evidently records the gift.[2] The Kapoteśvara temple of Chezrala shows from the remains of its constructions that it was originally a Buddhist *Caitya*, converted at a later date to a Śaiva temple, with the growing popularity of the religion in South India. The remains of Chezrala may be considered as one of the only two extant brick-built *Caitya* halls which have preserved their original structural condition, the other being at Ter, the ancient Tagara, in Sholapur dist. in the Nizam's dominions. Both are ascribed to the 5th c. A.D.[3] A number of stone inscriptions of the Ānandagotra kings, a dynasty which ruled about the 6th c. A.D., expressing their Buddhist faith are seen in the Caitya of Chezrala.[4] In Jagayyapeṭa, an inscription on a marble-slab in 5th 6th c. characters, under the figure of a Buddha, mentions Candraprabha, the disciple's disciple of Nāgārjuna; the preceptor of Candraprabha was Ācārya Jayaprabha. A similar slab has also been found from Ramireḍḍipalli.[5]

XXIV. Another example of rock-cut monasteries of the Gupta period lies in the Buddhist remains on the S a ṅ k a r a m hills in the Vizagapatam district. These caves are scattered on the hill and the remains consist of a number of *stūpas*, a series of rock-cut chambers and the foundations of an extensive monastic building. Some of the

1. *Art and Letters,* XXVIII, no. 2. Amaravati & its influences (later school).
2. Hultzsch, *SII.*, (I), p. 25.
3. P. Brown, *Ind. Architec.*, I, p. 50.
4. *MER.*, 1900, p. 5.
5. Burgess, *Amaravati & Jagayyapeṭa Stūpas.*

*stūpas* are the largest of their kind. From a survey, it seems that the site was a flourishing condition in the Gupta period, though its origin goes back a few centuries earlier.[1] Other places in this region which have yielded remnants of Buddhism are Nāgārjunikonda, Gunṭapalle, Ghanṭāsālā, Rāmātīrtham, etc. Copper images of Buddha found from Buddhāni show the typical characteristics of Gupta art in their costume and features. A figure from Amarāvatī and identified as Avalokiteśvara, has its counterpart in the collection of the British Museum, ascribed to the middle of the 8th c. A.D. Another figure of Vajrapāṇi in the British Museum, though mutilated, has fine executions like those at Ellora.[2] Casting images in metal seems to be a common practice of this period, not only in the southern part of India, but in northern part also. So bronze images of Buddha have been found not only from this area, but the bronze image of Buddha found from Sultangañje and now deposited in the Birmingham Museum, is one of the finest specimens of its kind. Incidentally we may refer also to the 80 feet high image of Buddha said to have seen by Hwen Tsang at Nālandā, though no further trace of the image have been possible to find.

The countries to further south have not yielded many Buddhist antiquities, though the Chinese travellers found the religion in fairly popular condition. In the Western coast, an inscription is found frem Goa (ancient W. Koṅkan). The copperplate was issued by certain Mahārāja Candravarman, an records the grant of a piece of land to a Buddhist monastery (Mahāvihāra) at Śivapura, located in Goa. This king was probably a scion of the Bhoja family ruling in that region during the 5th century, to which period the inscription is also ascribed on paleographic grounds.[3]

From the above survey, it may be concluded that though the form of the religion had undergone great changes, and was losing its hold, it was in a fairly flourishing condition during this period. The decline of Buddhism, however, is not disappearance in the proper sense of the term because it merged into Brahmanism. The religion of Buddha started as a protest against Brahmanic ritualism, but ended in being more ritualistic than ethical and philosophical. The line of demarcation between the Buddhists and the Brahminists was becoming narrower in the later part of our period of survey as is evident from some of the inscriptions stated above. The assimilation of Buddhism by

1. P. Brown, *Ind. Architec.*, I, p. 45; also ref. *ASI., Ann. Rep*, 1907-08.
2. *Cat. of the British Museum.*
3. *ABOR.*, XXIII, p. 510ff.

Brāhmanism was done by including Buddha in the list of ten Avatāras or incarnations of Viṣṇu or sometimes identifying him with Śiva. This process of assimilation manifested itself in an inscription in the Varāha Perumal temple, dating about the 7th c. A.D., where the Buddha is stated as one of the ten incarnations of Viṣṇu.[1]

In our period, the religion had travelled a long way from its primitive state, both in time as well as in form. But the destination was still farther, which was reached during the rule of the Pālas in Bengal, when the religion was turned into a ritualistic Tantric one. The Tantras had not yet reached its full-fledged form, but the faint traces of its advent are hinted in some of the literature of this period. The practice of mystic rites, if practised at all, was done in secret. Hwen Tsang mentions that at Kāmarūpa, there were 'secret devotees.' This statement may lead one to believe that it was a centre of Tantric Buddhists, but it cannot be stated definitely that the Buddhist Tantras found a resort here in that period. Kāmarūpa, or modern Assam was for a long time, even a few decades ago, considered to be a place of secret practices.

The sect of Buddhism prevalent at different parts of India at the period under our consideration, cannot be ascertained from the inscriptions of the period, because very few of the numerous inscriptions of this period state the particular sect to which they belonged. But the growing popularity of Mahāyāna is manifested by some inscriptions, reports of the Chinese pilgrims, and above all, by the vest number of images found all over the country. These figures include not only those of Gautama Buddha and the past human Buddhas, but a large number of Bodhisattvas, together with their respective Dhyānī Buddhas or spiritual fathers and their Śaktis or the female counterparts. In addition to these, there are the personified forms of the sacred literature of the Mahāyānists, like the Prajñāpāramitā, Mañjuśrī, and Mahāmāyuri etc. mentioned above.

Most of the institutions which had their beginning in previous centuries, continued to function in this period and many of those others which flourished in subsequent days, had their beginning in this period. This period may be called the mid-day of Mahāyāna Buddhism, when the Mahāyana was on the summit of its glory. Then it changed on and on, until losing its individual existence, it finally merged itself into the Hindu religion.

---

1. *ASI.*, Mem., 26, p. 5.

# Chapter - 37

# Buddhism in the Śuṅga Period

**Kunja Govinda Goswami**

The Śuṅgas or at least the founder of the Śuṅga dynasty was the performer of the *Aśvamedha* sacrifice. This is recorded both in literature and inscription. The *Mahābhāṣya*[1] of Patanjali and the *Mālavikāgnimitra* of Kālidāsa incidentally inform us that Puṣyamitra, the founder of the Śuṅga dynasty performed the *Aśvamedha* sacrifice, whereas from the Ayodhyā stone inscription of King Dhanadeva, we learn that general Puṣyamitra celebrated two horse-sacrifices.[2]

The cult of Gautama Buddha flourished during the rule of the Śuṅgas, although they were pro-Brahmanic. This is indisputably proved by a number of monuments and inscriptions scattered over the different parts of India. In this paper it is proposed to point out the evidences yielded by archaeological excavations and epigraphic researches:—

At B h a r h u t in Nagod State and S a n c i in Bhopal State there was in each of these places a *stūpa* at the centre surrounded by stone railings leaving an intervening space for *pradakṣiṇa* or circumambulation with approaches from four cardinal points through four gateways. The stone railing consisting of a number of pillars is joined together by a number of *Sūcis* or lenticular cross-bars and overlaid by *uṣṇīṣa* (coping stone). The circumambulation for the second time used to be performed by the pilgrims on a higher level through a terrace to be together by a approached by a staircase. The railing and the gateways were richly decorated with bar-reliefs for the purpose of arousing religious feeling in the minds of the pilgrims. Some of the decorative designs were of religious character while

---

1. "*iha Puṣyamitraṁ yājayāmaḥ*" under Pāṇini's Sūtra, III, 2. 123.
2. *Ep. Ind.*, vol. XX, p. 57.

others were simple auspicious symbols. There are to be found on the railings some non-Buddhist popular deities with subordinate position evidently for proclaiming that the deities belonged to the world (*arūpa*) and not *lokottara* like Buddha.

The illustrations and labels (written in *Brāhmī* characters of 2nd-1st centuries B.C.) found on the Bharhut railing offer a comprehensive picture of the state of Buddhism during the rule of the Śuṅgas.

As regards Buddhist pantheon, Gautama Buddha (*Sākya-muni*) and the past Buddhas e.g. (1) Vipaśyin, (2) Viśvabhū, (3) Krakucchanda, (4) Kanakamuni and (5) Kāśyapa are mentioned by name and indicated by individual symbols. No figure of Sākyamuni or any one of the earlier Buddhas is found there. Their presence is indicated in the following way:—

(1) *Gautama Buddha* is represented by a throne surrounded by two *triratna* symbols placed under the Bodhi tree and labelled as *Bhagavato*[1] *Saka munino bodho*. (Bharhut Ins. No. 270).

(2) *Vipaśyin* by a throne under a *Pāṭali* tree and labelled as *Bhagavato Vipasino bodhi* (Bh. Ins. No. 87).

(3) *Viśvabhū* by a throne under a *Śāla* tree and labelled as *Bhagavato Vesabhuno bodhi Śālo* [Bh. Ins. No. 117(b)].

(4) *Krakucchanda* by a throne under a *Śirīṣa* tree and labelled as *Bhagavato Kakusadhasa bodhi* [Bh. Ins. No. 293(a)].

(5) *Kanakamuni* by a throne under a *Udumbara* tree and labelled as *Bhagavato Konāgamanasa bodhi* [Bh. Ins. No. 294].

(6) *Kāśyapa* by a throne under a *Nyagrodha* tree and labelled as *Bhagavato Kasapasa bodhi* (Bh. Ins. No. 295).

For winning over the common people, the stories of the Jātakas were depicted on stone is the form of beautiful illustrations on the railings of Bharhut and Sāñci. Representations are found on the Bharhut railings from the following Jātakas:—

| Jātaka | | | Illustration No. |
|---|---|---|---|
| (1) Laṭukika | ... | ... | 253 |
| (2) Sujāta | ... | ... | 327 |
| (3) Kukkuṭa | ... | ... | 329 |
| (4) Nigrodhamiga | ... | ... | 337 |
| (5) Migapotaka | ... | ... | 343 |

| | Jātaka | Illustration No. |
|---|---|---|
| (6) | Makhādeva | 356 |
| (7) | Bhisa | 362 |
| (8) | Cammasātaka | 379, 381 |
| (9) | Ārāmadūsaka | 404 |
| (10) | Maṇikaṇṭha | 383 |
| (11) | Asadisa | 376 |
| (12) | Mahā-Janaka | 391 |
| (13) | Kapota | 406 |
| (14) | Dabbhapuppha | 412 |
| (15) | Dubhiya makkaṭa | 418 |
| (16) | Vessantara | 422 |
| (17) | Kinnara | 424 |
| (18) | Mahākapi | 35 |
| (19) | Kakkaṭa | 289 |
| (20) | Mūgapakkha | 290 |
| (21) | Vidhura-paṇḍita | 260 |
| (22) | Chaddanta | 291 |
| (23) | Alambusā | 225 |
| (24) | Mahā-Ummagga | 202 |
| (25) | Mahā-kapi II | 317 |
| (26) | Mahā-bodhi | 319 |
| (27) | Ruru | 129 |

Some illustrations connected with the life of the Buddha are also found on the Bharhut railings, but they do not contain any figural representation of the Lord. His presence is indicated by the symbols of wheel, triratna, Bodhi tree, throne, *stūpa* and footprints.

After the shaving of the head of Buddha, his lock of hair is represented to have been taken away by gods to Heaven and worshipped there (Illustration No. 182). Thereafter we find that Arhadgupta, the angel makes announcement of the inauguration of the Law of Buddha in the assembly of gods. (No. 183).

The Buddhist conception of sin and hell also is represented at Bharhut (Illustration Nos 313-316). The torments of a couple for killing, people by administering poison are depicted there.

The followers of the faith of Gautama Buddha came from various strata of the society. They belonged to widely distant places of the country. The gift of lithic pillars and cross-bars etc. at a place of Buddhist pilgrimage was considered an extremely religious act. And in this work both the monastic and the lay Buddhists used to take keen interest. It is found that pillars and other objects were dedicated by nuns some of whom were named as Phalgudevī (Ins. No. 13), Somā (Ins. No. 33), Somanā (Ins. No. 34), Nāgadevī (Ins. No. 85), Nāgilā (Ins. No. 17b) Budharakhitā (Ins. No. 131), Bhutā (Ins. No. 133), Badhikā (Ins. No. 150), Nāgā (Ins. No. 237) and Diganāgā (=Diṅnāgā) (Ins. No. 310).

Teachers of Buddhist literature, pupils and reciters also contributed their share in showing due regard to the religion of the great Master. Thus we find that Bhadaṁta Valaka (who was a *bhāṇaka* or a reciter) (Bharhut Ins. No. 30), Ārya Kṣudra, well versed in the *Suttantas* (cf. *Ayacula sutaṁtika*, Ins. No. 73), Buddharakṣita proficient in the *Five Nikāyas* (Ins. No. 127), Ārya Ṛṣipālita (who was both a reciter and superintendent of the construction work) (*navakamika*) (Ins. No. 183. b), Ārya Jāta, a master of the Piṭakas (*Peṭakino*) (Ins. No. 263) also made gifts. The sculptor (*Rūpakāraka*), (Ins. No. 180) was also not left behind. Gifts were also forthcoming from the royal household as well as from the ordinary run of people. As regards the latter, the inscriptions record a good number of names both male and female who took part in making gifts to the Buddhist *stūpa* at Bharhut. On the other hand it is evident from the inscription No. 16, at Bharhut that some gifts came from a royal consort *Nāgarakhitā*, wife of a certain king whose name is now mutilated. Another inscription (No. 108) records that the first pillar was the gift of *Cāpadevī* wife of *Revatimitra*, of Vidiśā (modern Besnagar in Gwalior state). The royal figure mounted on an elephant with a relic casket in hand just near the inscription (No. 108) is probably King Revatimitra of Vidiśā mentioned in the above record. This person is followed by a horseman holding a Garuḍa standard. This makes out the case that Revatimitra, who probably hailed from the royal family of Vidiśā was the owner of the Garuḍa standard and was thus very likely devoted to *Vaiṣṇavism*. Another figure in the Bharhut railing is also found to carry a Garuḍa emblem. Moreover we are aware that in the 2nd century B.C. the Greek ambassador Heliodoros came to Vidiśā from the Greek king of Taxila. He professed *Bhāgavatism*[1] and

1. *Arch. Sur. Ind. An. Rep.*, 1912-13. pp. 82f.

set up a pillar with a Garuḍa emblem in honour of god Viṣṇu. From these it transpires that Vidiśā was an important seat of Vaiṣṇavism in the Śaṅga period and that King Revatimitra was a devotee of Vaiṣṇavism.

That Buddhism was appreciated by the Hindu society is proved by the gift of *Cāpadevī*, queen of Revatimitra who appears to be a follower of Vaiṣṇavism. The person mounted on an elephant holding a relic casket in his hand has been taken by some to be King Revatimitra of Vidiśā. If this identification is correct, it may be said that Revatimitra was a tolerant king and came forward of his own accord to lead the procession for depositing the relics of the Buddha in the *stūpa* at Bharhut.

It has already been noticed to some extent that the gifts at Bharhut were coming not only from the Buddhist order but also from various ranks of people of other sects. But now we shall see that the Bharhut *stūpa* attracted devotees and pilgrims not only from the same locality or neighbouring places but also from very distant regions. Thus we find that gifts were made from Pāṭaliputra (mod. Patna) (Ins. Nos. 44, 67, 70), Vidiśā (mod. Besnagar in Gwalior state) (Ins. Nos. 108, 119, 291, 302) and Bhojakaṭa[1] (mod. Ellichpur district, Berar) (Ins. Nos. 248, 310) etc. There are some other place names which cannot be properly identified now, e.g. Moragiri (Ins. Nos. 173, 177, 303), Bodhicakra (Ins. Nos. 249), Purika (Ins. Nos. 69, 132, 252), the town of Karahakaṭa (Ins. Nos. 362, 6), Dabhina (Ins. No. 150), Cuḍathila (Ins. Nos. 85, 91) etc. Another place name, e.g. Nandinagara (Ins. No. 14), which occurs at Bharhut as well as at Sanchi cannot now be properly identified. So it seems that this Nandinagara had a very important part in the activities connected with Buddhism. The other important centres of Buddhism during the Śuṅga period were at Sanci, Bodhgaya, Sarnath, Lauriya Nandangarh and some other places.

At S a n c i also the lithic bas-relief contains copious illustrations from the Jātakas and interesting stories connected with the life of the Buddha. Representations from the Mahākapi Jātaka and Śyāma Jātaka etc. are found there. Here also the great Master has been represented by symbols e.g. the throne and pipal tree just as in Bharhut.

---

1. Bhojakaṭa-rajya is found in the Chammak inscription of Pravarasena II. Fleet, *Corp. Ins. Ind.*, III, pp. 236f.

The Sāñci inscriptions show that there was a good number of corporate bodies or families which made gifts to the Buddhist stūpa.[1] Sometimes the donation comes from the village as a whole (cf. 1. *vejajasa gāmasa dānaṁ* 1. 17 II. *Pāḍukulikāya gāmasa dānaṁ*. II. 1.). From another inscription which reads *Bodha-goṭhiya dhamavadhananā dānaṁ*. 1.25., it is evident that *goṣṭhī* or committee of trustees for looking after religious institutions of the Buddhists was in existence in about 2nd century B.C. As regards other corporate bodies which took part in the activities of the Sāñci *stūpas*, mention may be made of *daṁtakāras* or guild of ivory workers (cf *Ep. Ind.*, II. p. 378, No. 200, c 189; *Vedisakehi daṁta-karehi rūpakaṁmaṁ kataṁ,* (i.e. workers in ivory of Vediśā have done the carving).

Gifts were coming both from the monastic order as well as from the laity. Some of the donors both male and female were well versed in the *Suttapiṭaka* and the five *Nikāyas* (cf. I. 79. *Avisinaye Sūtātikiniya maḍala chikatikāye dānaṁ*=the gift of Avinisa who is well versed in *Suttapiṭaka,* an inhabitant of Maḍala Chikata) (cf also I. 60. *Devagirino pacanekayikasa bhichuno sa atevasi*=(gift of monk Devagiri expert in five *Nikāyas* along with pupils).

Among the donors, the trading communities such as the Seṭhs or Śreṣṭhis and their relatives take a prominent part, the weavers (sotika=sautrika. I. 196), carpenter (according to Bühler Vaḍaki or Vardhakin means carpenter No. 311) and royal scribe (*Rājalipikara* I. 49) etc. also find suitable mention in connection with making gifts to the *stūpas* at Sāñci.

The places whose people were attracted by the great Buddhist centre at Śāñci are the following among others:—(1) Ujjayin; (I. 27, 69, 95; C VI. 12, 49. 55-68, 70 77), Vedisa (modern Besnagar I. 38, 1, 117), Mahisati (Māhismati, mod. Mandhātā on the Narbada, I. 111), Pokhara (=Puṣkara near Ajmir, I. 106, I. 83, etc.), Pratiṭhāna Pratiṣ ṭhāna (mod. Paithan on the Godavarī, I. 12, 70), Erakina (Eran in the Sagar district of C.P. I. c 98), Tumbavana (=Tumain, Esagarh district, Gwalior State), Arāpāna, Bhogavadhana, Madhuvana, Navagāma, Kurara, Kuraghara and Nandinagara etc. the last of these names i.e. Nandinagara occurs apparently also in the place names mentioned in the Bharhut inscriptions. The lion's share of the expenses for the ornamentation of the Sāñci monuments was borne by the villagers.

1. *Ep. Ind.*, vol. II, pp. 87f.

Although the votaries of the Sāñci *stūpa* generally come from the Buddhist community, there were some persons whose names bore the stamp of other religions or who were actually non-Buddhists but made gifts to the *stūpas* out of liberal views. For instance, the names, (1) Agisimā (=Agni Śarmā, I. 69) (2), Bahadata (=Brahmadatta, I. 30), (3) Viśvadeva (I. 95), Mitā (I. 73), Yamarakhita (II. c. 20) etc. appear to have been mainly influenced by the vocabulary of the Vedic literature and might have been connected with the Vedic worship also. Similarly the terms Nāgā (I. 50. c. 45), Nāgadatā (I. 117), Nāgila (I. 84. 11. c. 1), Nāgadina (=Nāgadatta, I. 115) are the reminiscences of the existence of the snake worship; and Vinhukā (II. c. 24) (=Viṣṇukā) seems to be the evidence of *Vaiṣṇavism*; while Śivanadi (=Śivanandī. I. 46), Nadiguta (=Nandigupta. I. 58), Naṁdigiri (I. 108) show the influence of Śaivism. Some scholars find an implied reference to the cult of *Śakti* in the word Himadatā (=Himādatta, Himā being a name of Durgā, I. c. 63).

It goes without saying that at B o d h - G a y a in Bihar, illustrations from the life and activities of the Buddha are also found on the stone railings measuring 145ft. by 108ft. round the holy Bodhi tree (pipal tree). This spot of enlightenment is illustrated on the Bharhut railings as a holy edifice in the 2nd century B.C.

The Bodhi tree at Bodh-Gaya was surrounded by a sumptuous railing consisting of a covered gallery with open niches resting on pillars.[1] Pilgrims from distant places used to visit this sacred place even in the 1st century B.C. This is evident from an inscription written in the script of 1st century B.C. wherein it is said that Buddharakṣita, an inhabitant of *Tāmraparṇa* (Ceylon) made a gift there. (cf. *Buddharakhitasa Tabapanakasa dānaṁ*).[2]

In this period we find that the *dharma-cakra* has found a place in the temple along with the *triratna* placed on throne. The Bodhi tree also was illustrated as a symbol of worship by the pilgrims. Buddhist *caityas* and *stūpas* also were figured in the railings for the purpose of showing reverence to these symbols. Bodh-Gaya drew also the attention of royal patrons. At one place in a half medallion a goddess who may be taken as goddess of Fortune or Fertility is found standing on lotus and being bathed by two elephants. Below her, there

---

1. *Arch. Sur. Ind. An. Rep.*, 1908-09. pp. 141f.
2. N.G. Majumdar, *Guide to the sculptures in Indian Museum,* (=GSIM,) Part I, p. 67.

is an inscription in the Brāhmi characters of the 1st century. B.C. which says that Nāgadevī, wife of King Brahmamitra, made a gift there (cf. *Raño Brahma mitrasa pājāvatiye Nāgadevaye dana.*)[1]

During his visit to Bodh-Gaya Cunningham found several pillars of granite bearing inscriptions of gift in the characters used by Aśoka. One such inscription reads—*Ayāye Kuragiye dānaṁ*[2] i.e. gift of Āryā Kuragi. Although Cunningham took them to be the relics of the Maurya period, they were more probably the objects of the time of the Śuṅgas on account of the characteristic briefness of the inscriptions and their donative purpose.

Then we come to S a r n a t h, where Buddha after his great en lightenment turned the Wheel of Law (dharma-cakra) for the first time. This place continued to be one of the important centres of Buddhism during the Śuṅga period also. Apart from the structural evidences, several inscriptions written in the Brāhmī characters of that age were discovered in course of excavations. Some of them contain the names of donors with their places of residence. Donors used to come from widely distant regions as Ujjayini,[3] and Pāṭaliputra[4] (Patna). Here also the donors just as at Bharhut, and Sāñci made gifts of pillars (and probably cross-bars and copings etc.). It appears that the gift of pillars, cross-bars, copings and gateways etc. was regarded to be one of the essential features of religious acts during the Śuṅga period. An inscription discovered at Sarnath in the Brāhmī characters of the 2nd century B.C. records the gift of a base-stone by a nun *Saṁvahikā* by name [cf. *bhikhunikāye Saṁvahikāye dāna*(*ṁ*) *ala*(*ṁ*)*banaṁ*[5]].

So far as places of religious worship are concerned, Buddhism has left for the posterity a remarkable legacy. A place of religious importance of this period was brought to light a few years ago in course of archaeological excavations. N.G. Majumdar dug out a huge brick structure nearly 80ft. high taking a zig zag course and showing a number of re-entrant angles at *Lauriya Nandangarh* in the Champaran district of Bihar in 1936-37. This building was polygonal and star-shaped in plan, measuring 500 ft. across the centre and facing each cardinal point with a side 104ft. long. There are four sides each

1. N.G. Majumdar, *GSIM.*, Part I, p. 71.
2. Cunningham, *ASR.*, vol. I, p. 10.
3. *Arch. Sur. Ind. An. Rep.*, 1914-15, p. 121, II, PL. LXVIII. 9-10.
4. *Ibid.*, p. 122. V, PL. LXVIII, 14.
5. *Ibid.*, 1906-07, p. 95.

at a distance of 266ft. from the other. The space between the two sides in each of the quadrangles is covered by 28 smaller sides showing 14 re-entrant angles and as many as 13 corners.[1]"

In plan the monument is somewhat similar to the Main temple at Paharpur (District, Rajshahi) though the latter was built about six or seven centuries after the former which is more elaborate and stupendous. The Lauriya Nandangarh monument has at least five terraces one above the other and there is passage for circumambulation on three of them. The lowermost and widest terrace has a width of 32 ft. and the one above it is 14 ft. across.

The decoration of the structure is very plain and simple. This monument has been attributed to the Śuṅga period by the experts. In this connection the observation made by N.G. Majumdar may be quoted here. He says "There is evidence to show that this structure must have been erected not later than the 2nd century B.C. As a simple brick built edifice of such stupendous dimensions it is perhaps unparalleled in the whole range of monuments of the period to which it belongs. Although nothing definite has yet been discovered to throw light on the character of the monument it may be described as a Buddhist *stūpa* in absence of any evidence to the contrary.[2]"

In B e n g a l also some places particularly *Bangarh* (ancient Kotivarṣa) and *Tamluk* (ancient Tāmralipti or Tāmralipta) both in West Bengal felt the sweeping influence of Buddhism during the Śuṅga period. Because two terracotta sealings[3] bearing the names, *Bhutarakhita* and *Śamana Vilala* in *Śuṅga Brāhmī* have been discovered in course of excavations at the former place. The name Bhutarakhita was generally popular among the members of the Buddhist sect and occurs in one (No. 119) of the inscriptions of the Bharhut railings of the Śuṅga period.

At Tamluk, a terracotta tablet which was recently discovered, is supposed to contain a scene from the Chadanta Jātaka. From stylistic ground the tablet is ascribed to the Śuṅga period and is now exhibited in the Ashtosh Museum of Calcutta University. From these evidences it cannot be denied that Buddhism had a favourable ground in Bengal during the Śuṅga regime.

---

1. *Arch. Sur. Ind. An. Rep.*, 1936-37, pp. 47f.
2. *Ibid,* 1936-37, pp. 47-50.
3. K.G. Goswami, *Excavations at Bangarh,* pp.12, 36. PL. XXIV. b.

During the rule of the Indo-Greek Kings in the North-Western India in the 2nd and 1st centuries B.C. Buddhism played a prominent part in that region. Because some of the Indo-Greek rulers became patrons of Buddhism and one of them, *Menander*, became a convert to the faith of Gautama Buddha. Although according to tradition Aśoka is said to have taken the initiative for preserving the sacred relics of the Buddha constructing *stūpas* in different parts of India, documentary (i.e. inscriptional) evidences are available from the Śuṅga period to the effect that the disciples and devotees were then giving particular attention to the preservation of the corporeal remains of the Great Master in the *stūpas* throughout the country for the worship and benefit of the people.

From the Shinkot steatite casket inscriptions found in the Bajaur tribal territory beyond the borders of N.W. Frontier Province it is known that in the reign of king Menander, Viyakamitra[1] (=Vīryakamitra), apparently one of the feudatories (Apraca-raja) of the former placed the corporeal remains of the Lord *Śākyamuni* endowed with life *(praṇa-sameda-sarira)* in a casket. But in the latter part of the inscription it is stated by Vijayamitra apparently a successor of Viyakamitra that in course of time probably after the death of the depositor these remains were not treated with due honour, hence he (Vijayamitra who was a successor or subordinate ruler) re-established the sacred remains and made arrangements for their regular worship.

That the depositing of the corporeal remains of the Buddha was considered to be one of the main religious activities of this period is also proved by the Swat relic vase inscription of the Meridarkh Theodoros[2] of the 1st century B.C. It is stated therein that a Greek Provincial Governor (Greek Meridarkhes) Theodoros placed a casket containing the sacred relics of the Lord Buddha's body for the benefit of a large number of people *(bahujana-hitaye)*. It appears that the arrangement of the relic caskets was made in order to give something concrete to the ordinary followers of Buddhism as an object of worship.

It has already been pointed out that Buddhism made a favourable appeal to the foreigners and foreign rulers, some of whom became staunch devotees and generous patrons of this religion.

---

1. *Ep. Ind.*, vol. XXIV, p. 7.
2. Sten Konow, *Corp. Ins. Ind.*, vol. II, i. p. 4.

Buddhism made a rapid progress also in South India in 2nd-1st centuries B.C. This is proved by the Bhaṭṭiprolu Casket inscriptions[1] of the time of Kuberaka of the Kristna district of South India. It is stated therein that two caskets—one of stone and the other of crystal were dedicated by some individuals— Kura's father, Kura's mother and Kura himself and also another person named Śiva for depositing the corporeal remains of Lord Buddha. The *mañjuṣā* or stone casket was actually the gift of Kura and his father Banaba. There were other sets of stone caskets and crystal caskets being the gifts of a good number of individuals and corporate bodies and also of king Kuberaka himself. It is further mentioned that the figure of king Kuberaka, the donor was also sketched there apparently to add importance to the work. According to casket No. 2 (D) King Kuberaka has been stated to be the chief of the *Simha Goṣṭhī* clan, which dedicated another set of two caskets one being made of stone and the other of crystal. Casket No. 3 (B) records that the *goṣṭhī* or clan of Arahadina (Arhaddatta) also dedicated a set of one stone casket and a crystal casket and that the work was accomplished by one who drew the figure of king Kuberaka. It is to be noted that the king who was the patron as well as one of the essential figures in the act of dedication was represented by the artist both in name as well as in portrait on the caskets to commemorate the act of depositing the relic.

The practice of representing the figure of donors is also seen in the relief of the Andhra King Sātakarṇi at Nānāghāt.[2]

In the 2nd and 1st centuries B.C., there began to grow the art of excavating caves, caitya halls and vihāras (monasteries) for the Buddhists (especially for the Buddhist monks) in different parts of India. In this connection the names of Bhājā[3] (near Poona), Nāsik[4] (District Nasik), Mānmada[5] (Junnār) and Nānāghāt[6] (District Poona) appear uppermost in our mind. The cave architecture which received a strong support from the Buddhists and patrons of Buddhism made steady progress during this period. These places besides Bharhut, Sāñci and Bodhgaya were certainly of great importance from the

1. *Ep. Ind.*, vol. II, pp. 323f.
2. Coomaraswamy, *HIIA.*, p. 30.
3. *Ibid.*, fig. 29.
4. *Ibid.*, fig. 31.
5. *Ibid.*, fig. 30.
6. *Ibid.*, p. 30; *Arch. Sur. Rep. West. Ind.*, V. p. 64.

Buddhist point of view, Pilgrims and monks from all quarters used to flock to these places. Although the Sātavāhana kings were themselves strong supporters and staunch followers of the Brahmanical religion, yet they were liberal patrons of Buddhism, and the Buddhist cave architecture of Nasik and Nānā-ghāt etc. flourished under them. There is record to show that during the reign of king Kṛṣṇa of the Sātavāhana dynasty a cave was excavated by the officer-in-charge of the Śramanas at Nasik[1] (or by a Śramaṇa who was himself a *Mahāmātra* or officer at Nasik). The Nānāghāt caves contain lebels bearing the names of Simuka Sātavāhana, Devī Nāganikā, King Sātakarṇi; Kumāra Śaktiśrī and Kumāra Sātavāhana.[2]

---

1. *Ep. Ind.*, vol. VIII, p. 93.
2. *Arch. Sur. Rep. West. Ind.*, V, p. 64.

## *Chapter - 38*

# Buddhism in South-East Asia

**R.C. Majumdar**

### Beginning

According to a tradition preserved in the Ceylonese Chronicles. Buddhism was preached in Suvarṇabhūmi by the missionaries of Aśoka. Though the location of Suvarṇabhūmi is uncertain, some having identified it with Burma, others with Siam (Thailand), there is no doubt that it refers to some part of Indo-China. But the authenticity of the tradition itself is open to question, as no early and reliable evidence has been obtained so far in support of it. Nor can we accept the view that the first two disciples of the Buddha named Trapuṣa and Bhallika, who built a sanctuary over his relics in their native land, belonged to Burma, for the Utkala country, which is referred to in the canonical texts as their native land, is certainly to be identified with Orissa.

There is, however, no doubt that Buddhism obtained a definite footing in South-east Asia during the early centuries of the Christian era. This is proved by the discovery of the images of Buddha of the Amarāvatī style in Thailand (Siam), Annam (Campā), Sumatra, Java and Celebes. The representation of the Buddha by a symbol, such as *dharmacakra* (wheel of law), rather than a human figure, in some of the sculptures in Thailand, also support the introduction of Buddhism in this region at an early date.

### 1. Thailand

The early sculptures discovered in Thailand prove conclusively that Buddhism was introduced in this region at the beginning of the Christian era. A Wheel of Law, associated with figures of crouching deer, was dug up at Pra Pathom. Another early site, Pong Tuk, has yielded bronze Buddha images of the Amarāvatī style, which may be dated in the second century A.D. Buddhist images of the Gupta style, both of earlier and later type, have also been discovered. As the inscriptions, engraved on the latter, may be referred to the fifth and sixth centuries A.D., those of the earlier type probably belong to the fourth century A.D.

From this early period we may trace the uninterrupted progress of Hīnayāna Buddhism in this country. The Thai conquest of the land in the thirteenth century A.D. gave a great impetus to this religion. The Thai rulers were ardent followers of Hīnayāna Buddhism. We learn from the inscription of Rām Kamheng, that this famous king was an ardent follower of Hīnayāna Buddhism and decorated his capital Sukhodaya with temples, monasteries and images of Buddha at the close of the thirteenth century A.D. The Hīnayāna Buddhism of the Thais was sustained and influenced by Burma and the island of Ceylon. The intercourse between Mons of Lower Burma and Thailand were of long standing. A Thai king sent a messenger to Ceylon in A.D. 1361 who brought back with him a senior monk who reformed the religion. The Hīnayāna Buddhism with its Pāli canon flourishes even now in Thailand, Burma and Ceylon, and it is not therefore necessary to discuss its history in great detail.

## 2. Cambodia

Buddhism made its influence felt in Cambodia as early as the fifth century A.D., for king Jaya-varman of Fu-nan, who ruled towards the close of that century, sent an embassy to China in A.D. 503, with presents including an image of Buddha. An inscription of his son Rudravarman begins with an invocation to Buddha. From this time onward the prevalence of Buddhism is proved by inscriptions. But it had a set-back in the 7th century, and the epigraphic records indicate that Śaivism, not Buddhism, was the dominant religion of Cambodia. It is curious, in view of the present state of things, that very few kings of Cambodia, of whom we possess any epigraphic record, were followers of Buddhism. Sūryvarman I (IInd century A.D.) was a Buddhist, for he had the posthumous title *Nirvāṇa-pada*. But his inscription on a temple at Prah Khan[1] begins with an invocation to Śiva in the first verse, and to the Buddha in the second. Several inscriptions on the temple known as Prasat Ta Keo,[2] in honour of Yogīśvara Paṇḍita, the *guru* of king Sūryavarman, begin with

1. R.C. Majumdar, *Inscriptions of Kambuja*, p. 360.
2. *Ibid.*, pp. 351 ff.

invocations to Śiva and Viṣṇu, and refer to donations made to these gods. Jayavarman VII, perhaps the greatest king of Kambuja, was a Buddhist, and his Ta Prohm Inscription, dated A.D. 1186, gives a detailed list of his magnificent donations to this temple.[1] The merit of these pious works was to accrue to the king's mother so that she might obtain the state of Buddha (v. 141).[2] In addition to the kings mentioned above, high dignitaries like Kavīndrārimathana and Kīrtipaṇḍita, both belonging to the tenth century A.D., were ardent Buddhists, and the latter claimed to have lighted again the torch of the true law which the sins of the world had extinguished. The form of Buddhism referred to is clearly Mahāyāna.

But if we take the epigraphic data as a whole, there remains no doubt that Buddhism was never a dominant religion in Kambuja till the time of Jayavarman VII. But even the patronage of this great emperor did not establish Buddhism as a state religion, as it is now. It is interesting to note that during the reign of king Śrīndra-varmadeva, a later king, we find an inscription,[3] dated A.D. 1308, written in Pāli and referring to Hīnayāna form of Buddhism. The next two kings, Śrīndra-Jayavarman and Jayavarman-Parameśvara were followers respectively of Viṣṇu and Śiva.

The state of religion in Cambodia is described by Cheu Ta-kuan who visited the country in A.D. 1296. It appears that Hīnayāna Buddhism was in a flourishing state at this time. Yet the older inscriptions mostly refer to Mahāyāna doctrine. Taking everything into consideration, we are forced to the conclusion that it was the influence of Thailand (Siam) that gradually introduced a great change in the religion of Kambuja. On the whole Brahmanical religion, specially Śaivism, was dominant in Kambuja, though Mahāyāna Buddhism was also a powerful sect, up to the end of the thirteenth century A.D. But the political dominance of the Thais (of Siam) in Cambodia established the supremacy of Hīnayāna Buddhism which is now the only religion of the people.

### 3. Campā

The ancient Hindu colony of Campā corresponds, roughly, to the southern part of Annam. The early introduction of Buddhism in this region is indicated by an image of Buddha of the Amarāvatī style

1. *Ibid.*, pp. 459 ff.
2. *Ibid.*, pp. 474 ff.
3. *Ibid.*, pp. 533 ff.

at Dong-Duong. But there is no epigraphic reference to Buddhism before the 9th century A.D.[1] The Bakul Stelae Inscription,[2] datd A.D. 829, refers to the construction of two temples and two monasteries for Jina and Śaṅkara. Jina may denote either the Buddha or Mahāvīra, but as there is no evidence for the existence of Jainism in South-east Asia, Jina may be taken to denote Buddha. The long inscription on the four faces of a stelae found at Dong-Duong[3] records the installation of an image of Buddha in A.D. 875, and the foundation of a Buddhist temple and a monastery by the Buddhist king Indravarman. The remains of a Buddhist temple at this place, far greater in dimensions than the largest Brahmanical temple in Campā, prove that Dong-Duong (ancient Amarāvatī) in the province of Quang Nam was an important stronghold of Buddhism in Campā.

Many later kings patronised Buddhism, and monasteries and temples were built in different parts of the kingdom. Many Buddhist images have also been found in different parts of Campā.

I-tsing refers to the prevalence of Buddhism in Campā and remarks that the "Buddhists generally belong to the Āryasammitīya-nikāya and there are also a few followers of the Sarvāstivādanikāya." Thus Hīnayāna prevailed at the end of the seventh century A.D. But the inscriptions and images leave no doubt that the Mahāyāna soon occupied the dominant position in Campā. Particular reference may be made to An-Thai Stelae Inscription[4] dated 824 Śaka (=A.D. 902) which records the erection of a statue of Lokanātha by *sthavira* Nāgapuṣpa, the abbot of the monastery of Pramudita-Lokeśvara, and refers to Vajradhātu, Padmadhātu and Cakradhātu, Amitābha and Vairocana.

It is interesting to note that Buddhist and Śaiva temples and monasteries were often erected side by side, by the same donor, that the epithet Ḍamareśvara (lord of the *Bhūtas*), originally belonging to Śiva, was applied to Buddha, and that figures of Śiva decorated the Buddhist temples of Dong-Duong.

---

1. Many scholars find traces of Buddhism in Vocanh inscription, but I do not find anything definitely Buddhist in it. (Forthe inscription cf. R.C. Majumdar, *Champa*, Book III, p. 1). Coedes maintains that it is Budd-hist—*Les Ētats Hindouisés d'Indo-Chine et d'Indonésie* (1948), p. 74.
2. *Cbampa*, BK, III, p. 65.
3. *Ibid.*, p. 74.
4. *Ibid.*, p. 105.

## 4. Malay Peninsula

The well-known Buddhist formula '*ye dharmā hetuprabhavā*' etc. followed by another verse beginning with *Ajñānāc=cīyate karma*, is engraved on a slab of stone found amid the ruins of an ancient brick building at Keddah. The second verse alone is engraved on a piece of stone, probably a part of an old shrine, in the northern part of province Wellesley. Both these inscriptions have been referred to the fourth or fifth century A.D.[1] Three Sanskrit verses are inscribed on a clay tablet found near Keddah. They inculcate Mahāyāna philosophical doctrines of Mādhyamika school, and have been traced to a text entitled *Sāgaramati-paripṛcchā*, which is known only from a Chinese "translation."[2]

The inscriptions mentioned above also prove that Buddhist temples, both of brick and stone, were built in Wellesley Province and Keddah in the fourth or fifth century A.D. The great *stūpa* of Nakhon Śrī Dhammarāt and a number of temples surrounding it indicate the existence of a flourishing Buddhist colony in this region. A number of terracotta votive tablets found in neighbouring caves also show that a large number of Buddhist monks resided therein.

## 5. Indonesia[3]

Buddhism did not obtain a secure footing in Indonesia till after the fourth century A.D. At the time when Fa-hien visited Java there was very little trace of Buddhism in that island. But Guṇavarman, who belonged to the royal family of Kipin (Kāshmir or Afghānistan) but had taken to religion, preached Buddhism in Java early in the fifth century A.D., and it soon took deep root in the soil. As Guṇavarman translated a text of the Dharma-gupta sect, he must have belonged to the Mūlasarvāstivāda school, and it was evidently due to his influence that this sect became dominant in Java and the neighbouring islands.

The neighbouring island of Bali also came under the influence of Buddhism about the same time. For according to the *History of the Liang Dynasty* (A.D. 502-556), the earliest Chinese historical annals that give an account of this island, the king of Bali claimed that the wife of Śuddhodana was a daughter of his country.

---

1. R.C. Majumdar, *Suvarṇadvīpa*, Part I, pp. 88 ff.
2. *JGIS*, VIII, p. 2.
3. For the facts mentioned in this section cf. *Suvarṇadvīpa*, part II.

By the seventh century A.D. Buddhism flourished all over Indonesia, and Śrī-Vijaya in Sumatra became a stronghold of this religion. We possess an inscription, dated Śaka 606 (A.D. 684), of a Buddhist king of this country named Jayanāśa. There was a regular trade and maritime intercourse between Śrī-Vijaya and India. On his way to India the Chinese pilgrim I-tsing halted at Śrī-Vijaya for six months, and he again visited the place, after his return to China, in order to copy and translate the voluminous Buddhist texts which he had brought with him from India.

It is evident from I-tsing's statement that although Hīnayāna was dominant in these regions there were in Śrī-Vijaya a few who followed the Mahāyāna form of Buddhism. This is also proved by the inscription of Jayanāśa referred to above. It not only contains definite reference to the Mahāyāna doctrine, but the use of the word *vajra-śarīra* further indicates that this Mahāyāna was of the Tāntrik form known as Vajra-yāna, Mantra-yāna or Tantra-yāna.

Indonesia was visited by eminent Buddhist scholars from India such as Dharmapāla, a Professor of Nālandā in the seventh century A.D., and Vajrabodhi, a South Indian monk. The latter and his disciple Amoghavajra, who accompanied him, were teachers of Tāntrik cult and are credited with its introduction to China. Both of them halted at Śrī-Vijaya for five months on their way from Ceylon to China, early in the eighth century A.D.

Towards the close of this century the Mahāyāna cult acquired great predominance owing to the patronage of the Śailendras who ruled over the greater part of Indonesia. Two inscriptions, dated A.D. 778 and 782, refer to the construction of a temple of Tārā at Kalasan, and setting up of an image of Mañjuśrī at Kelurak by the Śailendra emperors. The latter was inspired by their *guru* Kumāra-ghoṣa, an inhabitant of Gauḍa. The Śailendra emperors were in close touch with the Pala emperor Devapāla of Bengal, and the Cola emperor Rājarāja, both of whom endowed the monasteries built by the Śailendras, respectively at Nālandā and Negapatam.

The Mahāyāna form of Buddhism has left permanent memorials in Java in the famous *stūpa* of Barabuḍur and a number of other magnificent temples erected during the Śailendra rule. The Javanese literature and the Buddhist images found in Java clearly indicate that all the essential features of Mahāyāna, even of its last phases, were fully developed in that island. As in India, a number of Hindu gods were adopted in the Buddhist pantheon, though they were relegated to an inferior position. New divinities were introduced, some of which, like Trailokyavijaya, Hevajra, Bhairava and Heruka, were of monstrous or terrifying appearance. The Tantra-yāna, including Kāla-cakratantra, prevailed both in Java and Sumatra. The famous king Kṛtanagara of Java was a devout follower of the Tantra-yāna or Vajra-yāna, and his drinking bout is approved in a Javanese historical text on the ground that he scrupulously followed the prescriptions of religion. King Ādityvaraman of Malayu in Sumatra, who was ruling as a vassal of Kṛtanagara in A.D. 1286, seems to have been a follower of the Bhairava cult.

As in India, there was a gradual rapprochement between Mahāyāna and Brahmanical religion. This was more clearly indicated in Indonesia by the fact that gradually Śiva, Viṣṇu and Buddha were regarded as identical and so were their Śaktis. A definite Śiva-Buddha cult existed in Java, and in modern Balinese theology Buddha is regarded as a younger brother of Śiva.

There are two Buddhist texts in Java which give an interesting insight into the developed form of Mahāyāna. The first, *Sang hyang Kamahāyānikan* is a free Javanese version of a Sanskrit original, interspersed with a number of original Sanskrit verses. It was probably composed in the Śailendra period (8th century A.D.), but was modified, about a century or two later, in a manner which has been regarded as a Hinduised or Śaiva version of a Buddhist original. It contains an exposition of the leading principles of Mahāyāna and gives an account of its theology according to the Yogācāra system. It brings the Hindu Trinity in organic relation with the Buddhist pantheon. The picture of Mahāyāna in Java which it unfolds shows a close resemblance with, but also minor differences from, the form of religion current in India.

The second text *Kamahāyānan Mantranaya* contains forty-one Sanskrit verses with Javanese commentaries. It contains an exposition of the Tantra-yāna or Vajra-yāna both in its theoretical and practical aspects. The five kinds of sensual enjoyments (*pañca-ma-kāra*) are clearly prescribed, and the devotee is forbidden to communicate the secrets of *vajra, ghaṇṭā* and *mudrā* to those who do not belong to the *Maṇḍala*.

## *Chapter - 39*

# Outlines of the History of Buddhism in Indo-China

**L. Finot**

### I

To many people, especially those who have access only to English books[1], the expression "Indo-Chinese Buddhism" means the religion actually professed by the two countries, Siam and Burma, which, together with Ceylon, form the geographical area of the Southern Buddhism. This view is deficient on two points: first it neglects all the eastern part of the Peninsula; secondly, it does not make any allowance for the long period during which a great part of Indo-China knew no other form of Buddhism than the Mahāyāna. Therefore, it will not be useless to trace, with more precision, the main lines of the history of Buddhism in these far-off countries. This history has grown in two different regions independent of each other and of unequal importance: the eastern coast (Annam) and the western part of the country (British Malaya, Siam, Cambodia, Laos, Burma).

The most ancient Hindu settlement on the eastern coast of the Indo-Chinese Peninsula seems to lie in the south of modern Annam between Cochin-China and the mountain range which terminates with Cape Varella near the modern town of Nhatrang. There is a Bhagavatī, which though does not date back to a very remote epoch (the existing buildings are of the 9th century A.D.), occupies the seat of a much more ancient sanctuary. According to a tradition preserved in an inscription of the 8th century, a Mukhaliṅga had been erected there by a king, Vicitrasagara by name, in the year of 5911 of the Dvāpara[2]

---

1. The exact and well-informed work of Sir Charles Eliot, *Hinduism and Buddhism*, London, 1921, ought to be set apart.

2. Pañca-sahasra-nava-śataikādaśe vigata-kalikālaṅka-dvāparavarṣe Srī-Vicitrasagara-saṃsthāpitaḥ Śrī-Mukhaliṅga-devaḥ. *Inscriptions sanscrites de Champā et du Cambedge, publiéesn par* A. Barth et A. Bergaigne. Paris, 1885-1893, p. 294. [This collection will be referred to henceforth under the form *ISCC*].

age. This fabulous date proves, at least, that the Sanctuary of Nhatrang was considered in the 8th century as being of an immemorial antiquity.

Not far from this place was found a Sanskrit inscription of great historical importance. It does not contain any date but its writing points, with a quasi certitude, to the third or the second century of our era.[1] It owes its origin to a king who claims to be a descendant of Śrī Mārarāja. The wear and tear of the stone does not permit of any precise conclusion as to the religion which the author of that work professed, but some expression such as "*prajānāṅ karuṇā...*, "compassion for creatures" "*lokasyāsya gatāgati*" "coming and going of this world," [*prajā*]*nāṃ priyahite sarvaṃ visṛṣṭaṃ mayā*, "all is given up by me for the satisfaction and good of creatures", might give out a Buddhistic inspiration.

It is possible that this Hindu colony was the nucleus of the kingdom of Champa which, according to the Chinese historians, was founded in the year 192 A.D. by an adventurer, in revolt against the imperial authorities of the province of Je-nan and extended rapidly towards the north up to the frontier of Tongking.[2] It might also stand for the kingdom of Pāṇḍuraṅga, which later on became a vassal principality of Champa.

The epigraphy of Champa (leaving aside the inscription of Vo-canh) is, at first, clearly Śaiva. It is in the 9th century only that Buddhism makes its appearance there. In the second quarter of that century, a Buddhist of Pāṇḍuraṅga, Samanta by name, dedicates two monasteries (Vihāra) and two temples to the Jîna and Śiva (Jīnaśaṅkarayos), the *praśasti* being written by his son, Sthavira Buddha-nirvāṇa.[3] From that time is noticed the close association of Buddhism with Śaivism which will remain up to the end is one of the salient features of religion in Champa, as in the other Hindu states of Indo-China.

Some twenty years later, the growing importance of Buddhism is affirmed by the foundation of the great monastery of Lakṣmīndra Lokeśvara,[4] a pious work of king Indravarman II who had assumed

1. Inscription of Vo-canh, published in *ISCC*, p. 191, and re-edited in the *Bulletin de l' Ecole Française d' extréme-Orient*, XV, 2, p.3. [This Bulletin will be referred to hereafter under the form *BEFEO*].

2. L. Aurousseau in *BEFEO*, XIV, g, p. 26.

3. *ISCC*, p. 237, no. XXV.

4. The ruins of this monastery are situated near the village of Dong-düong in the province of Quang-nam (Annam). They have been described by H. Parmentier in: *Inventaire descriptif des monuments chams de l' Annam*, vol. I, p. 439 ff. The inscriptions have been published in *BEFO*, IV 84 ff.

before his coronation the name of Lakṣmīndra Bhūmiśvara Grāmasvāmī[1] and after his death that of Paramabuddhaloka. In the foundation charter, the king glorifies simultaneously Lokeśvara and the Liṅga Bhadreśvara.

It is peculiar that in this monument dedicated to Lokeśvara not a single image of this Bodhisattva has been discovered but only some big statues of the Buddha represented as sitting in the European fashion with hands resting on his knees.[2]

In 902 A.D. in the same province Sthavira Nāgapuṣpa sets up a Lokanātha in the monastery of Pramudita-Lokeśvara which he held as a royal gift.[3] On that occasion he was pleased to give a resumé of the Mahāyānist theogony under the rather peculiar form it had taken in his own time.

*Vajradhātur asau pūrvvaṃ Śri-Śākyamuniśāsanāt*
*Śūnyo pi Vajradhṛddhetuḥ buddhānām ālayo bhavat//*
*Padmadhātur ato Lokeśvarahetur jinālayaḥ*
*Amitābhavacoyuktyā mahāśūnyo babhyūva ha//*
*Cajradhātur asau śūnyātīto Vairocanājñayā*
*Vajrasattvasya hetuḥ syāt tṛtiyo bhūj jinālayaḥ//*

"In the beginning Vajradhātu (who, though void, is the cause of Vajradhara) became, by the order of Śākymuni, the receptacle of the Buddhas. Then Padmadhātu, the great void, cause of Lokeśvara, in compliance with the word of Amitābha—became the [second] receptacle of the Buddhas. Cakradhātu, the ultra void cause of Vajrasattva became, by the order of Vairocana, the third receptacle of the Buddhas."

As is seen, we are completely here in Mahāyānism though the name has not been yet pronounced. This gap is going to be filled up. At the end of the twelfth century a petty king, reigning in Pāṇḍuraṅga, boasts of practising the dharma of Mahāyāna and in testimony of his faith, erects a Buddha Lokeśvara in the district of Buddhaloka.[4]

Afterwards we have no more document. Nevertheless, a fragment which seems to date from the second half of the thirteenth century

---

1. It was a custom in religious foundations to place the name of the founder before that of the devatā Lakṣmīndra Lokeśvara=Lokeśvara founded by Lakṣmīndra; Mahīndra-Lokeśvara=Lokeśvara founded by Mahīndrādhipati, etc.

2. Is it to be surmised that these images represent Lokeśvara under the aspect of Buddha, a form which is met with in China. (A.FOUCHER, *Iconographie bouddhique*, p. 195, no. 31: Mahācīne Buddha-rūpaka—Lokanāthaḥ)? *Cf.* infra the erection of a Buddha-Lokeśvara

3. *BEFEO*, XI, 277.

4. *BEFEO*, IV, 971, 927.

begins with the invocation *Oṃ namo buddhāya,* which at least proves that Buddhism was not yet extinct in that time.[1]

Iconography confirms the data of epigraphy: the soil of Champa has given in abundance bronze and stone statues of Buddha. Lokeśvara and Prajñāpāramitā. A number of clay medallions bearing images of Buddha and Lokeśvara were picked up in the caves of northern Annam.[2]

The conclusion of this review of our documentation both written and iconographic is that from the 9th century A.D. up to at least the 13th century the two great religions of Champa were, in the first place, Śaivism with the preponderance of the cult of the Liṅga and in the second place, Mahāyāna under the form of the cult of Lokeśvara and that these two cults, far from being mutually incompatible, were more or less intimately associated.

The next question arises: has the predominance of Mahāyāna been preceded by a Hīnayāna period? This is what would seem to come out from a passage of the Chinese pilgrim, I-tsing (*Record*, p. 12): "In this country (Champa), Buddhists generally belong to the Arya-sammiti-nikāya and there are also a few followers of the Sarvāstivāda-nikāya." Nevertheless this assertion seems open to doubt. The information of I-tsing about Champa is secondhand and the apparent precision with which are characterised the two sects of the Hīnayāna that were supposed to be found there must rather put us on guard than to inspire confidence. In any case absolutely nothing in the documents known up to the present, corroborates the assertion of the Chinese pilgrim.

Towards the end of the 15th century, Champa ceased to exist as an independent state. The Annamites of Tong-king formerly subjects of the Chinese empire having regained their autonomy in the 10th century had gradually extended their possessions towards the south at the expense of Champa. In their last raid (1471 A.D.), they seized and burnt down the capital and took possession of the whole kingdom where they introduced this mixture of Mahāyānism, Taoism and Confucianism which, together with the cult of the ancestors and of the genii, constitutes the Chinese religion. As to the pitiable remnants of Cham people, reduced to a few districts of Southern Annam, some of them practise Islamism, others a debased form of Hinduism wherein no trace of Buddhism is found.

---

1. A. BERGAIGNE, *L' ancicn royaume de Champa,* p. 70.
2. Mainly L. FINOT, *La religion des chams d' apres les monuments, BEFEO,* I, p. 12-33; H. PARMENTIER, *Inventaire descriptif des monuments chams,* Paris, 1909-1918, 2 vol.; Id. *Les sculptures chames au museé de Tourane,* Paris, 1922. (Ars Asiatica, IV).

## II

In its palmy days, Champa had as neighbour in the West a state which is known to us only through the Chinese historians and which consequently passes by the name they give to it, viz., Funan.[1]

It was a great empire which had the centre of its power in the territory of modern Cambodia and extended its suzerainty from the Lower Cochin-china to the Gulf of Bengal and from Upper Laos down to the Malay peninsula. It counted among its vassals, the Mons of Dvāravatī (Siam)[2] and the Khmers, then established on the Mekong in the region of Bassak (by 15$^0$ lat. north). Its history occupies the first five centuries of our era.

As in Champa so in Funan we meet with two main cults: one in the foreground, the Śaivism; one in the background but not negligible, the Buddhism—the two religions existing peacefully side by side. That is what we gather from the evidence of I-tsing.[3] "Setting out southwestwards (from Champa) one reaches within a month Pa-nan, formerly called Fu-nan. Of old it was a country, the inhabitants of which lived naked, the people were mostly worshippers of the devas; later on Buddhism flourished there but a wicked king has now expelled and exterminated them all and there are no members of the Buddhist brotherhood at all."

Concerning the preponderance of Śaivism in Funan, it may be noticed that although the head of the mission sent to the court of China in 484 A.D. Śājya Nāgasena was a Buddhist monk, still in his description of Funan he exalts especially the god Maheśvara (*BEFEO*, IV, 270). Nevertheless, Buddhism enjoyed a place of honour in this country. Some illustrious relics were preserved there, notably a hair of the Buddha, 12 feet long which the king presented to the Emperor in 539 A.D. (ibid, p. 281). Several bhikṣus of Funan went to China for the translation work of the holy books; among them were Saṅghapāla and Mandrasena at the end of the 5th and in the beginning of the 6th century (ibid., p. 294).

---

1. Funan probably corresponds to the Khmer word *vnam* "mountain." Possibly the kings of the country were called *Krung vnam* "kings of the mountain" like the Śailendras of Sumatra.

2. The existence of the kingdom of Dvāravatī is attested for the 7th century by the two histories of the T'ang Dynasty and by the pilgrims Hiuen-tsang and I'tsing who locate it between Śrīkshetra (Prome) and Cambodia, but it may be much older. The ethnic character of its population has been brought to light by G. COEDES, *Documents sur l' histore du Laos occidental, BEFEO,* xxv, pp. 115 ff. cf. *ibid*, iv, 223, note 5.

3. *Record,* p. 12.

Our information on Funan does not allow any conclusion as to the particular form of Buddhism which was reigning there. Perhaps several sects divided this vast empire among themselves.

In the south of Funan, the Malay peninsula was essentially a Buddhist country. The inscriptions found in the region of Ligor and in the province of Wellesly prove that in the 4th century A.D. there were some important Buddhistic centres on the coasts.[1] Other inscriptions discovered on the south of the isthmus of Krā dating from the 8th and 9th centuries witness the continuation of the same religion in those countries. One of them which commemorates the construction of three caityas in honour of Avalokitesvara, Buddha and Vajrapāṇi in 775 A.D. proceeds from the king of Śrī-Vijaya (Palembang).[2]

## III

Towards the middle of the 6th century, a political revolution broke out in the western Indo-china: the Khmers or Kambojas, till then vassal of Funan, overthrew the sovereign state and took its place.

It is no doubt to this event that I-tsing alludes in the passage quoted above, when he speaks of the wicked king who exterminated the Buddhists of Funan. We may be permitted to believe that the pious writer has strongly exaggerated this disaster, for, in 664 A.D., that is to say, only half a century after the conquest, and precisely at the time when I-tsing commenced his journey, the reigning king, in an inscription, praises two eminent Bhikṣus (bhikṣu-variṣṭhān) living in his kingdom both of whom are (said to be) "treasures of virtue, science, kindness, patience, charity, austerity and prudence" (*ISCC.*, p. 62). *Śīla-śruta-śama-kṣānti-dayā-saṃyamadhī-nidhī*.

All that could possibly happen was a strengthening of Saivism which was the religion of the Khmer kings, but there is not the least probability of a persecution or a *fortiori* of an extermination of the Buddhists by the new sovereigns. An inscription of the same epoch (7th century)[3] which associates in the same pious donation, the Buddha, Maitreya and Avalokiteśvara, proves that it was the Mahāyāna which was at that time the form of Buddhism prevailing in Cambodia, and as such it remained till the inroad of the Hīnayāna following the Siamese wars, towards the 15th century when a new religious era commences.

---

1. H. KERN. *Over eenige oude Sanskrit-opschriften van't, Maleische Schiereiland* (Verslagen en Mededeelingen, 1883). L. FINOT, *Inscriptions du Siam et de la peninsule Malaise* (Bulletin de la Commission archeologique de l' Indochine, 1910, p. 147).
2. G. COEDES, *Le royaume de Śrīvijaya* (*BEFEO,* XVIII, n° 6).
3. Inscription of Ampil Rolöm, *cf.* AYMONIER *Le Cambodge,* I, p. 449.

The most popular figure of the Mahāyānist pantheon in Cambodia is Lokeśvara. This merciful Bodhisattva is the great divinity of the kingdom; it is under his patronage that the capital is placed; it is his image that appears on the fronton of the *dharmaśālās* built along the roads in order to provide a shelter to the pilgrims.[1] He is very often associated with Prajñāpāramitā and Vajrapāṇi. It is especially in the 10th century that his cult seems to have been flourishing. He is still invoked in the inscriptions of the 12th century, but no more foundations made in his name are recorded and when the great Buddhist king Jayavarman VII founds hospitals in various provinces of his empire, it is no more under the patronage of Lokeśvara that he places them, although this was one of the essential functions of the great Bodhisattva—but under that of the mythical Buddha Bhiṣajyaguru and of his two assistants Sūryavairocana and Candravairocana.[2]

The Tantrism seems to have exercised very little influence upon the Khmer cults, although several images of Hevajra have been found in the ruins of Ankor. Generally speaking the Cambodian Mahāyāna gives an impression of laudable sobriety. We may gather an idea of it from some specimens of the invocations that ordinarily open the acts of pious gifts.

Inscription of Phnom Bantāy Nāṅ, A.D. (n° k. 214).

*namo stu paramārthāya vyomatulyāya yo dadhau*
*dharma-sambhogi-nirmmāṇa-kāyān trailogyamūrttaye//*
*bhāti Lokeśvaro mūrddhnā yo' mitābhañ jinam dadhau*
*mitaraśmiprakāśānām arkkendvor darśanād iva//*
*Prajñāpāramitākhyāyai bhagavatyai namo stu te*
*yasyāṃ sametya sarvvajñās sarvvajñatvam upeyuṣaḥ//*

"Homage to the Absolute, identical with the Void, who has taken the bodies of Law, Beatitude and Creation, to make from them the shape of the three worlds.

"Resplendent is Lokeśvara, who has placed upon his head the Jina Amitābha (Unlimited Light) as a consequence of his having ascertained the limited light of the Sun and the Moon.

"Homage to thee, Blessed One! who art called Prajñāpāramitā, in who the Omniscients have attained their Omniscience."

---

1. cf. L. FINOT, *Lokeśvara en Indochine*, in *Etudes asiatiques, publièes a Poccasion du 25 anniversaire de l' Ecole francaise d' Extreme-Orient*, Paris, 1925, T.I., pp. 227-256. ID. *Inscriptions d' Ankor et Dharmaśālās au Cambodge, BEFEO*, T. xxv.
2. Edict of the Hospitals: *BEFEO*, iii, 18 ff., 460, xv, 2, p. 108, 185. There was in Ceylon an Ārogyaśālā-Lokeśvara "Lokeśvara of the hospitals", FOUCHER *Iconographie bouddhique*, p. 193 et 212.

Inscription of Ta Prohm, 1186 A.D. (n° k. 273).

*Sambhāra-vistara-vibhāvita-dharmmakāya-*
*sambhoga-nirmiti-vapur bhagavān vibhaktaḥ/*
*yo gocaro jina-jinātamaja-dehabhājāṃ*
*vuddhāya bhūtaśaraṇāya namo stu tasmai//*

*vande niruttaram anuttaravodhimārggaṃ*
*bhūtārtha-darśana-nirāvaraṇaikadṛṣṭim/*
*dharmman trilokaviditāmaravandyavandyam*
*antarvasat-ṣaḍariṣaṇḍa-khaḍgam//*

*samyagvimukti-paripanthitayā vimukta-*
*saṅgo pi santatagṛhītaparārthasaṅgaḥ/*
*saṅgīyamāna-jinaśāsana-śāsitān yān*
*saṅgho bhisaṃhita hitaprabhavo vatād vaḥ//*

*trailokya-kāṅkṣita-phalaprasavaika-yonir*
*agrāṅguli-vitapa-bhūṣita-vāhu-śākhaḥ/*
*hemopavīta-latikā-parivīta-kāyo*
*Lokeśvaro jayati jaṅgamapārijātaḥ//*

*munīndra-dharmmāgrasarīṃ guṇāḍhyān*
*dhīmadbhir adhyātmadṛśā nirīkṣyām/*
*nirastaniśśeṣavikalpajālāṃ*
*bhaktyā jinānāṃ jananīṃ namadhvam//*

"To the Blessed One, whose previous merits, as a result of their growing, are manifested in the bodies of Law, Beatitude and Creation and who (thus) is divided, who is the domain of those put on the bodies of Jina or of Bodhisattva,—to the Buddha, the Refuge of the beings, homage!

"I adore the supreme way of supreme Illumination, the Only View through which the pure reality is perceived without any veil, the Law, most revered by all the immortals who know the three worlds whom the three worlds know, the sword that cuts down the thicket of the six inner enemies.

"He, who, although emancipated from all attachments, is putting obstacle in the way of perfect emancipation, nevertheless remains faithfully attached to the interest of others, teaches the world the doctrine of the Jina sung (by the councils) and has always the production of good in view,—may the Saṅgha protect you!

"Victorious is Lokeśvara, unique source of the fruits wished for by the three worlds, whose arms are like branches adorned with twigs that are his fingers, whose body is encircled by a liana which is the Brahmanic thread, and who is (thus) a living Pārijāta (Tree of paradise).

"With a pious love adore Her, who marches at the head of the Law of the king of munis, who is rich in virtue, perceptible to the sages only by means of introspection and who unfolds the tangle of all kinds of doubts, the (Prajñāpāramitā), mother of the Jinas!"

Of a more popular character is the cult of Bodhidhruma such as it appears to us in an inscription which is connected with one of the sacred trees planted on the terrace of the principal temple of the royal palace at Angkor Thom. That inscription (n°. k. 484) may be attributed to the reign of Jayavarman VII (12th century)

*Vrahmamūla Śivaskandha Viṣṇuśākha sanātana*
*Vṛkṣarāja mahābhāgya sarvāśraya phalaprada//*
*mā tvāśanir mmā paraśur mānilo mā hutāśanaḥ*
*mā rājā mā gajaḥ kruddho vināśam upaneṣyati//*
*akṣispandaṃ bhruvo spandan dussvapnan durvvicintitam*
*aśvattha śamayet sarvvaṃ yad divyaṃ yac ca mānuṣam//*

"Oh, Thou whose roots are Brahmā, trunk is Śiva, branches are Viṣṇu, Oh, Eternal One, king of the trees, Fortunate One! Universal Refuge, Giver of fruits!

"Let neither the thunder-bolt nor the axe, nor the wind, nor fire, nor the king, nor the furious elephant cause thy ruin.

"Eye-blinking, eye-brow-trembling, bad dreams, evil thoughts, O Fig-tree, dispel all these, whether divine or human!"

Under the reign of Sūryavarman I (1002-1049 A.D.) who, according to a Pāli chronicle,[1] was the son of the king of Śrī Dhammarāja (Ligor) and probably belonged to the Buddhist religion, as is shown by his posthumous name of Paramanirvāṇapada, the Khmers wrested from the Mons the valley of Menam. The first Khmer

1. *Cāmadevīvaṃsa*, cf *BEFEO*, XXV, pp. 23 ff.

inscriptions at Lopburi date from his reign.[1] One of them, the object of which is to lay down some rules and regulations for the temples, monasteries and hermitages, makes a distinction between the Sthaviras and the Mahāyāna Bhikṣus.[2] It is, therefore, probably on the Lower Menam that the Mahāyāna of the Khmers and the Theravāda of the Mons met. A little afterwards, the advance of the Khmers towards the North put them in contact with another race which was, in a short time, to drive them back on the Mekong and finally to wrest from them the hegemony of western Indo-china. It was the *Thai*, descended from Burma.

## IV

The first record of the introduction of Buddhism into Lower Burma is that of the Singhalese Chronicles (Dīpavaṃsa, VIII, 12, Mahāvaṃsa, XII, 6, 44) concerning the mission of the theras Soṇa and Uttara sent to Suvaṇṇa-bhūmi by the council of Pāṭaliputra during the reign of Aśoka. Admitting the historicity of this mission, it does not follow that it marks the beginning of a continued development of Buddhism in these countries. In fact, we lack information on the following centuries.[3] A flash of dim light shows us something of the religious state of Lower Burma towards the 6th century. We owe it to two documents found near Hmawza (Prome), the one is a pair of gold-leaves upon which is engraved the well-known "Thammapariyāya": *Ye dhammā* etc, followed by some other Buddhist formulas; the other is a terracotta tablet which bears a fragment of the Vibhaṅga.[4] All these texts are in Pāli and written in characters intimately connected with those which were in use in Southern India towards the 6th century of our era.

This is about the time when the study of the Pāli Piṭakas flourished in Kañcipuram (Conjeveram), under the direction of the learned commentator Dhammapāla.[5] Now, as Pegu, according to its own traditions, had a continued communication with Kañcipuram[6] it

---

1. *Ibid.*, p. 25.
2. *Aymonier, Le Cambodge*, II, p. 81.
3. Those of TARĀNĀTHA'S *Geschichte des Buddhismus*, p. 262, do not seem to have a very great value.
4. Cf. L. FINOT, *Un noveau document sur le bouddhisme Birman* (Journal Asiatique, 1912, 2, p. 121); ID. *Le plus anciens temoignage sur l' existence du canon pâli en Birmanie* (ID., 1913, 2, p. 193).
5. Ed. HARDY, *Ein Beitrag sur Frage ob Dhammapālaim Nālanda-saṅghārāma seine Commentare geschrieben* in Zeitschrift für D. Morgenl. Gesellsch., 1897, p. 126.
6. M.H. BODE, *The Pāli Literature of Burma*, p. 8.

is tempting to look to that country for the origin of the Hīnayānist school of Prome, which might have received from there through Thaton its religious culture. That school continued to prosper in the following centuries side by side with a community of Vaiṣṇavas, who has left some remarkable sculptures.[1] The exact time of the destruction of Prome is not known, but it is likely that it took place in the course of the 9th century.[2]

In 1057, Anuruddha, the king of Pagan, invaded the Delta, became master of Sudhammapura (Thaton) and brought back to his own kingdom the collection of the holy books in Pāli together with several learned monks and dethroned the sovereign. From that time, the Theravāda of Ceylon completely superseded the mighty sect of the Ari, whose cult was a mixture of serpent worship, spirit worship and Tantric Buddhism.[3] It is strange that Pegu, which was evidenty in a state of civilization more advanced than Pagan, should have left us no literary work anterior to the conquest of Anuruddha and that the first hearth of Pāli literature should have been kindled at Pagan.[4]

Thirteenth century witnesses a general advance of the Thai or Shan race, facilitated by the fall of Pagan dynasty, which followed the Chinese invasions. They overran rapidly the whole Burmese territory and passed onwards into the basin of Menam where they very soon came into conflict with the Khmers. Their first important conquest was that of Sukhodaya which was wrested from the Cambodian Governor who had charge of it—by two Thai chiefs. One of these, a vassal of Cambodia, transferred to his confederate the title of Śrī-Indrapatindrāditya, which he has received from his suzerain, and installed him as king in Sukhodaya. That event took place about 1250[5] A.D. The second successor of this king was his son Rāma Khamhéng, of whom we possess a long and curious inscription, drawn up towards the year 1292 A.D.[6] It tells us that the boundaries of his kingdom

---

1. R.C. TEMPLE, *Notes on Antiquities in Ramaññadesa,* Pl. XIII-XVI; L. de BEYLIE, *Prome and Samara,* pt. VII. p. 2,
2. M. Harvey, the last historian of Burma, places it "not long after A.D. 800" (*History of Burma*, p. 12). It can not be prior to the embassy of Piao to the court of China in 807 A.D. (PELLIOT, *Two Itineraries*, p. 163).
3. On the Ari, see the excellent memoir of Mr. Charles Duroiselle. *The Ari of Burma and Tantric Buddhism* (Arch. Survey Annual Report, 1915-16, pp. 79-93).
4. The first work is the Kārikā, a treatise on Grammer, written in 1064 A.D. by Dhammasenāpati, a Burmese of Pagan (M. H. BODE, *op. cit.*, p. 15).
5. G.COEDES, *Recueil des inscriptions du Siam. I. Inscription de Sukhodaya,* p.7
6. C.B. BRADLEY, *The Oldest known Writing in Siamese. The Inscription of Phia Rām Khamhaeng of Sukhothai* (Journal of the Siam Society, 1909); G. COEDES, op. cit., pp. 37 ff. (The extract given below is borrowed from Bradley slightly altered according to the emendations of Coedès).

extended in the North and the East, up to the Mekong, in the South, up to Ligor (Malay Peninusula) and in the west, up to Haṃsavatī (Pegu). It contains also interesting details on the state of Buddhism at Sukhodaya.

"People in this city of Sukhodaya are given to alms, are given to making offerings. Prince Rāma Khamhéng, lord of this realm of Sukhodaya, with the matrons and nobles of the city, their retinues of servants and maidens, the gentry one and all, both male and female, and the mass of common folk, have reverence for the teaching of Buddha. Every one of them keeps the precepts during the Varṣa. When Varṣa is over, there are the offerings of the Kathin for a month before they are ended. In these ceremonies, they present heaps of money, they present heaps of areca-nuts, heaps of flowers, cushions for sitting and cushions for reclining. The accessories of the Kathin which are offered each year amount to two millions. To perform these ceremonies of the Kathin, they go to the Forest-monastery yonder; and when they return to the town, the procession stretches in line from the Forest-monastery yonder unto the skirts of the plain. There everyone prostrates himself, while the air resounds with the sound of timbrels and lute, the sound of carolling and singing. Whoever likes to sport, sports; whoever likes to laugh, laughs, whoever likes to sing, sings."

"This city of Sukhodaya has four gates exceedingly great. The people throng and press each other fearfully there, when they come in to see him, (the Prince) burn candles, to see him play with fire within this city of Sukhodaya. In the midst of this city of Sukhodaya, there are temple-buildings, there are golden images of Buddha, there is one eighteen cubits high. There are images of Buddha that are great, there are images that are middle. There are temples that are great, there are temples that are middle. There are reverend monks, there are theras and mahātheras."

"Toward sunset from this city of Sukhodaya is the Forest-monastery. Prince Rāma Khamhéng made of it an offering unto Phra Mahāthera, the Saṅgharāja, the scholar who studied, the Tripiṭaka unto its end, the head of his order and above every other teacher in this realm. He came here from Śrī-Dharmarāja."

"In the midst of that Forest-monastery is a temple-building that is large, lofty and exceedingly fair. It has an eighteen-cubit image of Buddha standing erect."

From what precedes, it follows that the kingdom of Sukhodaya professed the Theravāda with Pāli as its religious language.[1]

---

1. For what follows, cf. Coedès *Inscription de Sukhodaya,* pp. 8 ff. and *Document sur la dynastie de Sukhodaya* (*BEFEO,* XVII, 2, pp. 36 ff.).

Rāma Khamhéng had as his second successor Lüthai, a cultured and learned king, author of a Buddhist Cosmology, entitled *Traibhūmi*. He ascended the throne in 1347 A.D., under the name of Dharmarāja. In 1361, he received the ordination and wore for a time the yellow robe.

At that time, in the Buddhistic world, a growing esteem was shown for the Sīhalagaṇa, a Singhalese sect,—founded in 1190 by the Talaing monk Chapaṭa—which admitted as valid only the ordinations dating back to the Mahāvihāra of Ceylon. It is under the influence of these ideas that Dharma-rāja called from Pegu the thera Sumana, disciple of the thera Udumbara, who had left Ceylon to settle in the Ramaññadeśa. The king of Nabbisipura (Chieng-ami) obtained afterwards from the king of Sukhodaya the permission that Sumana should be sent to him to restore the religion in his kingdom. Dharmarāja was a zealous follower of Buddhism, but this did not prevent him from raising, in the celebrated Mango-grove (Ambavana), by the side of the great monastery which was there (Ambavanārāma), statues of Maheśvara and Viṣṇu.

Under his successors Sukhodaya steadily declined before the growing power of the kingdom of Ayodhyā, founded in 1350, which reduced it first to a small vassal state, then, to complete subjection.

On the other hand, this new state repelled, towards the East, the Khmer kings who had to abandon their capital Angkor, probably in the course of the 15th century.[1] This event marks the disappearance of Hinduism and of Mahāyāna which had, for such a long time, reigned in Cambodia. The whole country now professes the Theravāda which the Thai influence introduced there at the end of the 13th century[2] and to which the triumph of Siam assured an uncontested hegemony.

1. *BEFEO,* XIII, 6, pp. 6 ff. and XVIII, 9. p. 27.
2. Tcheon Ta-Kouan (1296 A.D.) "The *Ch'u-Ku* shave their head..." (*BEFEO,* II, p. 148). *Ch'u-Ku*=Chan-Ku, "My lord" appellation of the monks in Siam. (ID., xviii, 9, p. 6) This precise detail shows clearly the Siamese origin of modern Buddhism in Cambodia.

## *Chapter - 40*

# Outlines of the History of Buddhism in Indo-China

**R.C. Majumdar**

In a valuable article on the above subject contributed by the distinguished Professor L. Finot in vol II of this Journal (pp. 673-689), the writer traces the existence of Buddhism in Campā up to the end of the twelfth century, and then remarks:

"Afterwards we have no more document. Nevertheless, a fragment which seems to date from the second half of the thirteenth century begins with the invocation "*oṃm namo Buddhāya*" which at least proves that Buddhism was not yet extinct in that time."

This statement must be due to an oversight on the part of the learned scholar. For the Kim Choua Inscription of Jaya Parameśvara-varman [Journal Asiatique, 1888 (1) pp. 92-93, no. 411] contains the names of Buddhist divinities such as Śrī Jina, Śrī Jina, Vṛddheśvarī, Śrī Jina Lokeśvara, Śrī Saugatadeveśvara and Śrī Jinadevadevī. The reign of Jaya Parameśvaravarman has to be placed in the second quarter of the 13th century A.D.

# Chapter - 41
# Buddhism in Ancient Kambujadesa
## (An Epigraphic Study)

**B.N. Puri**

Buddhism in ancient Kambujadeśa was characterised by two important features—its compatability with Brahmanism and its progress in the other way from Mahāyānism to Hīnayānism. In this respect it differed from Indian Buddhism which originated as a revolt against the existing socio-religious structure that recognised the hierarchy of the Brahmins, and stressed the conception of arhathood as the *summum bonum*. It is rather interesting to find that there is not a single record which could show the least sign of bitterness or antagonism between the two existing systems. On the other hand, we find Buddha being accorded a position in the Brahmanical trinity. The identification of Śaivism and Buddhism was complete and we find the trinity composed of Padmodbhava[1] (Brahmā), Ambhojanetra (Viṣṇu), and the Buddha (*Yaśca Padmodbhav = āmbhojanetra-Buddham*). One has also to commend the catholic spirit of the emperors whose personal faith in no way affected their outlook. We find that some of the prominent Buddhists in the state service shared that catholic spirit. Kavindrārimathana, who had set up a statue of Prajñāpāramitā, was above suspicion (*Buddhānām-agraṇīr api*) so far as his loyalty to the Brahmanical emperor and his state religion was concerned.

The earliest reference to Buddhism in Kambujadeśa is noticed in a record dating from the end of the sixth or the beginning of the seventh century A.D.[2] It records dedications of male and female slaves by Pon Prajñā Candra to the three Bodhisattvas, Śāstā, Maitreya and

---

1. Majumdar, *Kumbuja inscriptions,* No. 156, p. 399.
2. Aymonier, *Le Cambodge*, vol. 1, p. 442.

Avalokiteśvara. The Bodhisattvas are accorded the Khmer title *Vrah Kamratā āñ* which is also borne by the Brahmanical deities. Avalokiteśvara is not noticed in any other record, but we notice the form Lokeśvara for the first time in the Prasat Ta Kam inscription[1] dated in the Śaka year 713. Buddhism, however, appears to have been introduced earlier than the seventh century A.D., as we find in the Vat Prei inscription (Ba Phnom Dist) of Jaya-varman, dated in the Śaka year 587,[2] a reference to the two Bhikṣus Ratnabhānu and Ratna-siṁha whose sister's daughter was authorised and guaranteed the hereditary enjoyment of a religious property by king Jaya-varman in the year 587-565 A.D. There is no reference to any Brahmanical god, and the term Bhikṣu suggests that the family was Buddhist. In the Khmer text the donations by these two Bhikṣus were made in favour of *Vrāh* which is a vague term denoting Buddha, as well as Brahmanical gods, and also the King. We have, therefore, to take the character of the record from the reference to the Buddhist Bhikṣ us who are the donors.

There is no Buddhist record for a little over two hundred years, and here one has to believe the testimony of the Chinese pilgrim, I-tsing,[3] who suggests that Buddhism flourished in Fu-nan in early times but was then subverted by a wicked king whose identity is not established, but it is suggested that he might be either Bhavavarman or Ī-Śāna-varman or Jaya-varman. This state of stalemate seems to have continued. Although there is no reference to the persecution of Buddhists in Kambujadeśa, the absence of positive evidence throws some doubt on its flourishing nature. The Kok Samron inscription[4] (Siem Rap, Dist Battambang) record an invocation to Saṅgha, though Buddha and Dharma are also noticed in a subsequent verse (*namas Saṁghāya Sambuddharatnam praṇamāmi dharma*). This invocation to Saṁgha, and the reference to Buddha and Dharma reveal the Buddhist character of the record. The eulogy of King Rajendra-varman makes the record contemporary with that ruler who became king in the Śaka year 883=961 A.D. It is interesting to find that in another inscription[5] of the time of Rajendra-varman, dated in the Śaka year 883=961 A.D. from Pre Rup (Angkor region), the Yogācāra system is mentioned.

---

1. Majumdar, *op. cit.*, No. 52 A, p. 571.
2. *Ibid.*, No. 29, p. 37.
3. Takakusu, p. 12.
4. Majumdar, *op. cit.*, No. 100 E, p. 583.
5. *Ibid.*, No. 102, p. 233, v. 275

It is equally interesting to find references to other divinities of the Buddhist pantheon whose statues were set up in Kambujadeśa in that period. An inscription from Thma Puok[1] (Svay Cek in Battambang) of the time of Jaya-varman V, and dated in the Śaka Samvat 911=989 A.D. contains invocations to Buddha, Prajñāpāramitā, Lokeśvara, Vajrin, Maitreya and Indra. The six divinities were installed by the sage Padma-Vairocana and some of them may be identified with the image of the deities round the miniature temple. A little earlier in the year 903-981 A.D., an image of the mother of the Buddha was set up by Tribhuvanarāja. The inscription found at Phnom Bantay[2] (South of Angkor Bauray to the west of Battambang) invokes the Buddhist Mahāyāna divinities including Lokeśvara and Prajñā-pāramitā. Installation of the images of other Brahmanical divinities like Jagadiśvara and Trailoyanātha is also mentioned. They were set up by other members probably of the same family.

The most important record is the Phimanaka inscription[3] of Jaya-varman VII in which Trikāya, Buddha and Lokeśvara are invoked. The two queens of the emperor were Buddhist. The second one, who was the elder sister of the first one, was very learned and taught the Buddhist nuns of the convents of Nagendratuṅga, Tilakttara and Narendrāśrama. This elder sister had initiated the younger one into Buddhism during the absence of her lord and she could see his image after the performance of certain ceremony. On the return of her lord, a dramatic performance, of which the plot was drawn from the Jātakas, was made by a body of nuns recruited from cast away girls. After the death of the younger sister, the elder sister won the favour of the king who asked her to teach the Buddhist doctrines in various convents. The importance of this record lies in several ways. First, it shows that Buddhism was active in its proselytising spirit and it freely drew its members from the Brahmanical and royal families, and there were a number of convents for cast away girls. The Buddhist literature was equally popular and the Jātaka stories could form the subjects of dramatic performances so as to impress upon the masses the importance and divine character of the Buddhist Lord.

The School of the lower vehicle, namely that of Sthāviras, also flourished in Kambujadeśa, though it arrived here much later than

---

1. *Ibid.*, No. 113 A, p. 594.
2. *Ibid.*, No. 113, p. 299.
3. *Ibid.*, No. 182, p. 515.

Mahāyāna. Unfortunately, there is only one record[1] of the time of Sūrya-varman I dated in the year 944, 947 from Lopburi in the modern temple of Bang Pahin, but it was brought from Lopburi in Siam. The inscription contains an order of King Sūrya-varman laying down the regulation that in all sacred places, temples, monasteries and hermitages, the ascetics, the Sth*Ibid.*, No. 113 A, p. 594.viras (monks of the little vehicle) and monks of the Grand vehicle were required to offer to the king the merit of their austerities.

From the findspots of these records certain conclusions might be drawn. The Mahāyāna Buddhist records are found (in chronological order) in Prasat Takham (Siem Rap), Vat Prei (Ba Phnom), Kok Saman (Siem Rap), Pre Rup (Angkor region), Thma Puok (Savay Cak in Battambang), Phnom Bantay (south of Angkor) and Phimanaka (Angkor Thom). They suggest that Mahāyāna Buddhism was introduced from the north west and it came probably by the land route. The earlier wave of Hīnayānists from Ceylon seems to have come by the sea route. We learn from the Kok Svay Cek (two miles south of western Baray) inscription[2] of Śrīndra-varman that the king gave to *mahāthera* (the great monk) Sirindamoli a village, and a Vihāra was built in 1231 where an image of Buddha was installed. The king gave four villages to the monastery. This is the earliest epigraphic evidence for the introduction of Ceylonese Hīnayāna Buddhism in Kambuja. We might also consider here the evidence furnished by the Chinese sources on the state of Buddhism in ancient Fu-nan. We learn that a coral image of the Buddha was sent to the emperor Wu-ti (500-550) in 503 A.D., and the inhabitants of Fu-nan made bronze image of the heavenly genii with two or four heads and four arms. An image made of sandalwood was sent to the Chinese emperor by Liut'o-pa-mo (Rudra-varman) and in 539 he offered him a hair of the Buddha twelve feet long. The two monks who went to China to translate Chinese scriptures, namely Saṅghapāla and Mandra were also from Fu-nan. I-tsing while returning from India in 675 A.D. describes the country of Po-nan formerly called Fu-nan of which the people were originally worshippers of the devas, but later on Buddhism flourished there. A wicked king exterminated all members of the Buddhist brotherhood.[3] This suggests that Buddhism in its earlier phase flourished in the Ba Phnom region in the south-east.

1. *Ibid.*, No. 139, p. 343.
2. *Ibid.*, No. 188, p. 533.
3. Elliot, *Hinduism & Buddhism*, vol. III, p. 106.

As the Chinese evidence is earlier than the epigraphic records noticed above, it may be presumed that Buddhism came to ancient Kambujadeśa at a fairly early date, probably synchronising with the time of the second Kuṇḍinya, and it had a set back probably in the time of Bhava-varman or his successors. It, however, flourished, but from the 10th to the 13th century it was at its peak because of the patronage of the Khmer rulers like Sūrya-varman, called *Nirvāṇapada* and Jaya-varman VII who was considerably influenced by his talented sister-in-law who later on became his wife. These rulers did not alienate their devotion to the family deity, and Śaivism continued to be the state religion, despite their adherence to Buddhism. Another ruler Yaśo-varman established a Saugatāśrama like the Śaiva and Vaiṣṇava āśramas.

In the propagation of Buddhism some important state dignitaries also played a prominent part. These include Satya-varman[1] who was charged with the erection of the building known as Phimanakei, Kavindrārimathana[2] a minister under Rājendra-varman V and Jaya-varman V who erected many statues including those of Buddha, Vajrapāṇi, Prajñā-pāramita and Lokeśvara. Kīrti-Paṇḍita[3] was the minister of Jaya-varman V and it was due to his efforts that the pure doctrine of the Buddha reappeared like the moon from behind the clouds or the sun at dawn. This Kīrtipandita also introduced Buddhist books from abroad, and it is suggested that the *Śāstra Madhya Vibhāga* and the commentary on the *Tattva Saṅgraha*[4] were brought by him. These ministers were certainly Buddhists and they never let their personal religion interfere in their official duties and the state religion.

Another important point worth attention is that Buddhism was so much in line with Brahmanism that Buddha actually found a place in the Brahmanical trinity. In the Prasat Prah Khset inscription[5] of Udayārka-varman dated in the Śaka year 989 = 1067 A.D., there is a reference to the *liṅga* formerly given to king Sūryavarman by his minister Sarāma and to this were added images of Brahma, Viṣṇu, and Buddha, and the entire group called *Caturmūrti* was consecrated

1. Aymonier, vol. 1, pp. 261 ff; *Ibid.*, p. 123.
2. Majumdar, *op. cit.*, p. 331; *Ibid.*
3. Elliot, *op cit.*
4. *Ibid.*, Nanjio, Catalogue 1244, 1248.
5. Majumdar, *op. cit.*, No. 156, p. 399.

to Śiva. Buddha is associated with Rudra in another inscription. The Prah Put lo Rock inscription[1] (cave in Mt. Kulen) dated in the Śaka year 869=947 A.D. records in the Khmer text the installation of an image of Tathāgata (Buddha), Rudra and probably other gods in the holy cave. There is not the slightest doubt that Buddhism in ancient Kambujadeśa was not so violent against Brahmanism and the latter assimilated Buddha in its pantheon.

We also find charitable and missionary activities which were associated with Buddhism. Here one is reminded of the humanitarian activities of the Buddhist emperor, Aśoka. Jaya-varman VII issued an inscription from Ta Prohm near Angkor which opens with an invocation of the Buddha followed by Lokeśvara and probably Prajñā-pāramitā. It refers to an establishment with 18 principal priests (*adhi-kāriṇah*), 2740 priests and 2232 assistants and dancing girls. This record also refers to 102 hospitals in his kingdom of which a detailed description is noticed in another record[2] found a Say-Fong in Laos. It opens with an invocation to the Buddha who in his three bodies transcends the distinction between existence and non-existence, and then to the healing Buddha and the two Bodhisattvas who drive away darkness and disease. The hospitals were open to everybody without any distinction of caste.

It would, thus, appear from a study of the Kambuja records that there were probably two or three waves of Buddhist immigrants in that country, and they experienced an initial set back. From the tenth century onwards Mahāyānism flourished as an auxiliary to Brahmanism and not in a spirit of hostility. The assimilation of the Tathāgata in the Brahmanical trinity is a very important factor in the religious history of Kambuja, and it was one of the reasons for the rebuff given to Islam in Cambodia. Brahmanism did not stand in the prosperity of Buddhism and it flourished undisturbed and without any animosity from the State religion. In fact, we have cited instances of high dignitaries and even of kings patronising Buddhism. It seems that catholicity and toleration were the hallmarks in the history of Buddhism in ancient Kambujadeśa.

1. *Ibid.*, No. 90, p. 179.
2. Elliot, *op. cit.*, p. 124.

# *Chapter - 42*

# Eleven years of works on Buddhism in Europe

## (May 1936-May 1947)

**Marcelle Lalou**

### Generalities

The most general question is the one put by Jean Przyluski in *RHR*, July-August 1936, pp. 52-68, under the heading: *Y-a-t-il une science des religions?* (Is there a science of religions?) The current classification in monitheism, polyhteism, animism, hierarchy which lies on two fundamental ideas: notion of soul and notion of gods, is contestable. Numerous are the peoples who know neither soul nor god in the sense in which we take these words. Thus, in Buddhism in its ancient forms, water, subterranean world, trees, mountains, earth and atmosphere are inhabitated by numerous genii. Besides there is a pantheon of gods who are those of the old Aryan religion. Therefore, Buddhsim has inherited the Vedic polythesim and has even widened it because, in the ancient forms, there coexist a multitude of spirits scattered in the universe, a pantheon of ancient gods and the Buddha is greater than those who are new gods.

Is it animism or polytheism? Instead of choosing, the historians writing on Buddhism have declared, as they have not found either among the *devas* or among the *Buddhas* the characteristics attributed to divinity, that this religion had no god. Hence it is a religion which can be called animism, polythesim or atheism according to our point of view.

There exist three methods for explaining the resemblances of myths, symbols, and cults in the religions of different peoples, writes Maryla Falk (*Indologie auf den Wegen und Abwegen vergleichender Religionsforschung, PBO.*, 1937, pp. 18-37). These resemblances can be attributed: (1) to a primitive revelation, the same for all peoples,

(2) to the common ground of the peoples beliefs having the same ethnical origin, and finally (3) may be explained by historical influences of cultures and religions. Only the last two methods are scientific and the author opposes Coomaraswamy's interpretations particularly in his *Elements of Buddhist Iconography,* which constitute an evident return to the first method. The ideas of this last work, which affirms that Buddhism presents exactly the same truth as the Vedas and the Brahmanism, that the Buddha is nothing but the new form of Agni of Brahmā-Prajāpati and that the *dharmacakra-pravartana* is noting but the cretion of the world, is to be rejected.

In three articles (*New Contributions to the problem of the prehīnayānistic Buddhism, PBO.*, 1937, pp. 8-17; *Mit, Kult i etyka buddyzmu, Przeglad Wspolczesny,* 65, Cracovic, 1938, pp. 31-2), St. Schayet has indicated the main lines of his most recent ideas on the evolution of Buddhism, then he has developed them in the collective volume published at Warsaw under the heading *Les Religions de l' Orient* (The Religions of the Orient) (*Religie Wschodu,* Biblioteka Wicdzy, Trzaska, Evert i Michalski, Varsovie, 1938, 460 pp. 44 ill.). First he refutes the theories of Oldenberg, Geiger, Winternitz and Stcherbatsky who identify the Pāli tradition with the very doctrine of Buddha. Buddhism has never been a simple, moral doctrine, but was from its beginning a religion with its myth, its cult and its doctrine of salvation. The Mahāyāna is not posterior to the Hīnayāna and is connected directly with primitive Buddhism the fundamental dogmas of which seem to be: belief in metempsychosis; a cosmology distinguishing three spheres (*kāma, rūpa* and *arūpadhātu*); analysis of the human person into material elements: earth, water, air, fire, ether and a psychical element, *vijñāna;* conception of the salvation constituting the passage from the *rūpa* to the *arūpadhātū*, from the of perishable elements (*rūpa*) to that of the eternal *dharma*; a supreme aim to attain, the *acyuta-pada,* a summit from which there is no return to the *saṃsāra*; a doctrine of the *karma* which loses the automatic and magic character which it has in Brahmanism and identifies the *karma* no more with the act, but with the intention (however, like the *kleśa*, the *karma* is "physically" conceived as one of the substances that soil or purify the soul); method leading to slavation based on the moral discipline (*śīla*) and practice of the yoga (which is anterior to Buddhism as well as Brāhmanism, and which is probably pre-Aryan). The essential and the most original point of this statement relates to the belief in Buddha. Never Buddhism would have become a religion had there been no dogma of Buddha, of a perfect and superhuman Being who, if he is neither the creator of the world nor the power that directs the fate of men, is however endowed with all other attributes of divinity. The dogma of Buddha presupposes two beliefs: (1) existence of supernatural beings appearing at intervals of many thousands of years to show the path of salvation; (2) Gautama, of Śākya's tribe has been such a being. The term *tathāgata* which designates this supernatural being has certainly not been created by Buddhism, but must have already been known in the 5th century B.C. in N.E. India. Gautama by declaring that he is the Tathāgata, thus assigned to himself the dignity of Saviour. The term *tathāgata* is as much pre-Buddhistic as the term *Messie* is pre-Christian.

On the other hand, the theories of *nirvāṇa,* of *anityatā,* of *anātmavāda* seem to have been unknown to primitive Buddhism. They appear only in the Hīnayāna, in the doctrine which has evolved from the time when the distinction between monks living in monasteries and laymen has been created. This doctrine which has for ideal the state of Arhat, is born in the solitude of meditations and inspite of a-personalism with which it makes one of the bases of the Law, ends in a sort of soteriological egoism. Everybody can attain only his own salvation. The extension of the idea of impermanence to all the elements of reality (in primitive Buddhism only the elements *rupa* were considered as impermanent), the negation of the permanent soul which logically proceeds from it, the theory of *dharma* and of isolated *santāna* etc., are only the philosophical consequences of that monachal egoism.

The Mahāyāna is not an evolution of the Hīnayāna, but is connected to Buddhism of laymen who have not accepted the monachal exclusivism. It develops the doctrine of solidarity of all beings, which ends in the dogma of Bodhisattva, the perfect saint who renounces his *nirvāṇa* to bring salvation to the world. Then the author rapidly reviews the philosophical consequences of this attitude to devote more place for pure religious facts: creation of a new pantheon of Buddha, Bodhisattva, Dhyāni-Buddha, which is not the deification of saints, but which continues the mythological beliefs always vivid among the laymen and gives only a new form to ancient cults. The Mahāyāna, however, avoids the polytheism by admitting the dogma of Buddha's body (*dharmakāya*) of which the Buddhas are only hypostases. The distinction between *dharmakāya* and *rūpakāya* does revive the ancient distinction between *dharma* and *rūpa* of primitive Buddhism.

The statement ends with a brief description of Tantrism and with the analysis of the doctrine of plurality of truths which allows Buddhism to become a universal religion.

In *La délivrance aprés la mort dans les Upaniṣad et dans le bouddhisme primitif* (The deliverance after death in the Upaniṣads and in primitive Buddhism), J. Przyluski distinguishes four periods in the religious history of India: (1) sacrificial religions and, in the non-Aryan religions, doctrine of transmigration, (2) aristocratic religion in which the sacrifices of horses play an important rôle; immoratlity and ascension to heaven are assured only to some privileged beings; cosmic myths and solar myths; (3) immortality is no more the prerogative of someone, knowledge and faith enable a few to reach the world of Brahmā, the farthest realm in heaven (epoch of the most ancient Upaniṣad and primitve Buddhism); (4) the deliverance can be obtained during this life and the *nirvāṇa* is transformed into a state of soul. The way of obtaining the deliverance, according to some very ancient texts, is the practice of the *brahmavihāras* which appear to be of non-Aryan origin. (I. *Die Erlösung nach dem Tode in den Upanishaden und im ursprünglichen Buddhismus*. II. *Der Lebendig-Erlöste in dem entwickelten Buddhismus*. Eranos-Jahrbuch 1937, Rhein-Verlag, Zurich, 1938, pp. 93-136).

The same author and M. Falk recall that before the Buddhist influence, China, has elaborated a cosmo-physiology where microcosm and macrocosm are constructed on the same plan, where are put into correspondence the elements, the religions of the space, the colours, the organs, etc..., a system which has analogies with the conceptions which have been perpetuated in India from Atharva-Veda to Tantrism after passing through the Upaniṣad (*Aspects d'une ancienne-psycho-physiologie dans l'Inde et en Extréme-Orients, BSOS.*, 1938 pp. 723-8).

Criticising Stcherbatsky's theories and Mrs. Rhys David's theory. J. Przyluski shows that the theory of the *skandha* cannot be accepted as an element of ancient Buddhism and still less as the pivot of the whole doctrine. Indeed, three currents are to be distinguished: Man has been considered (1) as a plurality of centralized organs, (2) as a plurality of hierarchical organs, (3) as a couple of opposite elements because the same word (*rūpa*, for example) takes different meaning in the three systems. By analysing the theory of the *skandhas* and that of *smṛtyupasthānas*, one notices the interference of the three systems, specially of the second and third (*La théorie des skandha. Contribution à l'histoire du Budhhisme ancien, RO,* XIV, 1938, pp. 1-8).

M. Falk already finds the conception of *nāma-rūpa* in the Vedic myth of *puruṣa* who has been divided into a male being (*puruṣa* = *rūpa*) and a feminine hypostasis (*Vāc* = *nāma*). The speculation of *Upaniṣ-*

*ads* develops this mythical conception. The two primordial elements are different from each other and their first nature is obscured by the pluality of their manifestations. But the *ātman* continues the idea of the *puruṣa=rūpa* and the *brahman* represents that of *Vāc=nāma*. In the *Kaṭha-upaniṣad* and in the *Bhagavadgītā*, appears the equation *dharma=brahman*. This explains that in primitive Buddhism, the binomial *dharma-rūpa* corresponds to the Brāhmanic binomial *nāma-rūpa* (*Nāma-rūpa i dharma-rūpa. Zrodla i dzieje staroindyjskiej koncepcji (Nāma-rūpa et dharma-rūpa. Sources et histoire d' une conception indienne)*. Comptes rendus de l'Acad. polonaise des Science et Lettres, fév. 1938, No. 2, pp. 35-40). This article has been developed in a book bearing the same title and published in India.

The notion of Time in the Indian philosophy is analysed by St. Schayer in his *Contributions to the problem of Time in Indian Philosophy* (Cracovie, 1938, 76 pp.) which develops his communication to the 20th International Congress of Orientalists (summarized in *RCCIO.*, 1938, p. 40). The Time, or rather the year (*saṃvatsara*), is a mythological notion, entity engendered by the Androgynous Anthropos. The successive hypostases of the Time are: Prajāpati in the Brāhmaṇa, Amitāyus in Buddhism, and, in Hinduism, Kāla identified sometimes with Śiva, sometimes with Viṣṇu. In all the ancient systems, the Time is a very subtle, omnipresent, eternal substance, one and indivisible but physical. Such is the theory of the Mīmāṃsakas, of the Vaiśeṣika and part of a school of Vedānta. Past, present and future are but three "portions" of the homogeneous Time. This realistic analysis of Time is resumed by the *traikālyavāda* of the Vaibhāṣikas. Here, the hyopostasis of Time-substance is replaced by that of the existence's real phases of a *dharma*. This system is discussed in detail and the author seeks to elucidate, on the basis of the *Mahāvibhāṣā* and of the *Nyāyānuśāraśāstra*, certain problems left without explanation in the *Abhidharmakośa*.

This is to be compared with the *Abhidharma Documents, The Controversy of Time,* long notice published by La Vallée Poussin in *MCB.*, 1937, pp. 7-168, and the article by P. Mus: *La notion de temps réversible dans la mythologic bouddhique* (*AESHR.*, 1938-39, pp. 5-38). The latter author shows that ancient Buddhism established its doctrine of salvation on the contrast of two eschatologies: the circle of transmigration, the dive in the *nirvāṇa* which is the "Issue". Both of them escape our habitual representation of the "evolutive" time. It is only with the beginning of the Mahāyāna mythological Buddhism which begins, with Amitāyus, "Buddha with infinite age", a chronological primate, still deified in a later period by the Tantras, under the features of Mahākāla, "the Universal Time."

L. de La Vallée Poussin studies (according to the *Vibhāṣa,* the *Kośa* and Saṃghabhadra) four holy truths in relation with the apparent truth (*saṃvṛtisatya*) and the absolute truth (*paramārthasatya*), but the apparent truth is contained in the absoulte truth because nothing of what is void of *paramātha* can be called truth. Therefore there is only one truth and not a second one (*Documents d'Abhidharma. Les deux, les quatre, les trois Vérités. MCB.*, 1937, pp. 159-87). Then returning to his researches on the *Nirvāṇa,* he discerns in the Buddhistic sources, ancient or scholastic, two opposed moral tendencies: the intellectualist granting a place of choice to intelligence or *prajñā;* the mystic preferring above all calmness, concentration or *samādhi*. It is the eternal divergency between speculatives and ecstatics. In the school of the Sarvastivādin-Vaibhāṣika which combines *prajñā* and *samādhi* giving however preference to *prajñā* the two points of view are reconciled and it proposes two paths of *nirvāṇa* completing each other: the vision (*darśanamārga*) and the meditation (*bhāvanāmārga*); it subordinates *samādhi* and *prajñā* by making of the concentration the condition *sine qua non* of the exact knowledge. For Harivarman, the ecstasies are not necessary, the reason only leads to the vision of truths; he ignores the mystic of *nirvāṇa* and denies to the latter all objective reality considering it simply as the destruction of *dharmas*. However certain texts of Abhidharma, in Sanskrit and Pāli, and a few non-canonical works show the existence of a purely mystical Buddhsim where intelligence plays only a secondary rôle. The proposed ideal is the obtainment of the *nirodhasamāpatti*: supreme contemplation during which, devoid of consciousness and sensations, the saint gets into contact with the mystical entity *Nirvāṇa (Mūsila et Narada, Le Chemin du Nirvāṇa, MCB.*, 1937, pp. 189-222.

H. von Glasenapp, in many publications has studied the dharma theory. He finds its origin, as well as that of the doctrine of the *anātman* in the conceptions reflected in the Vedic texts up to the most ancient Upaniṣads, and also in the most ancient parts of the Pāli Canon. More abstract than the Jaina theory of the *karma-prakṛti,* both of them go back to the Vedic conceptions of fluids, powers or substances that fill the world and penetrate into men (*Zur Geschichte der buddhistischen Dharma-theorie, ZDMG.*, 1938, pp. 383-420; *Der Ursprung der buddhistischen Dharma-Theorie, ZDMG.*, 1939, pp. 242-66 and *Actes du XXe Congr. Intern. des Orientatlistes,* 1940, pp. 216-7, and *WZKM.*, 1939, PP. 242-66; *Entwicklungestufen des indischen Denkens.*

*Untersuchungen über die Philosophie der Brahmanen und Buddhisten*, Halle, 1940, 169 pp.)

In a voluminous book of 679 pages, J.C. Jenninghs has published a collection of historical texts translated from the Pālio originals to construct *The Vedāntic Buddhism of the Buddha* (London, Oxford Univ. Press, 1947). His arguments to support his Vedāntic and Stoic Buddhism raise internal as well as external criticism. He notices that, in his instructions to the first missionaries, Buddha speaks neither of new births nor of the personal act. To establish that Śākyamuni did not believe in the transmigration, the author has recourse to some purely logical arguments. Buddha has denied the existence of separate souls, now where there is no durable Self, there can be no transmigration of soul to a new body. The reasoning may appear irrefutable to our occidental logic. But the *ātman* of which Buddha denies the existence does not correspond exactly to our Aristotalian concept: it is not a *Soul,* it is a *Self.* Though being a susbsisting, eternal and immutable principle, it opposes itself diametrically to Becoming, to *Saṃsāra*. For the Hindus, the notions of *Ātman* and of *Saṃsāra* are contradictory. That is why the Upaniṣads and the Vedānta, which admit the existence of the *ātman* are brought to deny the reality of the worlds of the transmigration and to reject it in the realm of illusion or *māyā*. Inversely, Buddha who admits the reality of *saṃsāra* and the Law of production in dependence (*pratītyasamutpāda*) must deny the existence of an *ātman* which if immutable would have withdrawn from transmigration; that is why he imagined the painful and impersonal *skandha*, but capable of being carried away by act and passion in the cycle of Re-births. We do not believe in the Vedic and Stoic character of Śākyamuni's message says E. Lamotte who has written a long report on the work in *Art. As.* (X. 2, pp. 160-4). However, while according a place of choice to virtues of benevolence (*maitrī*) and pity (*karuṇā*), the primitive Buddhism was not at all devoid of altruistic tendencies.

C.G. Jung, in a psychological analysis of Buddhistic meditation, underlines that for the Indians, the reality resides not in the sensorial world, but in the internal experience. Contrary to the religious tendencies of the West the aim of which is the act, the Indian religions aspire at an inactive and unconscious psychical state which is considered as the supreme form of conscienciousness. The author seeks to explain from the psycho-analytical view the choice of the "subjects of meditation" and points out some striking coincidences between the methods of *dhyāna* and those of psycho-analysis. The subtle difference, but very important, which is observed between the Christian and the Buddhist having attained the summit of meditation is explained by the fact that Christian psychology is deeply attached to the conscience of "ego", whereas the oriental experience lies still on the stratum of the collective subconscious state (*Zur Psychologie östlicher Meditation*, *BSSAEO.*, *v*, 1943, pp. 33-53).

E. Abegg studies the whole outlook of Indian ideas on soul and its functions and presents a detailed analysis of Buddhist psychology, trying to sketch out its history (*Indische Psychologie*, Zürich, 1945, 133 pp.)

**Courses of Indo-Greco-Iranian Exchanges**

J. Przyluski in *Mani et Plotin* (*BCL.*, *XIX*, 1933, PP. 322-6) has shown that the Indian asceticism colours the religion of Mani and the philosophy of Plotin and when the latter thinks of establishing in Campania a city of sages, the new ideal which appears in his doctrine is well explained if a Buddhistic factor is intervened. Then he has shown that to the three Bodies of Buddha according to the Mahāyānic theory correspond the three Hypostases in the system of Plotin the statement of which clarifies some difficult points of the Buddhistic doctrine (*Les Trois hypostases dans l'Inde et à Alexandrie*, Bruxelles, 1935). In *Les sept puissances divines on Grèce,* he points out the analogies between the doctrine of Ajita Keśakamablain, contemporary of Buddha according to the Vinaya of the Mūlasarvāstivādins, and the system of Empédocle (*RHPR.*, s. d., pp. 255-62).

H. de Lubac, in *Texts alexandrins et bouddhiques* (*RSR.*, 1937, XXVII, pp.336-51), studies many original texts and finds in them the evidence of an anterior theory which offers a curious similarity with the Buddhist theory.

J. Filliozat identifies the doctrines described by St. Hippolyte with those of the Upaniṣads, specially of the *Maitrī Upaniṣad* and he gives some indications on the propagation in Occident, in the first centuries of our era, of the knowledge of Buddhist and at the same time Brāhmanic doctrine (*La doctrine des brāhmanes d'après Saint Hippolyte, RHR.*, 1945, pp. 59-91).

P. Demiéville, starting from a doctrinal stanza pronounced by Chen-sieou (606-706) and reproduced in the introduction of the *Sūtra de l'Estrade* (T'an-king) follows in the Chinese, Indian, Buddhist, Hellenic and Christian literatures the metaphor that presents mind as a mirror reflecting the divine knowledge (*Sinologica*, I, 2; Bâle, 1947).

In *Les sept pusissances divines dans l'Inde et en Iran* (*RHPR.*, s.d., pp. 500-7), J. Przyluski shows that the comparison of the series of divine powers according to Herodotus, the *Chādogya-upaniṣad,* the *Bṛhadāraṇyaka-upaniṣad* and the Buddhist *Mahāsamaya* indicates the changes undergone by the two Upaniṣads and the agreement of the *Mahāsamaya* and Iranian notions. After the period when the series of Herodotus corresponds to that of *Mahāsamaya*, the heptad is transformed. The plurality of elements stands more and more in the way of unique principle: Fire, *brahman*, Space or unlimited Time. Then he replaces in the cadre of the ethnical, economical and political realities the great theses of the Indian and Iranian philosophy. what is properly Indian or Iranian, is not such cultural elements, but the manner with which those elements are grouped to form an organic whole (*Les rapports entre l'Inde et l'lran depuis l'époque védique, RHR.*, 1940, pp. 5-24). The same author, changing the orientation of his researches, resumes the hypothesis that the Śākyas of the Himālaya bear a name akin to that of the Śakas or Scythians. He shows that, in the Indian tradition, the Śākyas of the Himālaya have ethnical affinities with different peoples living south of Pamir. Buddha being a Śākya, if the Śākyas are Scythians, one must admit that a Scythian invasion took place in India in the llth cent. B.C. at the lastest—nearly at the time of their expansion towards Iran, Crimea, and the valley of the Danube (*Nowveaux Aspects de l'Histoire des Scythes, RUB.*, 1937, pp. 1-30.

## Myths, Cults, Legends, Faiths

Faiths relating to Maitreya in Sérindia are studied by W. Baruch who follows them in the images, formularies and inscriptions of donation, Manichaean, Ouigour and Khotanese texts (*RHR.*, CXXXII, July-Dec, 1946, pp. 67-92).

E. Abegg who had written in 1928 *Der Messiasglanbe in Indien und Iran*, where he supported that the Indian Messianism is independent of the Iranian eschatology, exposes the evolution of the prophesies on future Buddha, in the Indian and emigrated literature. He underlines the association of this mythical personage with the idea of the *maitrī*, but, faithful to his theory, opposes the hypothesis of the Iranian origin of the myth, because it already appears in the most ancient strata of Buddhism (*Der Buddha Maitreya, BSSAEO.*, VII, 1945, PP. 7-37).

J. Przyluski and M. Lalou have published, in collaboration, three articles. One describes the evolution of faiths relative to the "Son of Brahma" the lists of which from the *Mahābhārata, Mahāsamayasutta* and its Tibetan and Chinese versions, from *Mahāgovinda*° and *Janavasabhasutta*, show a tendency to make into a hierarchy some forms less and less subtle. The Tibetan versions, reflect originals better preserved than the Pāli manuscripts; particularly, they introduce Hārītī in the old Buddhistic pantheon (*Notes de Mythologie Bouddhique. Les fils de Brahmā, HJAS.*, 1939, pp. 69-76). In other notes of mythology (*Yakṣa et Gandharva dans le Mahāsamayasuttanta, HJAS.*, 1938, pp. 40-6), the authors had compared a passage similar in the *Mahāsamaya* and its Tibetan versions, the *Āṭānāṭiya* and the *Mahāmāyūrī*, a passage which is the evidence of an ancient mythology where Vedic gods, *Yakṣa* and *Gandharva* were confused. Later on the classification becomes more and more precise, four groups of Genii are subdued to four Guardian Kings of the Quarters of Space, but one finds often, the archaic list subsisting side by side with the canonical classification. In the restitution of names of genii, preference goes to the non-Pāli tradition. Finally, the *Récits populaires et contes bouddhiques* (*JA.*, 1936, pp. 177-91) show that the study of Buddhist tales, popular stories for a long time orally transmitted before being fixed, could not be done according to the habitual processes of the literary criticism. The comparison and analysis of four tales common to the *Avadāna-śataka* and to the *Karma-śataka* show the principles which have guided the elaboration of Buddhistic tales: (1) purification of popular stories containing immoral elements (here, marriage between brother and sister): expurgation and addition of a morality; (2) transfer of certain motives of a tale to another, by analogy; (3) respect of disciplinary rules: modifications are made to obtain stories corresponding to the rules of Vinaya. On his side, J. Przyluski compares *gandharva* with *gardabha* and recalls the rôle played by the *gandharva* in the Buddhist theory of reincarnation (*Asses, Horses and Gandharvas, IC.*, III, 4, pp. 613-20); he points out that the Sanskrit *devamanuṣya* and Pāli *devamanussa* must not be rendered by "men and gods," but by "men-gods". The notion is not specifically Buddhistic; it exists simultaneously with that of the *Vidyādharas* of Brāhmaṇical literature and its diffusion is explained by the increasing importance of the magic in the first centuries of our era (*JA.*, 1938, pp. 123-8). At last, in *Inara and Indra* (*RHA.*, 1939, pp. 142-6) he exposes a Vedic myth showing Indra living among the Asuras in a female form among women and in a male form among men, and he points out a series of equivalent bisexual divinities of the Great Goddess.

The Chinese form of Avalokiteśvara (Kouan-yin) is also subject to a change of sex. E. Erkes resumes the obscure question of the date of this change and, according to Eberhard who has found in a text of 817 the mention of female Kouan-yin, he makes this date go back beyond the traditional Xth cent. On the other hand, always according to Eberhard, the change of sex of Avalokiteśvara would proceed from his identification with a goddess of the sailors who is still venerated to-day on the south-east coast of China. At last, a figurine of Kouan-yin, dated 556 and coming from North China, show some feminie peculiarities in its coiffure and mantle. Let us note that it does not concern Kouan-yin "with children", the only aspect considered to-day as an unequivocal feminine appearance, but of an isolated divinity, whose ambiguous sex appears already in North China in 556 (E. Erkes: *Zum Problem der veriblichen Kuanyin, Art. As.*, 1946, pp. 316-21).

M. Lalou studies the epic and Buddhist forms of the god Vaiśravana who is also Androgynous, and compares his aspect of god of Treasures with that of Gaṇeśa. The research is called forth and helped by some images found in Touen-houang (*Mythologic indienne et peintures de Haute-Asie.* I. *Le dieu bouddhique de la Fortune, Art. As.*, 1946, pp. 97-111 et *JA.*, 1937, pp. 301-2). It is also mythology subject in the *Rgyud Sumpa* and the *Lha klu chen-po thams-cad spyan-draṅ-pa,* mss. of Touen-houang, which the same author has edited and translated (*Notes de mythologie bouddhique,* 2, *HJAS.*, 1938, pp. 126-36).

The cosmogony has been studied by H. Günther (*Die buddhistische Kosmognie, ZDMG.*, 1944, PP. 44-83) according to the passage of the *Aggaññasutta* which describes the apparition of men on the earth. The author seeks to show that, in its essential features, the Buddhist cosmology continues the speculation of the Upaniṣads.

Lin Li-kouang has edited the Sanskrit, Tibetan and Chinese texts of the *Dharmasamuccaya* and gives a French translation of it. The first volume (Annales du Musée Guimet, tome 53, 292 pp., Paris, 1946) contains the first five chapters.

In *La Lumière sur les Six Voies. Tableau de la transmigration bouddhique d'après les sources sanskrites, pāli, tibétaines et chinoises en majeure partie inédites* (Paris, 1939, 330 pp.), P. Mus deals on the one hand with the Buddhist hells and, on the other hand, writes the history of the *Saḍgatikārikā,* which alludes to the cycle of the Apocrypha and to the Sanskrit tradition of Abhidharma. These *ṣaḍgati*° are attributed to Dhārmika Subhuti by Vasubandhu, and only some very late traditions, admitted nevertheless by Sylvain Lévi have claimed to confuse him with Aśvaghoṣa. The intervention of the Burmese Pāli scriptures regarding a *Lokapaññati,* causes P. Mus to show that this *Lokapaññati* is nearer to the Sanskrit tradition than to the Pāli valgate, which seems less strange if one remembers the relations between the

Magadhan Buddhism and the Burmese Buddhism already attested by the archacology. The whole study of the Abhidharma Sarvāstivādin will have to be taken up again in the light of Pāli Burmese. The Burmese documents are precious, not only for the exegesis of the texts and the study of the doctrines, but also for the literal criticism of the Buddhist Sanskrit badly fixed, badly preserved.

According to P. Mus, the early Buddhist art which "substitutes" in the representation of Buddha that of the places he sanctified by his visit is a survival of the primitive "participation". The symbols do not take the place of the Buddha, they *are* Buddha (*La mythologie primitive et la pensée de l'Inde, BSFP.*, pp. 84-126).

The problem of the representation of the holy place is resumed by Jean Przyluski in *La Participation* (Presses Universitaires de France, Paris, 1940, 167 pp.). The same author, by studying *Le Culte de l'étendard chez les Scythes et dans l'Inde* (*Zalmoxis*, 1938, pp. 13-9), points out the mixture of two religious notions: fixed column or mobile standard, carrying each a sacred emblem. He compares the finds made at Doura-Europos relating to the cult of the standard with this cult in ancient India according to the *Cakkavatti-sīhanādasuttanta* and shows the duality of the fixed and pacific god (stone column of the sedentaries) and of the ambulant and warlike god (standard of the nomades).

*The Stūpa.* P. Mus has grouped under a separate title the studies on the Bārābuḍur (analysed in *BIbl. B.* VI, 548; VII-VIII, 810) by adding a preface of 300 pp. Always in connection with the Javanese monument, he deals with the genesis of the Mahāyāna Buddhology, the origin of five Jinas who are hypostases of Śākyamuni. The aspect, the name, the emblem and the activity of each of the Jinas characterised an episode of the career of Śākyamuni: Vairocana, the first preaching at Benares and the four other Jinas, the four weeks following the Bodhi. From Benares, Śākyamuni-Vairocana dominates the symbolic square gathered around the Bodhi tree. The transcendent Buddha has created with his own body, by a mythical segmentation, the innumerable Tathāgatas, and the latter are grouped into a single one when a Buddha, appears on the Earth and preaches the Mahāyāna. This magical dispersion of Prajāpati in the person of gods of the world and his reconstruction in that of Agni identified with the complete circle of the regents of the Orients. The Mahāyāna central Buddha tends to follow the model of the Creator God of the Brāhmaṇas. It is to Brahmā Prajāpati, not to Viṣṇu, that Buddha owes his first attributes of the Lord of the Universe. The three bodies of the Buddha are considered as intermediary between Buddha and men.

On the other hand, J. Prezyluski has noted, according to the conceptions of the *Kāraṇḍavyūha,* that the seven terraces of the Bārābuḍur correspond to the seven (later on ten) steps in the career of the Mahāyānist saint. He notes also that the round terraces of the Bārābuḍur begin with the fifth storey, which agrees well with the description of the fifth earth in the *Akṣyupaniṣad (Les sept terrasses du Barabuḍur, HJAS.*, 1936, pp. 251-6). But it is difficult to consider the Bārābuḍur, which is a reduction of the cosmic mountain surmounted by 73 stūpas, simply as a stūpa. It is a construction that seals up the mystical union of the empire and the universe (*The terminal stūpa of the Bārābuḍur, JGIS.*, 1936, pp. 158-69).

G. Combaz offers a general view of *The Evolution of the Stūpa in Asia (Les symbolismes du stūpa, MCB.*, 1936, 125 pp. 49 fig.) and J. Buhot in *Notes d' Architecture bouddhique* studies the transformation of the hemispheric stūpa into a high square or octagonal tower transformation that he explains by the existence of a wooden revetment destined to protect the most venerated stūpas of India and which was soon considered as equivalent to the monument itself. As to the origin of the pagodas on hexagonal plan he thinks that it comes from a false interpretation of a model on square plan. (*RAA.*, XI, 4, 1937 and XIII, 1939-1942).

At last, in an article bringing together informations from the *Dulva* translated by M. Lalou, and remarks of Wogihara, L. de La Vallée Poussin studies the composing parts of the stūpa, their cult and the funeral usages (*Staupikam, HJAS.*, 1937, pp. 276-89).

W. Zinkgraff has studied the *Divyāvadāna (Vom Divyāvadāna zur Avadānakalpalatā*, Heidelberg, 1940) specially the *Śādūlakarṇāvadāna* and the *Padmaka*°. E.J. Thomas (*BSOAS.*, X, 3, 1940, pp. 654-6) corrects a passage of the Mākandika history (*Divyā*°, p. 579). Though the work has appeared in America, it is useful to compare with these two studies on the *Divyāvadāna,* the work of K.K.S Ch'en on the *Svāgatāvadāna* wherein is translated the Chinese version and wherein are discusseed the problems raised by the other texts (*A Study of the Svāgata Story in the Divyāvadāna and its Sanskrit, Pāli, Tibetan and Chinese Versions, HJAS.*, 9 fev, 1947, pp. 207-314).

Dschi Hian-lin has translated (*ZDMG.*, 97, 1943, pp. 284-324) seven stories of the *Mahāvastu* and to the Chinese Canon related to the Tokharian recension of the *Puṇyavantajātaka,* text edited and translated by G.S. Lane (*JAOS.*, 67, March 1947, pp. 33-53).

## Doctrines

K. Régamey inaugurating the *Publications of the Oriental Commission of the Warsaw Society of Sciences and Letters,* has edited, translated and commented upon the Chapters VIII, XIX, and XXII of the *Samādhirājasūtra (Three Chapters from the Samādhi°*, Warsaw, 1938) according to a manuscript of the Bibliothègue Nationale de Paris and the Chinese and Tibetan versions. It deals about a work preliminary to the complete edition of the *Samādhi°* planned by Schayer and Régamey. War and death of Schayer have delayed this publication for which the recent Gilgit finds will bring some precious elements of comparison.

The same author has published the Tibetan text of the *Bhadramāyākāravyākaraṇa*, accompanied with an introduction and an annotated translation. It is one of the small *sūtras* of the *Ratnakūṭa*, part of a series that Régamey intends to disclose to us. The original text is lost; two Chinese versions of which one goes back to the IIIrd-IVth century and a Tibetan translation and fragments of a Śaka paraphrase edited by Leumann are left (*Bibl. B* VI-VIII, 103). The central theme of the story is the legend of the magician Bhadra who, to compromise Buddha, invites him to a feast that he creates by magic on a heap of ordure (sweepings). Buddha omniscient foresees the trap. He accepts the invitation and by the power of his magic he subdues Bhadra by preventing him from destroying the illusory feast. Thereafter he preaches on the universal magic. Some reminiscences of the legend are found in the Dhammapada commentary, but it is only in the *Bhadramāyākāra°* that it serves as a point of departure for the development of the doctrinal theses. The quality of these two works makes us greatly regret their almost complete destruction during the Warsaw fires. Their author at least was saved and has been able to resume his scientific activity in the Universities of Lausanne and Fribourg.

When Régamey explains the method to be followed to edit the texts the original of which is lost, he considers that the restitution of the original text is practically impossible and that the method to be followed is (i) to edit all the versions (except the Chinese if it is already edited in *Taishō*), and (ii) to make a critical translation according to all the known versions, by mentioning all the variants, even the evident mistranslations to present the whole of the data, Sten Konow, on the other hand, has reconstructed the two first chapters of the *Daśasāhasrikā Prajñāpāramitā* in Sanskrit (Oslo, 1941), and compares the data that they provide on the *dharmas*, from which a Bodhisattva must be detached, with the lists of other Prajñāpāramitās, the *Dharmasaṃgraha*, the *Mahavyutpatti*, the Pāli Canon, the *Mahāvastu*, the *Lalitavistara*, etc.

The fragments of the *Saddharmapuṇḍarīka* found at Gilgit have been utilized by W. Baruch in *Beiträge zum Saddharmapuṇḍarīkasūtra*, Leyde, 1938, 100 pp., when he compares the Nepalese manuscripts, those fragments of Gilgit and the Chinese translations.

G. Tucci has discovered in 1939 in a monastery at La-lu, a short manuscript on palm leaves of a summary of the *Aṣṭasāhasrikāprajñāpāramitā* bearing the heading of *Prajñāpāramitāpiṇḍārtha* of Diṅnāga. He publishes it and translates it (*Minor Sanskrit Texts on the Prajnāpāramitā*, I. *The Prajñā-pāramita-piṇḍārtha of Diṅnāga, JRAS.*, Ap. 1947, pp. 53-75) and shows that Nanjio, followed by Bagchi, restores a title *Buddha-mātṛka-prajñāpāramitā-saṅgīti-śāstra* and mentions Nāgārjuna as author whilst the *Hōbōgirin* and the *Catalogue Tōhoku*, which restore a title *Ārya-prajñāpāramitā-saṃgraha-kārikā,* mention Diṅnāga as author. The document deals with "sixteen insubstantialities" and "ten distractions".

E. Obermiller has published at Moscow, in 1937 (*BB*, XIX, 125 pp.) the Sanskrit and Tibetan texts of the *Prajñā-pāramitā-ratna-guṇa-sañcaya-gāthā*.

A. Ferrari has published and translated the Sanskrit text of the *Arthaviniścaya*. She has filled up its gaps with the Tibetan version and has compared the Chinese version of Fa-hien and of Kin-tsun-che (Roma, Reale Accademia d'Italia, 1944). Then, in 1946, she published the edition and the translation of the Sanskrit text of the *Pāramitāsamāsa* of Āryaśūra, according to a manuscript preserved in the library of the Mahārāja of Nepāl, with the variants of the Tibetan version (Il *"Compendio delle Perfezioni" di Āryśūra,* Annali Lateranenso, X, Città del Vaticano).

E. Lamotte has published in eight years, three important works:

1. *Le Traité de l'acte de Vasubandhu* (*Karmasiddhiprakaraṇam*). Edition of the Tibetan version and French translation. Though the Tibetan and Chinese traditions place this treatise in the *śāstras* of the Great Vehicle, E. Lamotte regards the work as that of a Sautrāntika, because the author accepts the reality of exterior things, specially of *rūpa*, and his psychology of the *ālaya* has nothing in common with the idealistic system of the Vijñaptimātra. The translation of Chap. XVII of the *Madhyamakavṛtti* of Nāgārjuna and Candrakīrti shows how these authors refute the system of the Sautrāntika and of the

Sāṃmitiya and establish the position of the Mādhyamika on the non-existence of act, passion, body and "enjoyers", while recognizing a practical efficacy in the non-substantial act.

2. *La Somme du grand Véhicule d' Asaṅga (Mahāyānasaṃgraha), Tome I: Versions tibétaines et chinoise (Hiuan-tsang); Tome II: Traduction et Commentaire.* It is a critical edition of the Tibetan based on the comparison of the Tibetan version with the four Chinese versions of Buddhaśānta, Paramārtha, Dharmagupta and Hiuan-tsang. The Tibetan version is the base of the French translation and is accompanied with a continued series of explanations borrowed from the Indian commentaries. The first two chapters of the *Mahāyāna*°, published and translated, deal respectively with the *ālayavijñāna* and the *dharmalakṣaṇa*. There is still to be published the Vol. III: Sanskrit, Tibetan and Chinese Index, and the Vol. IV: Introduction containing a study on the Yogācāra literature and systematic statement of the doctrines of Asaṅga.

3. The beginning of the enormous *Mahāprjñāpāramitāśāstra de Nāgārjuna (Le Traité de la Grande Vertu de Sagesse.* Tome I, XXXIII+620 pp., Louvain, 1944), of which the author gives a translation enriched with notes where he tries his best to identify, through the whole canonical as well as extra-canonical Buddhistic literature, the quotations, without precise references abounding in the text.

W. Couvreur, after having shown that this *Mahāprajñāpāramitāśāstra* of Nāgārjuna, though belonging to the Madhyamaka school, borrows from the Sarvāstivādins the principal materials of Buddhology, compares the latter with the Tokharian fragments (*Tocharische Sprachreste*), published by Sieg and Siegling and ascertains between the two sources an almost perfect agreement with the marks (*lakṣaṇa*), the minor-marks (*anuvyañjana*) and the ten epithets of Buddha. Hastily perhaps, he concludes in favour of the Sarvāstivādin-Vaibhāṣika character of the Tokharian Buddhism. Indeed, it seems impossible to determine from which school the latter holds his doctrine by the mere fact of borrowing marks, minor-marks, etc., which were the common wealth of the Buddhist schools.

F. Weller has translated the *Yu-hsing-ching,* 2nd sūtra of the *Dīrghāgama* of the Dharmagupta, translated into Chinese by Buddha yaśas and Chu Fo nien in 412-413 A.D. (*Buddha Letzte Wanderung, MS.*, IV and V.)

D. Friedman has published the translation of the first chapter of the *ṭikā* of Sthiramati on the *Madhyāntavibhāga (Sthiramati*

*Madhyāntavibhāgaṭika, Analysis of the middle path and the extremes.* Utrecht, 1937), soon after when stcherbatsky had given the translation of the first chapter of this *Madhyāntavibhaṅga*, of the *ṭīkā* of Sthiramati and of the *bhāṣya* of Vasubandhu (*Madhyāntavibhaṅga. Discourse on discrimination between Middle and Extremes, ascribed to Maitreya and commented by Vasubandhu and Sthiramati*, transl., from the Sanskrit (and Tibetan), *BB*, XXX, Moscow-Leningrad, 1938).

A. Kunst has published in 1939, at Cracovie, the annotated translation of the *Anumānaparikṣā,* Chap. XVIII of the *Tattvasaṃgraha* with the commentary of Kamalaśīla and the Tibetan and Sanskrit text of the *kārikās (Problems der Buddhistischen Logik in der Darstellung der Tattvasaṃgraha*).

**Yoga and Tantrism. Medicine, Magic, Physiology**

L. de La Vallée Poussin tries to discover in the theistic and speculative Yoga traces of "pure" or "without Metaphysics" Yoga from which Buddhism originated (*Le Bouddhisme et le Yoga de Patañjali, MCB.,* 1937, pp. 223-42).

H. Von Glasenapp has published some articles on Tantrism and Śaktism (*OAZ.*, 1936, pp. 120-33), on Vajrayāna (*Die Entstehung des Vajrayāna, ZDMG.*, 1936, pp. 546-72), on the rites of initiations in the Javanese Buddhism (*OLZ.*, 1936, pp. 483-9 and 1938 pp. 201-4) and a book on the development of Buddhistic Tantrism in India as well as in Meridional, Oriental and Central Asia. He distinguishes pure Tantrism, devoid of erotic elements from Hindusim. The Buddhist Śaktism is studied with its secret doctrines, its rites and its metaphysical support (*Buddhistische Mysterien. Die geheimen Lehren und Rite des Diamant-Fahrzeugs,* Stuttgart, 1940, 201 pp.)

In *Yoga en Yantra in hunne beteekenis voor de Indische Archaeologic* (Leyde, 1946, 180 pp.), P.H. Pott distinguishes "two paths" in the Tantric yoga. He studies the object of meditation (*yantra*), their different developements, as the *maṇḍalas,* and the help that they bring for the study of the Tantric yoga, its symbols and cosmogonies. The symbols of the "left path" are inspired from a complex of ideas connected with death, cemeteries and associations that they evoke. The most remarkable centre of the microcosmic cosmogony of the left path is "the lotus of the heart (*ānanandakandapadma*) on the petals of which reside eight divinities. The author has found some constant groups of eight divinties, which can be connected with this lotus, like those of the divinities of the sacred cemeteries of Nepal. The study of these groups proves that there are two which are intermingled and which are the sources of the Buddhist Tantric pantheon.

The theories which retrace the origin of the yoga to a prehistorical technique of chamans are criticized by J. Filliozat. For him, the question is of a pneumatic conception of ancient Indian physiologists which is comparable to that exposed in the hippocratic treatise "Des Vents" (winds). There follows a note, which nobody will go there to search for, on the impropriety of the term "Illuminé" employed for translating "Buddha" (*Les origines d'une technique mystique indienne, RP.*, 1946, pp. 208-220.

In the course of researches of physio-pathological order on the cardiac arrhythmias two French specialist doctors have recognized the influence of the concentration of thoughts on the functioning of the circulatory system (C. Laubry and T. Brosse" *Documents recueillis auz Indes sur les "Yoguis" par l'enregistrement simultané du pouls, de la respiration et de l'électrocardiogramme, Presse Médicale,* no. 83, Oct. 1936).

*Le culte des nāga et la thérapeutique,* as it is exposed by a Tibetan text, has been translated and commented by M. Lalou. It is about a complicated ceremony, requiring the concentric presence, around a *maṇḍala*, of eight specimens of thirteen animals, from lizard to horse. The prayers and offerings of drugs do not determine a magical flux acting directly on the man for whom the cult is being celebrated: the medico-magical force released by the rite must be at first exerted on the sick *nāga* who consents then to the reflux of this force towards man (*JA.*, Jan-Mar. 1938, pp. 1-19).

Among the Tantric teachings attributed to Nāgārjuna, we find three important texts: a collection of therapeutic fomulae, a treatise on alchemy and a manual of sorcery. J. Filliozat shows that one has been right not to give too much of attention to these attributions and that those scientific and magical treatises are not particularly Buddhistic but simply Indian (*Nāgārjuna et Agastya, médecins,chimistes et sorciers, AXXCIO,* pp. 228-9). In a general study called *Magie et Médecine* (Paris, 1943, 147 pp.), the same author among other Buddhist subjects deals with the magic rôle of the *maitri*. He has also gathered some texts on the demoniac possession of the children. In *Le Kumāratantra de Rāvaṇa et les textes parallèles indiens, tibétains, chinois, cambodgien et arabe* (Cahiers de la Soc. Asiatique, 1937), he edits and translates a chapter of the *Rgyud bzi* the teaching of which is attributed to Buddha *Bhaiṣajyaguru.* He studies a Tantric complement to this text: *Lhan-thabs,* the Tibetan translation of the *Guhyāgnicakra,* the Chinese version of the *Rāvaṇa-kūmara-tantra* of the Chinese Tripiṭ -aka and similar non-Buddhist various texts.

## *Documents from High-Asia*

J. Filliozat and Hōryū Kuno have studied some Sanskrit fragments of the *Vinaya of the Sarvāstivādins* coming from the Pelliot mission and have compared them with the corresponding passages of the Chinese version (*JA.*, 1938, pp. 21-64).

By publishing in 1939, researches on the historicity of the texts of the *Mahāparinirvāṇasūtra* (*Beiträge zur Textgeschichte de Mahāparinirvāṇasūtra*, Göttingen, 1939, *NGGW.*, Fachgr. III, 2, pp. 55-94). In his researches E.Waldschmidt claims greater degree of authenticity of the Sanskrit tradition. This opinion has been contested by A.M. Piggazzalli (*Nuove tradizioni sulla morte del Buddha, Scientia,* 1931, 67, pp. 173-7) who is convinved of the authenticity of the Pāli Canon. E.Waldschmidt prepares the editions of the Sanskrit fragments of the *Mahāparinirvāṇasūtra* found at Turfan and he has resumed his researches by dividing into six groups the events occuring during Buddha's Parinirvāṇa. The first four groups are studied in *Die Uberlieferung vom Lebensende des Buddha* (Göttingen, 1944, 168 pp.).

Other Sanskrit fragments found in Turfan, those of the *Āṭānāṭikasūtra,* are utilized by H. Hoffmann in a general study of this interesting and difficult text (*Bruchstücke des Āṭānāṭikasūtra aus dem zentralasiatischen Sanskrit-kanon der Buddhisten.* Kleinere Sanskrit-text Leipzing, 1939, 105 pp.

F.W. Thomas has completed his researches undertaken in 1926 on *The Nam Language* (*JRAS.*, 1939, pp. 192-216) and on the same object, M. Lalou has noted that a long ms. found at Touenhouang, written in Tibetan scripts, is certainly a specimen of the same language (*JA.*, 1939, p. 453).

Three other documents coming from Touen-houang have been studied by M. Lalou. *A Touen-houang prelude to the Karaṇḍavyūha* (*IHQ.*, XIV, 1938, pp. 198-200) gives a summary of a mss. of the Tibetan Pelliot collection which contains a résumé of the *Valāhajātaka* and which describes the Great Hell (*Mahānaraka*) from which Avalokiteśvara takes out the beings when they pronounce a formula which is not: "*Oṃ maṇi padme hum*". In the same Indian review (*Tunhuang Tibetan document on a Dharmadāna* (*IHQ.*, XVI, 2, pp. 292-8) she gives the text and translation of an official relating to a gift of holy scriptures executed at Ça-cu (Touen-houang) and offered by Khrigeug-lde-brcan. At last, the *Notes à propos d'une amulette de Touen-houang. Les litanies de Tārā et la Sitātapartrādhāraṇī* (*MCB.*, IV) reproduce and explain one of the prettiest Tibetan documents of

Touen-houang preserved in Paris. It is an inscribed image; tweleve out of twenty four verses of litanies of Tārā that introduce the personages are found in a leaf of Central Asia, wrongly indentified by Hoernle with the *Mahāpratyaṅgiradhāraṇī*. There are indeed two *Pratyaṅgira°* and two *Sitātapatrā°*. One of the latter, anonymous, seems to be the prototype of the similar texts and the model of the amulet which has certainly been worn.

J. Bacot, F.W. Thomas and Ch. Toussaint have published *Documents de touen-houang relatifs à l'histoire du Tibet* (Paris, 1940-1946, 204 pp.). It concerns historical Annals, Chronicles and royal Genealogies. The first mention of Buddhism is found there under Khri sroṅ lde bean, end of the VIIIth Cent. (cf. *JA.*, 1937, p. 149).

W. Fuchs has published in *SPAW.*, XXX, 1938 under the heading *Huei-chao's Pilgerreise durch Nordwest-Indien une Zentral-Asien um* 726 a new translation and edition of the fragment of the journal of Huei-chao discovered in Touen-houang by Pelliot and which comprises the voyage from Magadha to Karashar.

J. Nobel had begun a very advanced study on the *Suvarṇaprabhāsottamasūtra* in a work which appeared at Leipzig in 1937. He has published at Leyde, in 1944, a second part uniquely consecrated to the Tibetan versions in which he utilizes four fragments of Touen-houang reflecting the most ancient Tibetan tradition.

E. Benveniste has pursued his works on the Sogdian documents of the Pelliot mission. Simultaneously have appeared the *Codices Sogdiani,* reproduction in fac-simile of the manuscripts of the Bibl. Nationale de Paris (publication of the Monumenta Linguarum Asiae Maioris, Copenhague), i.e., of all the texts edited, translated and commented in the two following volumes: (1) *Texts Sogdiens* (Paris, Geuthner, 1940, in quarto, 280 pp.) and (2) *Vessantara Jātaka* with, in appendix, the *Sūtra des Causes et des Effects* (Paris, Ceuthner, 1946, in quarto, 137, pp.). The *Textes Sogdiens* are of every sort; some of them cannot be identified; the whole of the collection is of great interest. E. Benveniste publishes at the same time an important glossary. In 1942, I. Gershevitch has corrected some lectures of Gauthiot according to the fac-simile of the *Vessantara (JRAS.*, 1942, pp. 97-101). W.B. Henning, in *BSOAS.*, XI, 4, 1946, pp. 713-40 has given an accout of the fac-simile of Copenhague and of the edition of E. Benveniste.

F. Weller utilizes the Tibetan and Chinese version of the *Vimalakīrtinirdeśasūtra* to interpret the Sogdian version published by Reichelt (*Zum sogdhischen Vimalakīrtinirdeśasūtra*, Leipzig, 1937) and enriches and corrects his article relating to the first part (*Bibl. B.*, VII-VIII, 179). In *MS.*, II and III, by comparing the Chinese version of Buddhabhadra, he annotates the Sogdian text on the Dhyāna also published by Reichelt.

F.W. Thomas, in *A Buddhist Chinese Text in Brāhmī Script (ZDMG.*, 91, pp.1-48) and H.W. Bailey in *Vajraprajñāpāramitā (ZDMNG.*, 92, M. 579-83), confront and justify their readings of a ms. from the Stein collection, being a fragment of the Chinese translation of the *Vajracchedikā* by Kumārajīva, transcribed in Brāhmi script.

The Kharoṣṭhī documents have been taken up again by T. Burrow in *The Language of the Kharoṣṭhī Documents from Chinese Turkestan* (Cambridge, 1937) and *Further Kharoṣṭhī Documents from Niya (BSOS.*, IX, pp. 111-24). Those texts are those published by Rapson, A.M. Boyar, etc. One of these, viz., No. 661 has been annotated by F.W. Thomas in *Some notes on Central Asian Kharoṣṭhī Document (BSOAS.*, XI, 1945, pp. 513-49). On his side, H.W. Bailey studies, under the title *Gāndhārī (BSOAS.*, XI, pp. 764-97), certain aspects of the middle-Indian dialect represented by the Aśoka inscriptions and the Kharoṣṭhī Documents of Central Asia, including the *Dharmapada* of Khotan. He had given the year before a new edition of the fragments of this *Dharmapada* reproduced photographically by Senart and Oldenbourg, with an index and Sanskrit equivalents.

The same author, H.W. Bailey, has pursued his works on the Khotanese in the *Rāma Story in Khotanese (JAOS.*, 1939, pp. 460-68) where the text is summed up and the forms of the proper names studied; in *Hvatanica II (BSOS.*, IX, pp. 69-78), where he discussed the meaning and etymology of numerous words contained in the glossary of Leumann; in *Hvatanica III (BSOS.*, IX, pp. 521-43 and 859-60) where he edited and translated, with a glossary and the restitution of the Sanskrit forms, a Sanskrit-khotanese bilingual preserved in the Bibl. Nationale de Paris and which is a conversation between as Indian bhikṣu and a man of Kan-tcheou; in *Kaṇaiska (JRAS.*, 1942, pp. 14-28; 250) he gives the text and translation commented with a Khotanese version of the legend of Kaniṣka. And he has published in 1945 a collection of Khotanese texts (*Khotanese Texts*, Cambridge University Press).

In the *JA.*, 1941-42, pp. 83-104, Sten Konow has published a *Note sur une nouvelly forme aberrante du khotanais* regarding a fragment of 62 lines found in the region of Tumśuq by Pelliot. The writing is that of the Koutchean mss. It is about the formula of the

Triple Refuge followed by the mention without great cohesion of the duty of the *upāsaka* towards the *Śikṣapāda*. There is a glossary-index with the transcription and an attempt of translation.

The works on Tokharian, since 1939, are pointed out by H. W. Bailey in *Recent Work in "Tokharian"* (Transactions of the Philological Society, 1947).

Anne-Marie Von Gabain has pursued the edition of Hiuan-tsang's biography in Ouigour by publishing four letters which form the end of the VIIth chapter. She gives the corresponding Chinese text (21 pp. notes, index, in *SPAW.*, XXIX, 1938, pp. 371-415).

D. Sinor argues about this work. He deals with the writing of the Ouigours, their dialects, their conversion into Buddhism. Buddhist texts have been translated in the *t'ou-kine* language as early as the VIth century and from the beginning of the 'turquisation' of Turkestan, we must take into account a turkish Buddhism (*A propos de la biographie ouigoure de Hiuan-tsang, JA.*, 1939, pp. 543-90). The same author has described (in Hungarian) 54 Turkish Buddhist texts. He has added a bibliography and a short study (in English) on Turkish Buddhism in Central Asia (*A Kozépázsia török Buddizmusrol. On Turkish Buddhism in Central Asia,* Budapest, 1939).

J. Przyluski has studied, in *Les Ugrya dans l'Inde (RO.*, 1939, pp. 1-6), the name Oḍḍiyāna=Tib. O-rgyan/U-rgyan and a series of geographical names which goes from Khotan to the Indus and continues in India up to Orissa and which seems to be explained by the migration of people whose name can be restored in the form Ugrya(n).

**The Artistic Expansions**

A. Foucher has published with Mme E. Bazin-Foucher, *La vieille route de l'Inde de Bactres à Taxila* (Paris, 1942, 173 pp. 32 p;., 34 maps; and 1947, pp. 174-426, 8 pl.) which forms the first part of a historical, geographical and archæological introduction to the works of the French Delegation in Afghanistan. In connection with it have to be mentioned the publications of Hackin on the excavations executed in 1936-37 on the sites of Begrām and Shotorak (*RAA.*, XII, 1938, pp. 2-11; *OAZ.*, 1938) and the work devoted to the block no. 2 of Begrām, with Mm. J.R. Hackin's collaboration; those of G. Ghirshman (*JA.*, 1943-45, pp. 59-71) and those of J. Meunié on the site of Shotarak (Paris, 1942, 70 pp. 42 pl.). The latter has found near Shotarak the runis of the convents where Kaniṣka kept Chinese hostages. (*Le couvent des otages chinois de Kaniṣka au Kapiśa. (JA.*, 1943-45, pp. 151-62). The site and almost each details correspond to Hiuan-tsang's description.

In 1938, W.W. Tarn published *The Greeks in Bactria and India* (Cambridge University Press, 339 pp.), field of researches also explored by Sten Konow: *New Traces of the Greeks in India* (*NIA.*, 1940, pp. 639-48); L. Bachhofer: *On Greeks and Śakas in India (JAOS.*, 1941, pp. 223-50), article discussed by Sir Johan Marshall, *Greeks and Śakas in India* (*JRAS.*, 1947, p. 3); P. Meile (*Les Yavanas dans l'Inde Tamoule, Mélanges Asiatiques (=JA.*, 1940-1941, pp. 85-123) showing that great care ought to be taken when interpreting the term *yavana* which does not always mean "Greek"; A. Foucher, *Le lieu de naissance du roi indo-grec Ménandre (AIBCR.*, 1939, pp. 541-57); *A porpos de la conversion au bouddhisme du roi Indo-grec Ménandre (AIBM.*, XLIII, 2, pp. 260-95); *Les satrapies orientales de l'empire achéménide (AIBCR.*, 1938, pp. 336-53).

J. Hackin, in L'*Art Bouddhique de la Bactriane et les origines de l'Art Gréco-bouddhique,* puts again the problem of the heads of Hellenistic character found in Kunduz, of the meeting of Buddhism and Hellemism. According to him Buddhism penetrated into Bactria as early as the IInd cent. B.C., and the Greco-Buddhist art has been born on the Bactrian soil.

The question has given rise to numerous researches where are integrated, though of an American author, those of B. Rowland Jr. In *Gandhāra and Late Antique Art: The Buddha Image (AJA.*, 1942, pp. 223-36), this author indicates that the wholesale production could not have begun in Gandhara before the 2nd cent. A.D. and that it must have been the work of artisans coming from the Roman Orient. Statues of Buddha from Haḍḍa show the Buddha dressed in the *himation* and not in the *saṃghati*. On his side, H. Buchtal draws the attention on the similarities between the art of Gandhāra and the Christian art of the IVth-Vth and subsequent centuries (*The Common Classical Sources of Buddhist and Christian Narrative Art, JRAS.*, 1943, pp. 137-48) which he explains not through the Hellenistic currents, but through the Roman expansion and he proposes to see, in the Gandhāra art, a "Romano-Buddhist" school. According to the date the Roman motives to which he refers, the most ancient image of Gandhāran Buddha cannot go back beyond the 1st. cent. A.D. (*The Foundations for Chronology of Gandhāra Sculpture, TOCS.*, 1942/43, pp. 21-32). The iconography of the episodes of the life of Buddha, such as it has been formed in Gandhāra, reflects an evolution of Buddhism. The progressive divinization of Buddha by the Mahāyāna and his representation in the human form correspond to a current of thought analogous to those that have brought at first the Romans to divinize their emperors and then the Christians to represent Jesus (*The Western Aspects of Gandhāra sculputre, PBA.*, 1945, 28 pp.)

For M. Grünwald (*Geistige und stilistische...Art. As IX*, 1-3, pp. 37-67), the analogies between the art of Gandhāra and of Turfan and the primitive Christian art are explained by the same Hellenic art influences. He establishes some parallels between the Chinese art of the 5th and 6th centuries and the passage of Byzantine art to the primitive Roman art and shows the convergences between the Chinese style of the Wei and T'ang epoch and the Roman sculpture of the 11th and 12th centuries. The stylistic characteristics of the Buddhist sculpture are compared, from the synoptic point of view, with that of the European sculpture of Middle-Age, and conceived as the expression of analogous spiritual tendencies.

With regard to Buddha's legend in the *Buddhacarita*, F. Weller admits as possible that, in the 1st cent. the figured representations have served as source of inspiration, hypothesis which can explain disharmonies otherwise enexplicable (*Schauplatz und Handlung im Buddhacarita, ZDMG.*, 1939, pp. 306-338). As for the Indian reliefs representing Channa who clings to the tail of Kanthaka, they must have been inspired by the Greek reliefs of Cavaliers (*Channa am Pferdeschweife, OLZ.*, 1941, pp. 377-88).

H. Lueders tries to solve the problems put forward by the identification of the Bhārhut sculputres; he is not of Barua's opinion, that all the representations are related to the *Jātakas* and he concludes by showing that there is not any disagreement between some representations and the tradition of the Theras, as it has been pointed out by A. Foucher and other authors (*Bhārhut und die Buddhistische Literatur*, Leipzig, 1941, 182 pp.).

M. Lalou, by comparing two texts dealing with the painted clothes (*paṭa*), the *Mañjuśrīmūlakalpa* and the *Tārāmūlakalpa*, has discovered that the first section of the last text is a plagiarism badly done of the first thirteen chapters and of the three-fourths of the fourteenth chapter of the *Mañjuśrīmūlakalpa* because the important iconographic descriptions of those chapters are incompletely adapted to their new aim. If the *Tārāmūlakalpa* had been utilized in the *Mañjuśrīmūlakalpa*, there would have been a number of false identification (*Mañjuśrīmūlakalpa et Tārāmūlakalpa, HJAS.*, 1 Nov. 1936, pp. 327-49).

A. Getty published in 1936, with a preface by A. Foucher: *Gaṇeśa. A Monograph of the Elephant-faced God* (Oxford, Clarendon Press, 103 pp. 40 pl.), where she follows the images of the god in the entire era of Buddhist diffusion, then, in 1940, she has presented a curious iconographic research on the mysterious Uga-jin, the god-serpent represented coiled up and with a man's head. Though this divinity is actually assimilated by the Japanese Buddhism (being the object of a secret cult), its traces are not found again in India. But it resembles closely the god of fertility adored in Iraq, at Babylon, and in Mesopotamia towards 3000 B.C., whose most ancient image is furnished by a seal of Suse. The author gives the hypothesis that it is a question of a secret form of the cult of Tanimuz and notes that the Mexican god of the creation is also represented under the form of a coiled serpent holding in his mouth a man's head. The relation of this god with Uga-jin is difficult to establish because certainly he is his contemporary, but the two symbols can be derived from the same god of fertility of Mesopotamia (*Uga-jin: the coiled-serpent God with a human head. Art. As.*, VIII, 1, 1940, pp. 36-48).

The *Indo-tibetica IV,* published by G. Tucci in 1941, exposes the results of the exploration of the temples situated on the road of Gantok to Gyantse. G. Tucci has already published the documents from the exploration of the temples of Tabo. Lha-lung and Chang (Haut-Kunavar) (*Indo-tibetica III, I templi del Tibet Occidentale e il Loro Simbolismo Artistico,* Parte I, *Spiti e Kunavar*, Rome, 1935), and he has again just started to resume his researches on the spot. These documents (one volume of plates reproducing the monuments and their decoration, and one vol. of inscriptions) are of great importance for the Mahāyānist iconography. Their abundance allows to retrace the evolution of the Tibetan art and to discover its principal courses in the XIVth and XV centuries.

The Lamaist Cathedral of Peking is studied by F.D. Lessing (*Yung-ho-kung. An iconography of the Lamaist cathedral in Peking,* Stockholm, 1942, vol. I, 179 pp., 32 pl.) which adds four rites to the descriptions of a part of buildings, a study on Pu-tai and four *Lokapālas,* notes on *saṃvara* and the translation of the inscriptions. The work will be complete in four volumes.

In *Les Influences et les réminiscences étrangères au Kondō du Hōryūji*. J. Auboyer replaces the paintings of Kondō in the historical *milieu* of the VIIth-VIIIth centuries, an epoch when are developed the post-Gupta art in India, Irano-Buddhist complexes of Afghanistan and Central Asia, the great ensembles of Central Java, etc.,...By minute comparisons, she concludes against the traditional opinion which saw in the frescos of Kondō a direct influence of *Ajantā* (nay even a production of the same atelier), in favour of the influences of meridional

India (Ellorā), of Afghanistan and specially of Central Asia carried through China (Paris, Geuthner, 1941).

In 1994, G. Coedès published a *Histoire ancienne, des Etats hindouisés d'Etrême-Orient* (Hanoi, 366 pp., tableaux, maps, index) which is at the same time the history of the Buddhist expansion in respect of religion as well as art, in South-East Asia (a second edition, carefully published, has just appeared in Boccard, Paris, 1948, Histoire du Monde, VIII-2, under the heading *Les états hindouisés d'Indochine et d'Indonésie*.

R. Le May has published *A Concise History of Buddhist Art in Siam* (Cambridge Univ. Press, 1939, 165 pp., 205 ill.) some elements of which have formed the subject of a communication of the author for the XXth International Congress of the Orientalists (*AXXCIO.*, pp. 200-7).

G. de Coral Rémusat, in *L' Art Khmer. Les grandes étapes de son évolution* (Paris, 1940, 137 pp.), deals with the Buddhist expansion: coexistence of Brahmanism and Buddhism at a remote date (Vth cent.); preponderance of Çivaism and persecution of the Buddhists (VIth-IXth cents. approx.) then greater and greater tolerance which ends under Jayavarman VII (XIIth-XIIIth cents.) in the preeminence of a Buddhism dominating and protecting Brāhmaṇical gods.

H. Parmentier has published a *Esquisse de l'art laotien (BAL.*, 1937), where he notes that images of Bodhisattva are nearly absent, probably because Laotian Buddhism is that of the Little Vehicle.

Ph. Stern, in *L'Art du Champa (ancien Annam) et son évolution* (Toulouse, 1942, 122 pp.), proposes a chronology based on a succession of styles which he has determined by the evolution of the decorative motives.

L. Bezacier has published *Essais sur l'art annamite* (Hanoi, 1944; 253 pp.). It seems that Buddhism has been implanted in Annam specially under the Chinese form from the XIth cent. In Tonkin, though the divinities bear the traces of Chinese influence, generally an Indian origin can be pointed out (*Le Panthéon des Pagodes, bouddhiques du Tonkin, BSEI.*, Saigon, 1943, 38 pp.).

The excavatios carried out in the Malay Peninsula are exposed and commented by H.G. Quaritch Wales in an article published in India (*IAL.*, 1938) and in *Recent Malayan Excavations and some Wider Implications (JRAS.*, 1946, pp. 142-9). The Buddhist finds are important. Likewise, in Sumatra, some Buddhist monuments, one statue of Buddha which belongs to the Vth cent. have been found up to the

N.W. of Palembang, (F.M. Schnitger: *The Quest for mysterious kingdom in Sumatra, ILN.*, 20th Nov. 1937, pp. 890-2).

**Religious and Laic Legislation**

M. Hofinger in his *Etude sur le Concile de Vaiśāli* (Louvain, 1946, 300 pp.) brings material relating to the Second Council. He has translated them from the canonical sources for which, by studying the formation of the Canon 'Scripturaire', he established a relative chronology. Following the same method of researches as J. Przyluski, M. Hofinger ends in a complete agreement with the results of the *Council of Rājagṛha*. He underlines that once more the Pāli Canon does not reveal a source of information superior to the Chinese and Tibetan canonical stories, it is even sometimes inferior to them.

R. Lingat in a study on *L'Influence Indoue dans l'ancien droit siamois,* shows that if since a long time one has recognized in the ancient Siamese right of the Ayuthia epoch some traces of Indian influence, the recent hypothesis: introduction to Siam by the Burmese, between 1569 and 1584, of a *Code of Manu*, is criticizable. He proposes another founded on some historical, archæological and linguistic facts: the *Dharmaśāstra* incorporated in the Siamese laws was in its primitive form a *dhammasattham* in circulation among the majority of the people of the kingdom of Dvāravatī and taken up by the Siamese immigrants. After the foundation of Ayuthia, the Siamese would have preserved the Code, of Indian origin, but skillfully transposed by the Mon on the Buddhist mode and would have translated and incorporated it in their legislation (*Institut de Droit comparé. Etudes de sociologie et d'dthnologie juridiques publiées sous la direction de René Maunier,* XXV, 1937, 29 pp.).

The same author devotes an important judicial study to the marriage of the *bikkhu,* to the fate of their abandoned wealth, to their succession and their will, the whole founded on the Buddhist monks Code of Discipline. (*Vinaya et droit laïque. Etude sur les conflits de la loi religieuse et de la loi laïque dans l'Indo-chine mahāyāniste, BEFEO.*, XXXVII, 2, 1937, pp. 416-77.

**Instruments of Work**

By publishing an illustrated study on the bricks of Gopālpur (*JRAS.*, 1938, pp. 547053) which date from the VIth century, E.H. Johnston has supplied J. Filliozat with some points of comparison with the Tibetan scripture which could have been known in Tibet a little before the traditional date, *i.e.*, before Thon-mi (VIIth century) (*JA.*, Apirl-June, 1939, p. 283). A bibliography of the history of the scripture has been published at Linz in 1836, by P. Sattler and G. van

Selle (*Bibliographie zur Geschichte der Schrift bis in das Jahr* 1930, 234 pp.) but it is insufficient concerning the Indian scriptures and specially those of the Buddhist texts of Central Asia and Nepal.

Four Grammars have been published in France:

*Grammaire laotienne,* by J.J. Hospitalier (Paris, 1937);

*Grammaire sanskrite élémentaire*, by L. Renou (Paris, 1946);

*Grammaire du tibétain littéraire,* by J. Bacot, (Paris, 1946);

*Grammaire de la langue mongole écrite,* by L. Hambis, (Paris, 1946).

and three in Germany:

*Tibetische National grammatik,* by Schubert, (Leipzig, 1937);

*Alttürkische Grammatik,* by A.M. von Gabain (Leipzig, 1941);

*Khotansakische Grammatik*, by Sten Konow (Leipzig, 1941).

The third fascicle of Hōbōgirin appeared in 1937. The article "maladie" (*byō*) by its importance excels a dictionary notice. J.Rahder is the author of an article on *jñāna.*

W. E. Soothill and L. Hodous have published *A Dictionary of Chinese Buddhist Terms* with a number of Sanskrit equivalents (XIX+510 pp., London, Kegan Paul, 1937).

A general study on the order of words in the Sanskrit and Middle-Indian prose: inscriptions of Aśoka, *Dīghanikāya* II, etc....has been published by J. Canedo (*Zur Wort-und Satzstellung in der Alt- und Mittelindischen Prosa,* Göttingen, 1937, 8°, 114 pp.).

H. Hendriksen has kept himself busy with the *Syntax of the Infinite Verb-Forms of Pāli,* Copenhagen, 1944, 169 pp.

In a short note: *Uber die Formel der vier edlen Wahrheiten* (*OLZ.*, 43, 1940, pp. 73-9), F. Weller shows that in a formula of "four noble truths", the faulty forms like *dukhanirodham,* etc. are explicable by *Māgadhī*.

G. Borsani has complied the complete list of the titles of all the divisions and subdivisions of the Pāli Tipiṭaka (*Prospetti e indice del Tipiṭaka,* Milan, 1942, 265 pp.).

J. Filliozat has published the first fascicle of his *Catalogue du fonds sanskrit de la Bibl. Nationale,* where he makes the historical account of the formation of the collections and describes the mss. of the collections of Hogdson and Burnouf (Paris, 1941). In the *Cataloue des mss. sanskrits et tibétains de la Société Asiatique*, the same author gives the inventory of the mss. offered by Hogdson of the Asiatic Society.

M. Lalou published in 1939 the tome I of the *Inventaire des mss. tibétanis de Touen-houang conservés à la Bibiliothèque Nationale* (Fonds Pelliot tibétain, Nos. 1-849) where excepting the texts relating to the Discipline, the majority of the Buddhist documents: collections or isolated texts are described. The tome II is ready for publication.

In the *Indian Texts Series,* G.P. Malalasekera published two volumes of his *Dictionary of the Pāli proper names.*

The activity of the Pāli text Society has been manifested of numerous publication; by I.B. Horner, for example, 3 volumes of translation of the *Vinaya,* the edition of the *Madhuratthavīlāsinī* and that of the commentary of Buddhaghosa on the *Majjhimanikāya (Papañcasūdani)*; A.P. Buddhadatta, B.C. Law, C.V. Joshi, J. Takakusu, M. Nagai, L. Babbit, D.L. Barua, J. Kennedy. S Gehman, H. Kopp, E.M. Hare, F.L. Woodward, have also published in the same collection some editions and translation. The vols. I and II of the *Dīghanikāya*, since long exhausted, have been reproduced photographically and the Pāli-English Dictionary is in progress of reedition (Parts III and IV appeared; Parts I-II and V-VII in the press).

## ABBREVIATIONS

| | | |
|---|---|---|
| AEHSR | = | Annuaire de l'Ecole des Hautes-Etudes. Sciences religieuses. |
| AIBC | = | Académie des Inscriptions et Belles-Lettres, Comptesrendus. |
| AIBM | = | Académie des Inscriptions et Belles-Lettres, Mémoires. |
| AJA | = | American Journal of Archæology. |
| Art. As. | = | Artibus Asiæ. |
| AXXCIO | = | Actes du XXe Congrès International des Orientalistes. |
| BAL | = | Bulletin des Amis du Laos. |
| BB | = | Biblitheca Buddhica, Moscou-Leningrad. |
| BCL | = | Bulletin de la Classe des Lettres...Académie Royale de Belgique. |
| BEFEO | = | Bulletin de l'Ecole française d'Extrême-Orient. |
| Bibl. B | = | Bibliographie bouddhique. |
| BSFP | = | Bulletin de la Société françasie de Philosophie. |
| BSOS-(BSOAS) | = | Bulletin of the School of Oriental (and African) Studies. |
| BSSAEO | = | Bulletin de la Société Suisse des Amis de l'Extrême-Orient. |
| HJAS | = | Harvard Journal of Asiatic Studies. |
| IC | = | Indian Culture. |
| IHQ | = | Indian Historical Quarterly. |
| ILN | = | Illustrated London News. |
| JA | = | Journal Asiatique. |
| JAOS | = | Journal of American Oriental Society. |
| JGIS | = | Journal of the Greater India Society. |
| JRAS | = | Journal of the Royal Asiatic Society. |
| MCB | = | Mélanges chinois et bouddhiques. |
| MS | = | Monumenta Serica. |
| NGGW | = | Nachrichten der Gesellschaft der Wissenschaften im Göttingen. |
| NIA | = | New Indian Antiqurary. |
| OAS | = | Ostasiatische Zeitschrift. |

| | | |
|---|---|---|
| OLZ | = | Orientalistische Literaturzeitung. |
| PBA | = | Proceedings of the British Academy. |
| PBO | = | Polski Biuletyn Orientalistyczny. |
| RAA | = | Revue des Arts Asiatiques. |
| RCCIO | = | Recueil des Communications. XXe Congrés International des Orientalistes. |
| RHA | = | Revue d'Histoire et d'Archéologie. |
| RHPR | = | Revue d'Histoire et de Philosophie religieuses. |
| RHR | = | Revue d'Histoire des Religions. |
| RO | = | Rocznik Orjentalistyczny. |
| RP | = | Revue philosophique. |
| RSR | = | Recherches de sciences religieuses. |
| RUB | = | Revue de l'Université de Bruxelles. |
| SPAW | = | Sitzungsberichte der Preussischen Academie... |
| TOCS | = | Transactions of the Oriental Ceramic Society. |
| WZKM | = | Wiener Zeitschrift für die Kunde der Morgenländer. |
| ZDMG | = | Zeitschrift der Deutschen Morgenländischen Gesellschaft. |